Table of Contents

Preface: Why You Need to Read This Book Right Now

In 2023, a woman in Japan received an urgent video call from her "boss" while she was at work. The person on the screen looked exactly like her boss, spoke in his voice, and even used his familiar tone and mannerisms. He urgently requested she transfer funds to a "supplier" as part of a last-minute payment. Trusting the face, voice, and authority of her boss, she complied — only to find out later that her boss had never called her. The "person" on the video call was an AI-generated deepfake.

This attack wasn't science fiction. It wasn't a theoretical warning about the "future of AI-driven threats." It was a real event, and it could happen to anyone. The attacker used modern AI tools to clone a voice, replicate facial expressions, and fool an intelligent, well-trained employee into handing over large sums of money. The world of cybersecurity has changed. Deepfakes, AI-driven malware, and rogue AI cyberweapons are no longer ideas from sci-fi movies. They are active threats happening right now, and if you're not prepared, you could be the next victim.

If you think, "I'm not important enough to be a target," you're precisely who attackers are looking for. Small businesses, families, and everyday people are the perfect targets because they don't think they're targets. Hackers no longer need to "guess passwords" or "hack firewalls" — they can simply trick you into giving them what they want. And they're using AI to do it faster, smarter, and at scale.

Why This Book Matters More Than Ever
This book isn't about fear — it's about power. It's about taking control. Attackers are getting smarter, faster, and more persistent, but with the right knowledge, you can always be one step ahead.

This book will teach you to spot scams, recognize fake voices, detect malware that evolves like a virus, and protect your business, your family, and your future.

This book isn't filled with fluff or abstract "theory." It's a training manual designed to help you master practical skills that will protect you from real-world threats. By the end of this book, you will be able to:

- Recognize Deepfake Attacks — Whether it's a "CEO" on a Zoom call or a "family member" calling from overseas, you'll know how to spot and stop these manipulative scams.
- Stop Ransomware Before It Locks Your Data — You'll learn how to defend against ransomware attacks that demand payments to unlock your files.
- Detect Self-Evolving Malware — You'll understand how AI-driven malware works, how it hides from antivirus tools, and how to catch it before it infects your devices.
- Build a Family Defense Plan — You'll create a "Family Password" to protect against deepfake voice scams targeting loved ones.
- Outsmart AI-Enhanced Phishing Attacks — AI can generate thousands of personalized scam emails, but you'll be able to recognize and report them before they trick you.

You'll also learn to think like an attacker. You'll see how cybercriminals use AI to create and run attacks, from AI-guided malware to sophisticated reconnaissance bots that scan for vulnerabilities in real time. But you'll also learn to think like a defender, using the same AI tools to track, detect, and stop attacks before they happen.

From The SolarWinds Attack to AI-Powered Cyber-Weapons
You may have heard of the SolarWinds attack in 2020, where a routine software update was hijacked and weaponized to infect over 18,000 organizations, including Fortune 500 companies and U.S. government agencies. Hackers inserted a backdoor into the update, allowing them to spy on organizations and steal sensitive data. It was one of the most sophisticated cyberattacks ever seen.

But since then, things have escalated. We've seen ransomware gangs like LockBit create "Ransomware-as-a-Service" platforms that rent ransomware kits to anyone who pays. We've seen the rise of deepfake-driven scams, like the case of a finance executive who was tricked by a "voice clone" of their CEO. And we've seen the potential for AI to generate autonomous cyber-weapons that can attack infrastructure without human oversight.

This book will prepare you for all of it. It doesn't just teach you about what happened in the past. It's about preparing you for the future.

Here's a look at some of the new and emerging threats this book covers:

- Self-Evolving Malware — Malware that "learns" as it spreads, changing its code to avoid detection.
- Deepfake Voice Cloning — How AI can clone voices with just a 10-second recording.
- AI-Generated Cyber Weapons — How rogue AI could be used as autonomous attack agents.
- AI-Driven Misinformation — Fake news, propaganda, and the impact of disinformation on society.
- Cryptojacking — Hackers secretly using your devices to mine cryptocurrency without your consent.
- Supply Chain Attacks — Why trusting third-party software providers can leave you exposed.
- Quantum Computing Threats — Why modern encryption could be broken by quantum computers.

You may not face every one of these threats, but all it takes is one. And most people aren't ready for any of them.

What Makes This Book Different?
Unlike other cybersecurity books that focus on definitions, principles, and theory, this book focuses on practical action. Each chapter is a mini-training course, with exercises, step-by-step guidance, and checklists. You'll get hands-on experience in how to:

- Stop a phishing attack in real time.
- Recognize and avoid deepfake scams.
- Set up AI-driven anomaly detection for your family or business.
- Protect your social media presence from fake accounts and scam messages.
- Build your own Cybersecurity Incident Response Plan.

We don't just talk about what to do — we walk you through how to do it. This is why the book includes chapters on Red Team vs. Blue Team exercises, a Cybersecurity Practice & Exercises section, and even a capstone challenge where you'll design your own cybersecurity system.

By the end, you won't just "know about" cybersecurity. You'll have the skills, tools, and knowledge to keep yourself, your family, and your business safe from the rapidly evolving threat landscape.

What's Next?

Every day, the attacks get more sophisticated. Hackers aren't just targeting big corporations anymore. They're coming for small businesses, remote employees, and ordinary people. They're weaponizing AI, building malware that evolves, cloning voices, and launching phishing campaigns at an industrial scale. The battlefield has shifted.

But so has the defense. AI is also your greatest ally. With AI on your side, you can spot the scams before they spot you. You can stop ransomware before it locks you out. And you can protect your family, your business, and your identity with AI-driven tools and anomaly detection systems.

This book will give you everything you need to fight back. You'll learn the most powerful concepts in cybersecurity — from zero-trust models and XDR systems to quantum-safe encryption and voice cloning defense strategies. Every chapter builds on the last, giving you the skills to think like an attacker, train like a defender, and act like a cybersecurity pro.

Whether you're a beginner, a business owner, or a professional looking to level up, this book is your complete guide to AI-driven cybersecurity. So turn the page and get ready to face the threats of today, tomorrow, and beyond.

Let's get started.

Chapter 1: Introduction to Cybersecurity

Why Cybersecurity Matters in an AI-Driven World

You're sitting at home when your phone buzzes. It's a call from your sister, Emma, who's been traveling overseas in Italy.

"Hey, I'm at the consulate, and I'm in a really bad spot," she says. Her voice is shaky, and you can hear faint background noises — footsteps, distant chatter. "I lost my wallet, and all my cards are gone. I'm trying to get my passport reissued, but I need $2,500 to process the fees. Can you send it to the consulate's bank account? I can send you the account info."

This sounds 100% legitimate. It's Emma's voice, her unique speech patterns, and you know she's in Italy. It all checks out. Without thinking twice, you send the money.

But here's the shocking truth: It wasn't Emma. It was a machine. Cybercriminals used AI-driven voice cloning technology to clone Emma's voice. They didn't even need a long recording — just 10 seconds of her voice from a prior phone call or social media post was enough for AI to recreate her speech, tone, and natural pauses. The "consulate" was a fake, and the bank account was controlled by cybercriminals. By the time you realize what happened, your money is gone, and the attacker has vanished.

This is the world of AI-driven cyberattacks. Hackers are no longer just sitting behind keyboards guessing passwords. They're using AI-driven deepfake technology to clone voices and trick family members into sending money. They're deploying self-learning malware that mutates every few seconds, evading even the most advanced antivirus systems. They're infiltrating global supply chains, turning trusted software updates into weapons. They're attacking power grids and hospitals with cyber-physical attacks that disrupt daily life.

Cybersecurity is no longer just about protecting computers and networks — it's about protecting your family, your finances, and your future.

As technology advances, so do the threats. Attackers are now leveraging AI to automate, evolve, and personalize attacks on a massive scale. But defenders have powerful tools too. With AI-driven anomaly detection, predictive threat detection, and autonomous response systems, you can stay one step ahead.

This book will teach you everything you need to know to protect your family, business, and personal devices from the latest threats. By the end, you'll be able to recognize the warning signs of an attack, deploy advanced AI-driven tools, and secure every aspect of your digital life.

Here's why cybersecurity matters now more than ever:
- The Rise of AI-Driven Attacks: Attackers are using AI to automate hacking, launch personalized phishing scams, and create deepfake voice scams that trick families and employees.
- Physical-World Consequences: Attacks on hospitals, power grids, and pipelines disrupt society in ways that go beyond "stolen data." Cyber-physical attacks turn digital vulnerabilities into real-world chaos.
- Your Personal Devices Are at Risk: Every phone, tablet, laptop, and smart home device is a target. From voice assistants (like Alexa) to smart cameras, attackers are exploiting IoT vulnerabilities with AI-driven attacks.

This book will teach you how to fight back. You'll learn to recognize the signs of an attack, avoid social engineering scams, and build a family defense plan to outsmart voice-cloning scammers. This is a battle of AI vs. AI — and the side with better AI wins.

Case Studies: Cybersecurity in the Real World
Cybersecurity is no longer a theoretical concept. The threats are real, and they affect individuals, families, and businesses on a daily basis. The following case studies illustrate how modern cyberattacks unfold in the real world — and they reveal the true cost of AI-driven cybercrime.

Deepfake Voice Scam (2023) — When AI Sounds Like Family
One day, Sarah, a mother of two, received a frantic call from her son, Josh.

"Mom, I'm in serious trouble. I need $2,000 right now, or I'm going to jail," said a voice that sounded exactly like Josh — down to his unique way of pausing between words. The panic in his voice convinced Sarah it was real. She didn't hesitate. She wired the money immediately.

But when she called Josh later to check on him, he had no idea what she was talking about. She had been scammed.

How did this happen? Hackers used AI-driven voice cloning technology. By capturing just 10 seconds of Josh's voice from a previous phone call, they trained an AI model to reproduce his voice. They then used that AI-generated voice to scam Sarah into sending money.

This isn't science fiction — it's happening right now. Hackers use AI-driven voice cloning tools like ElevenLabs, Resemble AI, and Voice.ai to reproduce voices that sound indistinguishable from reality. As AI models improve, these attacks will become more common, especially against seniors and vulnerable family members.

Key Lessons from This Attack:
- AI-Driven Voice Cloning is a threat to family security.
- Attackers can clone someone's voice using just 10 seconds of recorded audio.
- The best defense is to create a Family Password (discussed in Chapter 12) that no AI can guess or replicate.

Colonial Pipeline Attack (2021) — When Cyber Attacks Hit the Real World
The Colonial Pipeline is one of the largest fuel pipelines in the United States, supplying nearly half the fuel to the East Coast. But in May 2021, everything stopped. A ransomware attack shut down operations for days, causing panic at gas stations. Fuel prices skyrocketed, and some stations ran out of gas entirely.

What happened? Hackers deployed ransomware on Colonial's IT network, locking up files and demanding payment in cryptocurrency. While the attack didn't directly affect the pipeline's operational technology (OT), Colonial preemptively shut down its pipeline to prevent further damage.

The attack wasn't just about money — it was about infrastructure. It revealed how vulnerable critical infrastructure is to cyberattacks. If a hacker can shut down a single pipeline, they can shut down power grids, hospitals, and water treatment facilities too.

Key Lessons from This Attack:
- Ransomware isn't just a "data theft" problem — it can shut down entire industries.
- Critical infrastructure systems (like pipelines, hospitals, and power grids) are prime targets for cyber-physical attacks.

- Defenders must monitor for anomalies using AI-driven detection tools to spot unusual activity on OT systems.

Twitter Bitcoin Scam (2020) — The Power of Insider Access
On July 15, 2020, the world's most famous Twitter accounts — including those of Elon Musk, Bill Gates, and Joe Biden — began tweeting the same message:

"Send $1,000 in Bitcoin, and I'll send $2,000 back."

What happened? Hackers tricked Twitter employees into giving them access to internal admin tools. This allowed the hackers to post from high-profile accounts and promote a Bitcoin scam. The result? The hackers made over $100,000 in just a few hours.

Key Lessons from This Attack:
- Insider Threats are one of the biggest risks to companies.
- Attackers don't need to hack your systems — they just need to trick your employees.
- Companies should limit employee access to admin tools.

European Bank Voice Cloning Scam (2019) — $35 Million Gone in Minutes
In 2019, a bank manager received a call from what he thought was his boss. The boss needed to transfer $35 million to a supplier, and the request was urgent. The manager complied, transferring the funds to a foreign bank account controlled by scammers.

What made the manager believe it was real? The caller's voice sounded exactly like his boss. Attackers had used AI to clone the boss's voice.

Key Lessons from This Attack:
- Deepfake Voice Cloning can target companies, not just families.
- Banks, executives, and managers must be trained to spot these scams.

Cybersecurity is no longer an abstract concept or a problem for "other people." It's here, and it's personal. From deepfake voice scams that target your loved ones to ransomware attacks that shut down pipelines, the risks are more real and more personal than ever. Attackers are no longer guessing passwords or using brute-force attacks. They're wielding AI-driven tools that learn, adapt, and evolve — and they're coming for your family, your business, and your identity.

But here's the good news: You don't have to face this alone. For every tool the attackers use, defenders have AI-driven solutions that are smarter, faster, and more adaptive. This book will train you to recognize the warning signs of an attack before it happens. You'll learn how to spot deepfakes, outsmart phishing attempts, and defend against self-evolving malware. You'll build a personal defense plan, learn how to protect your business, and discover how AI can be your most powerful ally in this fight.

Up next, we'll explore the CIA Triad — the foundation of all cybersecurity. Every attack you'll encounter targets at least one of the three pillars: Confidentiality, Integrity, and Availability. Understanding how these pillars work is the first step toward mastering cybersecurity fundamentals and ensuring that, with the power of AI on your side, you'll never be caught off guard. Let's begin.

The CIA Triad (Confidentiality, Integrity, Availability)
Cybersecurity is built on a foundation known as the CIA Triad. No, it's not related to spies or secret agents — it stands for Confidentiality, Integrity, and Availability. These three principles form the core framework of every cybersecurity system. Every cyberattack, every breach, and every defense strategy revolves around these three concepts.

If you understand how these three principles work, you'll be able to spot weaknesses before attackers do. You'll also understand how modern AI-driven tools aim to protect these principles at every level, ensuring that your data, systems, and personal devices remain secure.

Here's a deeper look at each pillar of the CIA Triad, how cybercriminals target them, and how AI-powered defenses can help you fight back.

1. Confidentiality — Keep It Secret, Keep It Safe
What It Means
Confidentiality means keeping information private and accessible only to those who are authorized to see it. It ensures that sensitive information — like passwords, bank details, or health records — isn't exposed to unauthorized users. Imagine someone accessing your bank account, reading your personal messages, or seeing private medical records. Confidentiality exists to prevent that.

How Attackers Target Confidentiality

Attackers break confidentiality in several ways:

- Phishing Scams: Attackers trick you into giving up your login details, passwords, or other private information.
- Man-in-the-Middle (MITM) Attacks: Attackers intercept communications between you and a website, allowing them to eavesdrop on your private data.
- Data Breaches: Hackers break into databases and steal customer information, credit card numbers, and login credentials.
- AI-Driven Voice Cloning: Attackers use deepfake voice technology to impersonate loved ones and extract confidential information.

How AI Defends Confidentiality

AI plays a key role in data encryption, anomaly detection, and access control. AI can detect abnormal login attempts, flag strange behaviors (like logins from new locations), and block access before damage is done. Here's how AI helps protect confidentiality:

- Multi-Factor Authentication (MFA): AI systems enforce MFA by requiring additional steps (like a code sent to your phone) to verify user identity.
- Anomaly Detection: AI monitors login behavior and blocks access if an account is accessed from a suspicious location or device.
- Data Encryption: AI-driven encryption tools ensure that even if attackers steal files, they can't read them without the decryption keys.

Real-World Example

The Yahoo Data Breach (2013-2014) remains one of the largest breaches in history, with 3 billion user accounts compromised. Attackers exploited vulnerabilities to steal usernames, passwords, and personal data. Today, AI-driven monitoring tools can spot unusual activity early and alert users to potential breaches before they spread.

How to Protect Confidentiality

- Use Multi-Factor Authentication (MFA) on all your accounts.
- Never share your login details via phone, email, or text.
- Use encryption tools (like BitLocker or FileVault) to encrypt sensitive files on your devices.

2. Integrity — Trust the Data, Not the Hackers
What It Means
Integrity means ensuring that information is accurate, authentic, and hasn't been tampered with. Imagine if a hacker modified a hospital patient's medical record, changing their blood type from "O" to "A." The result could be life-threatening. Integrity ensures that files, transactions, and records are exactly as they were intended to be.

How Attackers Target Integrity
Attackers target integrity by modifying or corrupting files, documents, or system settings. Here are some examples:
- Ransomware: When ransomware encrypts your files, it alters the integrity of your system.
- Data Tampering: Attackers might alter transaction logs, medical records, or business files to sow chaos.
- Supply Chain Attacks: Attackers corrupt software updates to introduce backdoors or malware.
- Data Poisoning: Attackers manipulate the training data used by AI models, causing the model to learn incorrect patterns or behaviors.

How AI Defends Integrity
AI plays a critical role in file integrity monitoring (FIM) and real-time anomaly detection. Here's how it works:
- File Integrity Monitoring (FIM): AI constantly scans files and system configurations for changes. If any unauthorized changes are detected, an alert is triggered.
- AI-Driven Patch Management: AI automatically patches software to prevent attacks on unpatched vulnerabilities.
- Anomaly Detection: AI can detect unusual patterns in files, like unauthorized edits to sensitive documents.

Real-World Example
The Stuxnet Worm (2010) is one of the most well-known examples of an integrity attack. It targeted Iranian nuclear facilities, altering the control system's logic and making it look like everything was operating normally. In reality, it was sabotaging the nuclear centrifuges. This attack demonstrates how attackers can manipulate integrity to create false readings or reports.

How to Protect Integrity
- Install software updates and patches regularly to prevent integrity-based attacks.
- Use file integrity monitoring (FIM) tools like Tripwire to track changes to system files.
- Backup your files so you can restore them if ransomware alters them.

3. Availability — If It's Not Available, It's Useless
What It Means
Availability means ensuring that data, applications, and systems are accessible when they're needed. If a bank's app goes offline, customers can't access their accounts. If a hospital's network goes down, doctors can't access patient records. Availability means uptime, access, and service.

How Attackers Target Availability
Attackers target availability to disrupt business operations, cause downtime, and demand ransom payments. Here's how:
- Distributed Denial of Service (DDoS) Attacks: Attackers flood a system with traffic, making websites and servers inaccessible.
- Ransomware: By locking users out of their systems, ransomware disrupts availability.
- Server Exploits: Attackers find vulnerabilities in websites, apps, and servers, causing them to crash.

How AI Defends Availability
AI-driven systems ensure that services remain online, accessible, and stable even during attacks. Here's how:
- DDoS Protection: AI-driven tools (like Cloudflare) can detect and block DDoS attacks before they overwhelm a server.
- Load Balancing & Redundancy: AI ensures that if one server goes down, traffic is redirected to another server, ensuring uptime.
- Predictive Maintenance: AI can predict when hardware might fail, allowing companies to repair it before downtime occurs.

Real-World Example
In 2016, Dyn DNS was hit with one of the largest DDoS attacks in history, affecting services like Netflix, Amazon, and Twitter. Attackers used a botnet of IoT devices (like baby monitors) to flood Dyn's DNS servers with traffic. Today, AI-driven DDoS protection is used to identify and block abnormal traffic before it takes down an entire platform.

How to Protect Availability
- Use DDoS protection services (like Cloudflare) to block attacks on websites.
- Create system redundancies so you have backup servers and databases in case one fails.
- Back up your data regularly so you can restore it if ransomware attacks.

Why the CIA Triad Matters

Every attack you'll encounter — from ransomware to phishing, from DDoS to deepfakes — targets at least one part of the CIA Triad:

- Confidentiality: Attackers steal, eavesdrop, or spy on your data.
- Integrity: Attackers alter files, inject malware, or corrupt AI models.
- Availability: Attackers shut down services with DDoS or ransomware.

If you understand how these principles are attacked, you can better protect your personal devices, business systems, and family networks.

How AI Transforms Cybersecurity for Attackers and Defenders

AI is revolutionizing the world of cybersecurity, but it's not a one-sided affair. Attackers are using AI to supercharge their attacks, while defenders are using AI to create smarter, faster, and more adaptive defenses. This ongoing battle of AI vs. AI is shaping the future of cybersecurity.

From AI-driven malware that learns and adapts to predictive threat detection systems that spot attacks before they happen, the cybersecurity battlefield is no longer human vs. human — it's machine vs. machine. In this section, we'll explore how AI is used by attackers and defenders, and how you can use AI to stay one step ahead of the bad guys.

How Attackers Use AI to Launch Smarter, Faster Attacks

Attackers aren't relying on luck or manual effort anymore. They're using AI to automate everything from reconnaissance to execution. AI-powered attack tools can scan for vulnerabilities, automate phishing campaigns, and even mutate malware on the fly. Here's how attackers are using AI to gain the upper hand.

1. AI-Powered Phishing Bots

How It Works:

Phishing used to be simple — attackers would send generic "click here" emails. But today, AI-powered phishing bots create ultra-personalized phishing emails based on your online behavior. These bots scan social media, breach databases, and employee directories to generate messages that look like they come from trusted people or companies.

Example Attack:
Imagine you just bought a product from Amazon. Hours later, you get an email that looks exactly like an official Amazon shipping update. It says, "Your order was delayed, click here to track it." But the link leads to a fake Amazon login page designed to steal your credentials. AI-generated phishing emails can create these kinds of attacks automatically, using natural language processing (NLP) to sound human-like.

How to Defend:
- Use AI-based phishing filters (like those from Google Workspace) to block phishing attempts.
- Avoid clicking links from emails you didn't expect.
- Use password managers (like Bitwarden) to prevent you from entering passwords on fake sites.

2. Deepfake Voice and Video Impersonation
How It Works:
Deepfake technology uses AI-driven neural networks to clone human voices and faces. Attackers use this to impersonate CEOs, family members, and executives during phone calls, Zoom meetings, or video conferences. With just 10 seconds of recorded voice or video, they can create a digital clone that sounds and looks real.

Example Attack:
A bank manager receives a call from what he thinks is his CEO, instructing him to transfer $35 million to a "supplier's account" urgently. The voice is identical to the CEO, but it's a deepfake generated by AI. Thinking it's legitimate, the manager sends the money — only to later discover it was a scam.

How to Defend:
- Use a "Family Password" strategy (discussed in Chapter 12) for voice verification.
- Train employees to never trust voice-only verification for high-stakes transfers.
- Implement call-back verification protocols to verify sensitive requests.

3. AI-Driven Malware & Polymorphic Malware
How It Works:
Traditional malware can be detected because its "signature" (its code) stays the same. AI-driven malware mutates every few seconds, changing its structure to avoid detection. Attackers use mutation engines to create polymorphic malware, which looks like a new, unique file every time it runs.

Example Attack:
The Emotet malware is one of the most well-known polymorphic malware examples. It continuously changes its file structure, making it nearly impossible for traditional antivirus software to detect it. AI-driven mutation engines now allow attackers to create thousands of malware variants automatically.

How to Defend:
- Use behavioral-based antivirus (like SentinelOne) that detects actions, not file signatures.
- Deploy Endpoint Detection and Response (EDR) tools that analyze file behavior in real time.
- Use sandboxing tools that test files in a safe, controlled environment before opening them.

4. AI-Guided Social Engineering
How It Works:
Attackers use AI-driven social engineering to manipulate human behavior. By scraping social media and analyzing a target's online habits, attackers craft personalized attacks. Chatbots powered by AI can impersonate customer support agents, gaining the target's trust.

Example Attack:
An attacker pretends to be a support agent from your bank. Using an AI-driven chatbot, they convince you to "confirm your account details" via a link. Since it all happens through live chat, it feels more legitimate. Behind the scenes, the AI bot is pulling personalized details (like your name and recent activity) to make the scam more believable.

How to Defend:
- Verify all customer support interactions using official contact channels.
- Be skeptical of customer support agents asking for private info like passwords.
- Use browser-based anti-phishing extensions like Privacy Badger or uBlock Origin.

5. Adversarial AI Attacks
How It Works:
Adversarial AI attacks manipulate machine learning (ML) models by feeding them bad data. This technique is used to "fool" image recognition systems, spam filters, and even autonomous vehicle AIs. Attackers can add small, undetectable "noise" to images, causing AI to misclassify them.

Example Attack:
Attackers added small "stickers" to traffic signs, causing an AI-powered self-driving car to misread a "Stop" sign as a "Speed Limit 50" sign. Adversarial inputs like this are used to trick AI systems in both cybersecurity and physical security environments.

How to Defend:
- Train AI models to recognize adversarial inputs.
- Use Explainable AI (XAI) to detect abnormal outputs from machine learning models.

How Defenders Use AI to Build Smarter Defenses
For every tactic attackers use, defenders have a response. AI-driven defense tools are changing the way cybersecurity teams predict, detect, and respond to threats. Here's how defenders are using AI to win the battle.

Predictive Threat Detection
- Instead of waiting for attacks to happen, AI systems predict future attacks based on data patterns. If AI notices that ransomware is infecting companies in a particular industry, it can predict which companies will be attacked next.

Example:
- Darktrace, an AI-driven cybersecurity platform, monitors global attack patterns and uses predictive analytics to detect future threats. If 10 similar companies are hit with malware, it predicts that other companies in the same industry might be next.

Real-Time Anomaly Detection
- AI systems can detect unusual behaviors, like employees logging in from unusual IP addresses or logging in at 3 a.m. UEBA (User and Entity Behavior Analytics) uses AI to track normal user behavior, flagging suspicious activity automatically.

Example:
- If John from accounting suddenly logs in from Russia at 2 a.m., AI-driven anomaly detection software would flag it as suspicious and block access.

Automated Incident Response (SOAR)
- SOAR (Security Orchestration, Automation, and Response) platforms use AI to automate responses. If malware is detected, SOAR systems can automatically quarantine the affected device and trigger an incident response plan.

Behavioral Analytics & AI-Driven Password Managers
- AI-driven password managers generate long, random passwords and store them in encrypted vaults. No human guesses, no human errors.

Example:
- Tools like Bitwarden and 1Password create ultra-random passwords and warn you if your passwords have been leaked.

File Integrity Monitoring (FIM)
- AI tracks and monitors system files for changes. If a file is altered, an alert is triggered. This helps defend against ransomware and data tampering attacks.

The Future of Cybersecurity: AI vs. AI
Every attack you face — from phishing and malware to supply chain attacks — is being powered by AI-driven tools. But defenders aren't defenseless. They have AI-driven anomaly detection, predictive analytics, and EDR tools to spot and stop attacks. The battle isn't just humans vs. hackers anymore — it's AI vs. AI. The only question is which side has better AI.

With the right knowledge, tools, and strategies from this book, you'll have everything you need to build smarter defenses and fight back with AI on your side.

Chapter Conclusion: Master the Core, Master Cybersecurity
Cybersecurity is no longer just about firewalls and antivirus software — it's about mastering the principles of Confidentiality, Integrity, and Availability (CIA) and understanding how modern AI-driven threats exploit them. Attackers aren't relying on brute force anymore. They're automating everything — from AI-generated phishing emails to deepfakes impersonating loved ones, while polymorphic malware mutates faster than antivirus tools can detect.

But here's the key takeaway: for every method of attack, there is a stronger method of defense. By using predictive threat detection, anomaly detection, and AI-driven security tools, you can take control over your personal, family, and business security. The CIA Triad (Confidentiality, Integrity, Availability) will guide every security decision you make — from protecting your devices to safeguarding your data.

Next, we'll explore how AI plays a direct role in modern cybersecurity — both for attackers and defenders. This is where the real battle begins — AI vs. AI. Let's continue.

Chapter 2: The Role of AI in Cybersecurity

Introduction: The AI Revolution in Cybersecurity
Cybersecurity is no longer a battle fought between human hackers and human defenders. Today, it's a war where AI faces off against AI. The rapid evolution of artificial intelligence has created a paradigm shift in the way both attackers and defenders approach cybersecurity.

For years, cybersecurity relied on human analysts sifting through logs, responding to alerts, and manually mitigating threats. But the sheer scale and speed of modern attacks made this approach unsustainable. Today, attackers leverage AI to automate phishing emails, create self-evolving malware, and crack passwords faster than ever before. In response, defenders now rely on AI-driven systems for predictive defense, anomaly detection, and automated incident response.

This chapter explores how AI is transforming cybersecurity from every angle. We'll look at the key differences between traditional cybersecurity and AI-driven security, examine how AI enhances predictive defense, anomaly detection, and automation, and finally, reveal how attackers are weaponizing AI to outsmart even the most sophisticated defenses.

Traditional Cybersecurity vs. AI-Driven Security
1. Traditional Cybersecurity: Reactive, Signature-Based, Human-Driven
Traditional cybersecurity methods relied on human expertise and static rule-based systems. Key components included:
- Antivirus software that relied on known malware signatures.
- Firewalls that filtered traffic using static rules.
- Manual threat hunting where analysts manually review logs for suspicious activity.

While these methods were effective in the past, they have significant limitations:
- Reactive Nature: Traditional defenses only responded after an attack occurred.
- Human Fatigue: Analysts become overwhelmed by thousands of daily alerts.
- Static Detection: Signature-based systems fail to detect zero-day vulnerabilities or self-evolving malware.

2. AI-Driven Cybersecurity: Proactive, Adaptive, and Automated

AI-driven security introduces a fundamental shift in approach. Instead of waiting for an attack to happen, AI systems predict and prevent attacks before they strike.

Key components of AI-driven security include:
- Machine Learning Models that learn from historical data to predict and prevent attacks.
- SOAR Platforms that automate security incident response.
- Behavioral Analytics to identify anomalies in user and device behavior.

Example:
A traditional antivirus might scan for a known file hash, but AI-based solutions like Cylance and SentinelOne identify threats by analyzing file behavior, even if it's a brand-new variant of malware. This means AI detects zero-day threats that traditional antivirus tools miss.

AI's Role in Predictive Defense, Anomaly Detection, and Automation

1. Predictive Defense
Imagine being able to predict a cyberattack before it happens. Predictive defense allows security teams to stay ahead of attackers. AI systems analyze millions of data points in real-time and predict where future attacks are most likely to occur.

How Predictive Defense Works
- Historical Analysis: AI models identify patterns from previous attacks.
- Threat Intelligence Feeds: AI tracks live threat intelligence from global attack reports.
- Predictive Alerts: AI sends alerts if it predicts a ransomware campaign, phishing attack, or malware outbreak.

Example:
Predictive systems like FireEye Threat Intelligence can issue early warnings about ransomware campaigns before they begin, allowing companies to bolster defenses.

Key Benefits:
- Reduces response time to zero.
- Prepares defenders before attacks happen.
- Predicts ransomware trends and phishing scams.

2. Anomaly Detection

Anomaly detection is one of AI's most critical roles. Attackers may disguise their activity, but they can't hide their behavior. Anomaly detection identifies unusual patterns in user behavior, login activity, or system processes that don't fit the "normal" activity.

How Anomaly Detection Works

- User and Entity Behavior Analytics (UEBA): AI tracks user logins, file transfers, and access logs.
- Network Traffic Analysis: AI identifies abnormal traffic flows, which could indicate a DDoS attack or data exfiltration.
- Insider Threat Detection: If an employee suddenly accesses files at 3 a.m., AI flags this as abnormal.

Example:

Microsoft Defender for Identity tracks user activity in Active Directory environments and flags unusual activity, such as users logging in from different geographic locations within hours.

Key Benefits:

- Identifies insider threats and compromised accounts.
- Detects file exfiltration and anomalous login activity.

3. Automation in Cybersecurity

Automation is the answer to the growing skill gap in cybersecurity. With too few analysts and too many alerts, companies rely on SOAR platforms to automate routine security actions.

How Automation Works

- SOAR (Security Orchestration, Automation, and Response): Automates responses to incidents (like shutting down infected devices).
- Response Playbooks: AI-driven platforms trigger a sequence of actions when an attack is detected.
- Malware Containment: If AI detects ransomware, it isolates the infected system and blocks further access.

Example:

Palo Alto Cortex XSOAR automatically quarantines malware-infected devices and deactivates user credentials if a breach is detected.

Key Benefits:

- Reduces time-to-response from hours to seconds.
- Reduces false positives through machine learning.

How Attackers Use AI Offensively
Attackers are no longer relying on manual effort or guesswork.
With AI at their disposal, they can automate, predict, and
personalize attacks with precision and scale never seen before. The
following are the key offensive tactics attackers use to target
individuals, businesses, and entire organizations.

1. AI-Powered Phishing Bots (Spear Phishing & Whaling)

How It Works:
Traditional phishing emails were easy to spot — bad grammar,
generic wording, and suspicious links. But AI-powered phishing
bots are game-changers. They use Natural Language Processing
(NLP) to craft highly personalized messages based on your online
activity, social media posts, and company announcements.
Attackers scrape social media, LinkedIn, and breach databases to
create emails that look like they're coming from a trusted person,
such as your boss, a coworker, or even your bank.

Example Attack:
Imagine receiving an email from your "boss" while they're on a
work trip. The email says:

"Hey, I'm in a meeting with clients right now, but I need you to
wire $4,000 to our new supplier in Singapore. I'll explain later.
Here's the account: [Bank Details]. Can you handle this ASAP?"

It feels urgent, it looks real, and it's timed perfectly. AI-generated
phishing emails create this level of believability automatically.
Business Email Compromise (BEC) scams like these cost
companies billions every year.

How to Defend Against It:
- Use AI-driven anti-phishing filters (like those in Google
  Workspace) to detect unusual email activity.
- Verify high-risk requests via phone or secondary contact before
  taking action.
- Use Domain-Based Message Authentication, Reporting, and
  Conformance (DMARC) to stop email spoofing attacks.

2. Deepfake Voice & Video Impersonation (Voice Cloning Attacks)

How It Works:
Attackers use AI-driven voice cloning tools to replicate the voices of executives, family members, or trusted figures. With just 10-20 seconds of voice recording, tools like ElevenLabs, Voice.ai, and Resemble AI can create eerily accurate voice clones. Attackers then use these voice clones in phone calls, WhatsApp voice notes, or Zoom video impersonations.

Example Attack:
A finance executive receives a phone call from the "CEO" asking them to wire $250,000 for a "surprise merger announcement." The voice on the phone sounds exactly like the CEO — but it's actually a deepfake-generated voice. The scam works because voice biometrics (like tone, pitch, and rhythm) are replicated with near-perfection.

How to Defend Against It:
- Use the "Family Password" technique discussed in Chapter 12 for family calls and sensitive requests.
- Create a voice verification policy for executive financial approvals (require callback verification).
- Train employees to be skeptical of high-stakes requests made via phone or voice message.

3. Polymorphic & Self-Evolving Malware

How It Works:
Polymorphic malware changes its code every few seconds to avoid detection by antivirus tools. Attackers use AI mutation engines to modify malware automatically after each infection. These attacks are now evolving into self-learning malware that adapts based on the defenses it encounters. When antivirus tools recognize the malware, it "learns" from the detection and changes its attack pattern.

Example Attack:
The Emotet malware constantly changes its file structure to avoid detection, creating unique malware variants for every infection. Self-evolving malware is the next evolution, using AI to adjust and "learn" from its previous attempts. If an antivirus stops it once, the malware alters its attack strategy for the next target.

How to Defend Against It:
- Use behavioral-based EDR (Endpoint Detection and Response), which tracks behavior, not signatures.
- Deploy AI-driven malware detection tools like SentinelOne or CrowdStrike.
- Use sandbox environments to analyze file behavior before it can run on your system.

4. AI-Guided Social Engineering Attacks (Baiting, Pretexting, and Quid Pro Quo Scams)

How It Works:
AI has given social engineering a dangerous new twist. Attackers can use AI chatbots to engage with you in conversations, posing as customer support agents, coworkers, or family members. AI can impersonate chat agents on customer support portals or social media channels like WhatsApp, Discord, and Telegram.

Example Attack:
You message "customer support" on a company's website. The chat agent (actually an AI-driven bot) says:

"Hi [your name], I see that your account is locked. I can reset it for you, but I'll need your email and phone number for verification."

The bot learns from your responses and escalates the attack. Since the AI-driven chatbot sounds human, most people don't realize it's fake.

How to Defend Against It:
- Avoid sharing personal details in customer support chats.
- Verify the support number or website before initiating a chat.
- Don't trust chatbots with sensitive information. Call the company's official support line instead.

5. AI-Driven Password Cracking & Credential Stuffing

How It Works:
Attackers use AI to predict passwords. By analyzing leaked passwords from past breaches, AI models learn the most common password patterns, like "Name123" or "PetName2024". Tools like Hashcat and John the Ripper use AI to crack passwords in a fraction of the time it took before.

Example Attack:
With AI's ability to predict password patterns, attackers use "credential stuffing" to reuse stolen passwords from one platform (like a LinkedIn breach) on another platform (like Netflix or Gmail). If you reuse passwords across sites, attackers can easily breach multiple accounts.

How to Defend Against It:
- Don't reuse passwords across platforms.
- Use a password manager to create long, random, unique passwords for each site.
- Enable Multi-Factor Authentication (MFA) on all your accounts.

6. Adversarial AI Attacks (Fooling AI Defenses)

How It Works:
Adversarial AI attacks manipulate machine learning models by feeding them poisoned data. Attackers upload adversarial "noise" to images, files, or inputs, causing the AI to misclassify them. For example, a subtle alteration to a security camera feed could cause an AI-driven facial recognition system to mislabel a criminal as "Authorized Personnel."

Example Attack:
A self-driving car's AI sees a "STOP" sign as a "Speed Limit 50" sign after attackers placed stickers on the sign. This attack is possible due to adversarial inputs that exploit AI's reliance on pattern recognition.

How to Defend Against It:
- Use adversarial training to teach AI models how to recognize adversarial inputs.
- Rely on Explainable AI (XAI) to understand how AI systems classify inputs.

7. Reconnaissance and Vulnerability Scanning with AI

How It Works:
Attackers deploy AI-powered bots to scan thousands of websites for vulnerabilities simultaneously. These bots analyze software, servers, and APIs, searching for misconfigurations, exposed APIs, or unpatched systems.

Example Attack:
During the Log4j vulnerability incident, attackers used AI bots to scan every exposed web server, looking for companies that hadn't patched the Log4j flaw. Attackers breached thousands of servers in just hours.

How to Defend Against It:
- Use vulnerability management tools to identify and patch misconfigurations.
- Regularly scan for vulnerabilities with AI-driven tools like Tenable.io.
- Patch known vulnerabilities immediately when they're disclosed.

Conclusion: The Rise of Offensive AI
AI has transformed cybercrime from a manual process to a fully automated attack system. From deepfake impersonations to AI-guided chatbots and mutating malware, every attack has become smarter, faster, and more adaptive. Attackers use AI to predict passwords, clone voices, automate phishing, and find vulnerabilities.

But you're not defenseless. Every tactic attackers use has a corresponding AI defense. In Chapter 3, you'll learn how to defend against these threats, recognizing how AI-driven anomaly detection, EDR, and Zero-Trust systems give you the edge. The fight is no longer human vs. human — it's AI vs. AI.

Chapter 3: Cyber Threat Landscape

The <u>Five</u> Horsemen of Cybersecurity
For years, cybersecurity experts discussed the "Four Horsemen of Cybersecurity" — Ransomware, Phishing, Social Engineering, and Malware. But with the rise of AI, a new threat has emerged — one so powerful it can trick our most fundamental instincts. This threat is called Deepfakes, and it has become the Fifth Horseman of Cybersecurity.

This chapter will explore the Five Horsemen and explain how they work together to attack individuals, businesses, and entire nations.

The Five Horsemen are:

1. Ransomware — Encrypts your files and demands payment for decryption.

2. Phishing — Tricks you into handing over sensitive information or login credentials.

3. Social Engineering — Manipulates people into giving away secrets, passwords, or access.

4. Malware — A catch-all for malicious software, trojans, and ransomware delivery tools.

5. Deepfakes — AI-generated video, voice, or images designed to trick your senses and convince you to trust an attacker.

Attackers don't just rely on one of these methods. In most attacks, they combine multiple threats, like using phishing to deliver malware or using social engineering to enable ransomware. But the most dangerous of all might be Deepfakes — because they target your sense of reality itself.

Comprehensive Overview of Ransomware, Phishing, Social Engineering, Malware, and Deepfakes
In this section, we'll explore the details of each of the Five Horsemen. We'll see how they operate independently, but also how they are often combined in larger, multi-stage attacks.
- Ransomware: Encrypts your files and demands payment to unlock them.
- Phishing: Lures you in with fake emails or websites, stealing passwords and personal data.

- Social Engineering: Manipulates human behavior with pretexting, baiting, and impersonation.
- Malware: Installs malicious software on your system to spy, steal, or destroy.
- Deepfakes: Uses AI-generated video, voice, and images to deceive you into thinking you're interacting with a real person.

1. Ransomware: The Digital Hostage Crisis

The Rise of Digital Extortion
Imagine waking up one day and discovering that all of your files—your family photos, business documents, customer records, and critical company databases—are completely locked. A message on your screen reads:

"Your files have been encrypted. Pay $1 million in Bitcoin within 72 hours, or they will be permanently deleted."

This is the terrifying reality of a ransomware attack. Ransomware has become one of the most devastating cyber threats in the world. By targeting hospitals, corporations, government agencies, and individuals, ransomware attackers have found a highly profitable criminal model that exploits fear, urgency, and helplessness.

What is Ransomware?
Ransomware is a type of malware that encrypts the victim's files or systems, rendering them unusable. Attackers demand a ransom, often paid in cryptocurrency like Bitcoin or Monero, in exchange for a decryption key.

Unlike traditional malware that spies or steals, ransomware locks you out. This makes it different from viruses, worms, or Trojans. Its primary goal is to disrupt the Availability pillar of the CIA Triad (Confidentiality, Integrity, Availability).

Ransomware attacks have grown exponentially, with damages projected to reach $30 billion annually by 2025. Attackers often target essential services (like hospitals) where downtime is too costly to bear, increasing the chances that victims will pay.

How Ransomware Works: The 5 Stages of Attack
- 1. Infection (Delivery and Initial Access)
- 2. Installation and Execution
- 3. File Encryption
- 4. Ransom Demand
- 5. Payment or Recovery

1. Infection (Delivery and Initial Access)

The first step in a ransomware attack is to gain access to the victim's network, system, or device. Initial access is often achieved through the following methods:

- Phishing Emails: Attackers trick users into clicking malicious links or downloading infected attachments.
  - Example: A user receives an email claiming to be from "Microsoft Security" asking them to click a link to "fix an urgent issue."
  - How AI Makes It Worse: AI is used to create highly personalized phishing emails using data from social media profiles.

- Exploiting Vulnerabilities: Attackers exploit unpatched software vulnerabilities.
  - Example: The WannaCry ransomware attack in 2017 exploited the EternalBlue vulnerability in Windows' Server Message Block (SMB) protocol.
  - How AI Makes It Worse: AI-driven bots automatically scan the internet for vulnerable systems and deploy ransomware as soon as a weakness is detected.
- Malicious Downloads (Drive-By Downloads): Attackers plant ransomware on compromised websites, and users download it unknowingly.
  - Example: A user visits a legitimate website that has been hijacked. A hidden download installs ransomware in the background.

- Insider Threats: Employees with internal access may intentionally (or accidentally) install ransomware on the network.
  - Example: An employee clicks on a USB stick left in the parking lot, unknowingly launching ransomware.

2. Installation and Execution

Once the attacker gains access, the next step is to install and execute the ransomware on the target system. This phase involves running the ransomware file, which can be a .exe, .vbs, .js, or .bat file.

- Stealth Mode: Modern ransomware remains "silent" for several minutes or hours to avoid detection.
- File Persistence: Ransomware embeds itself in critical system files or startup files so it runs again every time the device reboots.
- Privilege Escalation: The ransomware seeks administrator privileges to infect system-wide files, not just local files.

Real-World Example:
- Ryuk Ransomware: Used by the Wizard Spider Group, it remains dormant for hours or days to avoid detection before launching its encryption attack.

How AI Plays a Role:
- AI-Driven Polymorphic Malware: Attackers use AI to create polymorphic ransomware that changes its code every few hours, making it undetectable to traditional antivirus software.
- Fileless Ransomware: Instead of installing traditional files, attackers use PowerShell scripts or in-memory execution to run the ransomware directly from system memory, leaving no trace on disk.

3. File Encryption

This is where the real damage happens. Ransomware scans the victim's system for specific file types (like .docx, .xlsx, .pdf, .jpg, .mp4, and .zip files) and encrypts them using strong encryption algorithms like AES-256 or RSA-2048.
- Encryption Techniques:
  - AES-256 (Advanced Encryption Standard): Symmetric encryption used to lock files.
  - RSA-2048 (Rivest-Shamir-Adleman): Public-key cryptography where only the attacker holds the decryption key.
- Speed of Encryption:
  - Modern ransomware can encrypt thousands of files per minute, thanks to multi-threading.
  - AI-Driven Ransomware selects which files to encrypt first (critical business files) and skips unimportant ones.

How AI Plays a Role:
- AI-Powered Target Prioritization: AI identifies which files are "most valuable" (like databases) and encrypts them first.
- Stealthy Encryption: AI adjusts the encryption speed to avoid triggering anomaly detection systems.

4. Ransom Demand

Once encryption is complete, the attacker displays a ransom note on the victim's screen. The note typically includes:
- Payment Instructions: Usually, victims must pay in Bitcoin or Monero (to maintain attacker anonymity).
- Deadline: Attackers impose a time limit, such as "Pay within 72 hours, or the ransom doubles."
- Proof of Decryption: Some attackers decrypt one or two files as proof they can decrypt the rest.

5. Payment or Recovery
At this stage, the victim faces a difficult decision:
- Pay Ransom: Some victims pay, hoping to restore their files.
- Restore from Backup: If backups exist, you can avoid paying.
- Do Nothing: In some cases, victims simply lose everything.

Real-World Case:
- Colonial Pipeline: The company paid $4.4 million in Bitcoin to the attackers.

How AI Helps Attackers in this Phase:
- AI-Driven Payment Tracking: Attackers use AI to track cryptocurrency payments and detect who paid and who didn't.
- AI Chatbots: Attackers use chatbots for "customer support" to negotiate with victims.

How to Defend Against Ransomware
Here are the most effective defenses against ransomware:
- Backups and Disaster Recovery: Maintain daily backups stored in offline environments.
- Endpoint Detection and Response (EDR): AI-based EDR tools like SentinelOne monitor system behavior and block suspicious activity.
- Patch Management: Many ransomware attacks (like WannaCry) exploited unpatched vulnerabilities.
- Zero-Trust Security: Reduce system access permissions to limit the spread of ransomware.
- AI-Powered Anomaly Detection: Use AI tools that monitor for sudden spikes in file modifications (a sign of encryption).
- Cybersecurity Awareness Training: Train employees to avoid phishing links, the most common ransomware delivery method.

Ransomware is rarely a "standalone attack." Instead, it works hand-in-hand with phishing, malware, and social engineering. Here's how they connect:
- Social Engineering: Attackers use social engineering to trick employees into downloading ransomware-infected files.
- Phishing: A phishing email may contain a link or file that triggers the download of ransomware.
- Malware: Attackers install backdoors and remote access trojans (RATs) to re-launch ransomware later.

Conclusion
Ransomware is one of the most profitable, scalable, and AI-driven threats. Attackers use phishing, vulnerabilities, and insider threats to launch attacks. But defenders aren't powerless. By using AI-driven EDR, anomaly detection, and backups, companies can detect, prevent, and recover from ransomware.

2. Phishing: The Art of Deception
Introduction: Why Phishing is the Most Dangerous Cyber Threat
Phishing is often called the "gateway" to other cyberattacks. Unlike ransomware, which focuses on encrypting files, or malware, which operates in stealth, phishing goes straight for human vulnerability. Phishing doesn't just attack computers — it attacks the human mind.

91% of all cyberattacks begin with a phishing email. From ransomware infections to corporate data breaches, most modern attacks start with one employee, customer, or partner being tricked into clicking a link, downloading a file, or sharing their password. In the era of AI-driven phishing kits, phishing attacks have become more personal, convincing, and scalable than ever before. Attackers are using Natural Language Processing (NLP) to write human-like messages, and AI-powered social media scrapers gather personal information to customize these attacks. The goal is simple: make you trust them.

This section provides an in-depth look at how phishing works, the different types of phishing attacks, and the techniques attackers use to manipulate their targets.

How Phishing Works: The 4-Stage Process
Phishing is simple at its core, but modern attacks have become more sophisticated thanks to AI and automation. Here's a step-by-step breakdown of how a typical phishing attack works:

1. Reconnaissance (Building the Target List)
Before launching a phishing campaign, attackers need targets. They research potential victims to make their attack more personalized and believable. This process is called Open Source Intelligence (OSINT), and attackers use publicly available information like:
- Social Media: LinkedIn profiles, Facebook posts, and other social sites provide valuable information about employees, job roles, and company operations.
- Corporate Websites: Attackers scrape employee names, email addresses, and job titles from company websites.
- Email Breach Dumps: Attackers use leaked email/password dumps from data breaches to identify active targets.

2. Attack Delivery (Getting the Victim to Click)
Once the target list is built, the attacker must deliver the phishing message. They choose from one of these methods:
- Email Phishing: The most common method. Victims receive an email with a malicious link or attachment.
- SMS Phishing (Smishing): Victims receive a fraudulent text message.
- Voice Phishing (Vishing): Attackers call targets, pretending to be customer service agents, IT support, or government officials.
- Social Media DMs: Attackers send messages on LinkedIn, Instagram, or Facebook Messenger with malicious links.

How AI is Used in Attack Delivery
- AI-Driven Personalization: AI scrapes social media data to personalize the message, making it more convincing.
- Natural Language Processing (NLP): Attackers use NLP to write better, more human-like emails that avoid spam filters.
- Phishing-as-a-Service (PhaaS): Attackers buy access to pre-built phishing kits, complete with AI-enhanced templates and scripts.

3. The Hook (Exploiting Trust)
Once the victim opens the email, the attacker needs to convince them to act. This could mean:
- Clicking a link: The link takes them to a fake website (like a fake PayPal login page).
- Downloading a file: The file may look like a legitimate PDF but actually installs malware.
- Responding to a request: The victim might be asked to reply with personal information (like bank details or a one-time password).

How AI Plays a Role in The Hook
- Adapting Real-Time Conversations: AI-powered chatbots respond in real time to victims who reply to phishing messages.
- Dynamic Phishing Pages: Attackers use AI-generated "fake login pages" that look identical to the legitimate site.
- Behavioral Analysis: AI tracks which types of messages people are more likely to click on, improving future campaigns.

4. The Catch (Exploitation)

At this stage, the attacker has achieved their goal. The victim has either:

- Entered Credentials on a fake login page (like Gmail or Office 365).
- Downloaded Malware that allows the attacker to remotely control the system.
- Transferred Funds via a fraudulent payment request.

Once credentials are stolen, attackers use them to log in as the victim and escalate their attack. This is often the start of a larger campaign involving ransomware, data theft, or corporate espionage.

Types of Phishing Attacks

1. Email Phishing

The most common form of phishing. Attackers send mass emails, often pretending to be banks, tech companies, or popular brands. The goal is to get as many people as possible to click on a link or download a file.

Example:
"Your PayPal account has been restricted. Click here to verify your information."

2. Spear Phishing

Unlike email phishing, spear phishing targets a specific individual or organization. Attackers do extensive research on their target, using data from LinkedIn, social media, and company websites to make the attack more convincing.

Example:
"Hi Sarah, this is Mark from HR. Please log in to our new employee benefits portal here."

3. Whaling

Whaling targets high-profile individuals, like CEOs, CFOs, and senior executives. Attackers impersonate board members or executives to convince employees to transfer large sums of money.

Example:
"This is your CEO. We need a wire transfer for $50,000 sent to this vendor ASAP."

4. Vishing (Voice Phishing)
Attackers call their victims, pretending to be bank representatives, tech support, or government officials. With AI voice cloning, attackers can now mimic the voice of CEOs or executives to trick employees.

Example:
"This is John from IT. We noticed suspicious login attempts on your account. Can you share your one-time password with me to secure it?"

5. Smishing (SMS Phishing)
Attackers send fraudulent text messages designed to look like they're from legitimate companies (like banks or shipping companies). The goal is to get the user to click a link or share their details.

Example:
"FedEx: We tried to deliver your package. Please click here to reschedule."

How Attackers Use AI in Phishing
- AI-Powered Personalization: Attackers use AI to scrape social media data to craft personalized messages.
- Deepfake Voice Phishing: Attackers use AI to create deepfake calls where they clone the CEO's voice to request wire transfers.
- Phishing-as-a-Service (PhaaS): Attackers buy pre-built AI-driven phishing kits from the dark web.

How to Defend Against Phishing
1. Email Security Solutions
- AI-Powered Email Filters: Tools like Barracuda Sentinel analyze and block phishing emails before they reach users.
- Anti-Spoofing (SPF, DKIM, DMARC): Prevents attackers from spoofing legitimate email addresses.

2. Employee Training
- Spot Red Flags: Teach employees to recognize:
  - Urgent language (e.g., "Act now!")
  - Misspellings or incorrect branding.
  - Suspicious links.
3. Zero-Trust Security
- Enforce Zero-Trust Authentication, requiring users to authenticate every login or sensitive action.
- Multi-Factor Authentication (MFA) ensures that stolen passwords alone are not enough.

4. AI-Driven Phishing Detection
- AI-Driven URL Analysis: Uses machine learning to detect malicious URLs embedded in emails.
- Behavioral Analytics: AI tracks normal user behavior and flags anomalies (like logging into Gmail from another country).

Phishing Case Studies
- Ubiquiti Networks Whaling Scam: Attackers impersonated executives and convinced employees to send over $46 million in fraudulent wire transfers.
- Twitter Hack (2020): Attackers used spear-phishing to obtain admin credentials, allowing them to tweet from high-profile accounts like Elon Musk and Joe Biden.

Conclusion
Phishing is the most widely used form of cyberattack. Attackers use it to steal credentials, install malware, and launch ransomware. With AI-driven spear-phishing, vishing, and whaling, these attacks have become more convincing. But with AI-powered email filters, user education, and Zero-Trust authentication, you can protect yourself and your business.

3. Social Engineering: Hacking the Human Mind

The Human Element in Cybersecurity
While organizations spend millions on firewalls, antivirus software, and endpoint detection, attackers are bypassing all of it by targeting the weakest link in the chain — humans. This is the essence of social engineering. It's not about hacking computers; it's about hacking people's trust, emotions, and cognitive biases.

Unlike phishing or malware, social engineering doesn't rely on code. Instead, it exploits human psychology using pretexting, impersonation, baiting, and authority manipulation. Attackers use tactics like urgency ("Act now!"), fear ("Your account has been compromised!"), and curiosity ("See what's inside this USB drive!") to get victims to act against their best interests.

With the advent of AI-driven social engineering tactics, attacks are becoming more scalable, targeted, and personalized. Deepfakes, AI chatbots, and behavioral analysis have supercharged the ability of attackers to manipulate people at scale. This section breaks down how social engineering works, the different attack techniques, and the best ways to defend against it.

What is Social Engineering?
Social engineering is the art of manipulating people into revealing sensitive information, granting access, or taking an action that benefits the attacker. Instead of hacking computers, attackers hack the psychology of humans.

Unlike malware, which relies on technical flaws, social engineering attacks target cognitive biases — the natural mental shortcuts people use to make decisions. Attackers manipulate these biases, such as:
- Authority Bias: Trusting figures of authority (like a "CEO" or "IT support agent").
- Urgency Bias: Acting quickly without thinking due to perceived time pressure.
- Curiosity Bias: Clicking on unexpected items (like "Employee Salary Data").

How Social Engineering Works: The 5-Step Process
1. Reconnaissance (Building the Backstory)
Before launching a social engineering attack, attackers gather as much information as possible about the target. The more personalized the attack, the higher the success rate. This stage is called reconnaissance. Attackers gather details using Open Source Intelligence (OSINT).

How Attackers Gather Intel:
- Social Media: LinkedIn, Facebook, and Instagram posts reveal personal info (like birthdays, vacations, and relationships).
- Company Websites: Attackers collect employee lists, job titles, and organizational structures from "About Us" pages.
- Data Breach Dumps: Leaked password databases are used to see if employees have reused credentials.
- Job Postings: Job listings reveal what software and technologies companies use, giving attackers insight into internal systems.

2. Pretexting (The Setup)
In this stage, the attacker creates a believable scenario or "pretext". They assume the identity of someone the victim trusts, like:
- IT Support: "This is the IT department. We noticed suspicious activity on your account. Please verify your password."
- Executive Impersonation: Attackers impersonate senior executives (like the CEO) to request urgent actions.
- Delivery Personnel: Attackers pose as couriers to gain physical access to secure areas.

How AI Plays a Role:
- AI Voice Cloning (Deepfake Audio): Attackers use AI-generated deepfake voices to impersonate CEOs and request wire transfers.
- Chatbots: Attackers use AI-powered chatbots to manipulate customer service reps into giving out information (like security questions or PII).

3. Engagement (Manipulation Begins)
Once the pretext is established, the attacker begins direct interaction with the victim. This can happen in person, over the phone, or via email. The attacker creates urgency or fear to force the victim to act quickly.

Examples of Manipulation Tactics:
- Urgency: "Your account will be locked in 10 minutes unless you verify it now."
- Fear: "The IRS has flagged your account for fraud."
- Authority: "This is John, the CEO. I need this wire transfer done in 30 minutes."

4. Exploitation (The Attack Happens)
At this stage, the attacker convinces the victim to click, act, or share sensitive information. This could mean:
- Providing Credentials: Entering a password on a fake login page.
- Sending a Payment: Transferring funds to a fraudulent bank account.
- Granting Access: Letting a "delivery driver" into a secure building.

5. Exit and Cover-Up (Cleaning the Tracks)
Once the goal is achieved, the attacker may attempt to cover their tracks to avoid being caught. This is common in long-term insider threat campaigns. They may:
- Erase Chat Logs: If they used social media DMs, they delete the messages.
- Remove USB Devices: If they dropped an infected USB in the company parking lot, they recover it later.
- Plant Backdoors: Attackers install backdoor malware to maintain long-term access.

Types of Social Engineering Attacks
1. Pretexting
Attackers pretend to be someone the victim trusts, such as:
- IT Support: "We need to check your account for suspicious activity. Please provide your login info."
- Police/Government Official: "This is Officer Smith from the IRS. We have flagged you for fraud."

2. Baiting
Attackers leave "bait" for the victim to discover. This could be a USB drive with the label "Employee Salaries" left in the parking lot. When an employee plugs it in, it installs malware.

3. Impersonation
The attacker physically enters a secure location by pretending to be someone else. Examples include:
- Fake Delivery Driver: Pretends to be a delivery driver to enter a restricted area.
- Fake IT Technician: Poses as an IT worker to gain access to company servers.

4. Tailgating
This is a physical access tactic where an attacker follows a legitimate employee into a secure area without swiping a badge.

5. Piggybacking
Similar to tailgating, but in this case, the attacker actively convinces someone to let them in. For example, "Can you hold the door for me? I left my badge at home."

How Attackers Use AI in Social Engineering
1. Deepfake Audio & Video
Attackers clone the voice of a CEO and call employees, asking for wire transfers. Deepfake video calls can also trick employees into trusting attackers.

2. AI Chatbots for Pretexting
Attackers deploy chatbots on social media platforms to trick users into giving away their information.

3. Social Media Scraping with AI
AI scrapes LinkedIn, Facebook, and Instagram for names, job titles, and personal details to craft more convincing pretexts.

How to Defend Against Social Engineering
1. Employee Training
Training employees to spot social engineering tactics is the most important defense. Key red flags include:
- Urgent requests for credentials.
- Requests for payments to "new accounts".
- Unexpected requests for "emergency help" from executives.

2. Multi-Factor Authentication (MFA)
Even if attackers obtain a password, MFA stops them from logging in. MFA requires a second form of authentication, like a mobile app or SMS code.

3. Zero-Trust Access Control
Never trust, always verify. Users must prove their identity for each request. Even if a CEO's credentials are stolen, MFA and zero-trust can prevent unauthorized actions.

4. Anomaly Detection with AI
AI tracks user behavior (like login times, devices, and geographic locations). If it sees a user log in from two countries in the same hour, it flags it.

Case Studies of Social Engineering Attacks
Twitter Bitcoin Scam (2020)
Attackers tricked Twitter employees into revealing admin credentials, which allowed them to hijack high-profile accounts like Elon Musk and Joe Biden to promote a Bitcoin scam.

USB Drop Attack (U.S. Government)
Attackers dropped USB sticks outside government buildings. Employees picked them up and inserted them into their computers, causing backdoor malware to be installed.

Deepfake Impersonation Scam (2024)
In early 2024, a finance employee at a multinational company's Hong Kong branch was deceived into transferring approximately $25.6 million. Scammers orchestrated a video conference using deepfake technology to impersonate the company's Chief Financial Officer and other staff members. Convinced by the authenticity of the meeting, the employee authorized 15 transfers to multiple bank accounts before discovering the fraud.

This incident highlights the growing sophistication of social engineering attacks leveraging artificial intelligence to create convincing impersonations.

Conclusion
Social engineering is one of the most dangerous attack methods because it targets people, not systems. It bypasses firewalls, antivirus software, and detection systems. Attackers use pretexting, impersonation, baiting, and tailgating to manipulate human emotions and behaviors.

With AI-driven voice deepfakes, chatbots, and social media scraping, social engineering attacks are becoming more personalized, scalable, and effective. The best defenses are employee training, MFA, and anomaly detection.

4. Malware: The Cybercrime Swiss Army Knife

When people hear the term "malware", they often think of computer viruses. But malware is far more than that. Malware, short for "malicious software", is a category of software designed to spy, steal, damage, or disrupt. It includes viruses, trojans, worms, spyware, ransomware, rootkits, and more.

Malware is a critical tool in the arsenal of cybercriminals, state-sponsored hackers, and ransomware gangs. While phishing attacks may trick users into revealing login details, malware allows attackers to take control of entire systems, spy on victims, and establish backdoors for future attacks.

With the advent of AI-driven malware, attackers now have the power to create self-evolving, polymorphic malware that changes its code every few minutes, making it almost impossible to detect. In this section, we'll explore how malware works, the different types of malware, how attackers use AI to enhance their tactics, and how you can protect yourself from these evolving threats.

What is Malware?

Malware (short for malicious software) refers to any software that is intentionally designed to cause harm to systems, steal information, or grant unauthorized access. Unlike ransomware, which locks users out, malware is more versatile. It can spy, steal, disrupt, and destroy.

Malware can be a standalone program, or it can hide inside other files, applications, or links. For example, a seemingly innocent attachment (like invoice.pdf.exe) might actually be a Trojan that installs a backdoor on your system.

How Malware Works: The 6-Stage Process
1. Delivery (How Malware Enters a System)

The first step in a malware attack is getting the malware onto the victim's system. Hackers use a variety of methods to deliver malware to unsuspecting users, including:

- Phishing Emails: A user clicks a link or downloads an attachment, thinking it's an invoice or report, but it installs malware.
- Drive-By Downloads: Hackers compromise legitimate websites, and when a user visits, malware downloads automatically.
- USB Drops: Attackers drop USB drives labeled "Employee Bonus Report" in parking lots. Curious employees plug them in, infecting the system.
- Software Exploits: Attackers exploit vulnerabilities in software (like Log4j or unpatched browsers) to install malware remotely.

How AI Plays a Role
- AI-Driven Reconnaissance: Attackers use AI to scan the internet for vulnerable systems and identify weak entry points.
- Automated Phishing Campaigns: AI can send thousands of personalized phishing emails in minutes, leading to a higher infection rate.

2. Installation (Setting Up Basecamp)

Once the malware is on the target system, it needs to embed itself into the system to ensure it isn't easily removed. Attackers often focus on persistence so that malware survives reboots and system cleanups.

Common Techniques for Installation
- Rootkits: Malware installs itself in the kernel (the core of the OS), making it nearly impossible to detect.
- Registry Manipulation: Malware adds itself to startup programs, ensuring it runs every time the system is booted.
- Hidden Directories: Attackers hide malware files in obscure directories or name them similarly to legitimate files (like winservices.exe).

How AI Plays a Role
- AI-Driven Rootkits: Attackers use AI to create smarter rootkits that stay hidden for longer periods.
- Polymorphic Malware: Attackers use AI to make malware change its code every few minutes, allowing it to bypass antivirus detection.

3. Command and Control (C2)

After installation, the malware attempts to connect to the attacker's server (called a Command and Control server or C2 server). This server sends instructions to the malware, telling it what to do next.

Actions the C2 Server Might Order
- Exfiltrate Data: Send back login credentials, financial info, or PII.
- Install More Malware: Deploy ransomware, spyware, or banking trojans.
- Launch DDoS Attacks: Use the infected device as part of a botnet.

How AI Plays a Role
- C2 Obfuscation: AI helps hide the location of the C2 server by frequently changing the IP address using Fast Flux networks.
- Behavioral Analysis Avoidance: AI tells malware to avoid activating when a sandbox or analysis environment is detected.

4. Propagation (Spreading to Other Devices)
Some malware, like worms, has the ability to self-replicate and spread. Unlike traditional viruses that need human interaction, worms spread automatically.

Propagation Methods
- Network Worms: Malware spreads to all devices on a connected network.
- File Infections: Malware attaches itself to files like Word documents or Excel spreadsheets, and when those files are shared, the infection spreads.

How AI Plays a Role
- Smart Propagation Paths: AI helps malware decide which devices to target first (like high-value servers).
- Self-Evolving Malware: Attackers use AI mutation engines to create thousands of malware variants that spread undetected.

5. Payload Execution (The Attack Begins)
At this point, the malware executes its main mission. This mission could be to:
- Exfiltrate Data: Send passwords, financial data, or customer records back to the attacker.
- Install Ransomware: Encrypt files and demand payment in Bitcoin.
- Destroy Data: Use wiper malware to destroy hard drives.
- Spy on Users: Use keyloggers to steal passwords as users type them.

6. Persistence (Staying in Control)
After the attack, the malware attempts to remain on the system for future use. This is especially common with backdoors and Remote Access Trojans (RATs). Attackers can access the system whenever they want, even after the initial attack is over.

Types of Malware
1. Viruses
Viruses attach themselves to other files (like .exe files) and spread when those files are shared.
- Example: The ILOVEYOU virus infected over 10 million users in 2000 by disguising itself as a "love letter" email attachment.

2. Trojans
A Trojan hides inside a legitimate-looking file but secretly carries malware.
- Example: Emotet Trojan originally posed as a banking app, but later turned into a delivery platform for ransomware.

3. Worms
Unlike viruses, worms self-replicate and don't need human interaction.
- Example: The Stuxnet worm was used to disrupt Iran's nuclear centrifuges.

4. Ransomware
Ransomware locks files and demands payment to decrypt them.
- Example: WannaCry affected 200,000 systems worldwide in 2017.

5. Spyware
Spyware tracks user activity and sends it back to the attacker.
- Example: Pegasus spyware was used to spy on journalists and politicians worldwide.

6. Keyloggers
Keyloggers capture and record keystrokes, stealing passwords and sensitive information.
- Example: Keyloggers are often included in Trojans and are used to steal banking passwords.

7. Backdoors
Backdoors allow attackers to maintain secret access to the system.
- Example: SolarWinds Attack (2020) included a backdoor trojan that let attackers control U.S. government networks.

How to Defend Against Malware
1. Use AI-Powered Endpoint Detection and Response (EDR)
   - AI tools like SentinelOne detect malware based on behavior, not just signatures.
2. Zero-Trust Security
   - Assume that every system, user, and device is untrusted. Limit access to sensitive areas.
3. Multi-Factor Authentication (MFA)
   - Even if malware steals credentials, MFA prevents logins.
4. Update and Patch Regularly
   - The WannaCry attack could have been stopped if users had patched their Windows systems.

Conclusion
Malware is the most versatile weapon in the attacker's arsenal. From ransomware to Trojans to spyware, it can steal, spy, and destroy. With AI-driven malware mutation engines and fileless malware, traditional antivirus tools are no longer enough. To stay safe, use AI-based EDR, anomaly detection, and Zero-Trust security.

5.Deepfakes: The Fifth Horseman of Cybersecurity

What Are Deepfakes?
Deepfakes are AI-generated video, audio, and images that look, sound, and feel real — but they aren't. Cybercriminals use deepfake technology to impersonate CEOs, employees, celebrities, or family members. Unlike older forms of social engineering (where attackers pretend to be someone else), deepfakes are far more convincing because they manipulate human trust through visual and auditory signals.

Deepfakes are created using AI models like GANs (Generative Adversarial Networks). These models learn to "mimic" the faces, voices, and behaviors of real people using publicly available media (like interviews, podcasts, and social media videos). Attackers can train these AI models to clone voices, create hyper-realistic video calls, or forge images that look like a real person.

Attackers aren't just using deepfakes for social engineering. They are using them for:
- Business Email Compromise (BEC): Attackers impersonate C-Suite executives during video calls.
- Financial Fraud: Attackers clone a CFO's voice to order urgent wire transfers.
- Disinformation Campaigns: Deepfakes are used to produce fake videos of public figures making controversial statements.
- Social Media Scams: Deepfakes are used to impersonate people on platforms like Instagram, TikTok, and Facebook.

Unlike phishing emails or social engineering scams, which can often be spotted if you know what to look for, deepfakes are dangerous because people trust what they see and hear.
Attackers are no longer just hacking systems — they're hacking human perception.

How Deepfakes Work
Deepfakes are made possible by advances in AI-driven content creation tools. Here's how they work:

1. Voice Cloning — AI models like Resemble.AI or ElevenLabs use audio samples from social media, podcasts, or phone recordings. Attackers only need 3-5 minutes of recorded voice data to create a near-perfect clone of a person's voice. They can then call family members or employees and pretend to be a trusted person.

2. Face-Swapping (Video Deepfakes) — AI-driven software like DeepFaceLab takes video footage of a real person and overlays the face of another person. This is how scammers create fake "live" Zoom calls or Teams calls where attackers pretend to be the CEO, CFO, or a key employee.

3. Synthetic Images & Photos — Attackers use GANs (Generative Adversarial Networks) to create images of "people who don't exist." These images are used to build fake LinkedIn profiles or create online personas. Check out thispersondoesnotexist.com for an example of how convincing these AI-generated faces can be.

4. Real-Time Deepfakes (Live Streaming) — Attackers can generate live, real-time deepfakes. This allows criminals to conduct video calls on Zoom, Teams, and Google Meet while pretending to be someone else. Attackers can move their lips and face in real-time, making it appear that the CEO is giving direct orders to employees.

Why Are Deepfakes So Dangerous?
Deepfakes are unlike any of the other Four Horsemen because they target our most basic instincts — sight and sound. If you see your boss on a Zoom call, you naturally believe it's them. If you hear your child's voice on the phone, you believe it's them.

But with Deepfakes, you can no longer trust your eyes or ears. This makes them particularly dangerous in the following contexts:
- Business Fraud (BEC - Business Email Compromise): Instead of relying on phishing emails, scammers can now send a "Zoom call" from your CFO or CEO and give verbal instructions for urgent wire transfers. This makes the attack seem far more legitimate than a simple email request.
- Family Scams (Voice Cloning Attacks): Scammers can use AI to clone the voice of family members (like children) and convince parents to send emergency money. "Mom, I'm in trouble! I need $500 now!" The parent hears their child's voice and immediately responds.
- Financial Fraud: Deepfakes are used to trick bank verification systems that rely on biometric voice recognition. Attackers can "speak" using the victim's voice and bypass voice-activated bank verification systems.
- Blackmail & Extortion: Attackers can generate fake compromising videos of executives or celebrities and use them as blackmail material. These attacks are particularly devastating in reputation-driven industries.

- Disinformation & Propaganda: Attackers can create fake video footage of political leaders to disrupt elections or influence public opinion. Imagine seeing a "breaking news" video of a world leader making threats of war — only to later discover it was a deepfake.

Deepfakes are a triple threat:
- They attack businesses through BEC and fraud.
- They attack families through voice cloning scams.
- They attack public trust through disinformation campaigns.

Real-World Case Study: $25.6M Deepfake CFO Scam
In one of the most infamous deepfake attacks, cybercriminals used a deepfake video call to impersonate a CFO.
What Happened:
- Attackers used DeepFaceLab to create a realistic video of the CFO on a Zoom call.
- Employees on the call believed they were speaking to the actual CFO.
- During the call, the "CFO" gave instructions to transfer $25.6M to a new vendor for a "business-critical deal."
- Believing it was a legitimate request, employees completed the wire transfer.
- The money was never recovered.

Lesson Learned: Even trained employees can be fooled when they see the face and hear the voice of their trusted CFO.

How to Defend:
- Use anomaly detection to flag unusual transactions.
- Verify instructions using a second form of authentication (like text or phone confirmation).
- Use Deepware Scanner to detect deepfake video/audio streams.

How to Defend Against Deepfakes
Unlike traditional threats like phishing, there's no "phishing filter" that can detect Deepfakes automatically. Since they attack our visual and auditory senses, defenses must be more advanced. Here's how to defend yourself:

1. Anomaly Detection — Use **XDR, EDR,** and **SIEM** tools to detect unusual network activity (like a sudden video call from a CFO).

2. Multi-Factor Verification — If you receive a strange request (like a wire transfer) during a video call, ask for secondary confirmation via email, phone, or Slack.

3. Family Passwords — Use a Family Password Strategy (see Chapter 12) to protect yourself from voice cloning scams. Create a secret "family-only" password that only family members know. If you get a phone call from "your child," you can verify them by asking them to give you the 15th letter of the password.

4. Deepfake Detection Software — Use tools like Deepware Scanner to analyze video and audio content for signs of AI-generated deepfakes.

5. Employee Training — Train employees to be suspicious of voice calls, video calls, or messages that require urgent financial action. Even if it looks like the CEO or CFO, confirm it out-of-band (via text, call, or a second channel).

Key Takeaways from Deepfakes
- Trust Nothing, Verify Everything: If a CEO gives you instructions during a Zoom call, confirm it out-of-band.
- Family Passwords Work: If you receive a call from a "family member" in distress, verify their identity with a secret password.
- AI Detection Tools Are Essential: Use Deepware Scanner to analyze video calls for signs of deepfake manipulation.
- Anomaly Detection (XDR, SIEM) Stops Fake Calls: Modern XDR systems can detect unusual login activity or unexpected video calls.

Deepfakes vs. Other Horsemen
- Ransomware locks files; Deepfakes lock your trust.
- Phishing attacks your email inbox; Deepfakes attack your vision and hearing.
- Social Engineering uses human trickery; Deepfakes automate and perfect this trickery.
- Malware runs silently; Deepfakes are loud and visible, but deceptive.

Conclusion
Deepfakes are the most insidious of the Five Horsemen because they target our most basic instincts — sight and sound. By using AI to clone faces, voices, and entire video calls, attackers can deceive even the most cautious individuals and employees. The infamous $25.6M CFO scam shows just how powerful this tactic can be when combined with urgency and authority. Unlike malware or phishing, deepfakes attack human perception directly, making it harder to detect and defend against. To protect yourself, you must adopt a "Trust Nothing, Verify Everything" approach and leverage tools like anomaly detection, family passwords, and AI-powered deepfake scanners.

Self-Evolving Malware — How AI-Driven Malware Learns as It Spreads

The Rise of Self-Evolving Malware
Traditional malware operates on fixed code. Once antivirus software identifies its "signature," the malware is easily detected and removed. But what happens when malware learns to evolve, adapt, and mutate like a biological virus? Enter Self-Evolving Malware — a new breed of AI-driven threats.

Unlike traditional malware, self-evolving malware can change its code, behavior, and appearance automatically, making it nearly impossible to detect using traditional signature-based antivirus systems. Thanks to AI mutation engines and machine learning models, these malware programs can evolve with every infection, learning from past mistakes to avoid detection.

The concept of "malware that learns as it spreads" is no longer science fiction. In fact, polymorphic malware and metamorphic malware already exist. Attackers are now combining these mutation techniques with AI to create self-evolving malware capable of bypassing even the most sophisticated detection tools. This section explores how self-evolving malware works, its lifecycle, its use of AI and machine learning, real-world case studies, and strategies for defense.

What is Self-Evolving Malware?
Self-evolving malware refers to malicious software that changes its code, appearance, and behavior as it spreads. Traditional malware relies on static code, but self-evolving malware uses AI algorithms to modify its structure on-the-fly. This makes it nearly impossible for antivirus software to recognize it.

Key Characteristics of Self-Evolving Malware:
- Polymorphic Code: The malware's code changes slightly each time it infects a new system, making it unique for every target.
- Metamorphic Malware: The malware completely rewrites its own code after each infection, making every instance unique.
- AI-Based Learning: The malware "learns" from its failures. If it is detected on one system, it adjusts its tactics for the next system.

How Self-Evolving Malware Works: The 5-Stage Lifecycle

1. Infection (Initial Entry and Delivery)
The first stage of any malware attack is gaining access to the victim's system. Self-evolving malware uses the same delivery methods as traditional malware, but with a twist — it learns from its previous infections to refine its approach.

Common Delivery Methods:
- Phishing Emails: Victims click links or attachments that download the self-evolving malware.
- Exploiting Vulnerabilities: Malware exploits unpatched vulnerabilities like Log4j.
- Trojanized Software: Malware is hidden inside "legitimate" software downloads.
- USB Drops: Attackers leave infected USB drives in public places to be picked up by unsuspecting employees.

How AI is Used at This Stage:
- Predictive Targeting: AI scans social media (LinkedIn, Facebook) to determine the best "human targets" for a phishing attack.
- Delivery Optimization: AI learns which delivery methods (email, USB, exploit) have the highest success rates and adapts accordingly.

2. Mutation (Polymorphic and Metamorphic Transformation)
Once inside the system, the malware undergoes self-mutation to avoid detection. This is where AI-driven mutation engines come into play.
- Polymorphic Malware: The malware's appearance changes slightly (like altering its binary code) but retains its core functionality.
- Metamorphic Malware: More sophisticated than polymorphic malware, it rewrites its entire code to create a fully unique version of itself.

How Mutation Happens:
- Code Shuffling: Instructions in the malware are re-ordered to look different but still execute the same logic.
- Code Encryption: The code is encrypted, and only decrypted when executed.
- Variable Renaming: Variable names and function names are randomly changed.
- Junk Code Insertion: Random, useless instructions are added to increase the file's complexity.

How AI Enhances Mutation:
- Mutation Engines: AI-driven mutation engines analyze antivirus tools and learn how to avoid them.
- Behavioral Adjustment: If malware is detected in a sandbox, it stops running. AI identifies "sandbox conditions" and adjusts its behavior to appear benign.

3. Propagation (Spreading to Other Systems)

Self-evolving malware spreads automatically, infecting multiple devices, files, and networks. It uses worm-like capabilities to replicate itself and jump from one machine to another.

Propagation Techniques:
- Network Worms: The malware looks for other devices on the same network and infects them.
- File Sharing: Malware attaches itself to files (like PDFs or Word docs) that are shared across a network.
- Remote Exploits: If the malware identifies a vulnerable device on the network, it targets it for infection.

How AI is Used in Propagation:
- Smart Targeting: AI prioritizes high-value targets (like servers or domain controllers) over low-value targets (like printers).
- Stealthy Spread: AI tracks user behavior and spreads only during "low-activity hours" (like after work hours) to avoid detection.

4. Attack (The Payload)

Once it has spread, the malware launches its payload. The payload could be ransomware, spyware, or a simple system wiper.

Types of Payloads:
- Data Exfiltration: Malware steals files, passwords, and keystrokes.
- Ransomware: Files are encrypted, and a ransom demand appears.
- Wiper Attack: The malware destroys data, making it unrecoverable.

How AI Enhances the Attack:
- AI-Driven Payload Selection: AI determines which payload is most effective for the victim (for example, ransomware vs. spyware).
- Time-Delayed Execution: Malware waits days or weeks before executing to avoid suspicion.

5. Learning and Evolution (The AI Feedback Loop)

This is where AI truly takes control. Self-evolving malware learns from its failures. If one version of the malware is detected by antivirus, the AI-driven engine makes improvements.

- Behavioral Adaptation: If sandboxing is detected, the malware "plays dead" and avoids detection.
- Feedback Loops: Malware reports back to the attacker on which infection methods worked, and AI adjusts future versions accordingly.
- Evasion Techniques: If malware was caught by behavioral analysis, AI adjusts the behavior to look more "human-like" next time.

How Attackers Use AI to Create Self-Evolving Malware
1. Polymorphic Mutation Engines
Attackers use AI mutation engines to change malware code every 30 minutes, creating millions of unique malware samples in a single day.

2. Adversarial AI
Attackers create adversarial inputs that fool AI-based malware detection systems. These inputs trick AI into classifying malware as "benign."

3. Malware-as-a-Service (MaaS)
Attackers buy "off-the-shelf" AI-enhanced malware from darknet marketplaces.

Real-World Examples of Self-Evolving Malware
1. Emotet Trojan
Originally a banking Trojan, it became an all-purpose malware delivery platform. It uses polymorphic techniques to avoid detection and adapts after each attack.

2. TrickBot
TrickBot's AI-enabled network prioritizes targets and decides whether to steal passwords or install ransomware.

3. Cerber Ransomware
Cerber's self-evolving nature allows it to mutate its appearance, making it unrecognizable to antivirus systems.

How to Defend Against Self-Evolving Malware

1. AI-Powered EDR (Endpoint Detection and Response)
Traditional antivirus is useless against self-evolving malware. Use AI-based EDR systems like SentinelOne.

2. Behavioral Analytics
Instead of relying on file signatures, behavioral analysis looks for unusual activity (like encrypting thousands of files).

3. Zero-Trust Security
Even if malware infects one device, it won't be able to move laterally to other devices.

4. Multi-Factor Authentication (MFA)
If credentials are stolen, MFA can still prevent attackers from logging in.

Conclusion
Self-evolving malware is the future of cyberattacks. Unlike traditional malware, it uses AI-driven mutation engines, behavioral learning, and propagation intelligence to remain undetectable. As attackers continue to innovate, so must defenders. With the use of AI-driven EDR, anomaly detection, and zero-trust architectures, organizations can protect themselves from this ever-evolving threat.

Supply Chain Attacks — How Attackers Exploit Supply Chains and How AI Defends Against Them

Why Supply Chain Attacks Are So Dangerous
When you think of "supply chains," you might imagine shipping containers, factories, and delivery trucks. But in the world of cybersecurity, supply chains aren't physical — they're digital. A supply chain in the context of cybersecurity includes third-party software, vendors, and service providers that organizations rely on to operate. Attackers know that the easiest way to breach a target is to compromise its suppliers.

A supply chain attack occurs when hackers compromise a supplier to gain access to a larger, more valuable target. Instead of hacking a well-protected Fortune 500 company directly, attackers hack one of its vendors, knowing that trust is automatically extended to suppliers. The SolarWinds attack is one of the most infamous supply chain attacks, affecting thousands of companies and U.S. government agencies.

In the age of AI, supply chain attacks have become more sophisticated. Attackers use AI to analyze supply chains, automate attacks, and identify the weakest links. Defenders, on the other hand, are using AI to detect anomalies, verify software integrity, and monitor vendor access.

This section explains how supply chain attacks work, real-world case studies, how attackers use AI to exploit them, and most importantly, how AI can defend against them.

What is a Supply Chain Attack?
A supply chain attack occurs when a cybercriminal compromises a third-party vendor or supplier to access the systems, data, or networks of a larger target. Instead of directly attacking the target, attackers use the "back door" provided by the supplier.

Supply chain attacks exploit the trust between organizations and their vendors. If a supplier's software update or patch is compromised, every client that installs it becomes infected. One successful attack on a supplier can affect thousands of companies at once.

Types of Supply Chain Attacks:
- Software Supply Chain Attacks: Attackers modify a legitimate software update to include malware.
- Hardware Supply Chain Attacks: Attackers tamper with hardware components, like motherboards or USB drives.
- Service Provider Attacks: Attackers compromise service providers like IT consultants or cloud platforms to access their clients.

How Supply Chain Attacks Work: The 6-Step Process
1. Target Identification
Attackers identify which suppliers or vendors to target. Instead of attacking a heavily protected company like Amazon, attackers focus on its smaller vendors, like software developers, shipping providers, or maintenance contractors.

How Attackers Identify Targets:
- OSINT (Open Source Intelligence): Attackers search LinkedIn for company partnerships and third-party suppliers.
- Third-Party Risk Platforms: Attackers analyze public records, breach databases, and vendor directories.
- Job Listings: Companies often list software tools and platforms they use in job postings, revealing supply chain dependencies.

How AI Plays a Role:
- AI-Powered OSINT: Attackers use AI to automate the scanning of LinkedIn, websites, and social media to identify third-party suppliers.
- Vulnerability Detection: AI scans vendors for software vulnerabilities and unpatched systems.

2. Initial Access (Compromising the Supplier)
Once the attacker identifies a vulnerable supplier, they focus on gaining access to the supplier's system.

Common Access Methods:
- Phishing: Attackers send phishing emails to supplier employees.
- Credential Stuffing: Attackers use leaked passwords from data breaches to access vendor systems.
- Exploiting Software Vulnerabilities: Attackers target suppliers with outdated or unpatched software.

How AI Plays a Role:
- Phishing Automation: AI generates phishing emails tailored to each vendor's employees.
- AI-Driven Password Guessing: Attackers use AI to brute-force passwords faster than traditional methods.

3. Supply Chain Infiltration (Backdooring the Software/Service)
Once attackers have access to the supplier's system, they modify the vendor's software, update files, or network connections.

How Attackers Infiltrate Supply Chains:
- Software Backdoors: Attackers insert backdoors into the vendor's software updates.
- Malware Injection: Attackers inject malware into libraries, APIs, or developer tools.
- Credential Theft: Attackers steal API keys, access tokens, and cloud service credentials.

Real-World Example:
- SolarWinds Attack: Attackers modified SolarWinds' Orion software update, affecting over 18,000 companies and government agencies.

How AI Plays a Role:
- Smart Backdoors: AI-based malware can detect if it is being run in a sandbox and "play dead" to avoid detection.
- Stealthy Injection: AI optimizes code injection techniques to avoid being flagged by antivirus or file integrity checkers.

4. Propagation (Spreading to Clients)
Once the supplier's system is compromised, the malware or backdoor spreads to all downstream clients (i.e., the supplier's customers).

How Propagation Works:
- Software Updates: Clients download infected updates from the supplier.
- API Calls: Malware spreads via legitimate API calls between suppliers and customers.
- Third-Party Tools: Attackers compromise third-party developer tools used by multiple organizations.

How AI Plays a Role:
- Smart Delivery: AI identifies when users are most likely to install updates (like after Patch Tuesday) and deploys malware accordingly.
- Automated Infection: AI automates the infection of every company that downloads the compromised software.

5. Command & Control (C2) and Attack Execution
Once the malware is installed on a client's system, it calls home to the attacker's Command and Control (C2) server. From here, the attacker can issue new commands, launch ransomware, or exfiltrate data.

6. Data Exfiltration and Persistence

Once access is established, the attacker's final goal is to steal, spy, or maintain backdoor access. They may:

- Exfiltrate Data: Steal customer data, financial information, and proprietary code.
- Install Ransomware: Encrypt files and demand payment from downstream customers.
- Maintain Persistence: Keep a backdoor for future attacks.

Case Studies of Supply Chain Attacks
SolarWinds Attack (2020)
Attackers infiltrated SolarWinds' Orion software update, affecting 18,000+ companies. Victims included U.S. government agencies and Fortune 500 companies.

Kaseya VSA Ransomware Attack (2021)
Attackers exploited a flaw in Kaseya's remote monitoring tool. The attack affected 1,500+ companies worldwide, with attackers demanding $70 million in ransom.

Log4j Zero-Day (2021)
Attackers exploited Log4Shell, a vulnerability in the widely used Log4j library. This open-source library was embedded in thousands of enterprise software systems.

How Attackers Use AI in Supply Chain Attacks
- AI-Powered OSINT: AI scrapes LinkedIn, GitHub, and job postings to identify potential vendor targets.
- Deepfake Emails & Calls: Attackers clone the voices of executives using deepfake audio to request unauthorized payments.
- AI-Driven Credential Cracking: AI speeds up password-cracking attempts, especially for weak, reused passwords.

How AI Defends Against Supply Chain Attacks

1. AI-Based Threat Intelligence
AI systems like CrowdStrike and SentinelOne track attack patterns, allowing organizations to spot supply chain compromises earlier.

2. AI-Powered Anomaly Detection
Instead of tracking file signatures, AI uses behavioral analysis to detect unusual activity (like a vendor suddenly accessing sensitive files).

3. Software Bill of Materials (SBOM) Verification
AI validates that software updates have not been tampered with.

4. Zero-Trust Security
If a supplier is compromised, Zero-Trust prevents the attacker from moving laterally through the system.

Conclusion
Supply chain attacks are some of the most dangerous and widespread attacks today. With AI-driven reconnaissance, attack automation, and C2 management, these attacks are only becoming more automated, stealthy, and scalable. Defenders must use AI-driven anomaly detection, Zero-Trust security, and automated patching to protect against future attacks.

Emerging Threats: The Next Generation of Cyber Attacks
The cyber threat landscape is evolving faster than ever before. While the Five Horsemen of Cybersecurity—Ransomware, Phishing, Social Engineering, Malware, and Deepfakes—represent the most well-known threats today, new attack vectors are rapidly emerging. Driven by advances in AI, IoT, blockchain, and cloud computing, these threats are more sophisticated, harder to detect, and capable of inflicting greater damage.

Cybercriminals are no longer working in isolation. They're using automation, machine learning, and AI-driven tools to launch complex, large-scale attacks. As new vulnerabilities arise, attackers are quick to exploit them, leaving traditional security measures scrambling to keep up. This section introduces you to the four key emerging threats that are expected to dominate the next 5-10 years. These aren't just "future risks" — many of them are already happening.

1. AI-Powered Cyber Attacks
What It Is:
Cybercriminals are now harnessing AI to supercharge their attacks, creating threats that are faster, more targeted, and much harder to detect. With AI, attackers can automate every stage of an attack, from reconnaissance to exploitation.

How It Works:
- AI-Powered Phishing: AI can generate highly personalized, human-like phishing emails using models like GPT. These emails are more convincing than traditional phishing attempts and harder to spot.
- AI-Driven Vulnerability Scanning: AI bots scan thousands of websites and networks looking for misconfigurations, outdated software, and known vulnerabilities.

- Malware with AI Mutation Engines: Polymorphic malware, powered by AI, changes its appearance after every detection, making it nearly impossible for signature-based antivirus tools to detect it.
- Automated Penetration Testing: Hackers now use AI bots to act as "red teams," automatically running attack simulations and identifying weak points in systems.

Real-World Example:
Hackers used AI to automate the creation of phishing emails during the Emotet campaign. AI-generated emails were hyper-personalized to employees, mimicking real communications from HR or payroll departments. As a result, click-through rates were 50% higher than standard phishing emails.

How to Defend:
- Use AI-driven threat detection tools (like EDR, XDR, and SIEM) that spot unusual system behavior.
- Deploy anti-phishing tools like Abnormal Security, which use AI to spot sophisticated phishing.
- Patch vulnerabilities frequently to prevent AI-driven bots from exploiting them.

2. Cryptojacking
What It Is:
Cryptojacking occurs when cybercriminals use your devices (PCs, smartphones, and IoT devices) to mine cryptocurrency without your consent. This attack drains your system's resources, reduces its lifespan, and drives up your energy bills. Unlike ransomware, cryptojacking operates silently, often going undetected for months.

How It Works:
- Drive-By Mining: Attackers inject cryptojacking scripts into websites. When you visit the site, your web browser is hijacked to mine cryptocurrency like Monero.
- Malware-Based Mining: Attackers install cryptojacking malware on your device. This malware runs in the background, using your CPU and GPU to mine cryptocurrency for the attacker.
- Cloud Cryptojacking: Hackers target cloud infrastructure (like AWS and GCP) to mine cryptocurrency using stolen cloud compute resources.

Real-World Example:
The Coinhive malware infected millions of websites, secretly turning website visitors' browsers into cryptocurrency miners. Thousands of companies unknowingly hosted Coinhive scripts on their websites, slowing them down and costing users massive electricity bills.

How to Defend:
- Use browser extensions like NoCoin or uBlock Origin to block cryptojacking scripts.
- Monitor cloud infrastructure for unusual CPU usage spikes (this often indicates cryptojacking).
- Use XDR and SIEM to track unusual processes on endpoints and detect high CPU usage from hidden mining software.

3. IoT Vulnerabilities
What It Is:
The rapid growth of smart devices (IoT) like smart locks, smart speakers, webcams, and wearable devices has created a massive attack surface. Many IoT devices have poor security, default passwords, and limited update mechanisms, making them prime targets for attackers. Cybercriminals use these devices to create massive botnets for DDoS attacks, steal private data, or access corporate networks.

How It Works:
- Botnet Attacks: Attackers compromise IoT devices and add them to a botnet to launch massive Distributed Denial-of-Service (DDoS) attacks.
- Eavesdropping & Surveillance: Attackers hack into smart home devices like cameras and speakers to spy on users.
- Data Exfiltration: IoT devices store user data, like voice recordings and location history, which can be stolen if attackers gain access.
- Pivoting into Networks: Attackers use weak IoT devices as a "jump point" to enter corporate networks.

Real-World Example:
The infamous Mirai Botnet attack compromised over 600,000 IoT devices like cameras, routers, and DVRs to launch a DDoS attack that brought down large parts of the internet in 2016. Attackers used default passwords on IoT devices to take control of them and launch attacks on services like Netflix, Twitter, and Reddit.

How to Defend:
- Change the default passwords on IoT devices.
- Use IoT firewalls and network segmentation to isolate smart devices from sensitive company networks.
- Use AI-driven anomaly detection to identify unusual device behavior (like an IoT camera sending data to an unknown IP address).

4. Social Media Exploitation
What It Is:
Cybercriminals use social media to gather intelligence on users, launch phishing attacks, and spread misinformation. AI bots and fake accounts now play a major role in social engineering campaigns on platforms like Twitter, Instagram, and Discord.

How It Works:
- Fake Accounts (Bot Networks): Attackers create thousands of fake social media accounts to distribute links, scams, and misinformation.
- Social Engineering Scams: Attackers befriend people online and convince them to send money or credentials (common on Discord and Telegram).
- Misinformation Campaigns: Attackers spread fake news or disinformation during elections, protests, or global events to influence public perception.
- Profile Takeovers: Attackers use stolen passwords to take over accounts and spread malware links.

Real-World Example:
The 2020 Twitter Bitcoin Scam was one of the most high-profile social media attacks. Attackers used insider access to take over the accounts of prominent figures like Elon Musk and Joe Biden, sending out messages that promised to double Bitcoin payments. Over $100,000 was stolen in a matter of hours.

How to Defend:
- Use two-factor authentication (2FA) on social media platforms.
- Be suspicious of unusual messages, especially those promising money, investment, or gifts.
- Use AI-driven fake account detectors like Botometer to spot fake followers and scam accounts.
- Limit what you post on social media (like birthdays, pet names, or other info attackers use for security questions).

5. AI-Augmented Social Engineering

What It Is:

Social engineering is one of the oldest attack methods in cybersecurity, but with AI, it has evolved into something far more dangerous. AI-Augmented Social Engineering allows attackers to use AI-powered tools like chatbots, deepfake voice cloning, and automated messaging systems to trick people into revealing sensitive information or taking risky actions. This approach makes attacks more convincing, personalized, and automated.

How It Works:

- AI-Driven Chatbots: Attackers use AI chatbots to impersonate customer support agents on platforms like Telegram, Discord, and live website support chats. These bots initiate conversations, ask for personal details, and often request payments or sensitive info.
- Voice Cloning (Deepfake Calls): Attackers clone the voices of CEOs, managers, or family members to make phone calls or send voice messages that sound real. These deepfake voice calls have led to successful scams where employees transferred large sums of money.
- AI-Personalized Phishing: Attackers use AI to create phishing emails that look highly authentic. Instead of "generic" emails, AI pulls personal information (like names, job roles, and company details) from social media to create convincing and personalized messages.

Real-World Example:

A 2023 incident involved an employee at a multinational company who received a phone call from someone who sounded like their CEO. The deepfake voice instructed the employee to wire over $243,000. Believing it was the CEO, the employee complied. The scam was only detected after the transfer was completed.

How to Defend:

- Family Password Strategy: Use a family password (explained in Chapter 12) to identify voice-cloning scams.
- Be Suspicious of Calls Requesting Urgency: If a call seems "urgent" or "time-sensitive," verify it through another channel.
- Watch for AI Chatbots: Be cautious of "live chat" support on websites, especially if it asks for passwords or payment information.
- Use AI Detection Tools: Tools like Deepware Scanner can detect deepfake audio or video.
- Be Aware of Personal Info Online: Limit the personal details you post on social media (like your voice, family names, and job role), as they can be used to train voice models.

Conclusion
The Five Horsemen of Cybersecurity are already formidable threats, but the next generation of threats is just as dangerous. AI-Powered Cyber Attacks, Cryptojacking, IoT Vulnerabilities, and Social Media Exploitation represent the next phase of cybercrime, where attacks are automated, large-scale, and adaptive. Attackers are no longer relying on brute force or simple scams — they're using AI, automation, and social engineering at scale.

To defend against these threats, you must adopt a Zero-Trust mindset, assume that every system is already compromised, and use AI-driven defenses like anomaly detection, multi-factor authentication (MFA), and XDR solutions. Companies and individuals alike must recognize that these threats will only grow more dangerous over the next 5-10 years.

"The next era of cybercrime will not be fought by humans alone — it will be fought by AI against AI."

This Emerging Threats: Next Generation of Cyber Attacks section gives the reader a forward-looking view of what's coming. It cements your book as a comprehensive guide, not only for current threats but also for future-proofing the reader's cybersecurity knowledge.

Additional Case Studies:

Ransomware Case Study: LockBit Ransomware
LockBit ransomware is one of the most notorious and successful ransomware strains in the world. First detected in 2019, it has grown to become one of the most profitable and prolific ransomware operations globally. LockBit is known for its Ransomware-as-a-Service (RaaS) model, where cybercriminals rent out the malware to affiliates, allowing even low-skill hackers to launch large-scale attacks.

Unlike earlier strains of ransomware like WannaCry, LockBit is highly advanced, using AI-based encryption algorithms, self-replication, and lateral movement techniques. It even features a "negotiation portal" where victims can engage with attackers.

How the Attack Works
1. Initial Access: Attackers gain access via phishing emails, stolen RDP (Remote Desktop Protocol) credentials, or exploiting unpatched software vulnerabilities.
2. Spreading Laterally: LockBit spreads automatically through the network, infecting as many devices as possible.
3. Encryption: It encrypts critical files using AES and RSA algorithms.
4. Ransom Demand: Victims are directed to a negotiation page where they can chat with attackers, negotiate ransom amounts, or "buy time" to extend deadlines.

Case Study: The 2022 Continental Attack
In August 2022, LockBit ransomware targeted Continental, one of the world's largest automotive parts suppliers. The attackers claimed to have stolen over 40 terabytes of sensitive data, including trade secrets and proprietary information.
- Attack Entry: Hackers gained access to Continental's internal systems via stolen VPN credentials.
- Data Stolen: Confidential files, research data, and intellectual property were stolen.
- Ransom Demand: The attackers demanded millions of dollars in ransom. Continental refused to pay, and in response, the stolen data was published on the dark web.

Why This Case Study Matters
- It highlights how stolen credentials (like VPN logins) can enable ransomware attacks.
- It demonstrates how RaaS (Ransomware-as-a-Service) allows even unskilled hackers to launch devastating attacks.
- It emphasizes the importance of multi-factor authentication (MFA) to prevent unauthorized access.

Key Takeaways
- AI's Role in LockBit: LockBit's use of AI-driven encryption and propagation algorithms enables it to self-spread quickly across networks.
- Prevention Tactics: Use Zero-Trust security models and enforce multi-factor authentication (MFA) for VPNs and RDP access.
- Lesson Learned: Never assume third-party credentials are safe. The attack on Continental underscores the risk of stolen login credentials.

Phishing Case Study: Ubiquiti Networks' $46M Loss via Whaling
Unlike traditional phishing, whaling targets senior executives like CEOs, CFOs, and VPs. Attackers trick executives or employees into transferring large sums of money by pretending to be senior leadership. Whaling attacks are larger, more targeted, and more costly than standard phishing attacks.

How the Attack Works
- Reconnaissance: Attackers gather information about the executives via LinkedIn, company press releases, social media.
- Impersonation: Attackers use AI-generated spear-phishing emails that mimic the CEO or CFO.
- Fraudulent Request: The attacker sends an email to the finance team, requesting an urgent wire transfer to a "new vendor."
- Execution: The finance department processes the payment, thinking it is legitimate.

Case Study: The $46M Ubiquiti Whaling Scam
In 2015, attackers launched a massive whaling attack against Ubiquiti Networks, a global technology company that manufactures networking equipment. The attackers impersonated a senior executive and tricked Ubiquiti's finance team into wiring $46 million to fraudulent accounts.
- How it Happened: Attackers spoofed the CEO's email address and pretended to be him. They sent emails to the finance department, urgently requesting a transfer.
- Losses: The company lost $46.7 million before the fraud was detected.
- Lessons Learned: The attack demonstrated how attackers can exploit the "authority bias" (trust in senior executives) and the lack of two-step verification for wire transfers.

Key Takeaways
- AI's Role in Whaling: Attackers use AI to clone executive voices via deepfake audio, convincing employees that they are talking to the real CEO.
- How to Prevent Whaling: Use AI-powered email filters to detect executive impersonation and require multi-factor approval for wire transfers.
- Lesson Learned: Don't trust email requests for wire transfers — always confirm with a phone call or alternate communication method.

Malware Case Study: Polymorphic Zeus Trojan

Polymorphic malware changes its code and appearance every time it infects a new system. Traditional antivirus software relies on "signatures" (unique identifiers) to detect malware, but polymorphic malware renders signatures useless by constantly changing.

How the Attack Works

- Initial Delivery: Attackers send malware-infected attachments (like Word or Excel files) via email.
- Polymorphic Transformation: Each new version of the malware modifies its binary code to create a "new" sample.
- Data Exfiltration: The malware steals passwords, bank information, and system credentials.

Case Study: Zeus Trojan (2007–Present)

Zeus Trojan is one of the most infamous malware strains of all time. Originally designed as a banking Trojan, it evolved into a polymorphic threat that became a tool for stealing bank credentials worldwide.

- How it Worked: Zeus was disguised as a legitimate banking app. Once installed, it stole login credentials for online banking.
- Polymorphic Engine: Zeus's code changes on each device it infects, making it nearly impossible for antivirus software to detect.
- Economic Impact: It has been responsible for billions of dollars in theft since its launch.

Key Takeaways

- AI's Role: Polymorphic malware like Zeus uses AI-driven mutation engines to change its structure every few minutes.
- How to Defend: Behavioral-based malware detection (like AI-driven EDR) can spot polymorphic malware.
- Lesson Learned: Signature-based antivirus is no longer sufficient. Companies need AI-driven endpoint detection and response (EDR).

Supply Chain Attack Case Study: NotPetya (2017)

The NotPetya attack was one of the most damaging cyberattacks in history, causing an estimated $10 billion in damages. It began as a supply chain attack on a Ukrainian tax software provider called MeDoc.

How the Attack Works
- Supply Chain Compromise: Attackers compromised a software update for the MeDoc accounting platform.
- Update Propagation: Thousands of companies that used MeDoc installed the infected update.
- Destruction: NotPetya acted like ransomware, but its true goal was to wipe data and cause system shutdowns.

Key Targets
- Maersk: The shipping giant lost $300 million in the attack.
- FedEx: The company's European operations were crippled.
- Merck: The pharmaceutical giant reported $870 million in damages.

Key Takeaways
- AI's Role: Attackers used AI-driven propagation engines to spread NotPetya across thousands of global organizations.
- How to Defend: Verify software updates using a Software Bill of Materials (SBOM).
- Lesson Learned: Don't trust software updates from vendors without integrity verification.

How to Protect Yourself From These Threats

Here's a Personal Cybersecurity Checklist to protect yourself from AI-driven attacks and emerging threats:

- AI-Powered Endpoint Detection and Response (EDR/XDR) — Use tools like CrowdStrike (https://www.crowdstrike.com/), SentinelOne (https://www.sentinelone.com/), or Microsoft Defender (https://www.microsoft.com/en-us/security/business/threat-protection/microsoft-defender) to detect and respond to malware, ransomware, and polymorphic threats. These systems spot anomalies and block malicious behavior in real time.

- Multi-Factor Authentication (MFA) — Protects against password theft and unauthorized access. Use authenticator apps like Google Authenticator (https://www.google.com/landing/2step/) or Authy (https://authy.com/) instead of SMS-based 2FA, which can be intercepted by attackers.

- Zero-Trust Security Model — Adopt a "trust nothing, verify everything" approach. Require verification for every action, user, and request, even within trusted networks. This approach limits access points for hackers and reduces the blast radius of a breach.

- Backups & Disaster Recovery — Create encrypted backups and store them offline. Use tools like Acronis (https://www.acronis.com/) or Backblaze (https://www.backblaze.com/) to create automatic, encrypted backups that can be restored quickly after a ransomware attack or system failure.

- Anomaly Detection & AI Monitoring — Use tools like Darktrace (https://www.darktrace.com/) or Microsoft Sentinel (https://azure.microsoft.com/en-us/products/microsoft-sentinel/) to monitor unusual behavior in your network. These AI-driven platforms detect anomalies in user activity, file access, and network traffic, identifying threats before they escalate.

- Family Passwords — Use a secret family password known only to family members to defend against voice cloning scams. Choose a password based on the chorus of a family-favorite song. If a family member calls for help, ask them for the 16th letter of the "family password" to verify their identity. Keep this password off all digital devices.

- AI-Powered Phishing Protection — Use anti-phishing browser extensions like Netcraft (https://www.netcraft.com/) and Avast AntiTrack (https://www.avast.com/antitrack) to block phishing links and scam websites. Many phishing scams use AI to personalize messages, but AI-powered tools recognize and block these attempts before you click.

- Voice Cloning Defense — Be suspicious of urgent phone calls requesting money or access to sensitive information. Use AI-driven scam call blockers like Hiya (https://hiya.com/) and Truecaller (https://www.truecaller.com/) to identify scam numbers. If someone claims to be a family member or colleague, ask them for your "family password" or challenge them with a specific question only they would know.

- IoT Device Security — Secure your smart devices by changing default passwords, disabling unnecessary features (like Universal Plug and Play (UPnP)), and regularly updating firmware. Use network firewalls like Firewalla (https://firewalla.com/) or Bitdefender BOX (https://www.bitdefender.com/box/) to protect all IoT devices connected to your home network.

- Cloud Security & Supply Chain Vigilance — Be cautious about third-party software and supply chain dependencies. Use Software Bill of Materials (SBOM) tracking tools to identify and audit dependencies. This approach prevents attackers from sneaking in backdoors via third-party software updates, as seen in the SolarWinds attack.

- AI-Driven Password Managers — Use Bitwarden (https://bitwarden.com/) or 1Password (https://1password.com/) to create long, random, and unique passwords for every account. Avoid using personal details (like pet names) that AI algorithms can predict.

- Block Cryptojacking Attempts — Use tools like Malwarebytes (https://www.malwarebytes.com/) to scan and block cryptojacking scripts that hijack your device's processing power to mine cryptocurrency.

Chapter Conclusion: Evolve to Survive — The New Threat Landscape

The modern Cyber Threat Landscape is no longer defined by a single type of attack. Instead, it revolves around the Five Horsemen of Cybersecurity: Ransomware, Phishing, Social Engineering, Malware, and Deepfakes. These threats now operate as coordinated, multi-stage attacks, with phishing emails delivering ransomware, deepfake calls tricking employees, and AI-powered polymorphic malware hiding in plain sight. Attackers leverage AI automation to supercharge each of these Horsemen, making them faster, more convincing, and harder to detect.

But these aren't the only threats. We must also defend against emerging threats like:
- Self-Evolving Malware — Malware that "learns" as it spreads, mutating its own code to stay ahead of antivirus software.
- Cryptojacking — Hackers silently hijack your CPU power to mine cryptocurrency.
- IoT Exploits — Attacks on smart devices like cameras, smart locks, and thermostats.
- Supply Chain Attacks — Hackers infiltrate trusted software vendors, delivering malware disguised as legitimate updates.
- AI-Powered Attacks — Attackers use AI to automate reconnaissance, craft phishing emails, and create polymorphic malware.

We are living in an era where AI-enhanced threats evolve faster than static defenses. For every security patch, attackers find a new method. Attackers are evolving — and so must we.

To combat these threats, you need to switch from reactive security to proactive security. No longer can you rely on traditional antivirus software alone. Zero-Trust models, AI-driven anomaly detection, and behavioral tracking are essential to staying ahead of these evolving threats.

Key Takeaways from Chapter 3
- The Five Horsemen of Cybersecurity — Ransomware, Phishing, Social Engineering, Malware, and Deepfakes are now interconnected and weaponized by AI.
- Emerging Threats — Self-Evolving Malware, Cryptojacking, IoT Exploits, and Supply Chain Attacks are on the rise, requiring proactive defense strategies.
- AI is the New Battlefield — Attackers use AI to evolve malware, crack passwords, and clone human voices. But defenders use AI too — through anomaly detection, AI-powered EDR, and predictive defenses.

Final Call-to-Action: Your Defense Starts Now
Your first step is to adopt a Zero-Trust security model. Trust nothing, verify everything. Use tools like Darktrace (https://www.darktrace.com/), Microsoft Sentinel (https://azure.microsoft.com/en-us/products/microsoft-sentinel/), and CrowdStrike (https://www.crowdstrike.com/) to monitor, detect, and respond to threats in real time.

Don't wait for an attack to "wake you up" to the danger. Be proactive. Here's a simple plan to get started today:
- Install an AI-driven EDR system like SentinelOne (https://www.sentinelone.com/) or CrowdStrike (https://www.crowdstrike.com/).
- Set up two-factor authentication (2FA) for every account you own. Use tools like Authy (https://authy.com/) or Google Authenticator (https://www.google.com/landing/2step/).
- Protect your home network using a firewall like Firewalla (https://firewalla.com/) or Bitdefender BOX (https://www.bitdefender.com/box/).
- Use password managers like 1Password (https://1password.com/) or Bitwarden (https://bitwarden.com/) to create long, unguessable passwords.
- Create a Family Password to protect against voice-cloning attacks. Keep it secret, off devices, and known only to your family.

Attackers are always one step ahead — but with AI on your side, you can stay two steps ahead.

This chapter has equipped you with the mindset, strategies, and tools you need to protect your family, business, and identity from AI-driven threats. As you move forward, remember this: Attackers adapt. So must you.

With every new chapter, your skills will evolve. By the end of this book, you'll be able to predict, detect, and block the attacks that most people won't even see coming. Let's continue.

Chapter 4: How Cybercriminals Think

Understanding the Hacker Mindset
To defeat your enemy, you must first understand their mindset. Cybercriminals are not just "hackers in hoodies" sitting in basements. They are part of an organized, evolving, and highly profitable ecosystem that includes state-sponsored hackers, hacktivists, criminal gangs, and ransomware affiliates.

While traditional motives like financial gain and espionage remain dominant, new motives such as cyber extortion, hacktivism, and chaos-for-hire have emerged. Today's attackers aren't just people — AI-powered attack bots are doing much of the dirty work. Attackers use AI-driven attack tools to automate reconnaissance, deliver sophisticated attacks, and evade AI-based detection systems.

This chapter dives into the psychology of cybercriminals, their motivations, and the cutting-edge tactics they use — including adversarial AI attacks and AI-driven hacking tools. By understanding their goals, motives, and tools, you can think like a hacker and defend like a pro.

Attack Motivations and Psychology of Cybercriminals

Who Are Cybercriminals?
Cybercriminals are not a monolithic group. They come from different backgrounds, have different goals, and operate with different levels of sophistication. Here's a breakdown of the key types:
- Script Kiddies: Inexperienced hackers who rely on pre-built attack tools and exploit kits.
- Hacktivists: Motivated by social, political, or ideological causes (like Anonymous).
- Cybercriminal Gangs: Organized groups running Ransomware-as-a-Service (RaaS) businesses, such as LockBit and REvil.
- State-Sponsored Hackers: Elite hackers working for nation-states to engage in cyber espionage, cyberwarfare, or sabotage (like APT29 (Russia) or APT41 (China)).
- Insider Threats: Disgruntled employees or infiltrators with access to internal systems.

What Motivates Cybercriminals?
Cybercriminals are motivated by one or more of the following drivers:

1. Financial Gain
   - Primary Motive: Most attacks are financially driven. Ransomware gangs aim to encrypt files and demand payment.
   - Attack Types: Ransomware, wire fraud, Business Email Compromise (BEC), and carding (stealing and selling credit card data).
   - Notable Example: The LockBit ransomware gang extorts companies for millions of dollars.

2. Espionage
   - Primary Motive: Espionage-driven attacks are often carried out by nation-states. The goal is to steal sensitive data, IP, or defense information.
   - Attack Types: Spear phishing, supply chain attacks, and Advanced Persistent Threats (APTs).
   - Notable Example: The SolarWinds attack by the APT29 (Russian intelligence) aimed to steal sensitive data from U.S. government agencies.

3. Political Ideology / Hacktivism
   - Primary Motive: Hacktivists attack companies, governments, or organizations they view as "immoral" or "unjust."
   - Attack Types: DDoS attacks, website defacement, and leaks of sensitive information.
   - Notable Example: The Anonymous collective attacked government websites to support social justice movements.

4. Revenge or Personal Grudges
   - Primary Motive: Disgruntled employees or former insiders may attack a company out of revenge.
   - Attack Types: Data leaks, sabotage, or deploying ransomware on internal networks.
   - Notable Example: An ex-employee of Tesla was caught sabotaging the company's internal systems.

5. Curiosity / Prestige
   - Primary Motive: Some hackers (especially Script Kiddies) attack systems to boost their reputation in online forums or hacking communities.
   - Attack Types: Website defacement, small-scale DDoS attacks, and bragging about exploits on forums like RaidForums.

6. Chaos-for-Hire
- Primary Motive: Some attackers launch destructive attacks for hire. Examples include the NotPetya malware, which pretended to be ransomware but was designed to destroy files permanently.
- Notable Example: The NotPetya attack, originally blamed on Russia, caused global destruction, crippling Maersk, FedEx, and pharmaceutical giant Merck.

Key Psychological Biases Attackers Exploit
Cybercriminals understand that humans are the weakest link in cybersecurity. They target human psychology through social engineering, phishing, and manipulation. Here's how:
- Urgency Bias: "Act now or lose access to your account!"
- Authority Bias: "This is your CEO. Send a wire transfer immediately."
- Curiosity Bias: "Click this link to see your confidential salary review."

Adversarial Attacks — How Attackers Fool AI Models with Adversarial Patches

The Silent Sabotage of AI Systems
As AI-driven defenses become more sophisticated, attackers have developed a strategy to exploit these systems. This method, known as an adversarial attack, targets the AI models themselves instead of the underlying software or human error.

Rather than launching a traditional attack, cybercriminals introduce small, undetectable changes to images, files, or datasets. These changes are so subtle that humans don't notice them, but AI models are fooled into making incorrect predictions, misclassifications, or dangerous decisions.

A famous example occurred when a "STOP" sign was modified using a small sticker, causing a self-driving car to misclassify it as a speed limit sign. While this may seem like a niche problem, adversarial attacks pose serious threats to AI-powered malware detection, facial recognition systems, and even medical AI models. This section explains what adversarial attacks are, how they work, and how attackers create and deploy adversarial patches. Real-world examples will illustrate the power of these attacks, and we'll also look at how AI-driven defenses can fight back.

What is an Adversarial Attack?
An adversarial attack is an attempt to fool an AI system by introducing small, deliberate changes to an input — such as an image, text, or audio file — causing the AI to misclassify or misinterpret the data. Unlike traditional cyberattacks, which rely on exploiting vulnerabilities in software or human error, adversarial attacks target the AI's decision-making process itself.

Attackers use adversarial perturbations — subtle changes to the input — to trick AI systems. For example, slight changes to an image (like pixel modifications) can cause a computer vision system to misclassify an image. To a human, the image of a dog may still look like a dog, but to the AI, it might be classified as a wolf or a cat.

How Adversarial Attacks Work
Attackers modify inputs in ways that aren't perceptible to humans but drastically affect AI models. These modifications can be applied to images, audio files, text, or even binary code in malware samples. The AI system, which relies on pattern recognition, becomes "confused" by the changes and misclassifies the input.

For example, in a malware detection system, attackers might modify the metadata, file headers, or hash values of a malicious file to make it look like a harmless document. The malware itself doesn't change in function, but it becomes "invisible" to AI-driven malware detection systems.

There are several key forms of adversarial attacks:
- Adversarial Perturbations: This involves making small, invisible changes to data, like altering a few pixels in an image, which causes the AI to misclassify it.
- Adversarial Patches: Attackers create physical patches, stickers, or patterns that disrupt AI vision models, like placing a sticker on a "STOP" sign to make it look like a "Yield" sign.
- Adversarial Examples: These are specific inputs that exploit an AI model's weaknesses. For example, attackers might slightly modify file headers or change binary code to fool AI-driven malware detection tools.
- Backdoor Attacks: Attackers insert hidden "triggers" in training data so that AI models misclassify specific inputs during testing or deployment.

What Are Adversarial Patches?
An adversarial patch is a specific type of adversarial attack in which attackers introduce physical stickers, patterns, or patches to an environment to confuse AI models. These patches are commonly used to disrupt computer vision systems like facial recognition, object detection, and self-driving car AIs.

The concept is simple but effective. Attackers design a sticker, QR code, or colorful pattern that disrupts the way AI detects or classifies an object. For example, placing a colorful sticker on a "STOP" sign might cause an AI-powered self-driving car to classify it as a "Speed Limit 45" sign. This misclassification could cause the car to drive straight through an intersection.

Here's how the process works:
- Attackers create a custom patch or sticker using AI-based optimization algorithms.
- The patch is tested against the AI system, with the goal of finding the simplest patch that can fool the AI.
- Once perfected, the patch is applied to a physical environment (like attaching it to a sign) or used digitally (like embedding it in malware samples).

How Adversarial Patches Are Created
Adversarial patches aren't random. They are created using sophisticated AI training models and optimization algorithms. Here's the step-by-step process of how attackers develop these patches:
- Generating the Patch
- Attackers use Generative Adversarial Networks (GANs) or other machine learning models to "train" the patch to be as effective as possible. The adversarial patch goes through multiple rounds of testing. Each time the patch fails to fool the AI, it "learns" from its mistakes and becomes more effective. The process is similar to how AI models are trained to recognize patterns, but in this case, the goal is to confuse the AI.
- Embedding the Patch
- Once the patch is optimized, attackers can apply it physically (as a sticker) or embed it digitally. For instance, the attacker might place a small, colorful QR code on a sign to confuse AI-powered object detection systems. In the case of malware, adversarial patches might be invisible modifications to the malware's binary file, like changing headers, padding, or hash values.

- Testing and Deployment
- Attackers run tests on the patch against the target system. If the AI system misclassifies the input, the attacker deploys the patch. If it doesn't work, the process repeats until the patch is fully optimized.

Real-World Examples of Adversarial Attacks

STOP Sign Attack
In one of the most famous examples, researchers applied small stickers to a STOP sign. The result? AI-powered self-driving cars misinterpreted the STOP sign as a "Speed Limit 45" sign. This could have deadly consequences in a real-world setting, as self-driving cars might fail to stop at intersections.

AI-Powered Malware Evasion
Attackers make small changes to malware, such as modifying the file header, changing the file signature, or altering binary code. These tiny modifications allow polymorphic malware to evade AI-based malware detectors. Unlike traditional antivirus tools that rely on file signatures, AI models analyze behavior. By introducing adversarial patches, attackers make the malware appear "harmless" to AI-driven detection.

Facial Recognition Evasion
Hackers wear colorful glasses or patterned masks to evade facial recognition. By applying adversarial patches on their clothing or faces, they can bypass AI-based facial recognition systems at airports, banks, and security checkpoints.

How Hackers Use AI to Create Adversarial Patches
Attackers use AI-driven adversarial generators to develop more effective patches. This is done using the same tools that companies use to train AI models. Here's how it works:
- Training the Patch: Attackers train an AI system (like a Generative Adversarial Network) to identify which changes will cause an AI model to misclassify the input.
- Generating Adversarial Examples: The attacker creates multiple versions of the adversarial patch, testing each version against a target AI system.
- Optimization: Over several iterations, the attacker fine-tunes the patch to ensure that it works on a wide range of images, files, or data inputs.

How to Defend Against Adversarial Attacks
Defending against adversarial patches is extremely difficult, as they exploit fundamental flaws in how AI perceives inputs. However, there are several strategies to mitigate the threat:

- Adversarial Training: Train AI models using adversarial examples to help them recognize perturbations.
- Robust Feature Engineering: Focus on creating models that pay attention to high-level patterns rather than low-level noise.
- Model Randomization: Use randomization at each layer of the AI model to make it harder for attackers to predict the model's behavior.
- Attack Simulation: Simulate adversarial attacks during AI training so the model becomes resilient to them.

Conclusion
Adversarial attacks are a game-changer for cybercriminals. By targeting the AI models directly, attackers bypass the traditional cybersecurity defenses. Adversarial patches, perturbations, and malware evasion tactics have the potential to compromise autonomous vehicles, malware detectors, and facial recognition systems.

The best defense is to use adversarial training, AI-driven anomaly detection, and Zero-Trust security models. In a world where AI is fighting AI, organizations must remain vigilant and adaptable.

How Hackers Use AI-Driven Attack Tools

The AI Arms Race
Cybercriminals have always relied on automation, but with the rise of AI-driven attack tools, their abilities have become more sophisticated, stealthy, and scalable. In the past, hackers had to manually create malware, write phishing emails, and find vulnerabilities. Today, AI does the heavy lifting. Attackers are no longer limited by time, resources, or technical expertise.

With AI, cybercriminals can automate large-scale attacks with precision targeting, faster execution, and better adaptability. AI doesn't just help attackers; it also makes them unpredictable and faster than traditional defenses. AI-driven attack tools allow even inexperienced "script kiddies" to launch devastating attacks.

This section explores how hackers use AI-driven attack tools to automate phishing, mutate malware, crack passwords, and bypass anomaly detection systems. We'll highlight real-world examples, emerging threats, and ways to defend against these AI-enhanced attacks.

What Are AI-Driven Attack Tools?
AI-driven attack tools are hacking platforms, bots, and malware that use AI to automate attack processes. Instead of relying on manual effort, attackers use AI to:
- Find vulnerabilities in real time.
- Generate personalized phishing emails using natural language generation (NLG).
- Create polymorphic malware that changes its code to avoid detection.
- Crack passwords faster than brute-force attacks.

These attack tools are often sold as part of "Attack-as-a-Service (AaaS)" offerings on the dark web. With no technical skills required, even low-level hackers can access AI-enhanced attack tools.

How Hackers Use AI to Supercharge Cyber Attacks

1. AI-Powered Phishing Tools
Phishing attacks have always been a major threat, but with the rise of AI-driven tools, phishing is now more targeted, scalable, and convincing than ever. Attackers use Phishing-as-a-Service (PhaaS) platforms to generate custom phishing emails and fake websites at scale.
How it Works
- Personalization with Natural Language Generation (NLG)
  - AI-driven attack tools analyze a target's LinkedIn, Facebook, and public data to create personalized emails that seem legitimate.
  - Tools like OpenAI's GPT models can create human-like email content, mimicking HR departments, CEOs, or customer support teams.
- AI-Generated Phishing Pages
  - AI creates realistic copies of login pages (like Microsoft 365 or Google Workspace) where victims unknowingly enter credentials.
  - Attackers use domain name generators (DGA) to register fake websites that look similar to real ones (like "mircosoft-login.com").
- Real-Time Adaptation
  - AI chatbots are used to respond in real time to targets via email, social media, or live chat systems.
  - For example, when a victim questions the authenticity of an email, the AI chatbot responds like a human to further convince them.

Example in Action
In a recent attack, hackers used AI-generated spear-phishing emails to impersonate LinkedIn recruiters. The email included a job offer that linked to a fake login page for the victim's email provider. The victim entered their credentials, which were instantly captured.
How to Defend Against It
- Use AI-powered email filters (like Barracuda Sentinel) to spot AI-generated phishing emails.
- Train employees to spot red flags, such as unfamiliar sender addresses, URL mismatches, and urgent calls to action.
- Use multi-factor authentication (MFA) so that even if credentials are stolen, the attacker cannot log in.

2. Polymorphic Malware & AI Mutation Engines
Hackers no longer create malware that stays static. Instead, they use AI-powered mutation engines to create polymorphic malware that mutates its code every few minutes. This makes it nearly impossible for traditional antivirus and endpoint protection systems to detect.
How It Works
- Mutation and Obfuscation
  - Polymorphic malware alters its binary structure (like rearranging its code) every time it infects a new system.
  - These changes are subtle and don't affect the malware's ability to function.
- Evasion of Signature-Based Detection
  - Since antivirus tools rely on signatures (unique hashes of files) to identify threats, polymorphic malware generates new signatures constantly.
  - As a result, each version of the malware has a different signature, making traditional detection methods useless.
- AI-Driven Learning
  - AI mutation engines analyze which changes were successful at bypassing antivirus detection and improve future mutations.

Example in Action
The Zeus Trojan is a well-known example of polymorphic malware. Every time it infects a system, it changes its code structure. This Trojan has been used to steal billions of dollars in banking credentials since its launch.
How to Defend Against It
- Deploy AI-driven endpoint detection and response (EDR) tools that detect behavior, not just signatures.
- Use anomaly detection to spot malware activity based on unusual file access, encryption attempts, and network traffic.

3. Password Cracking Tools with AI Assistance

Traditional password cracking relies on brute-force methods (guessing every possible combination) or dictionary attacks. AI has made these attacks much faster and more effective.

How It Works
- AI-Based Pattern Recognition
  - AI algorithms analyze previously leaked password databases to identify patterns in human password creation (like "123456" or "Qwerty2023").
  - AI predicts likely password combinations, making password guessing faster than traditional brute-force methods.
- Neural Networks for Password Cracking
  - Neural networks learn from leaked password datasets, and AI models predict human-like passwords based on trends.
- Password Profiling
  - Attackers use AI to analyze social media accounts, identifying potential password clues (like birthdates, pet names, and hobbies).

Example in Action

Hashcat, an advanced password cracking tool, uses AI-driven brute-force attacks. It can now guess complex 10-character passwords in hours instead of months, thanks to AI-assisted pattern prediction.

How to Defend Against It
- Use multi-factor authentication (MFA) to prevent logins even if passwords are stolen.
- Use long, complex passphrases instead of simple passwords (e.g., "CorrectHorseBatteryStaple").
- Employ password managers to create and store strong, unique passwords for every service.

4. Adversarial AI in Malware Evasion

Adversarial AI attacks involve fooling AI-based security systems. Attackers create small, imperceptible changes to files, images, or executable binaries to evade malware detection.

How It Works
- Adversarial Patches
  - Attackers modify the binary code of malware files by adding "adversarial noise" (like tiny, harmless changes) that confuse AI-based antivirus models.
- Evasion of Machine Learning Models
  - AI models predict whether a file is "malicious" or "benign." Attackers train adversarial AI models to identify how to make malware "look benign" to AI systems.

Example in Action
Attackers used adversarial AI patches to fool malware detection models. A ransomware file was modified so the malware scanner classified it as a harmless text file.

How to Defend Against It
- Use adversarial training to teach AI models how to recognize files with "adversarial noise."
- Use dynamic analysis tools that analyze malware behavior in a live environment, not just file attributes.

5. AI-Driven DDoS Botnets
AI has supercharged Distributed Denial of Service (DDoS) attacks, making them more adaptive and harder to stop. AI-driven DDoS bots can adjust attack strategies in real time.

How It Works
- AI bots constantly change IP addresses and traffic patterns to evade detection.
- AI bots adjust the rate and volume of attack traffic to stay under network rate-limiting thresholds.

Example in Action
The Mirai botnet was one of the first large-scale DDoS botnets. With AI, modern DDoS attacks use IoT devices (like security cameras) to launch AI-driven, adaptive DDoS attacks.

How to Defend Against It
- Use AI-driven DDoS protection tools, like Cloudflare's AI-based anomaly detection.
- Implement rate-limiting and geo-blocking to prevent unusual traffic spikes.

6. AI-Guided Social Engineering & AI-Powered Fraud
What It Is:
Social engineering has been a fundamental tactic for hackers for decades, but with the rise of AI, these attacks have become smarter, faster, and more deceptive than ever before. AI-Guided Social Engineering uses deepfake video calls, AI voice cloning, and automated chatbots to convince victims to share sensitive information or make unauthorized payments. Attackers no longer rely on manual persuasion tactics; instead, AI enables them to create highly convincing, automated social engineering campaigns.

How It Works:
- Deepfake Video Calls: Attackers use tools like DeepFaceLab and FaceSwap to create live video feeds of CEOs or managers. On Zoom or Teams calls, they impersonate executives and issue fraudulent instructions, like demanding wire transfers.

- AI-Driven Chatbots: Attackers create customer support bots that impersonate service agents on Telegram, Discord, or website live chats. The bots ask users to "verify their account" by entering sensitive information, like passwords or wallet keys.
- Voice Cloning: Attackers use AI-powered voice synthesis tools to clone the voices of CEOs, executives, or family members. They only need 30 seconds of audio to produce a convincing fake. The attacker then calls employees, family members, or business contacts to request urgent wire transfers or access to sensitive systems.
- Automated Fraud Playbooks: Using AI playbooks, attackers automate entire fraud campaigns, from reconnaissance to exploitation. These AI-generated "attack blueprints" show attackers which systems to target and which attack methods to use.

Real-World Example:
In one of the most famous cases, an accountant at a company in Japan received a video call from their CEO requesting an urgent wire transfer of over $400,000 USD. The call looked and sounded real — it showed the CEO's face on the screen, and the voice matched perfectly. But it wasn't real. The attackers had used AI-generated deepfake video and voice cloning to impersonate the CEO. The accountant only realized the mistake after the transfer had been completed.

How to Defend:
- The Family Password Strategy: This method, covered in Chapter 12, involves setting up a family-specific "password" that must be used during calls from "family members" to verify identity.
- Multi-Factor Authentication (MFA): Ensure wire transfers or payment requests are verified through a second channel, like an email or SMS, before action is taken.
- Video Verification Requests: During video calls, ask for visual proof like "Hold up three fingers" to prove the video feed is live. Deepfakes have difficulty responding to real-time physical requests.
- Deepfake Detection Tools: Use tools like Deepware Scanner to scan for signs of deepfake content. While these tools aren't perfect, they can identify early signs of manipulation.
- AI-Powered Anti-Fraud Detection: Companies like Darktrace and SentinelOne offer tools that can detect abnormal behaviors from employees, like sudden large payments or unusual wire transfers, and flag them as possible fraud attempts.

Conclusion

Cybercriminals have evolved from lone hackers to sophisticated organizations powered by AI-driven attack tools. As we've seen in this chapter, hackers no longer need to rely on manual techniques. Instead, they automate everything from password cracking and phishing attacks to AI-guided social engineering and deepfake video calls. With AI mutation engines, attackers create polymorphic malware that changes its code every time it infects a device, making traditional antivirus software obsolete. This chapter highlights how AI isn't just a tool for defenders — it's also the ultimate force multiplier for attackers. The ability for AI to adapt, learn, and automate entire attack sequences poses a critical challenge for cybersecurity professionals.

The addition of AI-Guided Social Engineering & AI-Powered Fraud has redefined the threat landscape. Attackers now use AI chatbots to impersonate customer support agents, deepfake video calls to impersonate CEOs, and voice cloning to fool employees into wiring large sums of money. This form of attack preys on human trust and urgency, and traditional training on "phishing awareness" is no longer enough. Companies and individuals must adopt new defensive strategies like the "Family Password" technique to counter these sophisticated attacks. Cybersecurity is no longer about "spotting typos in emails" — it's about verifying every interaction, every call, and every request, no matter how legitimate it appears.

To protect against this new wave of AI-enhanced attacks, organizations must rethink their defenses. Traditional static defenses, like signature-based antivirus, are no longer sufficient. Companies must deploy AI-powered anomaly detection and Extended Detection and Response (XDR) tools to identify abnormal user behavior, such as unexpected video calls or sudden requests for payments. As cybercriminals continue to harness AI to automate and scale their operations, defenders must match automation with automation. The most effective strategy is a combination of Zero-Trust architecture, multi-factor authentication (MFA), and constant anomaly detection. Understanding how hackers think — and how they use AI — is the first step toward staying one step ahead. This chapter has revealed their tactics, but the next step is to think like a hacker and act like a defender.

Chapter 5: Building Your Cybersecurity Toolkit

Your Arsenal Against Cybercrime
In the battle against cybercriminals, ransomware, malware, and adversarial attacks, your strongest line of defense is a well-equipped cybersecurity toolkit. Just as soldiers need weapons, shields, and armor, businesses and individuals need the right combination of software, hardware, and AI-powered tools to protect against modern threats.

Gone are the days when basic antivirus software and firewalls were enough. Modern attackers use AI-driven attack tools, malware mutation engines, and supply chain attacks to breach traditional defenses. To counter these threats, cybersecurity has evolved with the development of AI-driven defenses, smarter detection systems, and tools that predict and block attacks before they happen.

This chapter introduces the essential components of a modern cybersecurity toolkit. From firewalls and VPNs to AI-powered anomaly detection systems, we'll explore the tools that will help you stay one step ahead of cybercriminals.

Essential Cybersecurity Tools
In this section, we cover the core security tools that everyone should have, whether you're protecting a home network or a large enterprise.

1. Firewalls: Your First Line of Defense
A firewall is a security device (software or hardware) that acts as a gatekeeper for your network. It inspects incoming and outgoing traffic and allows or blocks it based on pre-defined rules. Think of it as a border checkpoint for your digital world.

How Firewalls Work
- Packet Inspection: Firewalls inspect "packets" (data units) and allow or block them based on security policies.
- Traffic Filtering: Firewalls block traffic from untrusted sources (like known hacker IP addresses) and prioritize trusted traffic.
- Stateful Inspection: Modern firewalls track connections and recognize if traffic is part of an established session (like a video call) or an unsolicited attack.

Types of Firewalls
- Hardware Firewalls: Physical devices connected to a network (like Cisco or Fortinet devices).
- Software Firewalls: Installed on operating systems (like Windows Defender Firewall).
- Next-Generation Firewalls (NGFWs): Use AI and machine learning to inspect traffic at a deeper level, identify anomalies, and block threats in real time.

Why You Need a Firewall
Without a firewall, attackers can scan open ports, send malicious payloads, and even exploit remote desktop access (RDP). Firewalls help block these access attempts before they reach your devices.

2. Antivirus & Endpoint Detection and Response (EDR) Tools
Antivirus software is one of the oldest and most recognizable cybersecurity tools. It scans files for malware signatures and removes known threats. However, traditional antivirus has major limitations because modern threats (like polymorphic malware) change constantly.

To combat this, Endpoint Detection and Response (EDR) was developed. Unlike antivirus, which looks for known "signatures," EDR monitors behavioral patterns. EDR uses AI to detect unusual activity on devices and endpoints.

How EDR Works
- Behavioral Analytics: EDR watches for unusual behavior (like a Word file encrypting 10,000 files in seconds — a sign of ransomware).
- Threat Containment: When EDR detects suspicious behavior, it can automatically isolate the device from the network.
- Real-Time Alerts: If malware is detected, security teams are notified instantly.

Why You Need EDR (Not Just Antivirus)
Traditional antivirus only recognizes known malware signatures. EDR detects unknown threats, including zero-day exploits, fileless malware, and polymorphic malware.

Examples of Popular EDR Tools
- SentinelOne (AI-driven)
- CrowdStrike Falcon (AI-driven)
- Microsoft Defender for Endpoint

3. VPNs (Virtual Private Networks)

A VPN (Virtual Private Network) encrypts your internet traffic and hides your IP address, making it impossible for attackers to track your online activity. VPNs also mask your location and prevent snooping on public Wi-Fi networks.

How VPNs Work
- Encryption: VPNs encrypt all internet traffic between your device and the VPN server.
- IP Address Masking: Websites you visit see the IP of the VPN server, not your real IP address.
- Access Restrictions: VPNs bypass geo-restrictions, allowing users to access content that may be blocked in their location.

Why You Need a VPN
VPNs protect against man-in-the-middle (MITM) attacks on public Wi-Fi. Without a VPN, hackers can intercept and steal passwords, payment info, and messages. VPNs also hide your online activity from your ISP (Internet Service Provider).

Recommended VPN Providers
- NordVPN (strong encryption, global coverage)
- ExpressVPN (known for speed)
- ProtonVPN (built with privacy-first design)

4. Password Managers

Weak passwords are responsible for 80% of data breaches. A password manager stores, generates, and encrypts strong, unique passwords for all your online accounts.

How Password Managers Work
- Password Storage: Passwords are stored in an encrypted vault accessible via a master password.
- Password Generation: They generate complex passwords like E1x%9Fp#6J instead of simple passwords like John1234.
- Auto-Fill & Syncing: They auto-fill passwords on websites and sync credentials across devices.

Why You Need a Password Manager
Attackers use AI-driven password crackers to guess human-created passwords. A password manager eliminates this problem by generating passwords too complex for AI-based brute force tools like Hashcat.

Top Password Managers
- 1Password
- LastPass (data breach issues, so use caution)
- Bitwarden (open-source and free)

AI-Powered Firewalls: The Next Generation of Network Defense

The Evolution of Firewalls
Traditional firewalls were once the primary gatekeepers of network security, acting like border checkpoints that allowed or denied access to incoming and outgoing traffic. While traditional firewalls are still useful, they are no match for the complexities of today's AI-driven cyberattacks. Attackers now use AI to generate polymorphic malware, mutate attack vectors, and create evasive phishing campaigns.

In response, AI-powered firewalls have emerged as a more advanced solution. Unlike traditional firewalls that rely on static rules, AI-powered firewalls can adapt in real time, learn from attack patterns, and automatically block threats. These firewalls combine machine learning, anomaly detection, and behavioral analytics to provide dynamic, real-time protection.

This section will explain what AI-powered firewalls are, how they work, key features, real-world examples, and why they are essential in modern cybersecurity defense.

What is an AI-Powered Firewall?
An AI-powered firewall is a next-generation security system that uses machine learning (ML) and artificial intelligence (AI) algorithms to monitor, analyze, and block suspicious network traffic. Unlike traditional firewalls that rely on pre-set rules, AI-powered firewalls are designed to learn from network behavior, identify anomalies, and detect previously unknown threats.

While traditional firewalls block traffic based on rules (e.g., "block all traffic from IP 192.0.2.1"), AI-powered firewalls analyze the context of network traffic, recognizing malicious behavior even if it's coming from a new, unknown IP. They can detect zero-day attacks, identify threats hidden in encrypted traffic, and even self-learn to adapt to new attack vectors.

How Do AI-Powered Firewalls Work?

AI-powered firewalls operate by using a combination of machine learning algorithms, behavioral analysis, and threat intelligence. Here's how they work step-by-step:

1. Real-Time Traffic Analysis
   - Data Ingestion: The firewall monitors all incoming and outgoing traffic from connected devices, IoT, & user endpoints.
   - Deep Packet Inspection (DPI): Unlike traditional firewalls, AI-powered firewalls inspect the entire contents of packets (not just headers) to identify potential threats within the traffic.
   - Content-Based Filtering: AI scans dsata for malicious patterns, scripts, or unusual payloads. If it detects something unusual, it triggers alerts.

2. Machine Learning for Anomaly Detection
   - Behavioral Analysis: The firewall observes "normal" network activity for a period of time, such as which devices are connecting, typical traffic volume, and login locations.
   - Anomaly Detection: If something "abnormal" happens (like an unusual IP address attempting to log in at 3 AM), the AI recognizes the anomaly and flags it as suspicious.
   - Adaptive Learning: Unlike static firewalls, AI-powered firewalls continuously learn from attack attempts. If an attacker uses new tactics, the system adapts to recognize those tactics in the future.

3. Automated Threat Response
   - Automated Blocking: If the AI-powered firewall detects suspicious traffic (like port scanning, brute-force attempts, or malware payloads), it can automatically block the source IP address.
   - Real-Time Updates: Threat intelligence feeds are updated in real time, giving AI firewalls the latest information on known threats, malware hashes, and bad IP addresses.
   - Quarantine: Suspicious files, IPs, or devices may be quarantined for manual review or automatic disconnection.

4. Predictive Threat Detection
   - Proactive Defense: Traditional firewalls wait for attacks to happen before blocking them. AI-powered firewalls predict and prevent attacks based on predictive models.
   - Zero-Day Attack Mitigation: Since zero-day attacks are unknown by definition, traditional firewalls often fail to block them. However, AI-powered firewalls can recognize behavioral anomalies associated with zero-day exploits, such as unusual file modifications, and block them.

85

Key Features of AI-Powered Firewalls

1. Deep Packet Inspection (DPI)
Traditional firewalls inspect only the metadata of a packet (like source IP, destination IP, and port number). AI-powered firewalls inspect the entire packet, including its contents. This allows the firewall to recognize threats hidden within encrypted traffic, malicious scripts, and payloads.

2. AI-Driven Threat Intelligence
AI-powered firewalls receive continuous threat intelligence updates from global attack databases. This allows them to recognize emerging threats, identify "bad actor" IP addresses, and block attacks before they impact the network.

3. Self-Learning and Adaptive Models
Unlike static firewalls, AI-powered firewalls adapt to changes in attack methods. If attackers change their IP addresses or use novel tactics, the AI firewall learns the new attack vectors. This self-learning ability makes them resistant to zero-day attacks.

4. Automated Response and Blocking
AI-powered firewalls are designed to automatically block threats without human intervention. If the firewall detects a brute-force login attempt, it can automatically block the offending IP address.

Real-World Examples of AI-Powered Firewalls

1. Palo Alto Networks (NGFW with AI)
Palo Alto's Next-Generation Firewalls (NGFWs) use AI to deliver real-time detection and blocking of advanced threats. It includes features like behavioral analytics, Zero Trust segmentation, and AI-driven threat intelligence. It is widely used in large enterprises, government agencies, and military networks.

Notable Features:
- WildFire: AI-powered malware analysis engine that detects unknown threats in real time.
- URL Filtering: AI recognizes and blocks malicious URLs, even if they are newly created (like "phishing" sites).
- Context-Aware Blocking: Uses AI to block specific user sessions instead of the entire IP.

2. Cisco Firepower

Cisco's AI-powered firewall provides automated detection and response to malware, ransomware, and network anomalies. The AI engine recognizes zero-day threats, uses encrypted traffic analysis, and deploys automatic blocking rules.

Notable Features:
- Behavioral Analytics: Identifies anomalies and unusual login behaviors.
- SSL/TLS Traffic Inspection: Detects malware in encrypted network traffic.
- Zero-Day Detection: Uses AI to recognize zero-day malware by analyzing behavioral anomalies.

3. Fortinet FortiGate (NGFW with AI-Powered Features)

Fortinet's FortiGate firewalls use AI-based intrusion prevention systems (IPS) to detect attacks that aren't recognized by traditional antivirus or malware detection. The FortiGuard AI system analyzes billions of threat feeds to provide real-time updates.

Notable Features:
- Threat Correlation: Correlates multiple attack signals (like brute-force logins + port scans) to identify an ongoing attack.
- AI-Driven IPS: Inspects encrypted traffic and identifies malware hidden inside TLS/SSL connections.
- Dynamic Risk Assessment: Monitors and calculates the "risk score" of devices, allowing suspicious devices to be quarantined.

Advantages of AI-Powered Firewalls

1. Proactive Defense
- AI firewalls predict and block attacks before they happen using predictive analytics. Traditional firewalls only respond to known attacks, but AI firewalls are proactive.

2. Zero-Day Threat Detection
- Traditional firewalls fail against zero-day exploits. AI-powered firewalls recognize anomalous behavior patterns (like unusual login attempts) and block threats before signatures are created.

3. Reduced Manual Intervention
- Traditional firewalls require security analysts to create rules and respond to alerts. AI-powered firewalls respond automatically to threats in real time, reducing the workload for IT teams.

4. Encrypted Traffic Inspection
- Attackers hide malware in encrypted traffic (HTTPS, TLS, etc.). AI-driven Deep Packet Inspection (DPI) can scan encrypted traffic, identify hidden payloads, and block ransomware downloads.

5. Faster Incident Response
- When an attack occurs, milliseconds matter. AI firewalls recognize anomalies and block attacks automatically.

Conclusion
AI-powered firewalls are no longer a luxury — they are a necessity. In a world where attackers use AI-driven malware, phishing generators, and polymorphic ransomware, companies can no longer rely on static, rule-based firewalls. AI-powered firewalls offer dynamic protection with predictive threat detection, anomaly-based blocking, and automatic quarantines.

If you're looking for the best protection, deploy tools like Palo Alto's NGFW, Cisco Firepower, or FortiGate. By using these firewalls, you can achieve a Zero-Trust architecture where nothing is trusted, and everything is verified.

Take Action
- Deploy an AI-powered firewall.
- Ensure your firewall inspects encrypted traffic (TLS/SSL).
- Prioritize Zero-Day Threat Detection using behavioral analysis.

AI-Driven EDR and XDR: The Future of Threat Detection and Response

From Antivirus to EDR to XDR
Gone are the days when antivirus software was enough to protect organizations from malware and viruses. As cyberattacks have become more advanced, automated, and AI-driven, security systems have had to evolve. Enter EDR (Endpoint Detection and Response) and XDR (Extended Detection and Response) — two of the most advanced threat detection tools available today.

While traditional antivirus software focuses on known malware signatures, EDR and XDR focus on behavioral analysis and anomaly detection. Powered by AI, they can detect unknown threats, zero-day attacks, and fileless malware by monitoring how files behave.

This section will explain the key differences between EDR and XDR, how they work, and why they are essential in modern cybersecurity. We'll also provide real-world examples, top tools, and recommendations on how to implement EDR and XDR in your cybersecurity strategy.

What is EDR (Endpoint Detection and Response)?
EDR (Endpoint Detection and Response) is a real-time detection and response system for endpoints, including laptops, desktops, servers, and mobile devices. Unlike traditional antivirus, which only scans for known threats, EDR tracks everything happening on the endpoint — processes, files, system changes, and user activity.

If the EDR system detects unusual behavior (like a file suddenly encrypting 10,000 files), it raises an alert and can automatically isolate the infected system to stop further damage. EDR also allows security teams to trace the attack's origin and see how it spread across the network.

How Does EDR Work?
- Data Collection
  - The EDR agent is installed on each endpoint (like laptops, servers, and desktops) and continuously collects data, including process activity, network connections, file executions, and system logs.

- AI-Driven Behavioral Analysis
  - Unlike traditional antivirus, EDR analyzes user behavior and file behavior. If a normal Word document suddenly starts encrypting files, that behavior would trigger a response from EDR.
  - The AI engine learns normal behavior for each system, so it can detect unusual patterns, even if it's a completely new attack.
- Threat Detection and Alerting
  - If unusual behavior is detected, the EDR agent raises an alert, detailing who, what, and when the incident occurred.
  - Unlike signature-based tools, EDR doesn't need to "know" what the malware looks like — it identifies threats based on behavioral anomalies.
- Incident Response and Containment
  - EDR can automatically isolate a compromised system from the network, stopping ransomware from spreading.
  - Security analysts can investigate the attack, view the chain of events, and roll back any unauthorized changes.

What is XDR (Extended Detection and Response)?

XDR (Extended Detection and Response) takes EDR to the next level. While EDR focuses on endpoint protection (like computers and servers), XDR extends protection across the entire environment, including:

- Endpoints (laptops, desktops, servers)
- Cloud (AWS, Azure, Google Cloud)
- Email and Collaboration Apps (Microsoft 365, Google Workspace)
- Network Traffic (firewalls, VPNs, and routers)

XDR correlates attack signals across multiple layers, which is crucial for detecting multi-stage attacks. For example, if an attacker gains access via a phishing email and moves laterally across a network, EDR might only see the endpoint behavior. XDR sees the entire chain of events from email to cloud to endpoints, giving defenders a clearer picture of the attack.

How Does XDR Work?
- Cross-Platform Data Collection
  - XDR gathers data from multiple sources, including endpoints, cloud environments, email gateways, and network traffic. This allows for a more holistic view of the threat landscape.

- AI-Driven Correlation and Analysis
  - AI correlates signals from multiple sources to detect multi-stage attacks. If a phishing email leads to lateral movement on the network, XDR sees the entire attack chain.
  - XDR correlates seemingly unrelated events to identify larger attack campaigns.
- Automated Incident Response
  - If XDR detects a threat, it can automatically block access to specific users, cloud services, or network locations.
  - It triggers automated incident playbooks that follow pre-configured rules, like locking down user accounts or blocking IP addresses.
- Threat Hunting and Investigation
  - XDR allows threat hunting, where analysts search for dormant threats using the data collected across endpoints, emails, and cloud apps.
  - Analysts can conduct root cause analysis to see how an attacker infiltrated the system.

Why Are EDR and XDR So Important?
- Zero-Day Threat Detection
  - Traditional antivirus can only detect known malware. EDR and XDR detect attacks with no known signature, such as zero-day exploits and polymorphic malware.
- Fileless Malware Detection
  - Fileless malware lives in memory (RAM) instead of hard drives, making it invisible to traditional antivirus. EDR and XDR detect fileless malware by monitoring process behavior.
- Real-Time Response
  - When EDR or XDR detects unusual behavior, it can automatically isolate the endpoint or block user access, preventing the attacker from moving laterally.
- Multi-Stage Attack Detection
  - EDR is limited to endpoint activity. XDR monitors the entire attack chain, from email phishing attempts to lateral movement within the network.

Key Features of AI-Driven EDR and XDR
- AI-Driven Behavioral Analysis: Monitors user behavior, file execution, and system changes to detect anomalies.
- Zero-Day Threat Detection: Recognizes and stops threats that have no known signature.
- Automatic Containment: Isolates infected endpoints from the network to stop the spread of ransomware.

- Cross-Platform Correlation (XDR): Tracks attacks from endpoints, cloud services, email gateways, and network traffic.
- Threat Hunting Capabilities: Security analysts can investigate threats, analyze attack chains, and respond proactively.

Examples of AI-Driven EDR and XDR Tools
- CrowdStrike Falcon
  - EDR + XDR Capabilities: Protects endpoints, cloud workloads, and network activity.
  - Key Feature: Uses AI-driven anomaly detection to identify fileless malware.
- Microsoft Defender for Endpoint (XDR)
  - XDR Capabilities: Protects endpoints, Microsoft 365 email, and cloud services.
  - Key Feature: Detects phishing, malware, and lateral movement across all Microsoft services.
- SentinelOne
  - EDR Capabilities: Detects, responds, and contains ransomware on endpoints.
  - Key Feature: Uses AI-based behavior tracking to detect new threats, including polymorphic malware.

Advantages of AI-Driven EDR and XDR
- Proactive Threat Detection
  - While traditional antivirus waits for an attack, EDR and XDR proactively scan for anomalies.
- Automated Response
  - When ransomware starts encrypting files, EDR automatically isolates the infected device, stopping the attack.
- Threat Hunting
  - With XDR's cross-platform tracking, security analysts can follow an attack from the point of entry (like an email) to where the attacker moves laterally (like accessing internal systems).
- AI-Powered Machine Learning
  - AI constantly analyzes patterns and behavior to detect new types of malware, including polymorphic and fileless malware.
- Multi-Layered Security (XDR)
  - XDR detects threats across cloud, email, endpoints, and networks, providing a full view of multi-stage attacks.

If you only have traditional antivirus, you are already two steps behind cybercriminals. Modern threats like ransomware, polymorphic malware, and fileless attacks require behavioral analysis, anomaly detection, and cross-platform tracking.

With AI-driven EDR and XDR, you can detect zero-day threats, block lateral movement, and stop attacks before they spread. Tools like CrowdStrike Falcon, SentinelOne, and Microsoft Defender for Endpoint use AI to predict, detect, and prevent attacks.

Take Action
- Upgrade from antivirus to EDR/XDR.
- Choose AI-driven tools like CrowdStrike Falcon or Microsoft Defender for Endpoint.
- Monitor for zero-day attacks, fileless malware, and multi-stage threats.

With AI-enhanced EDR and XDR, you'll have full visibility and control over endpoints, email, and cloud platforms — making it nearly impossible for attackers to hide.

The Core Components of a Strong Cybersecurity Toolkit
- Firewalls: Your first line of defense, monitoring and controlling network traffic.
- Antivirus & EDR (Endpoint Detection and Response): Protects devices from fileless malware, ransomware, and zero-day threats.
- VPNs (Virtual Private Networks): Encrypts your online activity and protects you on public Wi-Fi.
- Password Managers: Safeguards your credentials and prevents brute-force attacks.
- AI-Powered Firewalls: Uses anomaly detection, deep packet inspection, and AI to block unknown threats.
- AI-Driven EDR & XDR: Tracks attack chains across endpoints, cloud, and network traffic.
- AI-Driven Threat Intelligence: Collects real-time threat data from around the world, detects emerging threats, and blocks them automatically.

Each of these tools addresses different stages of an attack — from preventing attackers from getting in to detecting and responding to threats in real time.

Action Plan: How to Build Your Cybersecurity Toolkit
To build an effective cybersecurity toolkit, follow this 6-step approach:

1. Install an AI-Powered Firewall
Traditional firewalls aren't enough. Upgrade to a Next-Generation Firewall (NGFW) with AI-driven anomaly detection and encrypted traffic analysis. Look for features like deep packet inspection (DPI) and real-time IP blacklisting.
- Recommended AI-Powered Firewalls:
  - Palo Alto Networks (NGFW) - https://www.paloaltonetworks.com/
  - Cisco Firepower - https://www.cisco.com/c/en/us/products/security/firewalls/firepower-4100-series/index.html
  - Fortinet FortiGate (NGFW) - https://www.fortinet.com/products/next-generation-firewall

2. Use EDR or XDR for Endpoint Protection
Antivirus is no longer enough. Upgrade to Endpoint Detection and Response (EDR) or Extended Detection and Response (XDR) to detect and respond to fileless malware, zero-day attacks, and ransomware. Unlike antivirus, EDR/XDR can block malware before it executes, detect lateral movement, and quarantine infected devices.
- Recommended EDR/XDR Tools:
  - CrowdStrike Falcon - https://www.crowdstrike.com/
  - SentinelOne - https://www.sentinelone.com/
  - Microsoft Defender for Endpoint (XDR) - https://www.microsoft.com/en-us/security/business/threat-protection/microsoft-defender-endpoint

3. Use a VPN to Encrypt Your Online Activity
Whether you're working from home, traveling, or using public Wi-Fi, a VPN (Virtual Private Network) encrypts your data so that hackers, ISPs, and other snoopers can't see your activity. VPNs protect you from man-in-the-middle (MITM) attacks that can steal login credentials, payment info, and personal data.
- Recommended VPN Providers:
  - NordVPN - https://nordvpn.com/
  - ExpressVPN - https://www.expressvpn.com/
  - ProtonVPN - https://protonvpn.com/

4. Use a Password Manager

80% of data breaches result from weak passwords. Password managers generate strong, random passwords and store them securely. They also auto-fill your passwords when you log into apps or websites, so you never have to remember them.

- Recommended Password Managers:
    - 1Password - https://1password.com/
    - Bitwarden - https://bitwarden.com/
    - LastPass - https://www.lastpass.com/ (Note: Be cautious, as LastPass recently experienced security breaches.)

5. Deploy an AI-Driven Threat Intelligence Platform

Cybercriminals are always one step ahead, releasing new malware and phishing campaigns daily. To stay ahead, use an AI-driven threat intelligence platform that tracks global attack activity, predicts emerging threats, and automatically updates your blocklists, EDR, and firewalls.

- Recommended Threat Intelligence Platforms:
    - Recorded Future - https://www.recordedfuture.com/
    - IBM X-Force Exchange - https://exchange.xforce.ibmcloud.com/
    - ThreatConnect - https://threatconnect.com/

6. Monitor for Anomalies with AI-Driven Detection

No matter how strong your firewalls, VPNs, and EDR are, attackers can still get in. This is why anomaly detection is critical. Use tools like AI-driven anomaly detection to catch strange behaviors, such as file encryption, unusual logins, and abnormal network traffic.

- Recommended AI Anomaly Detection Tools:
    - CrowdStrike Falcon - https://www.crowdstrike.com/
    - SentinelOne - https://www.sentinelone.com/
    - Palo Alto Cortex XDR - https://www.paloaltonetworks.com/cortex/cortex-xdr

If you follow these steps, your business will be more secure than 95% of companies worldwide. Attackers may adapt, but with AI-enhanced predictive defense, you'll be ready for them.

Protect yourself. Protect your family. Protect your business.

"The attacker only has to succeed once, but with AI on your side, you can succeed every time."

Final Thoughts: Stay Ahead of Attackers
The most important lesson from this chapter is this: Cybersecurity is not "set it and forget it." Attackers evolve, mutate, and improve every day. Ransomware is now a billion-dollar industry, and attack tools are available to hackers as "services" on the dark web.

But there's good news. With the right AI-driven cybersecurity tools, you can stay one step ahead of attackers. While no single tool will stop every attack, layering multiple tools together creates a multi-layered defense that is incredibly hard to breach.

Conclusion: Bringing It All Together: Your Cybersecurity Arsenal
In today's fast-evolving digital landscape, having a well-equipped cybersecurity toolkit isn't just a "nice-to-have" — it's a necessity. The attacks of yesterday were simple viruses, worms, and spyware. But today, we face AI-driven malware, ransomware-as-a-service (RaaS), and adversarial attacks that mutate their behavior to avoid detection. To counter these threats, you need to combine essential security tools with modern AI-powered platforms to achieve multi-layered, proactive security.

This chapter has provided a comprehensive overview of the tools you need to protect yourself, your family, and your business. We explored everything from firewalls and antivirus to AI-enhanced EDR, XDR, and threat intelligence platforms. Each tool plays a unique role in protecting you from attacks, detecting threats, and responding to incidents in real time.

When combined, these tools form a Zero-Trust security model — a model where nothing is trusted by default, and everything is verified. By using AI-powered automation, anomaly detection, and predictive threat analysis, you no longer have to react to threats after they've caused damage. Instead, you can predict and block attacks before they occur.

Chapter 6: Family & Personal Cybersecurity

Why Family Cybersecurity is a Non-Negotiable Priority
In an era where nearly every device in our homes is connected to the internet, the concept of "home security" has shifted from physical locks and alarms to digital defenses and online protection. The modern family home is a playground for smart devices, online accounts, and ever-present connectivity, but it's also a prime target for hackers, scammers, and cybercriminals.

Cybercriminals are no longer just targeting large corporations — they're targeting you, your family, and even your children. Every smart TV, baby monitor, Wi-Fi camera, and connected device in your home is a potential entry point for attackers. Worse, scammers use social engineering tricks like phishing emails, vishing calls, and smishing texts to manipulate family members into sharing passwords, PINs, and personal data.

But here's the good news: You have the power to fight back. With the right tools, security habits, and knowledge, you can turn your home into a fortress of digital safety. In this chapter, we'll show you how to secure your family, protect your privacy, and stop scammers in their tracks.

Why Families are Prime Targets for Cybercriminals
If you think hackers are only interested in large companies, think again. Cybercriminals know that families are often easier targets because:
1. Lack of Cyber Awareness: Most families don't think about cybersecurity until after an attack happens.
2. Multiple Entry Points: Smart home devices, Wi-Fi routers, and children's devices all provide entry points for hackers.
3. Weaker Passwords: Many families use weak passwords, repeat passwords across multiple devices, or leave default passwords unchanged.
4. Children and Teenagers: Kids are often unaware of phishing attacks, gaming scams, and fraudulent apps. Hackers know this, and they use gaming platforms and social media to target children.
5. Social Engineering: Attackers pose as trusted sources (like "Amazon Customer Support" or "Tech Support") and manipulate family members into sharing information or clicking dangerous links.

These factors make families low-hanging fruit for attackers, but with the right security strategy, you can make your home much harder to breach.

What You Will Learn in This Chapter
By the end of this chapter, you will be able to:
- Secure every device in your home (like Wi-Fi routers, smart devices, and baby monitors) to prevent hijacking and botnet recruitment.
- Defend against social engineering scams targeting your family, including phishing, vishing (voice scams), and smishing (text scams).
- Create and implement a Family Password strategy to protect against AI-driven voice cloning scams and impersonation attempts.
- Build a Family Cybersecurity Action Plan with clear rules for online behavior, device usage, and scam detection for kids, teens, and adults.

We'll introduce specific AI-driven tools and services that make it easier than ever to protect your home. From smart Wi-Fi firewalls to scam-blocking AI phone apps, you'll learn how to leverage AI to create a proactive, always-on defense for your family.

Why You Need a Family Cybersecurity Plan
Imagine waking up one day to discover that a hacker has taken control of your baby monitor, or worse, that a scammer tricked your teenager into downloading a fake "game mod" that infects the entire family network with ransomware.

These attacks happen every day, and they're often preventable. But without a plan, your family is vulnerable to:
- Identity Theft: Children's identities are prized by hackers because they go undetected for years.
- Device Hijacking: Smart cameras, thermostats, and door locks can be hijacked remotely, giving attackers access to your home.
- Gaming Scams: Kids and teens are often tricked into clicking on links for free in-game currency, fake skins, or "hacks" that are actually malware in disguise.
- Social Engineering: Everyone in your family (kids, parents, and grandparents) is vulnerable to phishing emails, vishing calls, and "Amazon refund scams".

By building a Family Cybersecurity Plan, you'll ensure that every family member knows the rules. It's not just about installing software — it's about changing habits. Everyone in the home should know:

- How to recognize a scam.
- How to avoid risky online behavior (like downloading sketchy apps).
- What to do if something goes wrong (like a phone call from "tech support").

The 3 Pillars of Family Cybersecurity
This chapter is divided into three key sections. Each section tackles a crucial area of family cybersecurity, ensuring you have the tools, knowledge, and processes needed to protect your loved ones.

Section 1: Securing Smart Devices and Family Networks

- Learn how to secure your smart home devices, including smart thermostats, Wi-Fi routers, and baby monitors.
- Discover how hackers hijack IoT devices and how to prevent it with router-based firewalls and network anomaly detection.
- Get access to 10 actionable steps to lock down every device on your network.

Section 2: How AI Can Help Families Spot Social Engineering Scams

- Understand the rising threat of AI-driven voice cloning attacks and how hackers impersonate loved ones to steal money or information.
- Learn how AI-driven security tools (like scam call blockers, email spam filters, and phishing detection software) protect family members.
- Get step-by-step guidance on how to teach kids and teens to spot scams like game scams, Discord scams, and social media cons.
- Discover how call-blocking AI apps and phishing detection browser extensions protect you from scammers.

Section 3: Family Cybersecurity Action Plan

- Build your Family Cybersecurity Policy — a set of rules that every family member (kids, teens, and adults) follows to protect the household.
- Learn to set up daily, weekly, and monthly cybersecurity habits (like checking devices, updating firmware, and scanning for scams).
- Use checklists and printable worksheets to track your family's progress and keep devices safe.

Why AI is a Game-Changer for Family Cybersecurity
In the past, protecting your home meant installing antivirus software and hoping for the best. But today, AI offers advanced protection that predicts attacks before they happen. Here's how AI works in family cybersecurity:

- Spam and Scam Call Blocking: Apps like Hiya and Truecaller use AI to detect suspicious phone numbers. AI models track how scammers create new phone numbers and block them before they reach you.
- AI-Driven Email Filters: Email providers like Gmail use AI-based spam filters to recognize scam emails, phishing attempts, and fraudulent links.
- Anomaly Detection: AI-powered firewalls and network security systems (like Firewalla and TP-Link HomeShield) scan traffic for unusual activity, like a smart camera sending data to a suspicious server.
- Parental Controls with AI: Apps like Bark (https://www.bark.us/) and Qustodio (https://www.qustodio.com/) allow parents to set screen time limits, block harmful websites, and monitor for inappropriate content.

AI doesn't just react — it predicts. It sees attack patterns forming and prevents issues before they happen.

Your family's personal cybersecurity is no longer a passive activity. It's something you can actively control, protect, and monitor. Every connected device in your home represents a digital doorway. This chapter will show you how to lock every single one.

If you follow the guidance in this chapter, you'll go from being an easy target for hackers to being one of the hardest households to crack. With AI on your side, you'll see attacks forming before they hit. You'll spot scams before anyone in your family clicks on them.

Your family's online safety depends on what you do right now. Let's build your Family Cybersecurity Fortress together.

Securing Smart Devices and Family Networks

Why Securing Smart Devices Matters More Than Ever
The number of smart home devices in modern households has exploded in recent years. From video doorbells, smart thermostats, and baby monitors to devices like smart TVs, speakers, and robot vacuums, our homes have become more connected than ever. These devices, commonly referred to as Internet of Things (IoT) devices, make life more convenient but also introduce massive cybersecurity risks.

Cybercriminals have shifted their focus to smart homes because these devices are often under-protected and easy to compromise. Once an attacker gains control of a single device, they can:
- Spy on your family (via hacked baby monitors or security cameras).
- Launch ransomware attacks that lock you out of your devices.
- Steal sensitive information (like saved Wi-Fi passwords) to attack other devices.
- Recruit your devices into a botnet to attack larger targets.

This section will provide a step-by-step plan to secure smart home devices, protect your family's privacy, and prevent cybercriminals from turning your home into their next attack target.

What is a Smart Home and Why is it a Target?
A smart home is any household that uses devices connected to the internet to control appliances, security systems, and electronics. Examples include:
- Smart Thermostats (like Nest, Ecobee)
- Smart Cameras (like Ring, Arlo, Blink)
- Smart Plugs & Switches (like Kasa Smart Plugs)
- Smart Door Locks (like August Lock)
- Voice Assistants (like Amazon Alexa, Google Assistant)

These devices increase convenience but introduce security weaknesses. Many smart devices lack basic security features, ship with default passwords, or fail to receive regular security updates. Attackers exploit these flaws to hijack devices, spy on homes, and launch larger attacks using your devices as part of a botnet.

The Key Threats to Smart Devices
Before you can secure your home, it's important to understand the types of attacks that hackers use against smart devices.

1. Device Hijacking
Hackers hijack IoT devices, like baby monitors, security cameras, or smart assistants, to spy on users or control the device remotely. A hijacked baby monitor, for example, allows a hacker to watch and hear everything happening in your child's room.

Example:
In a famous 2019 case, a hacker hijacked a family's Ring Camera and spoke to an 8-year-old girl, pretending to be "Santa Claus." The attacker gained access through weak credentials and lack of multi-factor authentication (MFA).

2. Ransomware on IoT Devices
Ransomware doesn't just target files on your computer — it can also lock IoT devices. Imagine your smart lock refusing to unlock your front door or your smart thermostat blasting extreme heat until you pay a ransom.

Example:
Hackers have launched ransomware attacks against smart thermostats and smart home hubs, locking homeowners out of their own systems until a ransom is paid.

3. Privacy Invasion
Smart devices collect data about your routines, shopping habits, and conversations. Voice assistants (like Alexa) record voice commands, and smart TVs collect data on your viewing habits. Hackers who breach these devices can steal private information, track your behavior, and sell this data on the dark web.

4. Botnet Recruitment
When attackers hijack IoT devices, they often don't do it to attack you directly. Instead, they recruit your device to become part of a botnet — a network of hijacked devices that launch attacks on other victims. These botnets can be used in DDoS (Distributed Denial of Service) attacks against large companies, causing millions in damages.

10 Steps to Secure Your Smart Home

1. Change Default Passwords on All Devices
Most smart devices ship with a generic username and password,
like admin/admin or user1234. Attackers use automated tools to
search for devices that haven't had their default passwords
changed.
How to Fix It:
- Change the default password for each device during initial
  setup.
- Use a password manager like 1Password
  (https://1password.com/) or Bitwarden (https://bitwarden.com/)
  to create long, unique passwords for each device.

2. Enable Multi-Factor Authentication (MFA)
Even if hackers steal your password, they can't log in without the
second factor (like a text message code).
How to Fix It:
- Look for devices that offer MFA as an option (like Ring
  Cameras and Google Nest).
- Turn on MFA for the app used to control the device.

3. Separate Your Smart Devices on a Guest Wi-Fi Network
If an attacker takes over one device on your Wi-Fi network, they
can access other devices. But if you separate your smart devices on
a guest network, the attacker won't have access to everything.
How to Fix It:
- Create a separate guest Wi-Fi network for smart devices.
- Most modern routers (like Google Nest Wi-Fi and Eero) offer
  easy guest Wi-Fi setup.

4. Keep Firmware and Software Updated
Outdated firmware can have unpatched security flaws. Vendors
regularly release updates to patch vulnerabilities.
How to Fix It:
- Turn on auto-updates in the device settings (if available).
- Check the manufacturer's website for updates if auto-updates
  aren't available.

5. Turn Off Unused Features
If a device has features you don't use (like remote access), turn
them off.
How to Fix It:
- Disable remote access to devices like smart cameras and door
  locks.
- Turn off voice assistant recording on smart speakers.

6. Install an AI-Powered Wi-Fi Security Router

Smart routers now come with AI-driven threat detection that blocks unknown devices, detects anomalies, and flags security threats in real time.

How to Fix It:
- Use routers like Firewalla (https://firewalla.com/), Norton Core, or TP-Link HomeShield.

7. Use Network Anomaly Detection Tools

Anomaly detection tools alert you when new devices connect to your network or when existing devices behave unusually.

How to Fix It:
- Use the Fing app (https://www.fing.com/) to check which devices are connected.
- For deeper protection, use tools like Armis (https://www.armis.com/) for real-time monitoring of IoT device activity.

8. Disable Unused Ports and Protocols

Hackers look for devices with open ports. Ports are like "doors" into your devices.

How to Fix It:
- Disable UPnP (Universal Plug and Play) on your router.
- Disable any open ports that aren't in use.

9. Conduct Regular Security Audits

Review the devices connected to your home network. Look for old devices you no longer use.

How to Fix It:
- Use a tool like Fing to scan your network.
- Remove old or unused devices from the network.

10. Use Router-Based Firewalls

Some routers have built-in firewalls that block attacks at the network level.

How to Fix It:
- Use routers with built-in firewalls like Google Nest Wi-Fi, Eero Secure, or TP-Link HomeShield.

Recommended AI-Driven Security Tools for Smart Homes
- Firewalla (https://firewalla.com/) — AI-powered Wi-Fi security system.
- Armis (https://www.armis.com/) — AI-based anomaly detection for IoT devices.
- Fing (https://www.fing.com/) — Device tracker and network scanning app.

- Google Nest Wi-Fi — Built-in router firewall.
- TP-Link HomeShield — AI-driven security system for Wi-Fi networks.

Conclusion

Your smart home is only as secure as the weakest device on the network. By following these 10 essential steps, you'll protect your smart cameras, thermostats, and voice assistants from attacks. Don't wait until it's too late. Hackers are constantly looking for open devices. Use tools like Firewalla and Fing to track and secure your devices in real time.

By taking these simple actions, you can create a hack-proof smart home that protects your family, your privacy, and your peace of mind.

How AI Can Help Families Spot Social Engineering Scams

The Invisible Danger Lurking in Your Inbox and Calls
Imagine getting an email from "Amazon" telling you there's a problem with your order. Or a text message from your "bank" warning you of suspicious activity. These are examples of social engineering scams, and they're designed to manipulate your emotions into taking immediate action — like clicking a link, calling a fake customer service line, or providing sensitive information.

Social engineering attacks don't rely on technical hacking skills. Instead, they exploit human psychology. Attackers use tactics like urgency, fear, trust, and curiosity to trick family members into giving away passwords, clicking malicious links, or transferring money.

AI-driven protection has become essential in fighting social engineering attacks. Unlike human users, AI can detect patterns in scam messages and fraudulent phone calls. It identifies "red flags" in language, tone, and urgency that would fool most people.

This section will explain the following:
- How social engineering works (phishing, vishing, smishing, and tech support scams).
- The threat of AI-driven voice cloning attacks — how scammers impersonate family members, CEOs, and loved ones to request money or sensitive information.
- How AI-driven tools identify and block social engineering attempts (like scam blockers, anomaly detection, and browser protections).
- How to train your family to recognize these scams and build a family-wide Social Engineering Defense Plan.

What is Social Engineering?
Social engineering is when a scammer manipulates you into giving them access to your accounts, passwords, or financial information. Unlike malware, which directly infects your system, social engineering tricks you into giving access voluntarily.

These attacks work on the basis of urgency, fear, and authority. Attackers push you to "act fast" so you don't have time to think critically.

How to Outsmart Voice Cloning Scams
Imagine you're at work, and your phone rings. The number is unrecognizable, but the voice on the other end sounds painfully familiar — it's your child. They're crying, frantic, and they say, "I'm stuck at the airport, I lost my wallet, and I need you to send $1,000 right away. Please, mom/dad, it's urgent!"

The voice sounds so real that your heart races. You feel an instant need to act. But what you don't realize is that the "voice" you're hearing isn't your child at all. It's an AI-powered voice clone. Using AI voice cloning tools like ElevenLabs (https://elevenlabs.io/), scammers can recreate anyone's voice with just 20 seconds of audio. They might have pulled this audio from a social media post, voicemail greeting, or video your child posted online.

This attack is no longer theoretical — it's happening right now. Families have been scammed into sending thousands of dollars to fake "loved ones" in need.

How do you protect yourself? This is where the Family Password comes in (explained in Chapter 12). Instead of relying on your "gut feeling" or "trusting the voice," you ask for a secret family password — a specific word, number, or phrase that only your family knows. If the person on the other end of the call can't provide it, you hang up immediately

The Five Types of Social Engineering Scams

1. Phishing (Email Scams)
Phishing emails trick you into clicking on links that steal your passwords, financial info, or account access. Attackers disguise the email to look like it's from a trusted source (like PayPal, Amazon, or a bank).

How It Works:
1. The attacker sends an email disguised as a legitimate company (like PayPal).
2. The email includes a fake warning like, "Your account has been locked. Click here to unlock it."
3. The link directs you to a fake login page where you unknowingly enter your real credentials.

How AI Stops It:
- Email AI Filters (like Gmail's AI) analyze incoming emails and block phishing attempts based on suspicious language, links, and sender reputation.
- Browser Anti-Phishing Extensions like Bitdefender Anti-Phishing block websites that mimic popular brands.
- Machine Learning Models analyze message tone, urgency, and grammatical errors that humans might overlook.

2. Vishing (Phone Call Scams)
Vishing scams involve fake phone calls where the scammer pretends to be tech support, IRS agents, or customer service reps.

How It Works:
1. You receive a call from a spoofed number (like "Apple Support" or "Microsoft Support").
2. The caller claims your account has been "compromised" or "flagged for suspicious activity."
3. They ask for your password, Social Security number, or remote access to your device.

How AI Stops It:
- Call-Blocking Apps (like Hiya or Truecaller) use AI to detect caller reputation. If a number is flagged by thousands of other users as a scam, it is automatically blocked.
- AI-Based Caller ID Systems label calls as "Scam Likely" before you answer.
- Voice Analysis AI analyzes the tone, urgency, and voice patterns of the caller to flag potential vishing attempts.

3. Smishing (Text Message Scams)

Smishing involves fake SMS text messages that try to trick you into clicking on links.

How It Works:
1. You receive a text like, "Your package delivery is delayed. Click here to reschedule."
2. The link takes you to a fake login page that steals your username and password.
3. The scammer gains access to your shipping or payment accounts.

How AI Stops It:
- Spam Text Filters (like Google's SMS Filter) automatically filter scam texts into a "Spam" folder.
- AI Language Models scan text messages for words and phrases linked to scams (like "urgent," "limited time," and "click here").
- URL Scanners like Bitdefender Anti-Phishing flag fraudulent URLs linked in text messages.

4. Tech Support Scams

Tech support scams are fake calls, pop-ups, or alerts that claim your device is infected with malware. The goal is to make you pay for unnecessary "support services" or download malware disguised as a "repair tool."

How It Works:
1. You see a pop-up that says "Your system is infected!" with a phone number to call for "support."
2. If you call the number, a scammer asks for remote access to your computer.
3. They "show" you fake virus activity, then offer to "fix" it for a fee.

How AI Stops It:
- Browser Security Tools (like Microsoft SmartScreen) automatically block known scam pop-ups.
- AI Pop-Up Blockers stop pop-ups containing fake tech support messages.
- Scam Call Blocking Apps (like Truecaller) flag known scam numbers and prevent them from calling you.

5. Deepfakes

Deepfakes are AI-generated video, audio, or images designed to impersonate real people. This type of social engineering attack has become one of the most sophisticated threats in the world of cybersecurity. Unlike phishing or vishing, which rely on simple messages or phone calls, deepfakes use AI-generated media to create convincing imitations of voices, faces, and even full video calls.

The goal of deepfake attacks is to manipulate trust, convincing victims to share sensitive information, authorize large financial transactions, or grant access to accounts and systems. Attackers use AI-generated voice cloning and video manipulation to trick victims into believing they are speaking with a trusted person, like a CEO, family member, or bank representative.

How It Works:
1. Voice Cloning & Video Manipulation
   - Attackers use AI to clone the voice of a trusted individual, like a CEO, CFO, or family member.
   - This voice is used in a phone call, video call, or voicemail to deliver a convincing social engineering attack.
2. AI-Generated Video Calls
   - Attackers create a deepfake video feed of a CEO, executive, or manager on a video conferencing app (like Zoom or Teams).
   - The victim joins the call and sees what appears to be their boss, issuing direct orders to authorize wire transfers or approve access to secure files.
   - Victims trust the face and voice of the person on the call, making it one of the most effective and hard-to-detect scams.
3. Familiar Voices on Phone Calls
   - Attackers use stolen voice samples from YouTube videos, social media, and voicemail recordings.
   - The AI model learns how the person speaks, mimics their tone, and generates a perfect clone of the voice.
   - Victims receive a phone call where the cloned voice of a family member or loved one asks for emergency help, like money or private information.

Real-World Example:
The $25.6M Deepfake CFO Scam (2024)
- Attackers used a deepfake video of a CFO during a business video conference call.
- The scammer, posing as the CFO, convinced a finance executive to transfer $25.6M in multiple payments to several foreign accounts.
- Because the employee believed they were following direct orders from a company leader, they authorized 15 transactions before discovering the fraud.
- Takeaway: The employee trusted the face and voice of the "CFO" in the video call, highlighting the psychological power of deepfakes.

How AI Stops It:
- Deepfake Detection Tools
  - AI-powered deepfake detection software (like Deepware Scanner) analyzes videos and voices to identify subtle AI-generated artifacts.
  - Companies like Microsoft, Intel, and Google are developing tools to detect deepfakes before they go viral or cause damage.
- Voice Verification Protocols
  - Companies are encouraged to use multi-layered authentication when handling financial transactions, especially when instructions are given over the phone or video calls.
  - Family Password Strategy: Families and companies can create "verification questions" or use pre-determined "family passwords" to verify if the caller is legitimate. If the person on the call cannot answer the question correctly, it's a red flag.
- Training & Awareness
  - Train employees and family members to recognize the signs of a deepfake attack.
  - Signs include slight lip-syncing issues, unnatural facial movements, or unusual speech patterns.
  - Encourage users to verify sensitive financial requests through a second, secure communication channel.
- Multi-Factor Verification
  - Require an extra verification step for all financial transactions, payments, and security approvals.
  - If an executive asks for a large wire transfer, employees should use a second channel (like text, email, or an internal app) to verify the request before acting.

Why Deepfakes Are Dangerous:
- AI-Powered Trust Manipulation: Humans are hardwired to trust faces and voices, and deepfakes exploit that instinct.
- Difficult to Detect: Unlike phishing emails, deepfakes can bypass email filters, scam blockers, and traditional "warning systems."
- Business Impact: Deepfakes are now being used in business email compromise (BEC) attacks via video conferencing software (like Zoom, Google Meet, and Microsoft Teams).
- Hard to Train For: Employees are less familiar with deepfakes, making it difficult for them to recognize the warning signs.

How to Defend Against Deepfake Attacks
- Adopt a Family Password Strategy (detailed in Chapter 12)
  - How It Works: All family members agree on a "shared password" that only close family knows (like the 20th letter of a favorite song lyric).
  - Purpose: If a family member receives a call from "Mom" asking for money, they can ask, "What's the 20th letter of our family password?" If the answer is wrong, it's a scam.
- Use Multi-Factor Authentication (MFA)
  - Enable MFA on financial accounts, business logins, and bank apps.
  - If deepfakes trick one system (like a phone call), they won't be able to bypass a second layer of protection.
- Voice Verification Protocols
  - For Businesses: If a CEO or CFO requests a wire transfer, employees must confirm via a secure second channel like a company-issued chat app or in-person confirmation.
  - For Families: Use the Family Password strategy as a personal-level defense.
- Deepfake Detection Apps
  - Use tools like Deepware Scanner to detect audio and video deepfakes. These tools analyze the waveform, facial movement, and lip-syncing of voices and faces to detect AI manipulation.

Why Deepfakes Deserve Their Own Category
Deepfakes are more than just "social engineering" — they're an entirely new type of attack fueled by AI-generated deception. While phishing, smishing, and vishing rely on simple messaging, deepfakes exploit the visual and auditory trust instincts that humans have developed over thousands of years. The fact that deepfakes can use both video and voice at the same time makes them significantly more dangerous than traditional phishing or vishing scams.

How to Protect Your Family from Social Engineering
Here are specific actions you can take to protect your family from phishing, vishing, smishing, and tech support scams:

1. Install AI-Driven Call-Blocking Apps
   - Hiya (https://hiya.com/) and Truecaller (https://www.truecaller.com/) are apps that use AI to block scam calls.
   - They detect scam numbers before they ring and flag them as "Scam Likely."
   - These apps pull data from thousands of reports to identify common scam numbers.

2. Enable Browser Anti-Phishing Protections
   - Install Bitdefender Anti-Phishing (browser extension) to block fake websites.
   - Enable browser-based security settings (like Google Safe Browsing) to protect against fake login pages.

3. Teach Family Members to Spot Scams
   - Check the Sender's Email Address: Teach family members to look for fake email domains like "info@paypal-security-alerts.com" instead of the real "service@paypal.com."
   - Hover Over Links: Show kids and teens how to hover over links to see if the URL is fake.
   - Don't Answer Unknown Calls: Tell family members to send unknown calls to voicemail. Legitimate companies leave messages — scammers don't.
   - Be Suspicious of Urgency: Train family members to avoid "urgent" messages, such as "Act Now!" or "Limited Time Offer!"

4. Install Scam-Blocking Browser Extensions
   - Install browser extensions like Bitdefender Anti-Phishing or Avast Online Security.
   - These tools scan every link you click and block access to fake login pages.

5. Use Parental Control Tools
   - Use apps like Qustodio (https://www.qustodio.com/) and Bark (https://www.bark.us/) to monitor children's devices for signs of scam activity.
   - These apps notify parents if kids visit scam sites or engage with malicious messages.

Build a Family Password Strategy
One of the most important tools in your Family Cybersecurity Action Plan is the Family Password. This simple but powerful strategy protects against one of the fastest-growing threats of the decade — AI-powered voice cloning scams.

As discussed earlier, voice cloning allows attackers to steal someone's voice with as little as 20 seconds of audio. Attackers can call you pretending to be your child, parent, or sibling, using emotional urgency to manipulate you into sending money or sharing sensitive information.

With a Family Password, you can verify their identity on the spot. If they don't know the password, you know you're being scammed.

How to Create a Family Password
1. Choose a Source — Pick a song, movie, book, or other cultural reference that everyone in your family knows and loves.
2. Pick a Specific Line — Select a specific line, lyric, or phrase from that source. It should be something only your family remembers but isn't too obvious. Example: If the family loves "Bohemian Rhapsody" by Queen, you could select the 3rd line of the 2nd verse.
3. Create a Verification Method — When under pressure, it's hard to think clearly. So, establish a simple verification method. Example: If the password is "Is this the real life, is this just fantasy," you can challenge the caller with:
   - "What's the 8th word of our family password?"
   - "What's the 16th letter of our family password?"
   - "Recite the 2nd line of our family password."
4. Teach Your Family — Every family member should know the password, but it should never be written down, typed, or shared on a phone. This keeps the password out of reach of AI listening devices like Siri, Alexa, or Google Home.

Why Family Passwords Work
Attackers may have access to your social media, voice recordings, or email accounts, but they don't have access to this offline secret. It's something only your family knows, and since it's based on a shared memory, it's harder to forget.

Here's why this is AI-proof:
- AI can clone voices, but it can't predict your private family password.
- Attackers won't be able to answer questions like "What's the 12th letter of our password?" because AI models have no access to this private information.

Example in Action
You receive a call from someone pretending to be your spouse. The voice sounds real, but something feels off. To verify, you say:
"If this is really you, tell me the 6th letter of our Family Password."
If the caller responds incorrectly or hesitates, you immediately hang up.

Action Step: Set Your Family Password Now!
Set aside 10 minutes with your family to create a Family Password. Follow these simple steps:
- Pick a memorable song, movie, or quote your family knows.
- Select a key line, verse, or phrase.
- Teach every family member how to ask and answer questions about the password.
- Keep it off devices — no texting, no notes, and no voice recordings.

This 10-minute action could prevent your family from being scammed out of thousands of dollars.

Pro Tip: If you have younger children, turn it into a family game. Make it fun and memorable so they don't forget.

Conclusion: Stay Ahead of the Scammers
Social engineering is one of the most dangerous types of attacks because it targets human nature. Phishing emails, scam calls, and fake tech support are psychological hacks designed to manipulate your family members. But with AI-driven tools, you can fight back.

Take these actions now:
- Install Truecaller (https://www.truecaller.com/) or Hiya (https://hiya.com/) to block scam calls.
- Use Bitdefender Anti-Phishing to block fake sites.
- Train your family to recognize scam "red flags."
- Make a Family Password

With AI as your security partner, your family can spot scams before they strike. Stay alert, stay safe, and never trust the unknown.

Why Every Family Needs a Cybersecurity Action Plan
Cyberattacks don't just target large companies and governments. They target families, children, and home networks too. Hackers look for weak points like smart devices, kids' gaming accounts, and unprotected home Wi-Fi. Without a plan, your family's personal data, privacy, and even your finances are at risk.

A Family Cybersecurity Action Plan ensures that every family member knows the rules of online safety, understands how to recognize scams, and takes proactive steps to protect all household devices. This action plan isn't just for parents. Every family member — including kids and teens — has a role to play.

This section will help you create a practical and simple plan to protect your family. We'll cover:
1. Daily, weekly, and monthly cybersecurity habits.
2. How to create a Family Cybersecurity Policy that everyone in the house can follow.
3. Tools and resources to manage family security, including AI-driven parental control apps, device tracking tools, and scam-blocking software.

1. Daily, Weekly, and Monthly Cybersecurity Habits
The best way to protect your family is to build consistent habits. These small actions, when done daily, weekly, and monthly, keep hackers, scammers, and malware out of your home.

Daily Habits
- Check for Unusual Alerts: Review alerts from tools like Firewalla (https://firewalla.com/), Fing (https://www.fing.com/), and parental control apps like Bark (https://www.bark.us/).
- Teach Kids to Spot Phishing: Remind family members to double-check email senders and avoid clicking unknown links.
- Be Cautious with Downloads: Ensure that new apps, games, and downloads come from trusted app stores only (like Google Play and Apple's App Store).
- Don't Answer Unknown Calls: Use apps like Hiya (https://hiya.com/) or Truecaller (https://www.truecaller.com/) to identify potential scam calls.

Weekly Habits
- Scan Your Home Network: Use Fing or Firewalla to identify unknown devices connected to your Wi-Fi. If you see something unfamiliar, investigate and remove it.
- Review Smart Devices: Check for firmware updates on devices like smart speakers, thermostats, and baby monitors. Hackers often exploit outdated devices.
- Teach One New Skill to Kids: Each week, review an online safety skill with your children, such as how to spot phishing links or recognize scam phone calls.
- Check Device Permissions: Look at which apps on family phones and tablets have access to location, cameras, or microphones. Remove unnecessary permissions.

Monthly Habits
- Update Your Family Cybersecurity Policy: Have a family discussion about new scams or new security tools.
- Audit User Accounts: Review every account your family uses (like gaming accounts, streaming services, and social media) and change passwords if necessary.
- Review Parental Control Tools: Ensure that Bark, Qustodio (https://www.qustodio.com/), or similar parental control apps are still working properly.
- Review Passwords: Use a password manager like 1Password (https://1password.com/) or Bitwarden (https://bitwarden.com/) to review stored passwords and identify weak ones that need to be changed.
- Test Incident Response: Ask family members what they would do if they received a scam call, phishing email, or malware alert. See if they know how to react.

2. Create a Family Cybersecurity Policy

A Family Cybersecurity Policy is a list of rules that every family member follows to stay safe online. It's like having house rules for internet usage. These rules are especially helpful for children and teens who may not recognize risky behavior online.

How to Create a Family Cybersecurity Policy
- Define the Purpose: Explain to your family that this policy is designed to protect the entire family from online scams, hackers, and device takeovers.
- Set Basic Rules: Write down simple, clear rules for everyone to follow. Here are some essential rules:
  - No clicking on unknown links in texts, emails, or social media messages.
  - All new devices must be reviewed and secured before connecting to the network.
  - No downloading apps without parental approval.
  - Passwords must be unique for each account and stored in a password manager.
  - Multi-Factor Authentication (MFA) is required for all important accounts (like banking, email, and social media).
- Post the Policy: Print it out and place it somewhere visible (like on the fridge) so everyone remembers it.
- Review It Monthly: Revisit the policy once a month and update it if new threats emerge.

3. Tools and Resources for Family Cybersecurity
1. Parental Control Tools
Parental control tools help you manage screen time, block dangerous websites, and monitor activity on your children's devices.

- Qustodio (https://www.qustodio.com/): Monitors screen time, blocks specific websites, and tracks location.
- Bark (https://www.bark.us/): Uses AI to detect signs of cyberbullying, online predators, and scam activity in social media messages.
- Google Family Link (https://families.google.com/familylink/): Tracks kids' device usage, limits screen time, and prevents access to harmful content.

2. Scam-Blocking and Call-Blocking Tools
Scam blockers prevent robocalls, phishing calls, and tech support scams from reaching your phone.

- Hiya (https://hiya.com/): Blocks scam calls in real time.
- Truecaller (https://www.truecaller.com/): Uses crowdsourced reports to flag scam callers as "Scam Likely."

3. Password Management Tools
A password manager stores and protects your family's login credentials so you don't have to remember them.

- 1Password (https://1password.com/): Creates and stores long, unique passwords for every family member.
- Bitwarden (https://bitwarden.com/): Open-source password manager that's free for families.

4. Network Protection and Anomaly Detection
These tools track activity on your Wi-Fi network and alert you when unknown devices connect.

- Firewalla (https://firewalla.com/): Monitors home network activity and blocks suspicious traffic.
- Fing (https://www.fing.com/): Lets you see which devices are connected to your Wi-Fi at any time.

Chapter Conclusion: The New "Home Security System" is Digital
In the past, family safety meant locking the front door, installing alarms, and keeping your kids within view. But in today's connected world, the threats are digital. Hackers, scammers, and online predators aren't breaking into your house — they're sneaking in through your smart devices, phones, and gaming consoles.

The good news is that with the right tools, education, and planning, you can make your home one of the hardest targets for hackers to breach. By following this chapter's guidance, you will:

- Secure all smart devices (like smart speakers, baby monitors, and thermostats) so hackers can't hijack them.
- Spot and block social engineering scams (like phishing emails, vishing calls, and smishing texts) before they fool your family.
- Build a Family Cybersecurity Policy so every family member knows the rules for safe online behavior.

Your home should be a place of privacy, security, and protection. Hackers will look for easier targets. Scammers will move on to someone else. Your family will be protected, informed, and ready.

Key Takeaways from Chapter 6
1. Secure your family network with tools like Firewalla and Fing.
2. Prevent social engineering attacks with scam-blocking apps like Hiya and Truecaller.
3. Teach kids and teens how to recognize and avoid scams.
4. Set up a Family Cybersecurity Policy with rules for online behavior, device usage, and scam detection.
5. Setup a Family Password (revisited Chapter 12)

By building these habits, securing your devices, and using AI-driven tools, you'll turn your home into a digital fortress. No scammer, hacker, or botnet will stand a chance.

Take action today. Lock every digital door. Protect your family.

Chapter 7: Business Cybersecurity Essentials

Why Cybersecurity is Critical for Businesses

In the modern digital landscape, every business — regardless of its size — is a target for cybercriminals. While large corporations often make headlines when breached, small and medium-sized businesses (SMBs) are frequently the "low-hanging fruit" for hackers. Why? Because many small businesses assume "I'm too small to be a target," and as a result, they don't invest in proper cybersecurity measures. But here's the harsh reality: 43% of all cyberattacks target small businesses, and 60% of SMBs that suffer a cyberattack go out of business within six months.

The cost of a data breach is no longer measured in stolen files alone. It now includes reputation damage, lawsuits, regulatory fines, and ransom payments. Cybercriminals know that small businesses often lack dedicated IT security teams, and with AI-driven automation, they can launch large-scale attacks against thousands of businesses simultaneously. If your business relies on customer data, payment processing, or remote work, you are a target.

Cybercriminals have also adapted their tactics using AI, which allows them to automate reconnaissance, identify vulnerabilities, and launch customized attacks against businesses. AI-powered attack tools scan for weak points in company systems, like unpatched software, misconfigured cloud resources, and open API endpoints. This gives attackers a strategic edge, but it also provides defenders with powerful tools to fight back. By adopting cybersecurity frameworks and AI-enhanced detection tools, even small businesses can achieve the same level of security as Fortune 500 companies.

This chapter will provide business owners with the essential tools, strategies, and insights to secure their businesses against modern cyber threats. From adopting industry frameworks to leveraging AI-enhanced threat detection, you'll learn how to protect your company, your customers, and your brand reputation. By the end of this chapter, you'll be able to:

- Adopt a cybersecurity framework that aligns with your business size, industry, and risk level.
- Deploy AI-enhanced security tools that automate the detection and blocking of modern threats like ransomware, phishing, and malware.

- Identify and secure common attack vectors like insider threats, phishing emails, and ransomware.
- Lock down your cloud environment and protect against cloud misconfigurations, API vulnerabilities, and malware-infected applications.

With the right tools and knowledge, your business can become an impenetrable fortress in a world of cyber threats. Attackers might have AI on their side, but so do you. This chapter will show you how to use it.

Implement a Cybersecurity Framework
A cybersecurity framework is a structured, step-by-step system designed to help businesses identify threats, protect critical assets, detect intrusions, respond to incidents, and recover from attacks. These frameworks are not just technical guides — they are complete risk management blueprints that align with industry best practices.

Without a framework, businesses operate in a state of reaction. They only respond after an attack occurs, often suffering unnecessary losses. With a framework, businesses move from reactive to proactive, ensuring they can detect, respond to, and recover from threats before they cause damage. This structured approach provides clarity for business owners, IT teams, and leadership on how to manage cybersecurity risks.

Some of the most widely used cybersecurity frameworks include:
- NIST Cybersecurity Framework (CSF) — Used by thousands of businesses worldwide and required for many government contractors.
- CIS Controls — Provides 20 essential controls to protect businesses from attacks.
- ISO 27001 — A globally recognized standard that helps organizations establish a formal information security program.
- Industry-Specific Compliance — Sectors like healthcare (HIPAA) and finance (PCI-DSS) have their own frameworks to meet legal and regulatory standards.

The right framework depends on your business size, industry, and data sensitivity. For example:
- Healthcare companies follow HIPAA regulations, which demand the protection of patient health information (PHI).
- Financial services follow PCI-DSS to secure credit card information and prevent data breaches.
- Small businesses often use NIST CSF or CIS Controls to manage risks without the complexity of full ISO certification.

This section will show you how to choose, implement, and maintain a cybersecurity framework tailored to your business.

Why It Matters
If you don't have a cybersecurity framework, you don't have a plan. When an attack happens — like ransomware locking up your files or a data breach exposing customer data — you'll be stuck figuring out your response in real-time. This "panic mode" approach leads to mistakes, higher recovery costs, and long-term reputational damage.

On the flip side, having a framework in place means you already have a plan. Your team knows:
- What steps to take when a breach happens (because you've already run practice drills).
- Who is responsible for critical decisions (like shutting down systems or notifying customers).
- How quickly systems can be restored (because you've tested and timed your disaster recovery process).

With a framework, you aren't just reacting to cyberattacks — you're preparing for them. Your employees, vendors, and executive team all have a clear, shared plan on how to manage an attack from start to finish.

Step 1: Choose Your Framework
The first step is to choose a framework that fits your business needs. Here's an overview of the most widely used frameworks:

NIST Cybersecurity Framework (CSF)
- Who Uses It? Small businesses, government contractors, and IT service providers.
- Why Use It? It's one of the easiest to understand and implement. The framework outlines five key functions:
    - Identify — What are your critical assets (files, devices, software) that must be protected?
    - Protect — What security measures will you use (like firewalls, MFA, and encryption) to protect them?
    - Detect — How will you detect a cyberattack (like EDR or anomaly detection)?
    - Respond — How will you respond once an attack occurs (like shutting down devices or activating SOAR playbooks)?
    - Recover — How will you recover lost data and restore operations?

CIS Critical Security Controls
- Who Uses It? Small and medium-sized businesses (SMBs) looking for an entry-level framework.
- Why Use It? It's simple, with only 20 key controls (like securing accounts, updating software, and implementing access control).
- How It Helps: CIS offers a "checklist" approach, perfect for smaller businesses that don't have time for the complexity of ISO or NIST.

ISO 27001 (International Standard for Information Security)
- Who Uses It? Large enterprises, financial services, and global organizations with regulatory requirements.
- Why Use It? It's a globally recognized security standard that demonstrates compliance to customers and regulators.
- How It Helps: ISO certification shows customers and partners that you take cybersecurity seriously. It's essential for companies dealing with GDPR and privacy regulations.

Step 2: Implement the Framework
Once you've chosen a framework, it's time to implement it. This process can seem overwhelming, but it becomes manageable when broken into smaller tasks. Here's how to do it step-by-step:

Identify Critical Assets
- What are the most valuable systems, data, and devices in your business?
- This includes customer data, payment information, intellectual property, and essential software.

Secure Devices and Accounts
- Set up multi-factor authentication (MFA) on all admin accounts.
- Enforce role-based access control (RBAC) so employees only access systems they need.
- Ensure all devices (laptops, phones, tablets) have EDR (Endpoint Detection & Response) protection.

Adopt a Risk Assessment Process
- Identify potential risks (like ransomware, insider threats, and supply chain vulnerabilities).
- Run a Business Impact Analysis (BIA) to see what would happen if your systems were shut down for 48 hours.

Set Up an Incident Response Plan
- Create a step-by-step plan for responding to an attack (like ransomware or data breaches).
- Assign roles and responsibilities so everyone knows what to do.
- Run tabletop exercises — practice your response before an actual attack happens.

Use AI-Powered Detection and Response Tools
- Use tools like CrowdStrike, SentinelOne, and Darktrace to detect and block attacks in real time.
- Implement XDR (Extended Detection & Response) for email, cloud, and network threat detection.

Run Cybersecurity Drills and Tests
- Simulate a ransomware attack or phishing attack and see how employees respond.
- Test your ability to restore from a backup after a ransomware attack.

Step 3: Maintain and Continuously Improve
Cybersecurity isn't a "set it and forget it" task. Attackers evolve, and your defenses must evolve too.

Here's how to keep your framework effective:
- Audit Every 6-12 Months: Review your access controls, MFA, and system updates regularly.
- Stay Updated: Follow threat intelligence feeds (like Recorded Future) to learn about new threats.
- Rehearse Incident Response Plans: Hold "fire drills" for cyber incidents to make sure your team knows how to react.

Real-World Example
Target Breach (2013): The Target breach was one of the largest and most publicized breaches in the world. The attacker exploited a third-party HVAC vendor that had access to Target's internal systems. Because there was no formal security framework in place to monitor third-party access, the attacker used this entry point to steal the credit card details of over 40 million customers.

Lesson Learned: If Target had used a cybersecurity framework like NIST CSF, they would have known to:
- Identify third-party risk (the HVAC vendor).
- Protect sensitive systems (credit card databases) with segmented access.
- Detect unusual behavior (like a third-party vendor downloading 40 million records).

Key Takeaways
- Cybersecurity frameworks are essential for any business that wants to avoid "panic mode" when a breach happens.
- NIST CSF, CIS Controls, and ISO 27001 are the most widely used frameworks.
- Implementation requires focus on asset management, threat detection, and incident response planning.
- The only way to test your framework is to run drills and attack simulations to ensure employees know how to respond.

Call to Action
Don't wait until a ransomware attack happens to figure out your next step. Choose a framework, implement it, and run your first cybersecurity fire drill this week. Start small with the CIS Controls or go deeper with NIST CSF. The difference between reacting to an attack and having a plan in place could be the difference between survival and shutdown.

Use AI-Enhanced Security Tools to Automatically Detect and Block Threats

What It Is:
AI-enhanced security tools have revolutionized modern cybersecurity. Unlike traditional tools that rely on static rules and human intervention, AI-driven tools operate in real-time, learning from every threat they encounter. These tools don't wait for an attack to occur — they predict, detect, and block threats automatically.

In the past, businesses had to hire teams of security analysts to monitor activity, investigate threats, and respond manually. But with AI-enhanced security tools, businesses can now automate threat detection and incident response. From detecting zero-day malware to stopping phishing emails before they reach employees, AI-driven tools give small businesses the same level of protection as Fortune 500 companies.

Why It Matters
Hackers are using AI to supercharge their attacks, so businesses must use AI to defend against them. Attackers no longer target companies one at a time. Instead, they use AI-powered "attack bots" to scan thousands of businesses simultaneously, looking for weaknesses. If your business isn't protected by AI-enhanced detection tools, you won't even know you've been attacked until it's too late.

Without AI Tools:
- Attacks like ransomware, phishing, and malware may go unnoticed until damage is done.
- Businesses must rely on human security analysts to identify, investigate, and respond to every threat.
- Threats like fileless malware and polymorphic malware evade detection because they don't match known attack signatures.

With AI Tools:
- AI-powered systems detect threats instantly and respond without waiting for human intervention.
- Behavioral AI tracks patterns in user activity and identifies anomalies (like logins from suspicious locations).
- Threat intelligence from thousands of companies is pooled together, making AI smarter after every attack it encounters.

AI-driven tools are essential for small businesses that don't have large security teams. These tools level the playing field, giving small businesses access to the same capabilities used by large corporations.

Types of AI-Enhanced Security Tools

Endpoint Detection and Response (EDR)
EDR tools detect, investigate, and respond to threats on endpoints like laptops, desktops, and mobile devices. Instead of relying on antivirus signatures, EDR tools monitor behavioral changes on devices. If an employee suddenly downloads thousands of files or runs an unknown script, EDR will flag it as suspicious.

How EDR Works:
- Behavioral Analysis: EDR tools analyze how users and devices normally behave. If something "weird" happens (like running unknown scripts), it triggers an alert.
- Threat Containment: If ransomware is detected, EDR tools isolate the infected device to stop it from spreading.
- Automated Investigations: EDR tools like CrowdStrike and SentinelOne analyze how an attack started, identify "patient zero," and track how far the infection spread.

How to Get Started:
- Install CrowdStrike, SentinelOne, or Microsoft Defender for Endpoint on all laptops, desktops, and employee devices.
- Create rules to block untrusted scripts and limit employee permissions to reduce the attack surface.

Extended Detection and Response (XDR)
XDR extends beyond EDR to detect threats across email, cloud apps, endpoints, and networks. Instead of focusing on a single endpoint, XDR covers all entry points that attackers use to breach a system.

How XDR Works:
- Cross-Platform Threat Detection: XDR tracks anomalies across multiple platforms, from email accounts to cloud systems like Google Drive.
- Multi-Source Data Correlation: It correlates alerts from emails, devices, & user behavior to determine if an attack is in progress.
- Real-Time Response: If a phishing email is detected, XDR systems block all future attempts from the same source.

XDR is a must-have for businesses that have remote employees, cloud-based apps, and multiple third-party integrations.

How to Get Started:
- Use tools like Microsoft Defender for Identity, CrowdStrike XDR, or SentinelOne XDR to monitor email, cloud, and endpoint activity.
- Set up anomaly detection for unusual login times, large file transfers, and foreign IP logins.

Security Orchestration, Automation, and Response (SOAR)
SOAR tools allow businesses to automate their incident response. Instead of waiting for a human to respond, SOAR platforms trigger playbooks — a series of pre-programmed actions that activate when a threat is detected.

How SOAR Works:
- Automated Playbooks: When a ransomware attack is detected, SOAR tools automatically isolate the affected systems, alert key personnel, and begin disaster recovery protocols.
- Threat Escalation: SOAR can escalate incidents to senior management, legal teams, and law enforcement if a breach occurs.
- Automation: Common responses like disabling user accounts, isolating infected endpoints, or blocking IP addresses happen in seconds, not hours.

How to Get Started:
- Set up Cortex XSOAR or IBM Resilient to automate incident response.
- Create a ransomware playbook that automatically isolates infected systems and launches recovery protocols.

Threat Intelligence Platforms (TIPs)
TIPs collect data on threats from across the internet, including hacker forums, the dark web, and live threat feeds. This information allows you to identify potential attacks before they reach your business.

How Threat Intelligence Platforms Work:
- Data Aggregation: Threat intelligence platforms pull in real-time data on new malware, phishing domains, and hacking campaigns.
- Threat Scoring: Every new threat is scored for risk, so you can prioritize which threats deserve immediate attention.
- Proactive Blocking: If the platform identifies a malicious domain, it can automatically block it across all your apps, networks, and endpoints.

How to Get Started:
- Use platforms like Recorded Future, ThreatConnect, or Anomali to gather intelligence from global threat feeds.
- Set up alerts for threats targeting your industry (like ransomware gangs targeting healthcare or finance).

How AI Enhances Security Tools

AI-Powered Anomaly Detection
AI learns what "normal" user behavior looks like and flags any activity that doesn't fit that pattern. For example:
- If an employee logs in from a foreign IP at 2:00 AM, it gets flagged as suspicious.
- If an employee downloads 50,000 files in an hour, it triggers an alert.

AI-Powered Threat Hunting
Traditional threat hunting is manual, but AI threat hunters scan for suspicious patterns in real time. If AI spots malware that behaves like Emotet, it marks it as a "potential Emotet clone" and takes action.

AI-Driven Response Automation
With AI, incident response happens in seconds. Instead of calling a security analyst, SOAR systems isolate ransomware and quarantine infected devices automatically.

Real-World Example
Colonial Pipeline Ransomware Attack (2021): When ransomware hit the Colonial Pipeline, it disrupted fuel delivery for millions of people. The attack shut down critical infrastructure for over a week. One of the key failures was the lack of automated incident response. Colonial's response relied on manual decisions, which caused delays.

Lesson Learned: If Colonial Pipeline had used a SOAR platform, they could have instantly:
- Quarantined infected devices.
- Automatically launched a disaster recovery plan.
- Isolated network segments to prevent ransomware from spreading.

Key Takeaways
- AI-enhanced tools like EDR, XDR, and SOAR allow businesses to detect threats in real time and respond instantly.
- Use EDR to detect ransomware, use XDR to track cloud logins, and use SOAR to automate your incident response.
- Threat intelligence platforms provide an early warning system, letting you know about hacker campaigns before they affect you.
- With AI-driven detection tools, your business can respond to attacks in seconds instead of hours.

Call to Action
If your business still relies on human analysts for threat detection, it's time to make a change. Install an AI-enhanced EDR, XDR, or SOAR tool this week. Set up anomaly detection to flag unusual logins, file transfers, and large downloads. Create playbooks for ransomware and phishing. With these tools in place, you'll have a 24/7 automated security system that protects your business from threats before they cause damage.

Protect Your Business from the Most Common Attack Vectors

What It Is:
Cybercriminals don't reinvent the wheel every time they attack a business. Instead, they rely on proven, repeatable attack methods. By targeting well-known vulnerabilities and human behavior, they can exploit businesses of any size.

An attack vector is the entry point that attackers use to gain access to a system. It could be a phishing email, a ransomware download link, or an unsecured smart device. Understanding these vectors helps you block entry points before an attack happens.

The good news is that by focusing on the most common attack vectors, you can eliminate the vast majority of attack opportunities. Most successful attacks come from a small number of well-known tactics. This section will teach you how to recognize and protect your business from the most exploited attack vectors.

Why It Matters
Attackers aren't looking for "hard targets." They want easy wins. In fact, most successful breaches happen because of simple mistakes like:
- Employees clicking phishing emails.
- Misconfigured cloud storage.
- Weak passwords on admin accounts.

Cybercriminals know which attack vectors are most effective, and they use them on repeat. If you can eliminate these attack vectors, you can prevent most breaches. For example, simply enabling multi-factor authentication (MFA) can prevent 99% of credential-based attacks.

Knowing these attack vectors also helps you prioritize where to focus your defenses. If 90% of attacks happen via phishing, then training employees on phishing defense has a higher ROI than spending thousands on other security tools.

This section will cover the four most common attack vectors and how you can defend against them.

Common Attack Vectors and How to Defend Against Them

1. Phishing Attacks
What It Is:
Phishing is when an attacker pretends to be a trusted source (like Amazon, PayPal, or your boss) to trick employees into clicking a link or sharing sensitive information. Email is the #1 phishing channel, but attackers also use SMS (smishing) and phone calls (vishing).

How It Works:
- The attacker sends an email that looks legitimate.
- The victim clicks on a link or opens an attachment.
- The link downloads malware, or the attachment installs ransomware.
- Attackers may also ask for sensitive information (like login credentials) via a fake login page.

Example:
The 2016 John Podesta Phishing Attack targeted a key figure in the U.S. election. Podesta clicked a link in a fake Google login email, allowing attackers to steal his email credentials. This simple mistake changed the course of the 2016 presidential election.

How to Defend:
- Use AI-powered email security tools like Mimecast or Proofpoint to block phishing emails.
- Train employees to recognize phishing emails by looking for odd URLs, spelling errors, or urgency.
- Use multi-factor authentication (MFA) so stolen credentials alone can't be used.
- Encourage employees to verify suspicious requests directly with the sender.

2. Ransomware Attacks
What It Is:
Ransomware is one of the most devastating attack vectors. Attackers encrypt all your files and demand a ransom payment to unlock them. If you don't pay, you lose access to your files forever. Ransomware attacks are highly profitable for cybercriminals, which is why ransomware-as-a-service (RaaS) has exploded.

How It Works:
- Attackers use phishing emails, malicious websites, or infected USB drives to deliver the ransomware.
- Once ransomware installs, it encrypts files on your local devices and network drives.
- Attackers demand payment (usually in cryptocurrency) to decrypt the files.

Example:
The WannaCry Ransomware Attack (2017) affected over 200,000 computers in 150 countries. WannaCry exploited a Windows vulnerability (EternalBlue) that had not been patched by thousands of businesses. The attack caused hospitals, banks, and businesses to lose access to critical files, leading to massive financial losses.

How to Defend:
- Use Endpoint Detection and Response (EDR) tools like CrowdStrike to detect ransomware early.
- Keep all devices updated with the latest security patches.
- Use immutable backups (backups that cannot be changed or deleted) to ensure you can recover files.
- Practice "least privilege" access so employees can't accidentally trigger ransomware on shared drives.

3. Insider Threats
What It Is:
Insider threats come from employees, contractors, or partners who have legitimate access to your systems. Insiders can accidentally or intentionally leak data, steal intellectual property, or plant malware.

How It Works:
- Insiders may copy sensitive files to a USB drive before quitting a job.
- Disgruntled employees may delete important files on their last day.
- A careless employee may fall for a phishing attack, giving an attacker access to company systems.

Example:
The Tesla Insider Threat (2020) occurred when a disgruntled Tesla employee was caught sabotaging the internal network and sharing Tesla trade secrets with competitors. The attack was stopped when another employee reported suspicious activity.

How to Defend:
- Use User and Entity Behavior Analytics (UEBA) tools to detect unusual employee behavior.
- Limit data access to only the files employees need for their roles (role-based access control, RBAC).
- Set up data loss prevention (DLP) tools to block unauthorized file transfers to USBs or cloud apps.
- Monitor employee actions when they resign, as this is a high-risk period for insider attacks.

4. Cloud Misconfigurations
What It Is:
Many businesses rely on cloud platforms like AWS, Azure, and Google Cloud. But if those platforms are misconfigured (like having an S3 bucket open to the public), attackers can steal files without even hacking in. Cloud platforms are highly secure when configured properly, but many businesses make mistakes when setting them up.

How It Works:
- Attackers use tools like Shodan to scan the web for misconfigured AWS S3 buckets.
- If the bucket is public, they download files directly.
- Attackers also scan for exposed APIs and leaked access keys to access cloud platforms.

Example:
In 2017, the U.S. Department of Defense accidentally exposed classified data due to an unprotected S3 bucket. Over 100 GB of sensitive military files were accessible to anyone with a browser.

How to Defend:
- Use Cloud Security Posture Management (CSPM) tools like Prisma Cloud or AWS Config to scan for misconfigurations.
- Enable IAM role-based access control so employees only access the files they need.
- Use multi-factor authentication (MFA) for all admin accounts on AWS, Azure, and Google Cloud.

How to Protect Your Business from All Attack Vectors
While the four attack vectors above are the most common, they aren't the only ones. Attackers are constantly evolving their techniques, and businesses must stay ahead of the curve.

Here are 4 essential tactics that protect against ALL attack vectors:
- Endpoint Detection and Response (EDR) — Stops ransomware, malware, and insider threats.
- AI Email Filters — Blocks phishing emails from reaching employee inboxes.
- Cloud Security Posture Management (CSPM) — Detects cloud misconfigurations and enforces proper security policies.
- User Training and Awareness — Teach employees to recognize phishing, insider threats, and social engineering tactics.

Key Takeaways
- The four most common attack vectors are phishing, ransomware, insider threats, and cloud misconfigurations.
- Each vector requires a unique defense strategy, but AI-driven tools like EDR, CSPM, and anomaly detection protect against all four.
- Businesses that close these attack vectors can prevent the vast majority of cyberattacks.
- Attackers don't use one attack vector at a time — often, they combine them. For example, a phishing email might deliver ransomware, or an insider might be tricked into accessing a malware-laced link.

Call to Action
If you focus on closing these four attack vectors, you'll protect your business against the majority of cyberattacks. Install EDR, use CSPM, and train your employees to spot phishing emails.
Attackers might have new tactics, but they always rely on the same entry points. Close those entry points, and you'll stay ahead.

Cloud Security Threats
What It Is:
Cloud services have become essential for modern businesses, allowing them to store data, run applications, and collaborate online. However, with this convenience comes a new set of cybersecurity threats. Unlike on-premises systems, cloud environments are shared, remote, and accessible from anywhere, which creates more potential entry points for attackers.

Cloud security threats arise from misconfigurations, human errors, API vulnerabilities, and insider threats. The attack surface of cloud services grows as businesses add more tools, apps, and integrations. Hackers target these platforms because one small misconfiguration can give them access to everything. Attackers have exploited these vulnerabilities to steal sensitive data, hold companies hostage, and disrupt essential services.

Why It Matters:
A single misconfigured cloud storage bucket, like an exposed AWS S3 bucket, can allow attackers to download sensitive customer data without ever hacking a password. Attackers have used this tactic to breach companies like Capital One, exposing millions of customer records.

With more businesses shifting to the cloud, cybercriminals have also shifted their attention. Hackers now search for misconfigured cloud resources, vulnerable APIs, and over-privileged admin accounts to exploit. To defend against these threats, businesses must lock down their cloud environments, use automated monitoring tools, and continuously review permissions and access controls.

Types of Cloud Security Threats

1. Misconfigured Cloud Resources
What It Is:
A misconfiguration happens when a company sets up a cloud resource (like an AWS S3 bucket, Google Cloud storage, or Azure database) and leaves it publicly accessible by mistake. Instead of requiring a login, these resources are available to anyone on the internet. Attackers actively search for these "accidental backdoors" using tools like Shodan.

How It Works:
- Businesses create a cloud storage bucket to hold files.
- If the bucket's permissions are set to "Public," attackers can access it.
- Attackers download sensitive files (like customer data) and may even threaten to leak it unless a ransom is paid.

Example:
In 2017, the U.S. Department of Defense accidentally left 100GB of classified data exposed in an unsecured S3 bucket. The files were accessible to anyone with a web browser. It wasn't a hack — it was a misconfiguration.

How to Defend:
- Use Cloud Security Posture Management (CSPM) tools like Prisma Cloud or AWS Config to scan for misconfigured S3 buckets and storage files.
- Enforce least privilege — Cloud users and services should only have access to files they need.
- Turn on logging and alerting to get notified if anyone accesses sensitive storage.

2. Exposed and Vulnerable APIs
What It Is:
APIs (Application Programming Interfaces) allow cloud apps to communicate with each other. But when APIs are poorly secured, hackers can use them to bypass security controls. API vulnerabilities are one of the most overlooked cloud security threats.

How It Works:
- Developers create an API to connect services like payment systems or CRM tools.
- If the API does not require strong authentication, attackers can send requests directly to the API to extract data.
- Hackers may also "manipulate API requests" to force the system to give them access to sensitive data.

Example:
The Facebook API Data Breach (2019) exposed the private data of 540 million users. The breach occurred because the third-party app developers failed to properly secure their APIs, allowing hackers to extract private user information.

How to Defend:
- Require API authentication — Use OAuth 2.0 or token-based access to restrict API calls.
- Use rate limiting to limit the number of API requests that can be made per minute, reducing brute-force attacks.
- Conduct regular API security testing and use tools like Burp Suite or OWASP ZAP to detect vulnerable endpoints.

3. Cloud Account Hijacking

What It Is:
When attackers steal login credentials for cloud platforms (like AWS, Google Cloud, or Microsoft Azure), they gain control over the entire environment. Once inside, they can launch attacks, steal data, or create new administrator accounts.

How It Works:
- Attackers steal admin login credentials using phishing, brute force, or malware.
- They log into your cloud account and create a new "hidden" admin account.
- Attackers use this access to delete data, deploy malware, or steal sensitive files.

Example:
A well-known case of cloud hijacking happened when a cryptojacking malware attack used stolen AWS credentials to mine cryptocurrency using the victim's cloud resources. Attackers racked up thousands of dollars in AWS bills.

How to Defend:
- Use multi-factor authentication (MFA) for all cloud admin accounts.
- Set up risk-based login alerts so you get notified if someone logs in from a suspicious location.
- Limit the number of users with admin permissions and rotate admin credentials frequently.

4. Cloud Malware Injection

What It Is:
Attackers upload malware to cloud storage or cloud-hosted applications. If the malware goes undetected, it spreads to every user who downloads or interacts with the infected files.

How It Works:
- Attackers upload malware-infected files to cloud storage (like Google Drive or SharePoint).
- Employees download the file, and malware spreads through the company's network.
- Malware may steal sensitive data, launch ransomware, or create backdoors for later access.

Example:
The OneDrive Malware Campaign (2022) involved hackers uploading malware-laced files to OneDrive and sending fake "file sharing" links to employees. Clicking on the link downloaded malware, infecting users' devices.

How to Defend:
- Use AI-powered malware scanners on all files before uploading them to cloud storage.
- Implement read-only permissions for sensitive cloud storage locations.
- Use file integrity monitoring to detect when files are modified, deleted, or altered.

How to Secure Your Cloud Environment
Securing your cloud environment may sound complicated, but with Cloud Security Posture Management (CSPM) tools and AI-driven anomaly detection, businesses can eliminate most cloud risks.

Here's how to lock down your cloud systems:
- Enforce MFA — Multi-factor authentication prevents attackers from logging into admin accounts.
- Use Role-Based Access Control (RBAC) — Restrict access based on employee roles.
- Use CSPM Tools — Tools like Prisma Cloud and AWS Config scan for misconfigured cloud resources.
- Monitor Anomalies — Use AI-driven anomaly detection to identify unusual logins, API usage, or file access.
- Enable Logging — Set up logging for all cloud activity, so you know exactly who accessed which files.

Real-World Example
Capital One Breach (2019): A former AWS employee exploited a misconfigured AWS S3 bucket to steal the personal data of 106 million Capital One customers. The attacker extracted names, Social Security numbers, and bank details.

Lesson Learned:
- If Capital One had used a Cloud Security Posture Management (CSPM) tool, the misconfigured bucket would have been detected.
- If the company had used least privilege access, the attacker would not have been able to access customer records.

Key Takeaways
- Cloud threats include misconfigured storage, API vulnerabilities, hijacked accounts, and malware-infected files.
- Misconfigured cloud storage is the #1 threat, as attackers can access files without logging in.
- Businesses should use Cloud Security Posture Management (CSPM) tools to scan for misconfigurations.
- AI-driven anomaly detection helps identify suspicious logins, file transfers, and API calls.
- If you fail to secure your cloud systems, attackers can steal sensitive data, inject malware, or hijack your cloud infrastructure.

Call to Action
Don't wait for a cloud data breach to expose your company. Install a CSPM tool this week to find misconfigured S3 buckets, exposed APIs, and risky admin accounts. Turn on MFA for cloud accounts, and use AI-driven anomaly detection to detect unusual logins, file changes, and large downloads. Attackers target cloud platforms because of their complexity, but with CSPM, anomaly detection, and role-based access controls, your cloud will be as secure as any Fortune 500 company.

Conclusion: Business Cybersecurity Essentials

Cybersecurity is no longer an optional consideration for businesses — it's an absolute necessity. With the rise of AI-driven attack tools, even small and medium-sized businesses (SMBs) are prime targets. Attackers use automated scanning tools to look for weak points, such as misconfigured cloud services, exposed APIs, or employees who fall for phishing emails. Without a strong cybersecurity strategy, a single mistake can lead to ransomware infections, data breaches, or financial loss. The good news is that businesses can fight AI with AI. AI-enhanced security tools like EDR, XDR, and CSPM provide round-the-clock protection, automatically detecting threats, isolating malware, and blocking phishing attempts before they reach employees. By using AI to automate defenses, even small businesses can protect themselves like Fortune 500 companies.

To succeed, businesses must go beyond reactive security and embrace a proactive, multi-layered approach. This starts with implementing a cybersecurity framework like NIST, ISO 27001, or CIS Controls. Frameworks provide clear guidelines for risk management, threat detection, and incident response. Businesses must also leverage AI-enhanced security tools to block ransomware, malware, and insider threats. Tools like XDR for email and cloud protection, EDR for endpoint defense, and SOAR for incident automation allow companies to detect and respond to attacks in seconds instead of hours. But technology alone is not enough. Training employees to recognize threats like phishing emails and insider risks remains one of the most effective forms of protection.

By closing attack vectors, managing cloud security risks, and using AI-driven detection tools, businesses can achieve a level of protection once reserved for enterprise giants. Every step toward Zero-Trust security, role-based access, and anomaly detection strengthens the business's defenses. The cost of doing nothing is far higher than the investment in prevention. With AI as a defensive ally, small businesses can become hard targets for cybercriminals, forcing attackers to move on to easier prey. Your business doesn't have to be the weakest link in the chain. Adopt a proactive, AI-driven approach to security, and you'll be ready for whatever comes next.

What to Do Next
1. Install **EDR** and **XDR** Tools: Use CrowdStrike or SentinelOne to block ransomware.
2. Use Threat Intelligence Platforms: Use Recorded Future to track third-party risk.
3. Build a Cybersecurity Incident Response Plan: Your team should know exactly what to do if ransomware, phishing, or supply chain attacks happen.
4. Set Up Zero-Trust Security: Make sure only essential employees have access to critical files.

Call-to-Action: Take Control of Your Business Cybersecurity
Hackers don't sleep. They launch attacks 24/7 using AI to automate ransomware, phishing, and supply chain breaches. But you don't have to be a victim. By following this chapter's guidance, you'll create a security fortress that attackers will struggle to penetrate.

"Hackers only need to succeed once — but with AI on your side, you can succeed every time."

Use this chapter to build a cybersecurity framework, deploy AI-enhanced tools, and protect your business from the most common attack vectors. Attackers will always evolve, but with AI-driven predictive defense, you'll be ready for them.

Your business, your data, and your future depend on what you do right now. Take action, install the tools, and train your employees. This is how you win the war on cybercrime.

Chapter 8: Cyber Hygiene — Daily Habits for Staying Safe Online

Why Cyber Hygiene Matters More Than Ever
Imagine leaving your front door unlocked every day. It's only a matter of time before someone walks in. The same logic applies to cyber hygiene. If you don't maintain strong passwords, update your software, and protect your devices, you're inviting attackers into your digital home.

But there's good news: Cyber hygiene isn't difficult. In fact, most cyberattacks can be prevented by following a few essential daily habits. This concept is known as the "80/20 Rule" — 80% of cyber threats can be blocked with just 20% of the effort. By focusing on the most important habits, you'll prevent ransomware, phishing, and malware attacks before they start.

And with AI-powered tools, you don't have to do everything manually. Many tasks — like updating devices, managing passwords, and detecting unusual activity — can be automated.

This chapter will teach you how to maintain strong cyber hygiene using both manual habits and AI-driven automation.

What You Will Learn in This Chapter
By the end of this chapter, you will:
1. Understand the 80/20 Rule of Cyber Hygiene and how a few simple habits can prevent most attacks.
2. Learn the most important daily, weekly, and monthly habits to maintain good cyber hygiene.
3. Discover how AI-powered tools can automate repetitive tasks like password updates, network scans, and software updates.

The 80/20 Rule of Cyber Hygiene
What is the 80/20 Rule?
The 80/20 rule (also called the Pareto Principle) states that 80% of consequences come from 20% of causes. In cybersecurity, this means that most of your protection (80%) comes from just a few essential habits (20%).

The Core Concept:
If you focus on just a few critical actions (like updating software, using MFA, and managing passwords), you'll block the majority of attacks before they even start.

The 20% of Habits That Block 80% of Threats

Here are the most critical habits that have the biggest impact on security.

1. Use Multi-Factor Authentication (MFA)
Impact: Blocks 99.9% of account breaches.
Why It Works: Even if hackers steal your password, they can't log in without the second factor (like a code sent to your phone).

2. Update Software and Firmware
Impact: Stops zero-day exploits and unpatched vulnerabilities.
Why It Works: Attackers exploit old vulnerabilities in software like Windows, Chrome, and Zoom. Updates patch those flaws.

3. Use a Password Manager
Impact: Protects against password reuse and weak passwords.
Why It Works: Password managers create long, random passwords that attackers can't guess. Tools like 1Password (https://1password.com/) or Bitwarden (https://bitwarden.com/) store these passwords securely.

4. Limit Administrative Privileges
Impact: Prevents malware from installing system-wide.
Why It Works: If malware doesn't have "admin rights," it can't make system changes. Limit admin rights for employees and yourself.

5. Enable Firewalls and Use EDR
Impact: Blocks ransomware, malware, and hacker access.
Why It Works: Firewalls and EDR (Endpoint Detection and Response) monitor devices for threats and block unusual activity. Use Firewalla (https://firewalla.com/) or CrowdStrike Falcon (https://www.crowdstrike.com/) to protect devices.

How AI Helps You Achieve the 80/20 Rule
AI can help you automate these core habits so you don't have to manage them manually. Here's how:
- MFA Automation: AI can ensure MFA is enabled on all employee accounts.
- Automatic Updates: AI tools like Patch My PC automate software and firmware updates.
- Password Management: AI-powered password managers like 1Password detect weak passwords and suggest strong replacements.
- EDR Automation: AI-driven tools like CrowdStrike detect malware and quarantine it automatically.

Daily, Weekly, and Monthly Cyber Hygiene Habits
Daily Cyber Hygiene Habits
These are small daily tasks that take less than 5 minutes but prevent big problems.

1. Check for Unusual Notifications
   - Review alerts from tools like Firewalla and CrowdStrike for unusual device behavior.
   - If you see a new device connected to your Wi-Fi, investigate immediately.

2. Avoid Phishing Scams
   - Hover over links in emails before clicking.
   - Use email security tools like Microsoft Defender for Office 365 to block phishing links.

3. Don't Download Sketchy Files or Apps
   - Only download software from trusted sources like app stores or vendor websites.
   - Use AI-driven browser extensions like Bitdefender Anti-Phishing to block suspicious downloads.

4. Monitor Devices with AI Tools
   - Use Firewalla to track device activity.
   - Use Qustodio (https://www.qustodio.com/) for parental control on children's devices.

Weekly Cyber Hygiene Habits
Weekly habits are designed to catch vulnerabilities before attackers exploit them.

1. Review Device Permissions
   - Check apps and remove unnecessary permissions (like access to microphones or cameras).

2. Scan Your Wi-Fi Network
   - Use Fing (https://www.fing.com/) to scan your network for unknown devices.
   - Look for any new devices that shouldn't be there.

3. Check for Software Updates
   - Install updates for browsers, operating systems, and IoT devices.
   - Use a tool like Patch My PC to automate software updates.

Monthly Cyber Hygiene Habits
These larger tasks take a bit more time but reduce risk significantly.

1. Change Passwords for Key Accounts
   - Change passwords for admin accounts, email, and cloud services.
   - Use 1Password or Bitwarden to update passwords automatically.

2. Review Your Backup Strategy
   - Ensure your data is being backed up to the cloud.
   - Use backup tools like Acronis (https://www.acronis.com/) to test and verify your backups.

3. Review User Access
   - Remove access for ex-employees and contractors.
   - Limit admin privileges for employees.

How AI Tools Can Automate and Enforce Cyber Hygiene
How AI Tools Automate Cyber Hygiene
Manual tasks like checking updates, managing passwords, and scanning for threats are tedious. AI tools take over these tasks and run them automatically. Here's how.

1. Password Hygiene Automation
   - Tool: 1Password or Bitwarden
   - What it does: Identifies weak passwords and suggests new ones.

2. Patch Management Automation
   - Tool: Patch My PC
   - What it does: Automatically updates software on devices.

3. Threat Detection and Anomaly Monitoring
   - Tool: Firewalla, CrowdStrike, SentinelOne
   - What it does: Scans for unusual activity and quarantines malware automatically.

4. Device Tracking and Alerts
   - Tool: Fing, Qustodio, Bark
   - What it does: Alerts you if a new device connects to your Wi-Fi.

Chapter Conclusion: Habits That Protect Your Digital Life
Summary of Key Takeaways
- Follow the 80/20 Rule: Focus on 5 essential habits to block 80% of attacks.
- Adopt Daily, Weekly, and Monthly Cyber Hygiene Habits: Do small tasks daily, check Wi-Fi devices weekly, and review access monthly.
- Use AI Tools to Automate Tasks: Tools like Firewalla, 1Password, Patch My PC, and CrowdStrike automate everything from updates to password changes.

What to Do Next
1. Adopt 5 Essential Habits: Start using MFA, EDR, Firewalls, and Password Managers.
2. Use AI to Automate Repetitive Tasks: Set up Firewalla, 1Password, and Patch My PC.
3. Track Progress: Print a checklist of daily, weekly, and monthly habits.

"Good cyber hygiene is like brushing your teeth — small, daily actions prevent big, expensive problems."

By following the guidance in this chapter, you'll turn your devices, apps, and accounts into a digital fortress. No hacker, phisher, or botnet will stand a chance. Let me know if you'd like any changes or additions!

Chapter 9: Social Media Security

Privacy Settings & Platform-Specific Protection

Why Privacy Matters on Social Media
Imagine if every conversation you had, every vacation you took, and every thought you shared was broadcasted to the entire world. This is what happens when you don't control your social media privacy settings.

Social media is designed to make sharing easy, but it's also designed to collect and monetize your data. Everything you "like," post, or comment on is recorded, analyzed, and sometimes shared with advertisers, government agencies, or hackers. The result? Your private life is exposed to billions of strangers.

Here's the danger:
- Oversharing can lead to phishing scams, identity theft, and even physical danger (like home break-ins).
- Data tracking allows companies like Facebook, TikTok, and Instagram to create a digital profile of you — and advertisers pay for access.
- Third-party apps (like games, quizzes, or sign-in-with-Facebook apps) may access your personal information.

This section will show you how to take back control of your privacy. We'll walk you through the privacy settings of Facebook, Instagram, and TikTok, as well as give you general advice for platforms like LinkedIn, Snapchat, and Twitter.

By the end of this part, you'll be able to:
- Lock down your profiles so strangers can't see your personal information.
- Control what advertisers know about you (and how to block them).
- Stop third-party apps from collecting your data.

1. Privacy Protection for Each Platform
Facebook Privacy Protection
Why Facebook Privacy Matters
Facebook has faced criticism for sharing personal data with advertisers and third parties. But the bigger threat is oversharing. If your profile is public, anyone can see your photos, hometown, and even your workplace. Hackers and scammers use this information to create phishing attacks or trick you into sharing more information.

How to Lock Down Your Facebook Privacy
Here's how to secure your Facebook account in minutes.
- Limit Who Can See Your Posts
  - Go to Settings & Privacy   Privacy Shortcuts   Who Can See Your Posts?
  - Change this to Friends Only or Custom (Friends Except...).
- Control What Personal Info is Public
  - Go to Settings & Privacy   Privacy Checkup.
  - Make sure your birthday, phone number, and email are not visible to the public.
  - Change "Who Can Look You Up By Email or Phone?" to Friends Only.
- Review Third-Party App Access
  - Go to Settings & Privacy   Apps and Websites.
  - Remove apps you don't recognize or apps that haven't been used recently.
- Enable Two-Factor Authentication (2FA)
  - Go to Settings & Privacy   Security and Login   Two-Factor Authentication.
  - Enable 2FA using SMS or an authenticator app like Google Authenticator.
- Turn Off Facebook Activity Tracking
  - Go to Settings & Privacy   Off-Facebook Activity.
  - Clear all history and turn off future tracking.
- Block Ad Tracking
  - Go to Settings & Privacy   Ads.
  - Turn off personalized ads and tracking.

Pro Tip: Don't Share Vacation Photos in Real Time. If someone knows you're away from home, it makes your home a prime target for break-ins. Post vacation photos after you return.

Instagram Privacy Protection
Why Instagram Privacy Matters
Instagram is a visual platform, but every photo, story, or reel you post reveals more than just your creativity. Location data, timestamps, and people you tag can be used by stalkers, scammers, and hackers to track your movements and location. Instagram also allows unknown users to DM you, which increases the risk of scam messages.

How to Lock Down Your Instagram Privacy
Here's how to protect your Instagram account.
- Make Your Account Private
  - Go to Settings   Privacy   Account Privacy.
  - Toggle on Private Account.

- Restrict DM Requests from Strangers
    - Go to Settings   Privacy   Messages.
    - Change Allow New Message Requests to Only People You Follow.
- Hide Your Activity Status
    - Go to Settings   Privacy   Activity Status.
    - Turn off Show Activity Status so others don't see when you're online.
- Review Your Followers
    - Manually check for fake followers (accounts with no posts, odd names, or spammy behavior).
    - Remove followers you don't trust.
- Limit Story Viewers
    - When posting stories, tap Close Friends to share them with a select group of people.
    - Avoid sharing your location in stories, as it reveals your current location to strangers.

Pro Tip: Don't Tag Your Location in Real-Time. When you tag "Starbucks Downtown" in your story, you're letting everyone know where you are right now. Post the location after you leave.

TikTok Privacy Protection
Why TikTok Privacy Matters
TikTok is one of the most criticized platforms for its data collection practices. It tracks location, device IDs, app usage, and even your clipboard data. Beyond privacy risks, there's also a risk of inappropriate interactions with children, as TikTok is popular among younger users.

How to Lock Down Your TikTok Privacy
- Make Your Account Private
    - Go to Settings & Privacy   Privacy   Private Account.
- Control Who Can DM You
    - Go to Settings & Privacy   Privacy   Direct Messages.
    - Choose No One or Friends Only.
- Enable "Family Pairing" (For Kids/Teens)
    - Family Pairing links your child's TikTok to yours, giving you control of privacy settings.
    - Restrict who can DM your child or see their videos.
- Disable Personalized Ads
    - Go to Settings & Privacy   Privacy   Personalized Ads.
    - Turn off Personalized Ads to limit how TikTok tracks you.
- Turn Off Location Tracking
    - Go to your device's app settings (iOS or Android) and turn off location permissions for TikTok.

LinkedIn, Snapchat, and Twitter Privacy Tips
- LinkedIn
  - Turn Off Profile Visibility to limit access to your personal data.
  - Be aware of "Job Offer" scams that trick users into sharing personal information.
- Snapchat
  - Use Ghost Mode to prevent users from tracking your location on Snap Map.
  - Set story privacy to Friends Only.
- Twitter
  - Lock down your profile to be visible only to followers.
  - Disable location sharing when posting tweets.

Call-to-Action: Take Control of Your Privacy
Here's a simple checklist to lock down your social media privacy in 15 minutes or less:
- Set your Facebook profile to "Friends Only."
- Turn off tracking for Facebook, Instagram, and TikTok.
- Enable Two-Factor Authentication (2FA) for all platforms.
- Use TikTok's Family Pairing if you have kids or teens on TikTok.
- Turn on Private Mode for Instagram and TikTok.

"Your privacy is in your hands. Don't wait for a data breach to protect it."

Once you've secured your privacy, you'll have peace of mind knowing your information is safe from stalkers, scammers, and advertisers. In the next section, we'll show you how AI tracks fake accounts, scam messages, and misinformation — and how you can stay one step ahead of the scammers.

How AI Tracks Fake Accounts, Scam Messages & Misinformation

The Rise of AI in Social Media Threat Detection
Social media platforms like Facebook, Instagram, and TikTok are battling an invisible enemy every day — fake accounts, scam messages, and misinformation. Unlike traditional threats, these issues aren't just technical problems. They exploit human psychology, trust, and decision-making.

To fight back, social media platforms have turned to AI-powered detection systems. AI can scan billions of posts, messages, and accounts in real time, spotting suspicious behavior that humans would never catch. But hackers have AI too, and they're constantly creating new, more sophisticated fake accounts and scam tactics. This section will show you how AI tracks and removes fake accounts, scam messages, and misinformation, and how you can recognize and avoid these threats.

By the end of this part, you'll understand:
- How platforms like Facebook, Instagram, and TikTok use AI to protect users.
- The red flags for spotting fake accounts, scam messages, and fake news.
- How you can protect yourself from falling victim to scams and misinformation.

1. How AI Tracks Fake Accounts
Why Do Hackers Create Fake Accounts?
Fake accounts are used for many purposes, including:
- Spamming and Phishing: Sending scam DMs or comments with phishing links.
- Social Engineering: Pretending to be someone you know to trick you into sharing information.
- Influence Campaigns: Using fake accounts to spread disinformation or promote certain political messages.

How AI Detects Fake Accounts
AI algorithms scan three core data points to identify fake accounts:
- Behavior Analysis
  - AI tracks how often the account posts, who they follow, and how fast they like or comment on posts.
  - Example: A bot account might "like" 100 posts in 10 minutes — something no human would do.
  - AI identifies this unusual activity and flags the account.
- Profile Analysis
  - AI checks profile information, such as the profile picture, username, bio, and "About Me" section.

- If the profile picture is a stock image or AI-generated face, it's flagged as suspicious.
- Tools like Pimeyes (https://pimeyes.com/) allow you to reverse-search profile pictures to see if they are stolen.

1. Content Analysis
   - AI scans what the user is posting (images, comments, and links).
   - Example: If 80% of a user's comments contain the same spammy link, it's flagged as a bot.
   - AI also identifies the language used in messages. If it detects copy-pasted messages sent to multiple users, it marks the account as suspicious.

Red Flags of a Fake Account
You don't need AI to spot a fake account. Here's what to look for:
- No Profile Picture or a Generic Image (stock photos, AI-generated faces, etc.).
- Unusual Follower-to-Following Ratio (follows 5,000 people but has 2 followers).
- Low Post Count (only one or two posts on the entire account).
- Suspicious DMs (they message you out of nowhere with links or "urgent" requests).

How to Protect Yourself From Fake Accounts
- Use Reverse Image Search: Check if a profile photo is being used on other sites.
- Block and Report: On Facebook, TikTok, and Instagram, report fake accounts for review.
- Don't Click Links in DMs: If you didn't request it, don't click it.

"If an account feels suspicious, it probably is. Trust your instincts and report it."

2. How AI Tracks Scam Messages
What Are Scam Messages?
Scam messages are DMs (direct messages) or private messages sent by hackers to trick you into:
- Clicking a malicious link.
- Sending personal details (like passwords or banking info).
- Downloading malware disguised as a "file attachment."

How AI Detects Scam Messages

AI uses several techniques to identify scam messages. Here's how it works:

1. Natural Language Processing (NLP)
   - AI analyzes the words, phrases, and tone of messages.
   - It looks for words like "urgent, act now, your account is compromised" — classic scam tactics.
   - It flags unusual grammar, spelling errors, and phrases that are often seen in phishing attacks.
2. Link Analysis
   - AI scans links in DMs and checks if the link is malicious.
   - If the link leads to a known phishing domain, it's blocked.
   - Platforms like Instagram, TikTok, and Messenger automatically block harmful links.
3. Message Pattern Detection
   - If one person sends the exact same message to 100 users, AI detects the pattern.
   - The system sees that this "bot-like" behavior is not something a normal human would do.

Red Flags of a Scam Message

Here's how to recognize scam messages:
- Spelling errors and bad grammar.
- Messages that say "Urgent! Click this link now!".
- Offers that sound "too good to be true" (like winning a contest you never entered).
- Random messages from strangers asking for help or favors.

How to Protect Yourself From Scam Messages
- Don't Click Links in DMs (especially from strangers).
- Report Suspicious Messages on Facebook, Instagram, and TikTok.
- Block Suspicious Users who spam you.
- Use Bark (https://www.bark.us/) to monitor incoming DMs for scam links on children's accounts.

"If it feels too good to be true, it's probably a scam. Don't click that link."

3. How AI Tracks Misinformation
What is Misinformation?

Misinformation is false or misleading content spread online. Unlike scam messages, misinformation aims to influence people's beliefs and actions. It is often seen in:
- Fake News (like deepfakes and false articles).
- Misleading Clickbait Headlines.
- Hoaxes or Health Misinformation (like false health tips).

How AI Detects Misinformation
1. Content Analysis (Text Analysis)
   o AI scans news articles, captions, and headlines to detect factually incorrect claims.
   o Platforms like Facebook and Twitter check this data against trusted sources.
2. Image & Video Recognition
   o AI can detect if an image has been edited, distorted, or deepfaked.
   o AI tools like InVID (https://www.invid-project.eu/) can verify if a video is authentic.
3. Cross-Referencing With Fact-Check Databases
   o AI compares content with fact-checking websites like Snopes and PolitiFact.
   o If the claim has already been debunked, the post is flagged.

Red Flags of Misinformation

Here's how to spot fake news or misleading posts:
- Too Shocking or Outrageous — If it feels like "breaking news" but no major outlets report it, it's likely false.
- Unverified Sources — The post claims "Experts say" but never names the experts.
- Poor Design — Grainy images, typos, or "forwarded" messages are classic signs.

How to Protect Yourself From Misinformation
- Check Reputable Fact-Checking Sites like Snopes or FactCheck.org.
- Use browser extensions like NewsGuard to identify credible news sources.
- Don't Share Until You Verify — If you can't verify it, don't spread it.
- Read Community Notes on X (formerly known as Twitter) This crowdsourced feature allows users to add context or correct misinformation on posts

AI-Augmented Social Engineering
What It Is:
AI-Augmented Social Engineering is the next evolution of traditional social engineering attacks. In the past, attackers would rely on human intuition, guesswork, and manual effort to deceive victims. Today, AI-driven tools and bots have made these attacks more effective, faster, and harder to detect. AI can automate thousands of social engineering attempts at once, creating personalized phishing messages, crafting human-like customer service chatbots, and impersonating executives with voice or video deepfakes.

Unlike traditional social engineering, AI-augmented attacks scale massively. Attackers no longer need to create each phishing message or social media scam manually. Instead, they use AI to automate scams on social media platforms like Twitter, Facebook, and Discord, where unsuspecting users are most vulnerable.

How It Works
AI-Generated Phishing Messages
- Attackers use AI-driven natural language processing (NLP) models like GPT-style language models to write scam emails, texts, and social media messages. AI can mimic human writing, produce highly convincing text, and create personalized messages that are tailored to specific users.

Example:
- A fake "customer support" Twitter account appears in the replies of a customer's complaint tweet. The AI-generated reply says, "Hi, we noticed your issue and would love to resolve it. Please verify your identity by clicking this link." The link leads to a phishing page where the user enters their login details, which are then stolen.
- In a Discord scam, attackers send automated DM messages pretending to be from a server admin, asking users to "verify their account" or "claim a giveaway" by clicking a link. These messages are crafted using AI-driven conversational chatbots.

How to Defend:
- Use phishing detection tools that scan for suspicious shortened URLs (like bit.ly links) and detect unusual patterns in direct messages.
- Set up anti-phishing filters like Proofpoint or Mimecast to block phishing messages automatically.
- Train employees to never click on links sent by "support agents" in public Twitter replies or Discord DMs.

AI-Generated Chatbots for Social Engineering
- AI is also being used to create fake chatbots on websites, support portals, and messaging apps. While chatbots are typically helpful tools for customer support, attackers have figured out how to deploy fake AI chatbots to trick users into revealing personal information.

Example:
- A victim visits a website that claims to offer "instant tech support." They click on a chat icon and interact with an AI chatbot that asks for their name, phone number, and login details. The AI then uses social engineering prompts like "We need to verify your account for security reasons" to trick users into handing over sensitive information.
- Attackers use AI-generated "fake support bots" to impersonate well-known companies like Amazon or PayPal. These chatbots mimic the tone and structure of real customer support bots.

How to Defend:
- Don't trust unsolicited support chat links. Legitimate companies do not ask for login credentials in chat messages.
- Use browser extensions like uBlock Origin or anti-phishing extensions that block fraudulent chatbots.
- If you're unsure whether a chatbot is legitimate, visit the official company's website directly.

AI-Enhanced Deepfake Impersonation
- Deepfakes are now being used to conduct social engineering over video calls and voice calls. Attackers use AI voice cloning software to copy the voice of a company executive or family member. Using that voice, they can call employees, family members, or bank managers to trick them into approving payments or sharing security codes.

Example:
- The Deepfake CEO Scam in Japan: Attackers used a deepfake video call of a company's CEO to trick an employee into transferring money. The AI-generated deepfake perfectly mimicked the CEO's voice, face, and video mannerisms, convincing the accountant it was real.
- AI-Powered Voice Phishing (Vishing): Attackers use AI to clone the voices of C-suite executives (CEOs, CFOs) and call employees to ask for urgent wire transfers. Because the voice sounds legitimate, employees often comply without thinking.

How to Defend:
- Use a "Family Password" strategy (discussed in Chapter 12) for verification. This strategy requires employees or family members to answer questions only they would know (e.g., "What's the 12th letter of our family password?").
- Use call verification protocols for sensitive transactions. Employees should be required to verify video calls through secondary channels (like a Slack message) before sending money.
  - Use tools like Deepware Scanner to analyze videos and identify signs of deepfake tampering.

AI-Powered Bot Networks
- Attackers no longer rely on human effort to create fake social media accounts. Instead, they use AI-driven bots to create thousands of fake profiles on platforms like Instagram, Twitter, and LinkedIn. These bots are used to flood social media with scams, promote fake giveaways, and amplify misinformation.

Example:
- Fake Crypto Giveaways on Twitter: Attackers create thousands of fake Elon Musk, Binance, or crypto "influencer" accounts. These accounts all promote the same scam link, claiming "Send 1 Bitcoin, Get 2 Back!" The accounts seem credible because they reply to real Twitter threads, creating a sense of urgency.
- Fake Job Offers on LinkedIn: Attackers use AI to create profiles that look like legitimate job recruiters. They send messages to job seekers asking them to "complete a background check" on a third-party site (which is a phishing page).

How to Defend:
- Use Botometer to detect fake accounts on Twitter.
- Check for account age and activity — fake accounts often have few followers and were created recently.
- Avoid clicking on "Send X crypto, get 2X back" offers. No legitimate company will offer this.
- Report suspicious job offers on LinkedIn and use trusted job boards for employment applications.

AI-Enhanced Social Media Manipulation
- Social media platforms are ground zero for disinformation campaigns. Attackers use AI to spread disinformation, fake news, and conspiracy theories. Using AI-powered tools, cybercriminals can generate fake comments, fake accounts, and trending hashtags to manipulate public opinion.

Example:
- Election Disinformation Campaigns: During elections, AI bots create thousands of fake comments to sway public opinion. These comments may include false claims about candidates or urge people to boycott elections.
- Hashtag Manipulation: Attackers use bots to "trend" hashtags. For example, a small group of bots can make a hashtag like #BreakingNews appear as if it's going viral.

How to Defend:
- Don't trust "breaking news" from unknown social media accounts. Check with official news sites.
- Be aware of campaigns that attempt to influence your emotions with anger or fear. Disinformation often uses strong emotional triggers.
- Follow news from reliable sources with fact-checking processes, like AP News or Reuters.

Key Takeaways
- AI is supercharging social engineering. Attackers are no longer limited to human-crafted emails and phone calls. They use AI-driven bots, deepfake calls, and voice cloning to scale their attacks.
- Attackers can automate phishing messages, video impersonations, and scam bots on platforms like Twitter, LinkedIn, and Discord.
- Businesses and families must use multi-factor verification, fact-check suspicious messages, and verify video calls to ensure they're not being tricked by AI-powered scams.
- Tools like Botometer (fake account detector) and Deepware Scanner (deepfake detection tool) are essential for fighting back against AI-enhanced social engineering.

Call to Action
Social engineering is no longer just about "tricking people over email." It now involves sophisticated AI-powered tools, automated chatbots, and deepfake impersonations. To stay safe, use tools like Botometer, Deepware Scanner, and uBlock Origin. Train employees to spot AI-generated social engineering tactics, and implement call verification protocols to prevent video call scams. By recognizing how AI is used for social engineering, you'll be ready to fight back.

Tools to Protect Your Social Media Accounts
AI-Powered Tools to Protect Privacy, Block Bots & Detect Scams
You don't need to manage social media security on your own. AI tools can automate most of the work for you. Here's a list of essential tools you should install today.

1. Privacy Protection Tools
These tools ensure your personal data stays private and hidden from advertisers, trackers, and unwanted followers.

Privacy Badger (https://privacybadger.org/)
- What It Does: Blocks tracking cookies and social media trackers that track your behavior on other websites.
- How It Helps: Blocks Facebook, TikTok, and Instagram from tracking you when you browse the web.
- Action Step: Install the Privacy Badger browser extension (for Chrome, Firefox, or Edge).

uBlock Origin (https://ublockorigin.com/)
- What It Does: Blocks ads, trackers, and scripts that track you on social media sites.
- How It Helps: Prevents TikTok, Facebook, and Instagram from tracking you when you visit other websites.
- Action Step: Install uBlock Origin on Chrome, Firefox, or Edge.

2. Parental Control Tools
If you have children or teens on TikTok, Instagram, or Snapchat, you need to protect them from online predators, inappropriate content, and scam DMs.

Bark (https://www.bark.us/)
- What It Does: Monitors and alerts parents if a child receives scam messages, harmful DMs, or inappropriate content.
- How It Helps: Tracks TikTok, Instagram, Snapchat, and SMS text messages. Alerts parents if the child is being bullied, contacted by strangers, or exposed to risky content.
- Action Step: Install Bark on your child's phone and link it to your device.

Qustodio (https://www.qustodio.com/)
- What It Does: Tracks kids' screen time, app usage, and location.
- How It Helps: Gives parents control over how much time their kids spend on TikTok, Instagram, and Snapchat.
- Action Step: Install Qustodio on your child's device and set limits on app usage.

3. Fake Account Detection Tools

Firewalla (https://firewalla.com/)
- What It Does: Monitors your home network for suspicious devices, like unknown smartphones or tablets that connect to your Wi-Fi.
- How It Helps: Identifies devices linked to fake accounts and prevents unknown devices from connecting to your Wi-Fi.
- Action Step: Install a Firewalla device in your home and set up notifications for new devices on your network.

Pimeyes (https://pimeyes.com/)
- What It Does: Allows you to reverse-search profile pictures to see if your photo is being used on a fake social media profile.
- How It Helps: Scans the web for instances where your profile picture is being used on fake accounts.
- Action Step: Upload your photo to Pimeyes and review the results.

4. Scam Detection & Phishing Protection Tools

Microsoft Defender for Office 365 (https://www.microsoft.com/en-us/microsoft-365/security/defender-office-365)
- What It Does: Detects scam emails and suspicious links in social media emails (like password reset emails from Instagram, Facebook, etc.).
- How It Helps: Warns you before clicking scam links or phishing links.
- Action Step: Enable Microsoft Defender for Office 365 on your Microsoft 365 account.

Bitdefender Anti-Phishing (https://www.bitdefender.com/)
- What It Does: Scans links and web pages to ensure they aren't phishing sites.
- How It Helps: Stops you from clicking dangerous links in DMs, scam messages, and unknown texts.
- Action Step: Install the Bitdefender Anti-Phishing extension for Chrome or Firefox.

Daily, Weekly, and Monthly Security Habits
Daily Habits
These simple daily habits take less than 5 minutes and provide significant protection.
- Check for Fake Accounts: Look at your followers on TikTok and Instagram.
- Don't Click on Random Links in DMs: Most scam messages have "urgent" language to push you to click.
- Review DMs for Suspicious Messages: Block and report any DM that feels "off."

Weekly Habits
These tasks only take a few minutes but make a big impact.
- Check for Privacy Setting Changes: Platforms sometimes change privacy defaults.
- Review New Devices on Wi-Fi: Use Firewalla to review new devices on your Wi-Fi.
- Block Spam Followers: Check for spam followers on Instagram and TikTok.

Monthly Habits
Once a month, do these deeper security checks.
- Review Permissions for Third-Party Apps: Check TikTok, Instagram, and Facebook for apps linked to your account.
- Change Passwords for Social Media Accounts: Use a tool like 1Password to create strong, random passwords.
- Check for Data Breaches: Use HaveIBeenPwned (https://haveibeenpwned.com/) to see if your passwords were leaked.

Final Action Plan: Protect Your Social Media Today
Step 1: Lock Down Your Privacy
1. Set your Facebook profile to "Friends Only".
2. Make your TikTok and Instagram accounts private.
3. Review permissions for third-party apps connected to your social media.

Step 2: Protect Against Fake Accounts, Scam DMs, and Misinformation
1. Use Pimeyes to see if your profile image is being used in fake accounts.
2. Install Bark or Qustodio if you have kids on TikTok or Instagram.
3. Report and block fake followers on TikTok and Instagram.

Step 3: Install AI-Driven Tools
1. Install Privacy Badger and uBlock Origin on your browser.
2. Set up Firewalla to block unknown devices from joining your Wi-Fi.
3. Install Bitdefender Anti-Phishing to scan and block scam links.

Call-to-Action
"Your social media accounts are your most public asset — but they don't have to be vulnerable. By using AI tools, daily habits, and this action plan, you can stay one step ahead of scammers, bots, and hackers."

Privacy Enhancements for Hardcore Users
If you've followed all the steps in this chapter so far, you're ahead of 90% of social media users when it comes to privacy and security. But for those who want to go further — the hardcore privacy advocates — there are additional actions you can take.

These steps are for those who want to eliminate as much data exposure as possible. Whether you're concerned about advertisers tracking your every move or you simply don't trust social platforms with your personal information, this section provides advanced tactics to achieve true privacy and anonymity.

1. Request Data Deletion (GDPR/CCPA Requests)
Platforms like Facebook, Instagram, and TikTok are required to give users access to their personal data under laws like the General Data Protection Regulation (GDPR) and the California Consumer Privacy Act (CCPA). You have the legal right to:
- See what data they have on you (your activity, purchases, likes, comments, etc.).
- Request that your data be deleted from their servers.

How to Request Data Deletion on Major Platforms
Facebook/Instagram Data Deletion
1. Go to Settings   Privacy   Your Facebook Information.
2. Click Download Your Information (this will let you see everything Facebook knows about you).
3. Select Request Account Deletion to delete all your data.

TikTok Data Deletion
1. Go to Settings & Privacy   Manage Account.
2. Click Delete Account to remove your account and all stored data.
3. Alternatively, you can file a Data Access Request using TikTok's online form.

Twitter, LinkedIn, and Snapchat
- Twitter: Go to Settings   Your Account   Deactivate Your Account.
- LinkedIn: Go to Settings & Privacy   Account Preferences Close Your LinkedIn Account.
- Snapchat: Visit the Snapchat Account Deletion page (on a web browser) and log in to start the process.

Pro Tip: If you want to keep your accounts but delete stored data, look for "Download Data" or Request Data Access options. Platforms will give you access to all the info they have on you, which you can review and request to be deleted.

2. Block Third-Party Tracking (Like Facebook's "Off-Facebook Activity")
Did you know that Facebook tracks you even when you're not on Facebook? When you browse other websites, Facebook tracks your activity using "Off-Facebook Activity" data. This allows advertisers to retarget you with ads, but you can turn it off.

How to Turn Off "Off-Facebook Activity" Tracking
1. Go to Settings & Privacy   Settings   Off-Facebook Activity.
2. Click Clear History (this erases past activity).
3. Select Manage Future Activity and turn it OFF.

Pro Tip: If you use Google Chrome, install uBlock Origin or Privacy Badger to block Facebook trackers directly from your browser.

3. Control What Advertisers Know About You
If you've ever noticed an ad for a product you only thought about but never searched for, it's because advertisers are using predictive AI. Meta, TikTok, and Google analyze your behavior to predict what you want next. While you can't stop this entirely, you can reduce their ability to track you.

How to Opt Out of Targeted Ads
- Facebook/Instagram:
  o Go to Settings   Privacy   Ads Preferences.
  o Turn off Personalized Ads.
- TikTok:
  o Go to Settings & Privacy   Privacy   Personalized Ads.
  o Turn it OFF.
- Google/YouTube:
  o Visit adssettings.google.com and turn off Personalized Ads.
Pro Tip: After opting out of ads, clear your cookies and cache. Some trackers persist even after you change your settings.

4. Avoid Location Tracking (Stay Invisible)
Social media apps like TikTok, Snapchat, and Facebook can track
your physical location in real time. Here's how to stay off the radar.

How to Disable Location Tracking on All Platforms
1. On iOS/Android, go to Settings   Privacy   Location
   Services.
2. Disable location access for TikTok, Facebook, and Instagram.
3. On TikTok, go to Settings & Privacy   Privacy   Location
   Services   Turn Off Location Tracking.

More Tools for Advanced Users
For those who want an extra layer of protection, here are more
advanced tools for hardcore privacy advocates.

1. VPNs (Virtual Private Networks)
A VPN (Virtual Private Network) hides your IP address, so social
media platforms like TikTok, Facebook, and Instagram can't track
your location. VPNs also protect you from being tracked on public
Wi-Fi.

Recommended VPNs:
- NordVPN (https://nordvpn.com/): Excellent privacy, no-logs
  policy, and fast speeds.
- ExpressVPN (https://www.expressvpn.com/): Secure, fast, and
  works on most platforms.

Pro Tip: Always use a VPN on public Wi-Fi (like at cafes or
airports) to stop TikTok, Facebook, and Instagram from tracking
you.

2. Advanced MFA (Multi-Factor Authentication) Apps
Most people use SMS-based 2FA (like receiving a text code), but
this method is not secure. Hackers can SIM-swap your phone
number to intercept your SMS codes. Instead, use authenticator
apps.

Recommended MFA Tools:
- Authy (https://authy.com/): Backups and multi-device support.
- Google Authenticator (https://google.com/): Standard for 2FA,
  but no backups.

Pro Tip: Set up 2FA on all social media platforms, but never use
SMS-based 2FA. Switch to Authy or Google Authenticator for
maximum protection.

3. Browser Privacy Extensions

Browser extensions can prevent Facebook, TikTok, and other platforms from tracking you.

Recommended Extensions:
- Privacy Badger (https://privacybadger.org/): Blocks hidden trackers from TikTok, Facebook, and Instagram.
- uBlock Origin (https://ublockorigin.com/): Blocks pop-up ads, trackers, and malicious scripts.
- Ghostery (https://www.ghostery.com/): Blocks trackers and shows you which companies are trying to track you.

Pro Tip: Install uBlock Origin, Ghostery, and Privacy Badger together for maximum privacy protection.

4. Tools for Fake Accounts, Deepfakes & Scams
- Pimeyes (https://pimeyes.com/): Checks if someone is using your photo in a fake social media account.
- InVID (https://www.invid-project.eu/): Verifies if videos or images are authentic (great for spotting deepfakes).
- Bitdefender Anti-Phishing (https://www.bitdefender.com/): Detects and blocks phishing sites in DMs, comments, and links.

Pro Tip: Run a Pimeyes search on your profile picture to see if it's being used for fake accounts.

Chapter Conclusion: Protect Yourself from AI-Enhanced Threats
In this part, you learned how AI tracks fake accounts, scam messages, and misinformation. These threats are constantly evolving, but the platforms you use are fighting back with powerful AI systems.

Here's what you can do next:
- Check your followers for fake accounts on Instagram and TikTok.
- Don't click on suspicious DMs and report spam immediately.
- Use fact-checking tools like NewsGuard and InVID before sharing news.
- Use advanced privacy tools and techniques to stay anonymous.
- Protect your privacy on Facebook, Instagram, TikTok, LinkedIn, and more.

If you only take one message from this chapter, it's this:

"Every second you spend on social media, someone is collecting your data. But with privacy tools, daily habits, and advanced AI-driven security, you can take back control."

Chapter 10: Data Privacy & Online Identity

Understanding Your Digital Footprint
What is a Digital Footprint?
Imagine every click, tap, or swipe you make online leaves behind a trail of breadcrumbs. This trail is called your digital footprint. It's the combination of every online action, every login, every search, and every post you make across websites, apps, and devices. Even when you think you're "just browsing," your data is being collected.

There are two types of digital footprints:
1. Active Footprint: Data you intentionally share, like posting on social media, filling out forms, or commenting on blogs.
2. Passive Footprint: Data you unknowingly create, like your search history, IP address, location data, and activity from tracking cookies.

Example: When you log in to an e-commerce site and browse for shoes, that's part of your active footprint. But the site tracking your clicks, time spent on pages, and the items you hover over? That's your passive footprint.

How Your Data is Collected Online
Data collection happens every time you interact with the internet. This is how companies track you:
- Web Tracking (Cookies & Beacons)
    - Websites use cookies and invisible "tracking beacons" to see what you click, how long you stay on a page, and what pages you visit next.
    - Why it Matters: Data from cookies helps advertisers create targeted ads that "follow you" around the web.
- Search Engines (Like Google, Bing, and DuckDuckGo)
    - Every search you make on Google or Bing is stored, analyzed, and linked to your user profile.
    - Why it Matters: Google tracks your searches to predict your preferences, serve you ads, and customize your search results.
- Apps & Mobile Devices
    - Apps like Uber, Google Maps, and TikTok request access to your location, contacts, and even your clipboard data.
    - Why it Matters: Apps like TikTok have been criticized for logging keystrokes and copying clipboard data.

- Social Media & E-Commerce
  - Every like, comment, or share on social media platforms like Facebook or TikTok is added to your social graph — a collection of everything the platform knows about you.
  - Why it Matters: Platforms like Facebook analyze your behavior to sell "ad space" to advertisers, allowing them to target you based on what you post, like, and watch.
- IoT (Internet of Things) Devices
  - Your smart thermostat, smart TV, and smart fridge all collect behavioral data on you.
  - Why it Matters: Companies like Amazon and Google use data from your smart devices to create a profile of your daily habits.

How Your Data is Bought, Sold, and Shared
If you think only Google and Facebook know about you, think again. Your data is being sold to data brokers and other third parties every day. Data brokers collect and resell this information to advertisers, political campaigns, and even hiring managers.

How Data Brokers Collect Your Info
- Online Purchases: Retailers like Amazon, Walmart, and Etsy track your shopping behavior and sell the data to data brokers.
- Social Media Profiles: Public data, like your name, birthday, or location, is scraped from public social media accounts.
- Web Activity: Every time you visit a website that uses a tracking cookie (which is almost every site), that data is sold to data brokers.

How Data Brokers Sell Your Data
Data brokers package your information into "consumer profiles" that contain:
- Your name, address, phone number, and email.
- Your purchase history (like "frequent buyer of fitness products").
- Your social media activity (what you post, like, and share).

These profiles are then sold to:
- Advertisers: To target you with ads for products they know you want.
- Employers: Some hiring platforms use this data in background checks.
- Hackers: If data brokers get hacked (like Equifax), your data can end up on the dark web.

Example: If you've ever seen an ad on Facebook for a product you searched for 10 minutes earlier on Google, this is because data brokers are linking your activity across websites.

How AI Enhances Data Collection & Tracking
AI doesn't just collect your data — it processes, predicts, and personalizes it. Here's how:
1. Predictive Analytics
   - AI predicts your future actions (like which shoes you're about to buy) based on your browsing patterns.
   - Example: Amazon uses AI to suggest products you didn't even know you needed.
2. Behavioral Profiling
   - AI tracks your mouse movements, clicks, and page interactions to learn about your preferences.
   - Example: Netflix tracks what you pause, rewind, and rewatch to predict what shows you'll like next.
3. Advanced Ad Targeting
   - AI uses your previous ad clicks to serve you hyper-personalized ads.
   - Example: If you search for "best hiking boots," AI will track you across Facebook, TikTok, and Google to serve hiking boot ads.

How AI Anonymizes Your Data (Data Obfuscation)
If all this sounds overwhelming, don't worry — AI can protect you too. While most of the tracking discussed so far works against you, there are AI-driven tools that scramble, obfuscate, and anonymize your personal data. Here's how it works:

How AI Obfuscates Your Data
When you use privacy tools like Blur, MySudo, and Privacy Badger, AI works in the background to obfuscate (or "scramble") your data. Here's how:
- Data Scrambling: AI changes names, dates, and purchase details to make your data meaningless to trackers.
- Tokenization: Instead of storing your real credit card number, it replaces it with a "fake" credit card.
- Data Masking: AI hides personal information like your IP address by replacing it with a random IP.

Example: When you buy something online with Blur, the store only sees a fake credit card number. If the site gets hacked, your real card is safe.

How AI Encryption Works
Encryption takes your data and scrambles it into unreadable code. Only you (or people with a decryption key) can read it. Here's how it works:
- End-to-End Encryption (E2EE): Apps like ProtonMail and Signal ensure that only the sender and recipient can see the message.
- Bank-Grade Encryption: Services like Blur and MySudo use the same encryption that banks use to protect your sensitive info.

Example: When you send an email using ProtonMail, not even ProtonMail employees can read it. That's end-to-end encryption in action.

How AI Uses Obfuscation to Keep You Anonymous
- Anonymous Login Data: Services like Apple Sign-In give you an anonymous login option (instead of "Sign in with Facebook").
- Disposable Email Addresses: Use tools like SimpleLogin to create one-time-use email addresses for online accounts.
- Temporary Phone Numbers: Use MySudo to create "burner" phone numbers, so your real number is never shared.

Call-to-Action: Know Your Footprint, Control Your Data
Your digital footprint is bigger than you think, but with AI-driven tools, you can take back control. You now know:
- How your data is collected every day.
- How advertisers, data brokers, and hackers use it against you.
- How AI privacy tools like Blur, ProtonMail, and Privacy Badger anonymize and protect your data.

Here's what you can do next:
1. Use DeleteMe or Incogni to delete your data from broker databases.
2. Install Privacy Badger or uBlock Origin to block trackers.
3. Use Blur to mask your credit card info when shopping online.

"Every click, every search, and every purchase leaves a footprint. But with AI on your side, you can walk without leaving a trace."

Cleaning Up Your Digital Footprint

Imagine walking into a room filled with strangers, and every person knows your name, address, hobbies, and past purchases. Sounds unsettling, right? This is exactly what's happening online. Your digital footprint — the trail of information you leave behind — is accessible to advertisers, data brokers, hackers, and even people searching your name online.

But here's the good news: You can clean it up. By following a structured process to delete, anonymize, and block your personal data, you can reclaim control of your privacy. This part of the chapter will guide you through how to:

- Delete old accounts you no longer use.
- Remove your personal data from data brokers.
- Scrub your name, phone, and email from Google search results.
- Use powerful privacy tools to prevent your footprint from growing in the future.

If you've ever searched for your name online and been shocked by what you found, this section is for you.

1. Remove Your Data from Data Brokers
Data brokers like Acxiom, Spokeo, Whitepages, and PeopleFinder exist to buy, sell, and trade your personal information. These companies collect your name, phone number, address, purchase history, and more — all without your consent. This information is then sold to advertisers, spammers, and background check companies.

How Data Brokers Get Your Info
1. Public Records: Voter registrations, marriage certificates, and property purchases are public.
2. Web Tracking: Websites, apps, and e-commerce platforms sell your activity to data brokers.
3. Retail Purchases: When you sign up for store loyalty programs, your purchase history is sold.

How to Remove Your Info from Data Brokers
Option 1: Use Automated Data Removal Services
1. DeleteMe (https://joindeleteme.com/) — Removes your info from 50+ brokers automatically.
2. Incogni (https://incogni.com/) — Sends automatic removal requests to data brokers.
3. Kanary (https://www.kanary.com/) — Similar to DeleteMe but targets a wider range of brokers.

Pro Tip: These tools can save you hours of manual effort. They send data removal requests on your behalf and monitor for future reappearances.

Option 2: Manual Removal (Free, But Time-Consuming)
1. Acxiom: Visit https://www.acxiom.com/opt-out/ to submit a request to delete your data.
2. Spokeo: Go to https://www.spokeo.com/optout and follow the process.
3. WhitePages: Visit https://www.whitepages.com/suppression_requests to remove your phone number.

Pro Tip: Manual removal takes longer and may require identity verification. Be prepared to upload a photo of your ID for some requests.

Why This Matters
If you remove your info from brokers, it becomes harder for scammers to find you. Your phone number won't be listed on WhitePages, and hackers won't be able to find your address on Spokeo.

2. Delete Old Online Accounts

If you've been online for a while, you probably have old accounts on platforms like MySpace, Reddit, AOL, Yahoo, and gaming forums. These accounts are still active unless you close them, and they're a prime target for hackers.

How to Find and Delete Old Accounts
1. Use Deseat.me (https://www.deseat.me/)
   - What It Does: Finds all the accounts linked to your email address.
   - How It Helps: Automatically generates account deletion requests.
2. Use JustDelete.me (https://justdelete.me/)
   - What It Does: Provides direct links to delete old accounts on Reddit, LinkedIn, Yahoo, and more.
   - How It Helps: Tells you how difficult it is to delete each account (easy, medium, or hard).
3. Search for Your Email in Old Accounts
   - Go to Gmail, Yahoo, or Outlook and search for these terms:
     - "Welcome to"
     - "Account Created"
     - "Activate Your Account"
   - Look for any old platforms you forgot about and follow the process to delete them.

Pro Tip: Check for old social accounts on gaming sites (like Steam), forums (like Reddit), and email providers (like Yahoo, AOL, and Outlook). These old accounts are often forgotten but still contain personal data.

3. Remove Your Info from Google Search Results
If you've ever Googled your name and found your phone number or address, you know how scary it feels. But Google offers a process to remove sensitive info.

How to Remove Personal Info from Google
1. Go to Google's Remove Me Page: Visit https://support.google.com/websearch/answer/9673730.
2. Submit a Removal Request: Request the removal of phone numbers, email addresses, or addresses.
3. Monitor Your Name Regularly: Set up Google Alerts (https://www.google.com/alerts) with your name. If it appears in new results, you'll be notified.

Pro Tip: Use Incogni or DeleteMe to remove your name from data brokers, because if they remove your info, it will no longer appear in Google.

4. Tools for Privacy Enthusiasts
For hardcore privacy enthusiasts, basic privacy isn't enough. They want to be invisible online. Here's a list of advanced tools and techniques that will keep your data out of sight.

1. Disposable Emails and Phone Numbers
Tool: SimpleLogin (https://simplelogin.io/)
- What It Does: Creates temporary "burner" email addresses for online accounts.
- Why It Helps: Prevents companies from having your real email, so if it gets leaked, you won't be affected.

Tool: MySudo (https://mysudo.com/)
- What It Does: Creates temporary phone numbers and email addresses for sign-ups.
- Why It Helps: Protects your personal phone number from being spammed by marketers.

2. Anonymous Web Browsing
Tool: Tails OS (https://tails.boum.org/)
- What It Does: Runs a private, encrypted operating system on a USB drive.
- Why It Helps: Leaves no trace on the computer you're using.

Tool: Tor Browser (https://www.torproject.org/)
- What It Does: Routes your internet traffic through multiple servers, hiding your IP address.
- Why It Helps: Prevents anyone from tracking your browsing history.

3. Data Masking and Tokenization
Tool: Blur (https://abine.com/blur/)
- What It Does: Masks your credit card info with a "fake" card number.
- Why It Helps: If an e-commerce store gets hacked, your real card is safe.

Tool: Privacy.com (https://privacy.com/)
- What It Does: Creates virtual debit cards for online shopping.
- Why It Helps: Your real bank details are never exposed.

4. Password Management & 2FA
Tool: Authy (https://authy.com/)
- What It Does: Generates time-based codes for 2-factor authentication.
- Why It Helps: It's safer than SMS-based 2FA, which hackers can bypass.

Tool: Bitwarden (https://bitwarden.com/)
- What It Does: Stores your passwords securely in an encrypted vault.
- Why It Helps: Ensures that you never use the same password twice.

Call-to-Action: Clean Up Your Digital Footprint Today
Here's what to do next:
1. Delete Your Data From Data Brokers
   - Use DeleteMe, Incogni, or Kanary to send automatic deletion requests.
2. Delete Old Accounts
   - Use Deseat.me and JustDelete.me to track down old accounts.
3. Remove Your Info from Google
   - Use Google's Remove Me form to remove personal details from search results.
4. Use Advanced Privacy Tools
   - Install SimpleLogin, MySudo, Blur, and Privacy.com to protect your personal info.

"Every piece of personal data online is a target. Take back control. Clean up your digital footprint today."

AI-Driven Privacy Tools for Online Identity Protection

The Rise of AI for Privacy Protection
Most people think AI is only used for tracking and surveillance, but the truth is, AI can also be your greatest protector. Advanced privacy tools now use AI-driven obfuscation, encryption, and data anonymization to shield your identity online.

If you've ever used a masked credit card, a disposable email address, or an encrypted chat app, you've already benefited from AI-driven privacy protection. The next step is to learn how to use these tools proactively to protect your data, anonymize your activity, and make yourself invisible online.

This section introduces the most powerful AI-driven privacy tools available today. By the end, you'll know how to:
- Anonymize your personal data so websites can't track you.
- Use AI-powered tools to mask your credit cards, phone numbers, and emails.
- Deploy AI-driven encryption tools to keep hackers out of your messages, calls, and personal files.

1. How AI Anonymizes Your Data
AI doesn't just protect your data; it scrambles, masks, and encrypts it so that even if hackers get access, they can't use it. Here's how AI-driven anonymization works:

1. Data Obfuscation (Scrambling Your Data)
What It Is: AI takes your personal details (name, address, phone number) and replaces them with random characters or "tokens" that look like your data but aren't.
- How It Works:
  - AI creates a "masked" version of your credit card, so instead of using "4111-1111-1111-1111," you use a virtual card like "5300-4500-7864-0987."
  - If a hacker steals it, it's useless because it's not tied to your real card.
  - Tools That Use It: Blur, Privacy.com, and MySudo use obfuscation to create temporary, randomized data.

2. Tokenization (Replacing Data with Tokens)
What It Is: Instead of storing sensitive information (like credit card numbers or SSNs), AI replaces the info with unique "tokens". The real data is stored in a secure vault, and only the token is used online.

- How It Works:
  - You create a "virtual credit card" through Privacy.com.
  - When you pay at an online store, the store only sees the tokenized credit card number, not your real card.
  - If the store gets hacked, your real card remains safe.

Example: When you use Blur to create a "masked" phone number, the caller only sees the masked number. If the masked number gets leaked, you can delete it without changing your real number.

3. End-to-End Encryption (E2EE)
What It Is: Encryption converts your messages, files, and calls into unreadable code that only you (and the person you're communicating with) can read. No third parties, including hackers, can access it.
- How It Works:
  - Apps like ProtonMail, Signal, and WhatsApp use encryption to scramble your texts, emails, and voice calls.
  - Even if hackers steal the encrypted files, they can't read them without a decryption key.
  - Tools That Use It: ProtonMail, Signal, and encrypted messaging apps use E2EE encryption.

Example: If you send a message using ProtonMail, not even ProtonMail employees can read it. The message is encrypted before it leaves your device.

2. AI-Powered Tools for Privacy Protection

1. Masked Credit Cards & Payments
Tool: Privacy.com (https://privacy.com/)
- How It Works: Privacy.com allows you to create virtual credit card numbers for each purchase.
- Why It Matters: If a company gets hacked, your real bank info stays safe.
- How It Helps: Each payment gets a "disposable card" that can be canceled anytime.

Tool: Blur (https://abine.com/blur/)
- How It Works: Blur creates masked credit cards and anonymized payment details.
- Why It Matters: You can mask your email, phone, and card details for safer online shopping.
- How It Helps: If a website is breached, Blur's masked info is useless to hackers.

2. Disposable Emails & Anonymous Phone Numbers
Tool: SimpleLogin (https://simplelogin.io/)
- What It Does: Creates disposable email aliases.
- Why It Matters: Use a different email for every website so if one gets leaked, you're safe.
- How It Helps: You can disable specific email aliases if they start getting spam.

Tool: MySudo (https://mysudo.com/)
- What It Does: Creates temporary phone numbers and email addresses.
- Why It Matters: Use a "burner" phone number when signing up for apps, services, and websites.
- How It Helps: If a spammer gets the burner number, you just delete it.

Pro Tip: If you sign up for every social media platform using a MySudo phone number and a SimpleLogin email, you'll never have to share your real details.

3. Anonymous Browsing & Location Hiding
Tool: Tor Browser (https://www.torproject.org/)
- What It Does: Encrypts your internet traffic and hides your IP address.
- How It Helps: Websites can't see your location or identity.

Tool: Tails OS (https://tails.boum.org/)
- What It Does: Runs a privacy-first operating system from a USB.
- How It Helps: No trace of your activity is left on the computer.

Tool: NordVPN (https://nordvpn.com/)
- What It Does: Hides your IP address and encrypts your web traffic.
- How It Helps: Prevents websites and platforms from tracking your location.

4. End-to-End Encrypted Messaging & Email
Tool: ProtonMail (https://proton.me/)
- What It Does: Provides encrypted email that only you and the recipient can read.
- How It Helps: If your email gets hacked, the encrypted data can't be read.

Tool: Signal (https://signal.org/)
- What It Does: Sends end-to-end encrypted messages, calls, and videos.
- How It Helps: Protects you from surveillance, hackers, and cybercriminals.

Chapter Conclusion: Protect Your Identity, Anonymize Your Data
Your online identity is priceless, and in today's world, it's under constant threat from advertisers, hackers, and data brokers. AI-driven privacy tools offer the best way to protect your information, anonymize your activity, and keep you safe.

Here's what you've learned:
- How AI anonymizes your personal data through obfuscation, encryption, and tokenization.
- How to mask your credit card, phone number, and email using tools like Blur, Privacy.com, MySudo, and SimpleLogin.
- How to stay anonymous online using VPNs, Tor Browser, Tails OS, and encrypted messaging apps like ProtonMail and Signal.

Call-to-Action: Lock Down Your Identity Today
Here's what to do next:
1. Anonymize Your Payments
   - Create a Privacy.com account and start using virtual credit cards for online purchases.
2. Mask Your Phone and Email
   - Use SimpleLogin for disposable email addresses.
   - Use MySudo to create burner phone numbers.
3. Use Anonymous Browsing Tools
   - Download Tor Browser to stay anonymous while browsing.
   - Use Tails OS if you want to leave zero traces on your computer.
4. Lock Down Your Communications
   - Switch to ProtonMail for encrypted emails.
   - Use Signal for private, encrypted messaging.

"Your data is your power. Protect it, anonymize it, and reclaim your privacy."

Chapter 11: Device Security: Phones, Laptops, and IoT

Why Device Security Matters
Imagine waking up to find your phone has been hacked. Your text messages were read, your banking app was accessed, and a hacker has locked you out of your own accounts. It sounds like a nightmare, but for thousands of people, this is their reality. Now, imagine looking at your smart home camera feed, only to see the lens moving on its own, scanning your living room. A hacker is watching you.

This might sound like something from a movie, but it's happening every day. Hackers aren't just targeting corporate systems — they're targeting you. Why? Because your phone, laptop, and IoT devices are easier to hack than corporate systems. Cybercriminals know that individuals don't have security teams, and most people don't take device security seriously until it's too late.

Here's the scary truth:
- IoT devices are wide open to attacks. Many smart devices ship with default passwords like "admin" or "password" that hackers can guess in seconds.
- Your phone is the #1 device hackers target. From SMS phishing (smishing) to spyware apps that track your every move, phones are a hacker's favorite tool.
- Laptops are data goldmines. Hackers target your laptop to access your emails, documents, passwords, and payment details.

These aren't just "what-ifs" — they're happening right now. Take a look at some of the biggest device security incidents from recent years:

Recent Real-World Device Hacks
1. Hacker Speaks to Child Through a Smart Camera
- Targeted Device: Ring Smart Camera
- How It Happened: The hacker accessed a family's Ring security camera, took control of it, and began speaking directly to the child.
- What Went Wrong: The family never changed the default password on their Ring device, and the hacker used a password database to "guess" their login.
- Lesson: Change default passwords on all smart devices.

2. The SIM-Swap Attack That Drained $24 Million from a Bank
- Targeted Device: Smartphone (via SIM Swap)
- How It Happened: Hackers convinced the victim's phone carrier to issue a new SIM card for the victim's phone number. Once they had control of the phone number, they intercepted all 2FA (two-factor authentication) codes, accessed the victim's bank accounts, and stole $24 million.
- What Went Wrong: The victim relied on SMS-based two-factor authentication (2FA), which can be intercepted.
- Lesson: Never rely on SMS 2FA. Use an authenticator app like Authy or Google Authenticator instead.

3. Mirai Botnet Hijacks Over 100,000 IoT Devices
- Targeted Devices: Smart Cameras, Smart Plugs, and Routers
- How It Happened: Hackers launched the Mirai Botnet, a malware that scans for IoT devices with default passwords. Once infected, these devices were used to launch one of the largest DDoS attacks in history.
- What Went Wrong: Thousands of devices still had factory-default passwords like "admin" and "1234."
- Lesson: Change default passwords on every IoT device.

These aren't isolated incidents. Every day, hackers target ordinary people — not just corporations. Your phone, laptop, and smart home devices are at risk. But here's the good news:

With AI-driven monitoring tools, device encryption, and simple security habits, you can protect your devices from being exploited.

This chapter will show you how to:
1. Protect your phones, laptops, and tablets from spyware, malware, and device hijacking.
2. Secure smart devices like smart locks, smart speakers, and webcams to stop hackers from spying on you.
3. Use AI-driven monitoring tools to detect unusual behavior on any device (like devices turning on at odd times).

Why Device Security is Critical in an AI-Driven World
In the past, device security was about keeping viruses off your computer. Today, it's about defending against AI-driven attacks that operate at machine speed. Hackers are no longer guessing your passwords manually — they're using AI to predict and crack passwords. They're not sending one phishing email at a time — they're sending thousands with AI-written language that's more convincing than ever.

AI-powered threats can:
- Break into devices faster by guessing passwords with machine learning algorithms.
- Track your location and monitor device usage to identify weak points.
- Exploit human error (like forgetting to update firmware) to gain access to IoT devices.

But here's the good news:
- AI can protect you, too. New tools like Firewalla, Norton Mobile Security, and Bitdefender IoT Security use AI to detect unusual device behavior.
- AI can recognize normal patterns of use for your phone, laptop, and smart devices, so if something unusual happens (like your camera turning on at 3 AM), you'll be notified.

How Attackers Exploit Devices
To understand how to protect your devices, you must first understand how hackers attack them. Here's a look at the most common attack methods:

1. Phone Attacks
- Smishing: SMS phishing messages trick you into clicking a malicious link.
- Spyware: Hidden apps log your calls, texts, and GPS location.
- SIM-Swap Attack: Hackers hijack your phone number, take over your 2FA codes, and access your bank.

2. Laptop Attacks
- Keyloggers: Hackers install a small program that records every keystroke (passwords, emails, etc.).
- Phishing: Hackers send fake login pages for Gmail, Amazon, or your bank to steal your password.
- Malware: Viruses infect your laptop and give hackers full control.

3. IoT Device Attacks
- Camera Hijacking: Hackers take control of your smart home cameras (like Ring, Nest, and Arlo).
- Device Takeovers: Hackers use default passwords to take control of smart locks, smart thermostats, and smart plugs.
- Botnet Recruitment: Your smart devices are added to a hacker's botnet (like Mirai) and used to attack websites.

What Happens If Your Devices Get Hacked?
If a hacker gains control of your phone, laptop, or IoT devices, the consequences can be far more severe than you think. Here's what can happen for each type of device:

1. If Your Phone Gets Hacked
Your phone is the gateway to your online identity. If a hacker takes control of your phone, they can:
- Access your two-factor authentication (2FA) codes: Many people rely on SMS-based 2FA, but if a hacker executes a SIM-swap attack, they'll receive all 2FA codes meant for you.
- Read your private messages: Apps like SMS, WhatsApp, and even encrypted apps like Signal can be accessed if your phone is unlocked or if a spyware app is installed.
- Gain access to your banking apps: Banking apps like PayPal, Venmo, and CashApp can be opened and drained if a hacker has access to your phone.
- Track your GPS location: Many spyware apps secretly track your phone's location in real time, allowing the hacker to know where you are at any moment.
- Turn on your microphone or camera: Spyware can secretly activate your phone's camera or microphone, letting hackers see and hear you without your knowledge.

2. If Your Laptop Gets Hacked
Your laptop is a goldmine for hackers because it often contains all your passwords, personal documents, and browsing history. Here's what a hacker can do if they gain control:
- Log every keystroke you type: A keylogger records everything you type, including passwords, credit card info, and private emails.
- Access your webcam: Hackers can remotely activate your webcam to spy on you. If you've ever noticed the webcam light turning on without your permission, it might already be happening.
- Steal sensitive files and photos: Personal files, resumes, contracts, and tax returns stored on your laptop are prime targets. Hackers can upload these files to their own servers.
- Access your saved passwords: If you store passwords in your web browser (like Chrome, Safari, or Firefox), hackers can steal them.
- Install ransomware: A hacker can lock you out of your own device and demand a ransom payment to unlock it.
- Access your email accounts: Many people log into Gmail, Outlook, or work email via laptops, and once a hacker controls your laptop, they have full access to your inbox.

3. If Your IoT Devices Get Hacked

IoT devices (like smart locks, smart cameras, and smart thermostats) often have weak security, making them easy targets for hackers. Here's what a hacker can do if they take control:

- Spy on you through smart cameras: Hackers can watch live feeds from Ring, Nest, and Arlo cameras. There are cases of hackers speaking to children through hacked smart cameras.
- Take control of smart locks: If hackers gain access to smart locks on your home, they can unlock your doors remotely.
- Join your devices to a botnet: Hackers can turn IoT devices into "zombies" used to attack other networks. Your smart fridge, smart TV, or smart lightbulbs could be part of an attack without you knowing it.
- Exploit voice assistants: Hackers can hijack devices like Amazon Alexa or Google Home to give voice commands that purchase items or reveal your personal information.
- Control your thermostat and smart appliances: Hackers can overheat or freeze your home by controlling your smart thermostat. They can also turn on smart ovens, refrigerators, or dryers to cause disruption.

Why This Matters

Hackers know that your phones, laptops, and IoT devices are the key to your identity, finances, and personal security. If they gain control of any one of these devices, they can access your private information, spy on your home, and even steal your bank funds. But it doesn't have to be this way. With the right combination of password security, two-factor authentication, encrypted messaging, and AI-driven monitoring tools, you can prevent hackers from gaining control of your devices.

Up next, we'll cover how to secure each of these devices, starting with phones, laptops, and tablets.

Securing Personal Devices (Phones, Laptops, and Tablets)
Your phone, laptop, and tablet are more than just devices —
they're gateways to your online identity, finances, and personal
security. Hackers know this, which is why they target them with
spyware, ransomware, and phishing apps. The good news? You can
protect yourself with the right tools, apps, and features.

How Hackers Attack Personal Devices
How Hackers Attack Phones
- Spyware Apps: Malicious apps secretly record your phone
  calls, log keystrokes, and track your location.
- SMS Phishing (Smishing): Attackers send text messages with
  malicious links, tricking you into revealing personal
  information.
- App Cloning: Attackers create fake versions of popular apps
  (like banking apps) and trick users into downloading them.
- Zero-Click Exploits: Hackers exploit vulnerabilities in
  messaging apps, like iMessage or WhatsApp, where users don't
  need to click anything for the attack to succeed.

How Hackers Attack Laptops
- Keyloggers: Small malware files that secretly record every
  keystroke you type, including passwords, emails, and payment
  details.
- Ransomware: Attackers lock you out of your laptop and
  demand a ransom to unlock it.
- Phishing Emails: Fake emails with links to fraudulent login
  pages steal your credentials.
- Drive-by Downloads: Simply visiting a compromised website
  can install malware on your laptop.

How to Protect Your Devices (Tools, Apps, and Features)

1. Phone Security Tools & Features
Use an Authenticator App (Not SMS 2FA)
- Why it Matters: Hackers can steal SMS 2FA codes using a
  SIM-swap attack, but apps like Authy (https://authy.com/) and
  Google Authenticator (https://google.com/) make this
  impossible.
- How to Do It:
  a. Install Authy or Google Authenticator on your phone.
  b. Update your 2FA methods on Google, Facebook, and
     banking apps to use the authenticator app instead of SMS.
- Install Anti-Spyware & Malware Detection Apps
- Why it Matters: Spyware can steal your calls, messages, and
  GPS location without you knowing.

- Tools to Use:
  - Malwarebytes Mobile (https://www.malwarebytes.com/) for Android phones.
  - Lookout Mobile Security (https://www.lookout.com/) for iOS and Android devices.
- How to Do It: Download one of these apps and scan your phone for malware and spyware.

Use Lock Screens & Biometric Authentication
- Why it Matters: If your phone is stolen, a thief can access everything unless you lock it.
- How to Do It:
  - Use biometric security (fingerprint or face unlock).
  - Set a 6-digit PIN instead of a 4-digit PIN.
  - Set a "lock screen timeout" so your phone locks after 30 seconds of inactivity.

Prevent Spyware by Managing App Permissions
- Why it Matters: Apps often ask for unnecessary permissions (like access to your location, contacts, and camera).
- How to Do It:
  a. Go to Settings　Privacy.
  b. Review which apps have access to your microphone, camera, contacts, and GPS.
  c. Turn off access for any app that doesn't absolutely need it.

Activate Device Encryption
- Why it Matters: If a thief steals your phone, encryption ensures they can't access your files.
- How to Do It:
  - For iPhone: It's enabled by default if you set up a passcode.
  - For Android: Go to Settings　Security　Encrypt Device.

2. Laptop Security Tools & Features
Full-Disk Encryption (FDE)
- Why it Matters: If a hacker steals your laptop, they can access files on the hard drive — unless it's encrypted.
- Tools to Use:
  - BitLocker (for Windows 10/11) — Built-in encryption tool.
  - FileVault (for macOS) — Apple's built-in full-disk encryption.
- How to Do It:
  - On Windows, go to Settings　Update & Security　Device Encryption.
  - On macOS, enable FileVault in System Preferences　Security & Privacy.

Use a Password Manager
- Why it Matters: Storing passwords in your browser is risky. A password manager keeps your passwords encrypted.
- Tools to Use:
  - 1Password (https://1password.com/)
  - Bitwarden (https://bitwarden.com/)
- How to Do It:
  - Download a password manager.
  - Import existing passwords and create strong, unique passwords for each site.

Anti-Malware & Anti-Phishing Protection
- Why it Matters: Hackers use malware and phishing emails to trick users into downloading malicious files.
- Tools to Use:
  - Malwarebytes (https://www.malwarebytes.com/) for malware protection.
  - Bitdefender (https://www.bitdefender.com/) for real-time threat detection.
- How to Do It:
  - Install Bitdefender or Malwarebytes and enable real-time scanning.

Securing IoT Devices (Smart Locks, Smart Cameras, and Smart Home Hubs)
How Hackers Exploit IoT Devices
How IoT Devices Are Exploited
- Default Passwords: Most IoT devices ship with default logins like "admin" and "password."
- Unpatched Firmware: Manufacturers fail to update IoT firmware, leaving devices open to attack.
- Open Ports: IoT devices often have open ports that hackers can scan and attack remotely.

How to Lock Down IoT Devices (Tools, Tips, and Best Practices)
1. Change Default Passwords on IoT Devices
- Why it Matters: Hackers scan the web for IoT devices with default passwords.
- How to Do It:
  - Log into your router, smart cameras, or smart home hub.
  - Change the default password to a strong, random password.

2. Turn Off Remote Access
- Why it Matters: If you can access your device remotely, so can hackers.
- How to Do It:
    - Turn off "Remote Access" in the settings for devices like Ring, Nest, and Arlo cameras.

3. Keep Firmware Updated
- Why it Matters: Many IoT devices have unpatched vulnerabilities.
- How to Do It:
    a. Go to your device's settings.
    b. Enable Automatic Updates or check for updates weekly.

4. Use a Firewall for Your Entire Network
- Why it Matters: A network-level firewall blocks malicious traffic before it reaches your IoT devices.
- Tools to Use:
    - Firewalla (https://firewalla.com/) — Monitors every device on your network.
    - Bitdefender BOX (https://www.bitdefender.com/solutions/box.html/) — Scans for device threats.
- How to Do It:
    - Install a Firewalla device on your network.
    - It will alert you if a new device connects, allowing you to block or approve it.

5. Disable Unnecessary Features
- Why it Matters: Features like UPnP (Universal Plug and Play) create unnecessary vulnerabilities.
- How to Do It:
    - Access your router's settings.
    - Disable UPnP, remote access, and guest Wi-Fi.

6. Use AI-Driven IoT Monitoring
- Why it Matters: AI-powered tools like Firewalla can detect and block unusual activity on your smart home devices.
- How to Do It:
    - Install Firewalla to track smart camera activity.
    - Get real-time alerts if a hacker tries to control your camera or smart lock.

AI-Driven Device Monitoring
How AI Identifies "Normal" Behavior
Imagine having a personal security guard for every device you own
— your phone, laptop, smart cameras, and smart locks. But unlike
a human guard, this one never sleeps, never takes breaks, and can
detect subtle changes in device behavior that humans would miss.
This is the power of AI-driven device monitoring.

AI doesn't just block known threats. It actively learns the "normal
behavior" of your devices. It tracks when you log in, where you log
in from, which apps you use, and when you use them. If anything
unusual happens — like a sudden login from another country or a
smart camera turning on at 3 AM — AI detects it instantly.

Here's how AI defines "normal" behavior for each device:
- Phones: Tracks location, time of day, app usage, and login
  history.
- Laptops: Tracks mouse movements, login times, locations, and
  browser usage.
- IoT Devices: Monitors when devices turn on/off, device activity
  times, and IP addresses used.

Example: If your Ring camera turns on at 3 AM, but it's usually off
at that time, AI will flag it. This could be an early sign of someone
trying to control the camera remotely.

Pro Tip: AI doesn't just monitor your devices — it predicts
potential threats. If it sees a pattern (like repeated failed login
attempts on your phone), it can trigger an automatic lockdown or
alert you.

**How AI Tracks Unusual Activity on Phones, Laptops, and IoT
Devices**
When a hacker takes control of one of your devices, they act
differently than you. AI knows how you behave and recognizes
patterns. If a hacker does something unusual, AI spots it. Here are
a few examples of how AI tracks unusual activity:

1. Phone Tracking
- New Device Logins: If your Apple ID or Google account is
  accessed from a new device, AI notices.
- Unusual Locations: If your phone is accessed from a country
  you've never been to, AI flags it.
- Unauthorized App Permissions: Some apps secretly request
  new permissions (like access to your microphone or camera) —
  AI can spot this behavior.

- Unusual Battery Usage: Spyware apps use battery power in the background. If battery usage spikes for no reason, AI can detect it.

What You Can Do:
- Enable Google Play Protect on Android.
- Use apps like Lookout Mobile Security to monitor app permissions and device activity.
- Use Find My iPhone and Find My Device (Android) to track and lock lost or stolen phones.

2. Laptop Tracking
- New IP Logins: If your Gmail or social media accounts are accessed from a different IP address (like a hacker's VPN), AI flags it.
- Sudden Spike in CPU Usage: If malware or ransomware is running, you'll see a CPU usage spike. AI can detect this and block it.
- Unusual File Access: If a file you haven't touched in months is suddenly opened, AI can alert you.
- USB Device Insertion: If someone inserts a USB drive into your laptop (like in a hotel, airport, or shared workspace), AI tracks it.

What You Can Do:
- Install Malwarebytes (https://www.malwarebytes.com/) for real-time threat detection.
- Enable IP-based security notifications for your accounts (like Google or Microsoft).
- Turn on Ransomware Protection in tools like Bitdefender (https://www.bitdefender.com/).

3. IoT Device Tracking
- New Device Connections: If a new smart device (like a rogue security camera) tries to connect to your Wi-Fi, AI blocks it.
- Unusual Device Activity: If a smart camera suddenly activates at an odd time, AI flags it as abnormal.
- Botnet Detection: If your IoT device (like a smart plug) starts sending excessive data packets, it may have been recruited into a botnet like Mirai.
- Open Port Detection: AI scans for open ports on IoT devices and alerts you to potential threats.

What You Can Do:
- Use Firewalla (https://firewalla.com/) to monitor every device on your network.

- Install Bitdefender BOX
  (https://www.bitdefender.com/solutions/box.html/) for
  complete network-level protection.
- Regularly check for open ports using tools like ShieldsUP by
  Gibson Research.

Tools to Monitor and Control All Devices on Your Network
Now that you know how AI identifies threats, you need to know
the tools that give you full visibility and control of every device
connected to your network. With the right tools, you'll know if a
new device tries to connect, if your smart lock is accessed at 2 AM,
or if a hacker is attempting a brute-force login on your laptop.

1. Firewalla (https://firewalla.com/)
- What It Does: Monitors every device on your home network
  for unusual activity.
- How It Works: Alerts you when new devices join your Wi-Fi or
  if IoT devices behave abnormally.
- How It Helps: Blocks unknown devices, flags unusual activity,
  and protects your home network from threats.

2. Bitdefender BOX
(https://www.bitdefender.com/solutions/box.html/)
- What It Does: Protects every device on your home network —
  from laptops to smart TVs and IoT devices.
- How It Works: Scans for malware, botnet attacks, and
  abnormal device behavior.
- How It Helps: Prevents devices from being recruited into
  botnets, detects new devices, and notifies you of suspicious
  activity.

3. Fing (https://www.fing.com/)
- What It Does: Lists every device on your network so you can
  see who's connected.
- How It Works: Scans for new devices and notifies you when
  new ones connect.
- How It Helps: Identify devices you don't recognize, such as a
  hacker's phone or laptop connected to your network.

IoT Vulnerabilities and Emerging Threats
The Internet of Things (IoT) has rapidly become a vital part of
everyday life, with billions of smart devices controlling everything
from home security cameras to industrial control systems. While
IoT offers convenience, automation, and efficiency, it also expands
the attack surface for cybercriminals. Unlike traditional devices,
IoT devices often lack strong security protections, making them
prime targets for hackers.

Why It Matters:
The number of IoT devices is expected to reach over 75 billion by
2025, and each device represents a potential entry point for
attackers. Cybercriminals have already exploited IoT vulnerabilities
in botnet attacks, ransomware schemes, and supply chain attacks,
often using AI-powered tools to scan for weak devices. The stakes
are even higher when these devices are used in hospitals, factories,
and critical infrastructure.

This section breaks down the most pressing IoT vulnerabilities,
provides real-world case studies, and offers practical defenses that
individuals and businesses can implement.

**1. Case Study: The Mirai Botnet — The Attack That Changed
Everything**
What Happened?
In 2016, a group of attackers created the Mirai botnet, which
infected over 600,000 IoT devices such as IP cameras, DVRs, and
baby monitors. By exploiting devices with weak default passwords,
the attackers turned these devices into a powerful botnet army that
could launch Distributed Denial of Service (DDoS) attacks.

The Attack:
On October 21, 2016, the Mirai botnet launched a DDoS attack on
Dyn, a major DNS service provider. As a result, major platforms
like Twitter, Netflix, Reddit, and Spotify were knocked offline for
hours.

How It Worked:
- Attackers scanned the internet for IoT devices with
  weak/default credentials.
- Once a device was identified, Mirai installed malware that
  allowed it to become part of a botnet.
- The botnet sent a flood of traffic to Dyn, overwhelming its
  servers and causing internet outages across the U.S.

Key Takeaway:
The Mirai botnet demonstrated how default passwords could be exploited on a mass scale. Devices like baby monitors, smart locks, and security cameras became soldiers in a botnet army, attacking critical services. This attack highlighted the need for strong passwords, firmware updates, and IoT-specific firewalls.

How to Defend Against It:
- Change default passwords on all IoT devices.
- Use IoT firewalls to block unauthorized connections.
- Implement anomaly detection to identify and quarantine rogue IoT devices.

2. Advanced IoT Threats: Hardware Backdoors, Ransomware, and API Exploits

Attackers are constantly looking for new ways to infiltrate IoT devices. While the Mirai botnet exploited weak passwords, modern attacks are becoming more advanced. Hackers now target hardware, firmware, and APIs to gain persistent control over IoT devices.

Hardware Backdoors
Some IoT devices are manufactured with pre-installed backdoors. These hidden access points allow manufacturers (and sometimes attackers) to bypass security protocols and control devices remotely.
- Example: Certain IP cameras and smart home hubs have been found to contain secret admin accounts that cannot be disabled.
- How to Defend: Only purchase devices from trusted brands with strict supply chain security audits.

Ransomware on IoT Devices
Attackers can "brick" (permanently disable) IoT devices using ransomware. This is known as a bricking attack, where the device becomes unusable unless the victim pays a ransom.
- Example: Attackers could lock a business's smart thermostats during a heatwave, demanding payment to restore functionality.
- How to Defend: Regularly update IoT firmware and keep backups of device configurations.

API Exploits
IoT devices use APIs (Application Programming Interfaces) to communicate with cloud services. Attackers exploit weak APIs to send malicious commands to IoT devices.
- Example: Attackers exploited APIs in the Tuya Smart Home platform, giving them remote control over thousands of smart home devices.
- How to Defend: Implement API security tools like API gateways and limit API permissions for third-party apps.

3. Emerging IoT Threats (2024-2030) — What to Expect Next
The future of IoT security is deeply tied to the rise of 5G networks, autonomous vehicles, and smart cities. As connectivity increases, so do attack vectors. Here are the top emerging threats on the horizon:

5G-Driven IoT Attacks
With 5G networks enabling more IoT connections than ever, attackers have more targets to choose from. Since 5G operates at faster speeds and lower latency, attackers can launch botnet attacks faster and with more precision.
- Example: In a 5G-enabled smart city, attackers could use IoT sensors from traffic lights, cameras, and connected vehicles to coordinate a large-scale DDoS attack.
- How to Defend: Use network segmentation to isolate IoT devices from each other and from critical systems.

AI-Driven IoT Malware
Attackers are using AI to develop polymorphic malware that adapts and mutates its code. This makes it nearly impossible for traditional antivirus software to detect.
- Example: AI-driven malware could target industrial IoT (IIoT) devices in smart factories. Once installed, it could evolve, rewrite its own code, and evade detection for months.
- How to Defend: Use AI-driven Endpoint Detection and Response (EDR) to detect malware based on behavior instead of code signatures.

Cyber-Physical Attacks via IoT
IoT devices are now embedded in critical infrastructure (like power grids, healthcare devices, and factory robots). Attackers can use IoT vulnerabilities to cause physical harm.
- Example: A hacker could disable IoT-controlled medical devices (like infusion pumps) in a hospital.
- How to Defend: Implement air-gapped networks for critical infrastructure, which physically separate devices from the internet.

4. How to Defend Against IoT Vulnerabilities
The best approach to IoT security is a combination of Zero-Trust principles, AI-driven anomaly detection, and strong device management. Here's a summary of how to defend against IoT threats:
1. Adopt Zero-Trust for IoT Devices
   - Assume every IoT device is untrustworthy by default.
   - Only allow explicit access permissions for devices.
   - Restrict IoT communication to essential services only.
2. Update Firmware Automatically
   - Ensure automatic firmware updates are enabled for all IoT devices.
   - If an update cannot be automated, use a checklist to ensure devices are updated monthly.
3. Anomaly Detection for IoT
   - Use AI-driven anomaly detection to monitor unusual device behavior.
   - If a device starts sending data to a foreign IP address, it should be flagged immediately.
4. Encrypt IoT Data
   - Implement end-to-end encryption for all IoT communications.
   - Use VPNs for IoT devices that need to communicate with cloud services.
5. Use IoT-Specific Firewalls
   - Install dedicated IoT firewalls (like Firewalla or Palo Alto IoT Security) to filter inbound and outbound traffic.

Chapter Conclusion: Lock Down Your Devices — Stay Ahead of Tomorrow's Threats
Your phone, laptop, and smart home devices are no longer just personal tools — they are gateways to your finances, identity, and family security. If a hacker takes control of even one of these devices, they can infiltrate your entire digital life. From accessing bank accounts and stealing personal photos to taking over your smart home security system, the consequences can be devastating. But you're not helpless. With the right approach, you can lock down your devices and fortify your personal security. By leveraging the latest advances in AI-driven security tools, anomaly detection, and Zero-Trust architecture, you can stay ahead of even the most sophisticated attackers.

Attackers are looking for low-hanging fruit — unencrypted devices, default passwords, and outdated firmware. But when you implement the right security protocols, you make it too difficult for attackers, and they'll move on to an easier target. Locking down your devices isn't just protection — it's prevention.

Final Checklist: Lock Down Your Devices
1. Phones
Your phone is the ultimate attack target because it contains passwords, email access, bank logins, and messaging apps. Here's how to secure it:
- Enable device encryption on iOS or Android.
  - iOS Encryption Guide: https://support.apple.com/guide/iphone/encrypt-your-iphone-iphf8c74f083/ios
  - Android Encryption Guide: https://support.google.com/android/answer/9456711?hl=en
- Use Authenticator apps (like Authy or Google Authenticator) for two-factor authentication (2FA) instead of SMS.
  - Download Authy: https://authy.com/download/
- Install spyware and malware detection apps like Lookout Mobile Security.
  - Lookout Mobile Security: https://www.lookout.com/
- Set strong PINs (at least 6 digits) and enable biometric security (Face ID, fingerprint).
- Avoid using auto-fill for passwords on your mobile browser. Use a password manager instead (like Bitwarden or 1Password).
  - Get Bitwarden: https://bitwarden.com/
  - Get 1Password: https://1password.com/

2. Laptops
Your laptop is where most work, finances, and personal information are stored. It's a hacker's dream to gain access to your files. Here's how to lock it down:
- Turn on disk encryption (use FileVault on macOS or BitLocker on Windows) to secure your files.
  - FileVault Encryption Guide for macOS: https://support.apple.com/en-us/HT204837
  - BitLocker Guide for Windows: https://support.microsoft.com/en-us/windows/bitlocker-overview-and-requirements-46b3b04f-dcfd-76a7-6323-8f29fa9e2376
- Install anti-malware tools like Malwarebytes, Norton, or Bitdefender.
  - Download Malwarebytes: https://www.malwarebytes.com/
  - Download Norton Antivirus: https://us.norton.com/
  - Download Bitdefender: https://www.bitdefender.com/
- Use a password manager (like Bitwarden or LastPass) to store and generate strong, unique passwords for all your accounts.
  - Get Bitwarden: https://bitwarden.com/
  - Get LastPass: https://www.lastpass.com/

- Set a strong login password (use a passphrase, not a simple password) and enable auto-lock after 5 minutes of inactivity.
- Turn on firewall protection on Windows (Windows Defender Firewall) or macOS (Firewall in System Preferences).
  - Windows Defender Firewall Guide: https://support.microsoft.com/en-us/windows/turn-microsoft-defender-firewall-on-or-off-ec0847eb-3b75-483e-8e1d-4e39d6f46542
  - macOS Firewall Setup: https://support.apple.com/guide/mac-help/block-connections-with-the-firewall-on-mac-mchlp2591/mac

3. IoT Devices (Smart Locks, Smart Cameras, Smart Hubs)
IoT devices control our homes, from thermostats to security cameras. Hackers can use them as backdoors to access your network. Here's how to secure them:
- Change default passwords on every smart device.
- Install an IoT security firewall like Firewalla, Armis, or Bitdefender BOX.
  - Get Firewalla: https://firewalla.com/
  - Learn More About Armis: https://www.armis.com/
  - Get Bitdefender BOX: https://www.bitdefender.com/box/
- Disable Universal Plug and Play (UPnP) on your router. This feature allows devices to talk to each other, but hackers can also use it to infiltrate your devices.
- Install firmware updates for IoT devices regularly to patch known vulnerabilities.
- Segment your network: Use a guest network for IoT devices so they can't directly communicate with your main network.
  - How to Set Up a Guest WiFi Network: https://www.howtogeek.com/425735/how-to-set-up-a-guest-wi-fi-network-in-your-home/

Call-to-Action: Take Control of Your Device Security
"Your phone, laptop, and smart home devices are your most vulnerable targets. If a hacker gets control of your devices, they get access to everything."

But it doesn't have to be that way. Here's what to do next:
1. Install Firewalla or Bitdefender BOX to monitor your smart home.
- Firewalla: https://firewalla.com/
- Bitdefender BOX: https://www.bitdefender.com/box/

2. Encrypt your devices (phones, laptops, tablets) with FileVault or BitLocker.
- FileVault Setup: https://support.apple.com/en-us/HT204837
- BitLocker Setup: https://support.microsoft.com/en-us/windows/bitlocker-overview-and-requirements-46b3b04f-dcfd-76a7-6323-8f29fa9e2376

3. Install AI-driven security tools like Malwarebytes, Lookout, and Authy.
- Malwarebytes: https://www.malwarebytes.com/
- Lookout Mobile Security: https://www.lookout.com/
- Authy: https://authy.com/download/

4. Enable MFA (Multi-Factor Authentication) on all devices and accounts. Use an app like Authy or Google Authenticator instead of SMS-based 2FA.
- Authy: https://authy.com/download/
- Google Authenticator: https://support.google.com/accounts/answer/1066447?hl=en

The Future of Device Security
The future of device security will be defined by AI vs. AI — AI-driven attackers vs. AI-driven defenders. While attackers use AI to automate attacks, defenders are fighting back with AI anomaly detection, Zero-Trust architecture, and adaptive endpoint defenses. Your phone, laptop, and IoT devices are on the frontlines of this battle.

New threats are constantly emerging. AI-driven malware, deepfake attacks, and ransomware on IoT devices are on the rise. Your defense should evolve too. The key to staying secure is to adopt an approach of continuous learning, constant updating, and critical thinking.

Remember: Attackers are looking for the easy targets. By following the checklist provided here, you make yourself a hard target. Hackers want fast, easy wins, and a secured device isn't worth their time. Take action today and you'll be ahead of 95% of people still using weak passwords, outdated software, and default device settings.

"Don't wait for an attack to lock down your devices. Take action now, because the next attack is already being planned."

With the right AI-driven protection, Zero-Trust principles, and strong encryption, you can keep your family, business, and personal identity safe. Your phone, laptop, and smart devices aren't just electronics — they're digital keys to your life. It's time to lock them down for good.

Chapter 12: Email & Password Security

How to protect your email accounts and passwords from hackers using MFA, passwordless authentication, and AI-resistant strategies.

Why Email & Password Security Matters
Your email account is the master key to your entire digital life. If a hacker gains access to your email, they can reset passwords for every app, bank account, and social media profile you own. From there, they can steal your identity, drain your bank accounts, and impersonate you.

But email accounts aren't just hacked by guessing passwords anymore. Hackers now use AI-driven password cracking tools that can predict and guess passwords at speeds no human could match. If you're using an old, simple password like "123456" or "password123", these AI tools can crack it in milliseconds.

This chapter will teach you how to:
- Create uncrackable passwords that resist AI-driven attacks.
- Enable MFA (Multi-Factor Authentication) to lock down your email.
- Use biometrics and passwordless authentication to eliminate the need for passwords entirely.
- Prevent AI-driven password cracking and protect your digital identity.

By the end of this chapter, you'll have a bulletproof strategy to secure your email and passwords against any threat — human or AI.

How Hackers Crack Passwords
To protect yourself from hackers, you first need to understand how they attack your passwords. Hackers no longer rely on trial-and-error guessing. They use AI-powered tools that can crack billions of password combinations in seconds.

How Passwords Get Hacked
1. Brute Force Attacks
Hackers use AI-powered password cracking tools that try every possible combination of letters, numbers, and symbols. These tools can attempt millions of guesses per second.
- How It Works: The AI generates every possible combination (like "aaaa," "aaab," "aaac," etc.) until it finds your password.

- How Fast It Works: AI tools like Hashcat and John the Ripper can try 100 billion password combinations per second.
- How to Defend Against It: Use a long password (16+ characters), and avoid simple words or patterns like "abc123."

2. Dictionary Attacks
Instead of guessing random letters, hackers use "dictionaries" of commonly used passwords (like "password123" or "qwerty").
- How It Works: Hackers load a file containing millions of commonly used passwords and check if yours is one of them.
- Example: If you use "ILoveCats2024", it's in most hacker dictionaries.
- How to Defend Against It: Use randomized passwords instead of meaningful ones. Tools like Bitwarden or 1Password can generate complex, random passwords.

3. Credential Stuffing
If one of your passwords gets leaked in a data breach, hackers will try that same password on all your other accounts.
- How It Works: Hackers buy stolen password databases on the dark web and try them on other websites.
- Example: If your email and password from an old MySpace account are leaked, hackers will try those same credentials on Gmail, PayPal, and Facebook.
- How to Defend Against It: Use different passwords for every account and enable MFA (Multi-Factor Authentication).

4. Phishing Attacks
Hackers trick you into revealing your password by sending fake emails that mimic real companies.
- How It Works: You receive an email that looks like it's from PayPal or Google. The email says, "Your account is at risk — click here to log in." If you click, you're sent to a fake login page. If you enter your password, hackers steal it.
- How to Defend Against It: Use a password manager like Bitwarden or 1Password. These tools recognize fake websites and won't autofill your credentials on phishing pages.

5. AI-Driven Attacks (The New Frontier)
AI can predict human behavior, and it can predict your passwords too.
- How It Works: AI analyzes leaked passwords from past data breaches to detect human patterns (like common words, pet names, and birth years).
- Example: If you use a password like "Emma2024", AI predicts it because it knows humans like to combine names and years.

- How to Defend Against It: Use a random password generator from tools like Bitwarden. The more random and long the password is, the harder it is for AI to crack.

6. AI-Powered Phishing and Deepfakes
Hackers now use AI-driven phishing emails and deepfakes to trick you into revealing your passwords through hyper-personalized messages, video calls, and voice impersonation scams.

How It Works:
AI tools like GPT-style language models generate emails that look like official messages from companies like Microsoft, Google, or PayPal. These messages are personalized, free of spelling errors, and designed to trigger urgency. Attackers also use AI-powered deepfakes to impersonate company executives or family members in video calls or phone calls. The impersonator may claim to be in a rush, asking for urgent access to passwords, login credentials, or security codes.

Example:
An employee receives a video call from what appears to be their CEO, urgently asking for access to an admin account. The "CEO" is actually a deepfake video call created by hackers using AI. The employee, believing it's a real emergency, shares the password, giving attackers full access to the company's network.

How to Defend Against It:
- Verify all video and voice calls. If someone calls asking for access to sensitive systems, confirm their identity via a second channel, like Slack or SMS.
- Use tools like Deepware Scanner to detect deepfakes in video calls.
- Train employees on the "Family Password" strategy (discussed in Chapter 12) to protect against deepfake voice impersonations.
- Use phishing protection tools like Proofpoint and Microsoft Defender for Office 365 to block AI-generated phishing emails.

AI-Powered Phishing: Smarter, Faster, and Harder to Detect
Attackers no longer need to write phishing emails by hand. With the power of AI-driven natural language generation (like ChatGPT-style models), cybercriminals can produce thousands of realistic, perfectly written phishing emails in minutes. These messages are free of spelling errors, formatted like official company announcements, and even customized using your personal information from social media, leaked data breaches, and online profiles.

Why It's Dangerous:
Unlike older phishing emails that were obvious due to bad grammar and "Nigerian prince" storylines, AI-powered phishing emails look professional and perfectly mimic emails from real companies. Attackers can even use AI to predict what message will trigger your emotions (like fear, urgency, or curiosity) to make you click. Imagine receiving an email that says:

"Suspicious Login Alert: We've detected login activity on your account from Los Angeles, California. Click here to verify it was you."

Since the message mimics alerts from Google, Facebook, and other platforms, most people click on the link without thinking. Once they enter their password on the fake page, attackers steal it.

How to Defend Against It:
- Use multi-factor authentication (MFA) so that even if attackers steal your password, they still can't log in.
- Don't trust "Urgent Login Alerts" sent via email. Instead, go directly to the app (like Gmail) to check for alerts.
- Enable AI-driven phishing detection tools like Proofpoint or Microsoft Defender for Office 365 to block phishing emails before they reach your inbox.

How to Protect Your Email & Passwords
Now that you know how hackers attack, it's time to build a fortress of protection. The following steps will keep your email and passwords uncrackable, unhackable, and untouchable.

1. Use MFA (Multi-Factor Authentication)
Even if a hacker steals your password, they won't be able to log in if you have MFA enabled. MFA requires a second step (like a phone app or fingerprint) to access your account.

How to Enable It:
- Download an Authenticator App: Use Authy (https://authy.com/) or Google Authenticator (https://google.com/).
- Turn on MFA: Log into your email accounts (like Gmail, Outlook, and Apple) and activate 2-Step Verification.
- Avoid SMS-Based 2FA: SMS can be intercepted through SIM-swap attacks, so use an authenticator app instead.

2. Use Biometrics & Passwordless Authentication

Passwords can be stolen, but your fingerprint, face, or retina scan can't. Modern phones, laptops, and apps support passwordless authentication.

How It Works:
- Biometrics: Use your fingerprint or face to log in instead of a password.
- Passkeys: Websites like Google and Apple support "passkeys" that let you log in with FaceID or TouchID instead of a password.
- Hardware Tokens: Physical devices like YubiKey (https://yubico.com/) create an unhackable second layer of security.

What You Can Do:
- Enable biometric login on Gmail, Microsoft, and PayPal accounts.
- Use YubiKey for physical key-based logins.
- Switch to passwordless login where possible (many companies now support it).

3. Use Strong, Random Passwords

The most important rule: Don't create your own passwords. Let AI do it for you.

How to Create Uncrackable Passwords:
- Use a Password Manager: Use Bitwarden (https://bitwarden.com/) or 1Password (https://1password.com/).
- Generate Random Passwords: Create passwords like vT9!xs84Jn&5Zq.
- Use Unique Passwords for Every Account: If one password gets leaked, you won't lose access to everything.

4. Use a Password Manager

Remembering passwords is hard. That's why people reuse the same ones. Stop doing that. A password manager stores your passwords securely and autofills them when needed.

Best Tools for Password Management:
- Bitwarden (https://bitwarden.com/) — Free, open-source, encrypted vault.
- 1Password (https://1password.com/) — Paid service with family sharing options.

How It Works:
- Store your passwords in a password vault.
- Autofill passwords when you log in.
- Never reuse passwords.

Create a Family Password: Your Best Defense Against AI Voice Cloning Attacks

The Story: How a Hacker Stole a Family's Trust
Meet Sarah, a working mom with two kids. One day, she receives a call from a familiar voice — her brother, Jake. He sounds stressed.

"Hey, I'm in a bind right now. My wallet was stolen, and I'm stranded. Can you send me $1,500 via Venmo?"

The voice sounds exactly like Jake. Same tone, same speech patterns, and even his quirky way of pausing before certain words. Sarah is alarmed but wants to help her brother, so she transfers the money immediately.

Later that day, she texts Jake to check on him. But Jake replies:

"What are you talking about? I never called you."

That's when Sarah realizes she's been scammed. But how did it happen?

Here's the shocking truth: AI voice cloning technology was used to recreate her brother's voice. Hackers had called Jake days earlier with a "robocall" scam. When Jake answered, the hacker's system recorded just 10 seconds of his voice. This small recording was enough for the AI to replicate his voice — and with it, they scammed his sister.

This story is not an exaggeration. Attacks like this are happening today. With the rise of AI-driven voice cloning tools like ElevenLabs, Resemble AI, and Voice.ai, hackers can recreate a person's voice with just 10 to 20 seconds of recorded speech. This is why it's critical to create a Family Password that even the best AI can't guess or replicate.

How AI Voice Cloning Works
1. The Hacker Calls & Records a Voice
   - A hacker places a robocall to someone in your family (like Jake).
   - When Jake answers the phone and says, "Hello, who is this?" the AI captures those few words.
2. AI Clones the Voice in Seconds
   - The hacker runs Jake's voice through an AI tool like ElevenLabs or Voice.ai.
   - The AI creates a model of Jake's voice, mimicking his speech patterns, tone, and inflection.
3. The Hacker Calls a Family Member (Sarah)
   - The hacker, using the cloned voice, calls Sarah pretending to be Jake.
   - They sound so realistic that Sarah believes she's talking to her brother.
4. They Trick You Into Sending Money or Info
   - The hacker asks for personal information (like a birth date) or requests an urgent transfer of funds.
   - Since Sarah trusts the voice on the line, she complies.

This technique is called AI-Driven Impersonation Fraud, and it's becoming one of the fastest-growing attack methods today. Voice cloning, AI-powered robocalls, and voice synthesis are no longer sci-fi concepts — they are happening right now.

Why You Need a Family Password
If someone calls you, claiming to be a family member, how can you tell it's them? You might recognize their voice, but as we've seen, AI can replicate voices perfectly.

That's where a Family Password comes in. Think of it as a secret shared only by you and your loved ones. It's not stored on any phone, laptop, or smart speaker. It's a human-level authentication tool that can't be cloned or stolen.

Here's how it works:
- If you receive a call from someone claiming to be a family member, ask them a specific question related to the Family Password.
- For example:
  - "What is the 20th letter of our family password?"
  - "What is the second word of our family password?"
- Since only family members know the password, a hacker (and their AI) won't be able to answer.

How to Create a Family Password
Step 1: Get the Family Together
Gather everyone who needs to be included in the Family Password. This includes parents, siblings, and children who are old enough to understand.

Important: Leave all electronic devices in another room. No phones, laptops, tablets, smartwatches, or smart speakers (like Alexa, Siri, or Google Home) should be present. Why? Because these devices can listen, record, and store information. You don't want your Family Password being recorded.

Step 2: Choose a Song Everyone Knows
Pick a song that every family member knows. This could be:
- A favorite childhood song
- A family favorite from road trips
- A hit from a classic movie or TV show

Why a Song?
- Everyone remembers songs, so it's easier for the whole family to recall.
- Songs are long, so you'll have a large "pool" of letters to choose from.
- It's hard for an AI to guess a password that's a chorus from a song.

Step 3: Choose a Chorus (or 4 Lines) as the Password
Pick a memorable part of the song — typically the chorus. Here's an example:

♫ "Don't stop believin', Hold on to that feelin', Streetlights, people, oh-oh-oh" ♫

For this example, you'll use only the letters (not punctuation) to create the Family Password. So, it looks like this:

DontstopbelievinHoldontothatfeelinStreetlightspeopleohohoh

This long password is impossible for hackers (and their AI) to guess. It contains lowercase letters, uppercase letters, and randomness that can't be predicted.

Step 4: Practice Using the Family Password
Make sure everyone knows the Family Password. To test it, ask questions like:
- "What is the 16th letter of our Family Password?"
- "What is the 3rd word of our Family Password?"

Since everyone in the family knows the song, they can count the letters or words to answer. But here's the key: A hacker using an AI voice clone won't know how to answer.

Step 5: NEVER Store the Password on Any Device
Don't write the Family Password on your phone, laptop, or notepad app. The whole purpose is to ensure no device ever knows it. This ensures AI voice bots, malware, and hackers can't steal it. Keep it in your head and in your heart, not on paper.

How the Family Password Stops Hackers
When a hacker calls and pretends to be a family member, you have a built-in security test:
1. Ask a Verification Question
- "What's the 20th letter of our Family Password?"
- "What's the 4th word of our Family Password?"

2. Wait for Their Answer
If the person on the other end pauses, hesitates, or gets it wrong, you know it's a scam. A real family member will know it instantly.

3. If They Fail, Hang Up
If the caller fails, hang up and call the family member directly. Do not call back the same number — the scammer may have spoofed it.

Chapter Conclusion: Lock Down Your Security with Family Passwords and Strong Email Protection

Hackers are getting smarter, but so are we. AI-driven threats like voice cloning, deepfake impersonations, and credential theft have made it clear that the old methods of "recognizing a voice" or "relying on a strong password" are no longer enough. Attackers aren't just targeting your devices — they're targeting your family, identity, and financial accounts. But with the right strategy, you can outsmart them every time.

Here's the two-part action plan for securing your family and your online identity.

1. Lock Down Your Email & Passwords

If a hacker gains access to your email, they gain access to everything — your bank accounts, social media profiles, and even your personal identity. Your email is the master key to your entire digital life, and protecting it is non-negotiable.

Here's how to secure your email and passwords:
- Use Multi-Factor Authentication (MFA): Add an extra layer of protection with an authenticator app like Authy (https://authy.com/) or Google Authenticator (https://support.google.com/accounts/answer/1066447).
- Switch to Passwordless Login: Use biometrics like FaceID or fingerprint authentication instead of passwords whenever possible.
- Use a Password Manager: Generate strong, random passwords and store them securely using tools like 1Password (https://1password.com/) or Bitwarden (https://bitwarden.com/).
- Never Reuse Passwords: Every account needs a unique password. Reusing passwords gives hackers access to everything if just one of them gets leaked.

Pro Tip: "The most valuable thing a hacker can steal is your email. If they get access, they get everything. But with strong passwords, MFA, and passwordless logins, you can make yourself untouchable."

2. Create a Family Password (Your Best Defense Against Voice Cloning)

With the rise of AI-driven voice cloning, scammers are no longer strangers calling with fake stories — they can now sound exactly like your mom, brother, or child. They know where your loved ones are (thanks to social media) and can even reference specific details that make them seem authentic. This is why it's essential to have a secret Family Password that no AI can guess.

Here's how to create a Family Password:
- Gather the Family: Call a family meeting where everyone agrees on one shared password. This password should be known only to your family and should never be written down or saved on a device.
- Choose a Song or Poem: Select a song that all family members know and like. Use the first few lines (at least 4) as your Family Password.
- Memorize It: Do not store this password on phones, laptops, or voice assistants like Alexa, Siri, or Google Home. It must live only in human memory.
- Verification Questions: If you get a suspicious call claiming to be from family, ask them, "What's the 15th letter of our Family Password?". No AI-driven voice scammer will be able to answer that.

Pro Tip: "Your Family Password is a human-level security key. No AI can predict it, and no hacker can guess it."

Final Takeaway

Attackers are constantly upgrading their tactics, but you now have two of the most powerful defenses on your side:

1. Advanced email security using MFA, passwordless logins, and password managers.

2. The unbreakable Family Password that no AI can predict or replicate.

By following these steps, you'll have a foolproof system for protecting your family, your devices, and your identity. It's time to outthink, out-train, and outsmart the hackers. You now have the tools. All that's left is action.

Chapter 13: Social Engineering & Phishing Defense

How AI improves phishing detection (like scam email filters) and how to recognize scams that slip through AI-based filters.

Why Social Engineering & Phishing Are the #1 Threat
When most people think of cyberattacks, they imagine hackers using advanced code to break into systems. But in reality, 90% of successful hacks start with social engineering — tricking people into giving up their passwords, personal info, or access to secure systems. The most common form of social engineering? Phishing. Phishing attacks are so effective because they target human psychology. Instead of hacking your device, hackers hack your mind. Phishing emails, fake phone calls, and deceptive texts make you feel rushed, scared, or emotional, leading you to click on links or share sensitive information.

Here's the scary part: AI has supercharged phishing. Hackers now use AI to create ultra-realistic phishing emails that are almost impossible to detect. These emails use perfect grammar, mimic trusted brands, and are customized just for you. Worse yet, some phishing attempts slip past even the best AI-powered spam filters.

This chapter will teach you how to:
- Use AI-powered tools to block phishing emails and scam messages.
- Recognize the signs of a phishing scam when they slip past AI filters.
- Protect yourself against social engineering attacks through practical defense strategies.

How Hackers Use Social Engineering & Phishing
What is Social Engineering?
Social engineering is the art of manipulation. Hackers don't just rely on code — they rely on human error. Social engineers use deception, fear, and urgency to trick people into giving up passwords, sending money, or granting access to sensitive systems.

Common Social Engineering Tactics:
- Pretexting: The hacker pretends to be someone trustworthy (like IT support or a bank representative).
- Baiting: The hacker offers something desirable (like a free download) in exchange for login details.
- Phishing: Hackers send fraudulent emails or texts designed to steal your information.

- Vishing (Voice Phishing): Hackers call you pretending to be from "customer support" or "bank fraud protection."
- Tailgating: In physical spaces, a hacker might follow an employee into a secure building without swiping a keycard.

How Phishing Works
Phishing is the most popular form of social engineering because it's cheap, scalable, and highly effective. It's responsible for 90% of all breaches. Here's how it works:

1. The Setup: Hackers create a fake email, text, or phone call that looks legitimate (like a message from Amazon, Google, or your bank).

2. The Bait: The message contains a sense of urgency (like "Your account has been locked!") or an enticing offer (like "You've won a free iPad!").

3. The Hook: The message includes a link to a fake login page that looks identical to the real website. If you enter your email and password, hackers now have your credentials.

4. The Catch: Once the hacker has your credentials, they log into your bank, social media, or email account, lock you out, and take over.

How AI Supercharges Phishing Attacks
Hackers no longer create phishing emails by hand. AI does it for them. Using natural language processing (NLP), AI-generated phishing emails look almost perfect. The grammar is flawless, the logos are crisp, and the tone feels genuine. Worse still, AI can personalize phishing attacks just for you.

Here's how AI makes phishing more dangerous:
- Personalized Emails: AI tools like ChatGPT can create personalized messages using public data (like your LinkedIn profile).
- Grammar-Perfect Messages: In the past, phishing emails had spelling errors, but with AI, hackers can generate professional, mistake-free messages.
- Custom Email Domains: Hackers register similar-looking email domains (like "paypal.com" instead of "paypal.com") and AI designs them to look identical.
- Real-Time Customization: AI can generate messages "on demand" so every recipient gets a unique email, making them harder for spam filters to detect.

How AI Improves Phishing Detection
While hackers use AI to enhance phishing attacks, cybersecurity defenders also use AI to block them. The good news is that spam filters have become more intelligent than ever before. Email providers like Google, Microsoft, and Yahoo now have AI-powered filters that automatically block phishing messages before they ever reach your inbox.

Here's how AI filters phishing attempts:
1. Email Pattern Analysis
AI scans millions of incoming emails and looks for patterns that suggest phishing.

What It Looks For:
- Suspicious Domains: Does the sender's email look like "paypa1.com" instead of "paypal.com"?
- Link Analysis: AI scans links to see if they point to known malicious websites.
- Urgent Language: Phrases like "Click Now!" or "Urgent Action Required" raise red flags.

2. Machine Learning (ML) Models
AI systems like Google's TensorFlow analyze which emails users flag as spam. Over time, these ML models learn to recognize new phishing techniques.

What It Does:
- Learns from Phishing Reports: If millions of users mark an email as spam, AI learns what to look for in the future.
- Detects New Phishing Tactics: Hackers constantly change their tactics, but AI constantly adapts.

3. Natural Language Processing (NLP)
NLP enables AI to detect tone, intent, and urgency in emails.
What It Detects:
- Urgent Warnings: Messages like "Act Now!" or "Account Suspended!" trigger phishing alerts.
- Request for Personal Info: If the email requests passwords, MFA codes, or SSNs, it's flagged as suspicious.

AI-Powered Phishing Filters (Tools to Use)
- Google Gmail Spam Filter: Gmail's AI blocks 99.9% of phishing emails.
- Microsoft Defender for Office 365: Enterprise-level protection for businesses using Office 365.
- SpamTitan (https://www.spamtitan.com/): AI-powered anti-phishing software for business email.

How to Recognize Phishing Scams (Even When AI Fails)
While AI spam filters are 90% effective, some phishing emails still slip through. That's why you must know how to recognize phishing scams on your own.

How to Recognize Phishing Emails
1. Look at the Sender's Email
   - Hackers use email addresses like paypal.com instead of paypal.com.
   - Check for minor spelling errors in the email address.
2. Check for Urgency
   - Phishing Messages Use Urgency: "Your account has been locked!" or "You have 24 hours to act!"
   - If the email makes you feel rushed, stop and verify it.
3. Hover Over Links
   - Before you click a link, hover over it to see where it goes.
   - If it says paypal.com.support.io, it's fake. Legitimate companies don't use extra domains.
4. Watch for Unusual Requests
   - No legitimate company will ask for your password, MFA code, or Social Security Number.
   - If the message asks for this info, it's 100% a scam.
5. Use an AI-Powered Phishing Detection Tool
   - Use services like Bitdefender, Norton 360, and Microsoft Defender to flag emails before you see them.

Chapter Conclusion: Outsmart Hackers with AI Defense
Social engineering and phishing will never go away. As long as humans make mistakes, hackers will exploit them. But with AI-powered spam filters and personal awareness, you can spot and avoid these scams.

Here's what to do next:
   - Enable AI spam filters in Gmail, Microsoft 365, and Yahoo.
   - Be skeptical of urgent emails (especially those claiming "Your account has been locked!").
   - Learn to identify suspicious links by hovering over them before clicking.
   - Report phishing attempts in your email (this teaches AI filters to block future attacks).

"Hackers will always target the human mind. But with AI-powered spam filters and a sharp eye, you can block phishing scams before they block you."

Chapter 14: Cybersecurity for Remote Work

AI tools for monitoring remote employee behavior and creating a Zero Trust security model for remote work.

The New Normal of Remote Work
Remote work has become the new standard for millions of employees worldwide. While it offers flexibility and freedom, it also comes with serious security risks. Employees now connect to company systems from personal devices, public Wi-Fi, and home networks, creating countless entry points for hackers.

For cybercriminals, this shift is a dream opportunity. No longer do they need to attack a company's well-protected corporate network. Instead, they target unsecured home Wi-Fi routers, personal devices, and shared family networks.

The solution?
1. AI-driven monitoring tools that watch for unusual employee behavior.
2. A Zero Trust security model that assumes every connection is a potential threat.

In this chapter, you'll learn:
- How to use AI tools to monitor remote employee activity.
- How to create a Zero Trust security model to protect sensitive company data.
- Practical steps you can take to secure your remote work environment.

Why Remote Work Poses a Unique Security Challenge
The New Attack Surface
The traditional office network had clear boundaries. Employees worked on-site, used company devices, and connected through a secure firewall. But now, employees are spread out across homes, cafes, hotels, and airports.

This shift has massively expanded the "attack surface" for hackers. Instead of having to penetrate a company's central network, hackers now have a wide range of weaker entry points to attack, such as:
- Personal Wi-Fi routers (often with default passwords)
- Personal laptops and smartphones (which may lack endpoint security)
- Unsecured public Wi-Fi networks (like those in airports and cafes)

The Hacker's Perspective
Here's how hackers see the remote work landscape:
1. Unsecured Devices: Employees use personal laptops with no antivirus or malware protection.
2. Weak Passwords: Home users may use weak passwords on Wi-Fi routers, laptops, and email.
3. Unencrypted Communications: Employees may send sensitive company data over unsecured Wi-Fi.
4. Phishing Emails: Employees are more vulnerable to phishing at home, especially if there's no spam filter.

Real-World Example
During the COVID-19 pandemic, ransomware attacks skyrocketed as hackers targeted remote workers. A single click on a phishing link could lock down an entire company's systems, forcing them to pay millions in ransom.

AI Tools for Monitoring Remote Employee Behavior
Why Monitoring Matters
When employees work from home, IT teams lose the ability to see what's happening on their devices. Are employees accidentally downloading malware? Are they copying sensitive files to personal drives? Without visibility, companies are flying blind.

AI-powered employee monitoring tools fill this visibility gap. They analyze user behavior and look for signs of suspicious activity. If AI sees an employee sending large amounts of data to a personal Gmail account, it raises an alert.

What AI Monitors
AI doesn't just look for malware — it tracks employee behavior to detect insider threats. Here's what it watches for:

1. Unusual File Transfers
- AI tracks if an employee uploads a large number of files to personal cloud storage (like Google Drive, Dropbox, or OneDrive).
- If an employee suddenly transfers 1 GB of files to their personal email, it triggers an alert.

2. Unusual Login Locations
- AI tracks employee logins (location, device, and IP address).
- If the same user logs in from New York at 9 AM and Tokyo at 9:05 AM, AI knows it's a problem.

3. Time-Based Anomalies
- If an employee logs in at 2 AM when they've never done that before, it could be a sign that their account is compromised.

4. Abnormal Device Behavior
- If a laptop suddenly connects to multiple devices (like an external USB drive), it could mean data theft is occurring.
- AI flags unusual file changes on company systems (like deleting thousands of files at once).

Best AI Tools for Remote Work Monitoring
Here are some of the top tools for AI-driven employee monitoring:

1. Teramind (https://www.teramind.co/)
- What It Does: Tracks user activity (screenshots, file transfers, app usage) in real time.
- How It Helps: Monitors remote employees for unusual behavior (like large file transfers).
- AI Features: Uses AI to detect deviations from an employee's normal activity patterns.

2. ActivTrak (https://www.activtrak.com/)
- What It Does: Tracks employee productivity, app usage, and risk indicators.
- How It Helps: Identifies risky employee behavior (like connecting to personal cloud storage).
- AI Features: Uses AI to detect employees who exhibit behaviors consistent with insider threats.

3. Microsoft Defender for Endpoint (https://www.microsoft.com/)
- What It Does: Protects employee devices and detects unusual login locations.
- How It Helps: AI flags impossible logins (like logging in from New York and Tokyo within 5 minutes).
- AI Features: Detects device behavior changes, risky app usage, and phishing attacks.

Creating a Zero Trust Security Model for Remote Work
What is Zero Trust?
Zero Trust is a security model based on one simple idea:

"Trust no one, verify everything."

In a traditional security model, employees inside the office were trusted. But in Zero Trust, every connection must be verified — even if it's coming from a trusted employee. This means every login, every file transfer, and every app connection is double-checked.

How to Implement Zero Trust for Remote Work
Here's how to create a Zero Trust environment for remote work:

1. Use Multi-Factor Authentication (MFA) Everywhere
   - Add an extra step (like a 6-digit code or fingerprint) for every login.
   - Use Google Authenticator or Microsoft Authenticator.
   - Require MFA for access to email, VPNs, and cloud storage.

2. Use Role-Based Access Control (RBAC)
   - Only grant employees access to the files they need.
   - Don't let every employee access all company data.
   - Example: Sales reps shouldn't access accounting files.

3. Enable AI-Driven Risk Detection
   - Tools like Microsoft Defender analyze logins, file transfers, and app usage.
   - Use AI to detect unusual patterns (like employees copying files to USB drives).

4. Use Secure Access Service Edge (SASE)
   - SASE combines VPNs, firewalls, and Zero Trust into one system.
   - It verifies every connection, whether it's from a home office, coffee shop, or hotel Wi-Fi.

5. Enforce Conditional Access
   - Only allow logins from certain devices, locations, or times.
   - If an employee tries to log in from a suspicious location (like a new country), block them.
   - Use Microsoft Conditional Access to enforce these rules.

The Role of AI in Zero Trust
Zero Trust isn't just a security philosophy — it's enforced by AI-driven verification systems. AI scans logins, file transfers, app usage, and device behavior. If anything looks abnormal, Zero Trust kicks in and requires re-verification.

Chapter Conclusion: The New Rules of Remote Security
Remote work is here to stay, but so are hackers. As employees access company files from home, airports, and cafes, the risk of compromise increases.

The best way to protect against this is to:

1. Use AI-driven employee monitoring tools like Teramind, ActivTrak, and Microsoft Defender.

2. Create a Zero Trust security model that assumes all connections are suspicious.

3. Require MFA, role-based access, and AI anomaly detection for every login, every file transfer, and every device.

"Remote work doesn't have to be a security risk. With AI-driven monitoring, Zero Trust, and smart tools, you can protect your employees from anywhere in the world."

Chapter 15: AI-Driven Detection & Response

Why AI-Driven Detection & Response Matters

The New Reality of Cybersecurity: Why Traditional Methods No Longer Work

Imagine you're running a business with 10,000 employees spread across the globe. Every second, thousands of emails are sent, millions of data packets flow through the network, and hundreds of employees log in and out from remote devices.

Now imagine that a hacker is hiding in that sea of traffic. They're not using old-school malware that can be caught with a simple antivirus scan. Instead, they're moving laterally, exploiting new vulnerabilities, and using AI-powered attack tools to blend in with normal traffic.

Would you be able to spot them?
This is where AI-driven detection and response comes in. Unlike traditional methods that rely on known attack patterns (signatures), AI looks at behavior, context, and anomalies. It can detect threats that no human could see — and it can do it in milliseconds, not hours.

What Is AI-Driven Detection & Response?
AI-Driven Detection & Response is the use of artificial intelligence (AI) and machine learning (ML) to monitor, detect, and respond to cybersecurity threats. Unlike older security tools that rely on signature-based detection (like antivirus software), AI can recognize patterns of behavior — even if the attack has never been seen before.

Instead of asking:
"Does this file match the signature of a known virus?"

AI asks:
"Is this file behaving in a way that's similar to malware?"

This difference is crucial. Hackers have learned how to change the "signatures" of their malware to avoid detection. But with AI-based detection, it doesn't matter. The AI tracks how the file behaves, not just how it "looks."

How Traditional Detection Methods Fail

Signature-Based Detection (used by traditional antivirus software) only works if the malware has been seen before.

- Problem: Hackers create new, never-before-seen versions of malware, and antivirus software misses it.
- Example: Polymorphic malware (like modern ransomware) changes its code every time it infects a system, so it can avoid signature detection.

Rule-Based Detection (like firewalls) relies on static rules set by humans.

- Problem: Hackers can exploit "zero-day vulnerabilities" (flaws that haven't been patched yet).
- Example: A firewall rule might block traffic from "bad" IP addresses, but attackers can use a VPN to disguise their IP.

How AI-Driven Detection Solves These Problems

1. Behavioral Analysis — AI doesn't rely on signatures. Instead, it tracks how files, devices, and users behave. If a file suddenly starts encrypting all your files, it knows it's ransomware — even if it's a brand-new version.

2. Anomaly Detection — Instead of following static rules, AI tracks what's normal for each device and user. If a user logs in from New York at 9 AM and then from Hong Kong at 9:15 AM, AI knows it's a "Impossible Travel" anomaly and flags it.

3. Predictive Analysis — AI doesn't wait for the attack to happen. It predicts it. AI can detect early signs of an attack, like small increases in CPU usage or file access rates, and stop the attack before it escalates.

4. Real-Time Automated Response — The average time for a company to respond to a breach is 277 days. With AI, that response time can drop to seconds. AI can automatically block access, quarantine files, and trigger alerts without waiting for human intervention.

Why Speed Matters: The Attack Timeline

If a hacker gets access to your system, they don't wait around. Here's what typically happens:

- First 5 minutes: The hacker steals login credentials (like username and password).
- Next 10 minutes: They move laterally to other systems on the network.

- Next 15 minutes: Ransomware is deployed, encrypting files at lightning speed.
- Within 30 minutes: The entire network is locked down, and a ransom message appears on employee screens.

Traditional security tools operate on a delay. It can take hours (or days) for human analysts to detect an attack. But with AI-driven detection, every second counts. AI can detect and respond to threats in real time — sometimes before the attack even happens.

The Role of AI in Modern Detection & Response
So, what exactly does AI do in this process? Here are the core roles AI plays in Detection & Response:

1. Anomaly Detection
AI tracks user and system behavior to detect deviations from "normal."
- Example: If an employee suddenly starts downloading files at 2 AM (when they usually work from 9-5), AI flags this as a suspicious event.
- AI's Role: AI looks for patterns, like unusual logins, large file transfers, or connections to unusual IP addresses.

2. Predictive Threat Detection
AI doesn't just react — it predicts threats before they happen.
- Example: If AI detects that a hacker is scanning your network for open ports, it can predict an attack is coming.
- AI's Role: By spotting early indicators of an attack, AI can activate "predictive blocking" to shut down the threat before it becomes a breach.

3. Automated Incident Response
Once a threat is detected, AI takes action — automatically.
- Example: If a ransomware attack begins encrypting files, AI can automatically quarantine the affected endpoint.
- AI's Role: AI doesn't need human input to act. It can block users, quarantine devices, and shut down access instantly.

4. Self-Learning AI Models
AI gets smarter every day. It learns from past attacks and becomes better at identifying new ones.
- Example: If a phishing attack bypasses spam filters, AI "remembers" that attack and updates its models to catch similar ones in the future.
- AI's Role: Every attack makes AI stronger. This is why AI-based antivirus tools get smarter over time, unlike traditional antivirus, which only works on known threats.

Tools and Systems That Use AI-Driven Detection & Response

1. XDR (Extended Detection & Response)
   - What It Does: XDR monitors every system in the organization (email, endpoints, cloud, servers, and more).
   - How AI Helps: AI connects the dots between devices. If AI sees an attack on your email system, it automatically checks to see if that attack is present on your endpoints (like phones, laptops, or servers).

2. EDR (Endpoint Detection & Response)
   - What It Does: EDR monitors devices (like phones, laptops, and desktops) for suspicious activity.
   - How AI Helps: If AI detects ransomware on an employee's laptop, it can isolate that laptop before the infection spreads to the rest of the company.

3. SIEM (Security Information and Event Management)
   - What It Does: SIEM tracks security logs from thousands of devices.
   - How AI Helps: AI analyzes these logs in real-time, looking for patterns. Instead of waiting for a human to read the logs, AI detects threats in milliseconds.

How AI Turns Cybersecurity Teams Into Superheroes
Before AI, cybersecurity teams were like firefighters, constantly putting out fires after the damage was done. But with AI-driven detection, they become proactive defenders. Here's how AI helps security teams:
   - Cuts Response Time from hours to seconds.
   - Reduces False Positives, which means less "alert fatigue" for analysts.
   - Predicts Attacks, stopping them before they happen.
   - Learns from Each Attack, so the system is smarter every day.

Case Study Example:
A ransomware attack on a company network starts at 9:03 AM. The attack is detected by an XDR system using AI, which notices unusual file encryption behavior. By 9:05 AM, the affected computer is quarantined automatically, and the attack is stopped. Without AI, that attack would have encrypted the entire network, causing millions in damages.

Call to Action: What Should You Do Next?
If you want to stay ahead of hackers, you need to use AI-driven detection and response. Here's what you should do:
1. Invest in XDR, EDR, and SIEM tools that use AI-driven detection.
2. Demand Explainable AI (XAI) so you know why alerts are triggered.
3. Eliminate delay — use AI-driven automation to respond instantly.

"Hackers are using AI to attack you. It's time to use AI to fight back."

Key Detection Tools — XDR, EDR, SIEM, and AI's Role in Each
- Modern cybersecurity depends on three powerful detection tools: XDR (Extended Detection & Response), EDR (Endpoint Detection & Response), and SIEM (Security Information and Event Management). While each of these tools plays a unique role in threat detection, they are far more effective when used together — especially when enhanced by AI and machine learning. This section will walk you through how these tools work, how AI improves them, and how they form a unified defense system to protect against even the most advanced attacks.

What Are Detection Tools (XDR, EDR, SIEM)?
To understand how XDR, EDR, and SIEM protect your business, it's essential to understand their roles individually.

What is EDR (Endpoint Detection & Response)?
EDR (Endpoint Detection & Response) focuses on protecting the devices that employees use every day. This includes laptops, desktops, smartphones, tablets, and IoT devices. Hackers love targeting endpoints because they often have weaker security than corporate servers. EDR tools continuously monitor these devices, looking for unusual behavior or signs of malware.

How EDR works:
- Real-Time Device Monitoring: EDR tracks every action on a device, including what files are accessed, what apps are running, and what files are downloaded.
- Attack Detection: If a device starts acting suspiciously (for example, if it suddenly starts encrypting large batches of files), EDR flags it as a possible ransomware attack.
- Response and Containment: If a threat is confirmed, EDR can automatically quarantine the device to prevent malware from spreading across the network.

How AI improves EDR:
AI enhances EDR by using behavioral analysis instead of relying on traditional malware signatures. AI learns what "normal" behavior looks like for each user and device. If a laptop suddenly begins transferring files to an unknown USB drive, AI recognizes this as abnormal and triggers an alert. Unlike traditional antivirus software, which can only recognize previously known malware, AI can detect brand-new malware by analyzing its behavior.

Examples of EDR tools include CrowdStrike Falcon, SentinelOne, and Microsoft Defender for Endpoint. These tools incorporate AI models that automatically detect, block, and quarantine malware threats.

What is XDR (Extended Detection & Response)?
XDR (Extended Detection & Response) extends the capabilities of EDR beyond just endpoints. While EDR focuses on devices like laptops, XDR includes email systems, cloud services, and servers. Hackers don't just attack employee devices — they also attack email platforms (like Gmail or Microsoft 365) and cloud storage (like OneDrive or Google Drive). XDR unifies these tools so that threats in one area (like email) can be connected to threats in another area (like endpoints).

How XDR works:
1. Multi-Vector Threat Detection: XDR tracks threats across multiple points of entry, such as laptops, cloud storage, and email accounts.
2. Attack Correlation: XDR connects the dots between multiple attacks. For example, if a phishing email contains a malicious link, and an employee clicks it, XDR can track the attack from the email platform to the endpoint where it was opened.
3. Response and Containment: XDR can block access across multiple systems. If ransomware is detected on one laptop, XDR can block access to related cloud files to prevent the spread.

How AI improves XDR:
AI enhances XDR by making it more adaptive and predictive. Unlike human analysts, AI can correlate attacks in real time, recognizing that a phishing email, a malicious file, and a suspicious login are all part of the same threat actor's attack. AI systems like CrowdStrike XDR and SentinelOne XDR offer full attack timelines, helping companies track every step a hacker takes from initial compromise to data exfiltration.

What is SIEM (Security Information and Event Management)?
SIEM (Security Information and Event Management) is the central brain of cybersecurity operations. While EDR and XDR track endpoints and cloud apps, SIEM tracks the logs and security events from every system in the network — servers, firewalls, VPNs, cloud storage, and email systems. SIEM provides cybersecurity teams with a dashboard where they can see every event happening in real time.

How SIEM works:
1. Log Collection: SIEM pulls in security logs from firewalls, routers, servers, VPNs, and every system in the IT environment.
2. Threat Detection: SIEM uses AI and anomaly detection to scan the logs for suspicious patterns, such as failed logins, repeated password attempts, or logins from unusual locations.
3. Incident Response: When SIEM spots a threat, it sends alerts to security analysts or triggers automated responses (like blocking a suspicious IP address).

How AI improves SIEM:
AI makes SIEM far more effective by correlating multiple events into a single threat. For example, instead of treating "five failed logins" and "unusual file access" as separate alerts, AI connects them as part of the same attack. This reduces alert fatigue for human analysts, who would otherwise have to sort through thousands of disconnected alerts.

SIEM tools that use AI include Splunk, IBM QRadar, and Elastic SIEM. These platforms analyze millions of log entries in real time, identifying and correlating threat activity that would be impossible for human analysts to catch on their own.

How AI Enhances XDR, EDR, and SIEM
AI plays a different role for each of these tools:
- For EDR: AI detects anomalies on individual devices (like a sudden increase in file encryption).
- For XDR: AI connects multiple attacks from different sources (like email, cloud, and devices) into one unified view.
- For SIEM: AI scans through thousands of event logs and groups related alerts into a single "incident" to reduce alert fatigue.

By combining these three tools, AI creates a multi-layered defense system. If EDR misses something, XDR catches it. If XDR misses it, SIEM's log analysis will find it. This ensures that no threat goes undetected.

How XDR, EDR, and SIEM Work Together

While EDR, XDR, and SIEM are powerful on their own, they become exponentially stronger when they work together. Here's how it works:

1. Anomaly Detected (EDR): A laptop detects that an employee is downloading a suspicious file from the internet. EDR triggers an alert.
2. Threat Correlation (XDR): XDR tracks that same file to the email system and identifies that it was originally sent through a phishing email.
3. Alert Raised (SIEM): SIEM tracks related connections between this file and activity on the employee's account. If SIEM sees multiple failed login attempts or other anomalies, it raises the threat level.
4. Automated Response (XDR + EDR): XDR quarantines the affected laptop, and EDR prevents the file from spreading to other endpoints.

This process happens in minutes or even seconds, thanks to AI's ability to automatically detect and connect the dots between multiple threat vectors.

Case Study: How AI-Driven Detection Stopped a Supply Chain Attack

A global supply chain company was attacked through a third-party vendor's email system. Here's how XDR, EDR, and SIEM worked together to stop it:

- Phishing Email (XDR): An employee received a fake invoice email containing a malicious PDF. XDR identified the suspicious link in the email and flagged it as a potential threat.
- File Execution (EDR): The employee opened the PDF, but EDR recognized the file was attempting to access sensitive files. EDR quarantined the laptop immediately.
- Log Correlation (SIEM): SIEM correlated all the activity — the email, the file download, and the laptop quarantine — into a single alert for security analysts.
- Company Response: The company used XDR and EDR to quarantine other laptops that had received the same phishing email, blocking the attack before it could spread further.

Without AI, the threat would have spread to hundreds of devices before human analysts even noticed. With AI, the threat was stopped in real time.

AI Bias in Cybersecurity

Why AI Bias Is a Threat to Cybersecurity
AI is revolutionizing cybersecurity, enabling faster detection, prediction, and response. But there's a hidden risk that often goes unnoticed — AI bias. Bias in AI systems can lead to false positives, missed threats, and flawed decision-making. In cybersecurity, where every second counts, AI bias can mean the difference between stopping a breach and letting it succeed.

Unlike humans, AI models are trained on data, and if that data is flawed, biased, or incomplete, the AI's decisions will be flawed too. This problem is even more critical in cybersecurity, where detecting anomalous behavior is essential. If AI mistakes normal behavior for a threat, it creates unnecessary alerts. If it fails to recognize actual threats, the consequences can be catastrophic.

In this section, you'll learn:
- What AI bias is and how it appears in cybersecurity systems.
- How AI bias affects anomaly detection, behavioral analysis, and threat identification.
- How to identify, reduce, and prevent AI bias in cybersecurity tools like XDR, EDR, and SIEM.

By the end of this section, you'll understand how to spot bias in AI-driven detection tools and ensure your security systems are accurate, fair, and effective.

1. What is AI Bias in Cybersecurity?
AI bias occurs when AI systems make incorrect predictions or decisions because of flaws in the data, models, or algorithms used to train them. Since cybersecurity relies on anomaly detection, bias in AI models can lead to:
- False Positives: Normal activity gets flagged as suspicious (like employees working at unusual hours).
- False Negatives: Genuine threats (like malware) go undetected because the AI doesn't recognize them.
- Over-Alerting: Security analysts are flooded with alerts that lead to "alert fatigue," where important threats get missed.

Why Bias Exists in AI Models
AI models are only as good as the data they are trained on. If the data is biased, the AI inherits that bias. Here are the most common sources of AI bias:
- Data Bias: If the training data used to create the AI doesn't include certain threat behaviors (like new malware tactics), the AI won't recognize them in the real world.

- Selection Bias: If data samples aren't representative of the full spectrum of threat behaviors, the AI will be "blind" to certain types of attacks.
- Human Labeling Errors: Humans label training data (like "This is a threat" or "This is safe"). If they label something incorrectly, the AI learns the wrong lesson.
- Overfitting Bias: If an AI model "over-learns" from specific training data, it might become too rigid, flagging only known attacks and missing anything slightly different.

2. How AI Bias Affects Detection, Anomaly Analysis, and Threat Identification

AI bias can disrupt detection, especially in XDR, EDR, and SIEM systems that rely on machine learning to identify threats. Here's how it affects each component:

Anomaly Detection
Anomaly detection identifies "unusual" behavior that doesn't fit the normal activity pattern. But if AI's definition of "normal" is flawed, it leads to incorrect decisions.

How Bias Affects Anomaly Detection
- False Positives: If AI is trained on narrow or incomplete data, it might think legitimate user behavior (like an employee working late) is a threat.
- False Negatives: If the AI hasn't seen a specific attack pattern before (like a zero-day attack), it might fail to flag it as abnormal.

Example
Imagine an AI model trained on employee login data. If most employees log in between 9 AM and 5 PM, the AI might flag any login outside these hours as "suspicious." But in a global company, employees may log in from different time zones. This is an example of bias caused by poor data sampling.

Behavioral Analysis
Behavioral analysis tracks how users interact with systems (like file access, login patterns, and data transfers). If AI models only "understand" one type of user behavior, they will flag other behaviors as threats.

How Bias Affects Behavioral Analysis
- Insider Threat Detection Failures: If the AI is trained on normal employee behavior but not on insider threats, it won't recognize an insider attack.
- Missed Threats: If employees' work habits change (like working from home), the AI might think this change is "normal" and miss legitimate threats.

Example
If an employee typically downloads 10 files per day and suddenly downloads 1,000 files, AI should flag this as unusual. But if AI is trained on biased data that assumes employees only ever download 100 files, it might miss the anomaly entirely.

Threat Identification
AI models must recognize specific types of malware, ransomware, and phishing attempts. But if the AI is trained on a small sample of known threats, it won't recognize newer or more sophisticated attacks.

How Bias Affects Threat Identification
- Overfitting: If AI is trained on only one type of ransomware, like WannaCry, it might miss other variants like LockBit or BlackCat.
- Generalization Errors: AI might think that similar-looking files are safe if it was trained on only one type of malware signature.

Example
If hackers modify malware so it looks slightly different (by changing the file's hash), an AI trained on previous versions won't recognize it as malware. This is a form of data bias, where the training set failed to include multiple malware variants.

3. How to Prevent and Reduce AI Bias in Detection Tools
Reducing AI bias requires effort at every stage of the AI development process — from data collection to model training. Here's how to prevent and reduce AI bias in cybersecurity tools like XDR, EDR, and SIEM.

1. Use Diverse Data Sets for Training
Training AI on data from one company, one country, or one type of malware will create a biased model. Instead, train AI on global data that includes threats from many regions and industries.

What to Do:
- Use open-source threat intelligence feeds to ensure your AI sees a wide range of attack data.
- Train AI on diverse attack tactics (like phishing emails from different languages, file hashes from multiple ransomware types, etc.).

2. Continuous Testing and Retraining of AI Models

AI models degrade over time, especially as new threats emerge. Continuous retraining keeps AI "fresh" and reduces bias caused by older data.
What to Do:
- Update AI models at least monthly.
- Include zero-day malware in training data whenever possible.

3. Leverage Explainable AI (XAI)

XAI (Explainable AI) provides explanations for why the AI flagged certain threats. This allows human analysts to spot potential bias and correct it.
What to Do:
- Ask for XAI tools from your security vendors (like Splunk and CrowdStrike).
- If AI flags a legitimate user as a threat, review the AI's reasoning to identify possible bias.

4. Use Human Oversight and Human-in-the-Loop (HITL) Models

AI isn't perfect, which is why human analysts must verify AI decisions. Humans correct AI's mistakes and provide better training data.
What to Do:
- Use Human-in-the-Loop (HITL) systems, where human analysts review and correct AI alerts.
- Allow security teams to submit "false positives" so the AI can learn from its mistakes.

5. Regularly Audit and Review AI Models for Bias

Auditing an AI system involves testing it with edge cases (unusual behaviors) and seeing how it responds. If it flags too many false positives or misses legitimate threats, you know the AI model is biased.
What to Do:
- Conduct quarterly bias audits on AI-driven security systems.
- Use "synthetic users" with unusual behavior patterns to see if the AI falsely flags them.

Case Study: How AI Bias Led to a Failed Detection
The Incident
A global financial institution implemented a new AI-based XDR system to protect its global workforce. The system was trained using historical user login data from employees based in North America. Since most employees in North America worked 9 AM to 5 PM local time, the AI's model learned that this was "normal behavior."

However, as the company expanded its remote workforce in Europe, Asia, and the Middle East, employees in these regions logged in during what the system perceived as "unusual hours." Employees in Europe would log in at 3:00 AM North American time, while employees in Asia would log in during what would be considered "late at night" by the system's logic.

The AI saw this as an anomaly, triggering "suspicious login" alerts. Every day, thousands of these alerts flooded the company's Security Operations Center (SOC). Security analysts, overwhelmed by the flood of false positives, started ignoring these alerts — the same alerts that were intended to flag actual threat activity.

The Problem
1. The AI's training data only included employee behavior from North American time zones.
2. The model was biased toward time-based login activity, leading to the assumption that all logins during "odd hours" were suspicious.
3. The lack of global data diversity caused thousands of false positives, wasting the SOC team's time and slowing down their response to actual attacks.

How It Was Resolved
The company took action to retrain the AI model and prevent future bias. Here's how they solved the issue:
- Global Data Collection: They retrained the model using login data from all employee locations, including time zones in Europe, Asia, and the Middle East. The updated data set reflected the actual work habits of employees around the world, ensuring that the AI recognized "normal" for one region is not the same as "normal" for another.
- Time-Zone Awareness: The AI was updated to consider time zones when analyzing login behavior. Instead of using a "one-size-fits-all" approach, the AI now adapts its definitions of "normal behavior" based on the local time of the user's region.

- Customizable Thresholds: The company created new custom alert thresholds for login anomalies. For example, logins at 3:00 AM local time would no longer be flagged if they occurred within a region where it was considered "business hours."
- Explainable AI (XAI) Integration: They implemented XAI so human analysts could see why the AI flagged an alert. When an alert was flagged, the XAI system displayed a message like, "Login flagged because it occurred outside normal business hours for North America." This allowed analysts to quickly dismiss false positives and focus on real threats.
- Human Oversight and HITL (Human-in-the-Loop) Review: To prevent bias from creeping back into the system, the company implemented a Human-in-the-Loop (HITL) process. Analysts could review alerts and provide feedback on whether an alert was a true positive or a false positive. This data was fed back into the AI, allowing it to re-learn and correct its biases.

The Lesson
If you train an AI model using data from only one region, department, or time zone, it will make biased decisions. To prevent this, organizations should:
- Train AI models on diverse, global data sets that reflect real-world behaviors.
- Make the AI context-aware (so it understands time zones, roles, and user behaviors).
- Use XAI to understand why AI makes decisions.
- Add human oversight to allow analysts to correct the system's assumptions.

"If your AI can't see the world, it can't protect it."

How to Spot AI Bias in Detection Tools
One of the most important skills for cybersecurity analysts is learning how to spot AI bias in detection tools like XDR, EDR, and SIEM. Here's how to recognize the signs of bias in your security systems.

1. Red Flags of AI Bias in Detection Systems
Look for these indicators that your AI system may be biased:
- Excessive False Positives: If employees in certain departments, shifts, or regions trigger a high number of false alerts, this is a sign that the AI model might be overfitting on specific data.
- Regional Alert Imbalances: If certain geographic regions have more "anomalous activity" than others (like employees in Asia triggering more login alerts than employees in North America), this suggests the training data was regionally biased.

- Alert Fatigue in the SOC: If SOC analysts start ignoring certain types of alerts (like late-night logins) because they believe they are always false positives, it could mean the AI has flawed anomaly definitions.
- Limited Detection of Emerging Threats: If malware with new signatures isn't detected, it may indicate the training data only included older malware.
- Alert Disparity by Device Type: If Android users trigger more alerts than iOS users, it could signal bias in how AI models were trained on certain device types.

2. How to Spot AI Bias in XDR, EDR, and SIEM Systems
How to Spot Bias in XDR
- Login Behavior Bias: If employees logging in from global locations are flagged more than employees in the headquarters, this suggests the XDR model was trained with region-specific login data only.
- Email Alerts Bias: If phishing alerts only trigger on emails in certain languages (like English) but fail to flag attacks in other languages (like French or Japanese), it indicates a language training bias in the XDR's natural language processing (NLP) engine.

How to Spot Bias in EDR
- Device-Specific Bias: If EDR flags more alerts from Android devices than iPhones, it could indicate that the AI was trained on iOS malware samples only.
- Behavioral Anomaly Bias: If EDR constantly flags USB drive usage as "unusual" but ignores legitimate file transfers, it may be because the AI was trained on devices without USB usage patterns.

How to Spot Bias in SIEM
- Alert Clustering Errors: If SIEM creates multiple alerts for one event (instead of grouping them into one), it may signal a correlation bias.
- False Grouping of Unrelated Alerts: If SIEM connects a user's VPN login with a failed file transfer as part of a "related event," but the two actions are unrelated, it suggests SIEM's event correlation logic is flawed.
- Underreporting of Certain Attacks: If SIEM underreports certain attacks (like malware) but over-reports others (like failed logins), it suggests data imbalance bias in how threats were labeled in the training data.

Examples of AI Bias in Detection Tools

Example of Bias in XDR
An XDR system only recognized phishing emails in English but failed to detect phishing emails written in Spanish. This was because the model was trained using English-language phishing samples only. As a result, employees in Latin America were hit with a massive phishing attack that went undetected.

Example of Bias in SIEM
A financial company experienced an attack on a server, but SIEM failed to link it to earlier attacks on employee endpoints. Why? The SIEM system only had log data from servers but didn't track logins from endpoints. This disconnect in data sources resulted in false negatives — the SIEM didn't see the bigger picture.

Example of Bias in EDR
An EDR system flagged any attempt to copy files to USB drives as suspicious. But for employees in the legal department, copying files to USB drives was part of their daily tasks. This led to constant false positives, and SOC analysts began ignoring the alerts, which allowed a real insider threat to go unnoticed.

Emerging Threats to AI-Driven Detection & Response
As defenders use AI to strengthen cybersecurity, attackers are evolving their tactics to exploit weaknesses in AI-driven anomaly detection, machine learning models, and security operations centers (SOCs). From poisoning AI training data to deploying AI-augmented malware that can outthink traditional detection systems, attackers are now directly targeting the AI systems designed to protect us. This new battleground requires defenders to rethink how they train, monitor, and deploy AI-based security tools.

1. Data Poisoning: How Attackers Sabotage AI Models
What It Is:
Data poisoning is a tactic where attackers corrupt the training data used by AI models. Since machine learning models are only as good as the data they learn from, if attackers can control or manipulate that data, they can "teach" AI to ignore real threats or produce false positives. This tactic is especially dangerous for anomaly detection tools like SIEM, XDR, and EDR, which rely on training data to recognize unusual activity.

How It Works:
1. Attackers inject "bad data" into the training set that AI models use to learn what "normal" activity looks like.
2. The corrupted data tricks the model into allowing malicious activity (like malware) to appear as "normal" behavior.
3. This creates false negatives — the AI system fails to detect attacks in progress.

Real-World Example:
An attacker targets a company's SIEM (Security Information and Event Management) system by repeatedly generating fake "benign" login attempts from foreign IP addresses. Over time, the SIEM system learns to ignore logins from those IP addresses, believing they are "normal." Later, the attacker uses those same IP addresses to launch a ransomware attack. Since the IPs have already been "trusted" by the AI model, the attack goes undetected.

How to Defend Against Data Poisoning:
- Train on diverse datasets: Don't rely on one source of training data, especially if it comes from a single geographic region or user group.
- Use adversarial testing: Before deploying an AI model, subject it to "poison tests" where you introduce fake data and see if it responds correctly.
- Regularly re-train AI models: Periodically retrain anomaly detection models with new, clean data to prevent corruption.
- Use Explainable AI (XAI) to identify which data points the model is prioritizing. If it's prioritizing poisoned data, defenders can manually correct it.

2. AI-Augmented Malware: How Attackers Use AI to Outsmart Defenders
What It Is:
AI-augmented malware is a new generation of cyberweapons that leverage AI mutation engines, self-learning code, and adaptive behavior. Unlike traditional malware, which follows pre-programmed instructions, AI-augmented malware can "think" in real time, changing its attack strategy based on the environment.

How It Works:
- Attackers use AI mutation engines to create polymorphic malware that changes its file signature every few minutes.
- Malware monitors its own environment, checking for detection tools (like sandboxes or EDR tools) and changing its behavior accordingly.
- The malware "learns" from past failures and adapts its strategy, making future attacks more successful.

Example of AI-Augmented Malware:
- Polymorphic Malware: Polymorphic malware like Emotet and TrickBot changes its code every time it infects a new system. But with AI-augmented malware, this process becomes fully autonomous. AI mutation engines generate thousands of malware variants per hour, far faster than human hackers could do manually.
- Fileless Malware: Attackers use AI to control fileless malware that lives in system memory, making it impossible to detect with signature-based antivirus software. The malware can "watch" the processes it interacts with and adapt to avoid being flagged.

How to Defend Against AI-Augmented Malware:
- Use AI-driven EDR and XDR to detect unusual file behavior, not file signatures.
- Deploy behavioral anomaly detection tools that identify changes in user or system activity, not just file signatures.
- Use sandbox evasion detectors that spot when malware "plays dead" in a virtual environment.
- Update models frequently, so AI-augmented malware cannot learn to "trick" the system.

3. AI-Driven Security Operations Centers (SOCs)
What It Is:
The rise of AI-driven SOCs (Security Operations Centers) is transforming how organizations detect and respond to threats. AI-SOCs are SOCs that rely on AI tools for threat detection, alert prioritization, and incident response. Instead of relying on human analysts to identify threats, AI-driven SOCs use anomaly detection, machine learning, and predictive analysis to automate the detection of cyberattacks in real time.

How It Works:
- AI tools (like EDR, XDR, and SIEM) collect security data from servers, devices, and cloud environments.
- The AI-SOC automatically prioritizes alerts, reducing "alert fatigue" for human analysts.
- Automated threat detection systems launch playbooks and responses when an attack is detected, like blocking an IP or isolating a device.

Real-World Example:
Many large enterprises now use AI-driven platforms like Darktrace and Microsoft Defender for Endpoint. These tools constantly analyze traffic, detect anomalies, and predict which areas are most likely to be attacked.

How to Defend:
- Adopt SOAR platforms (Security Orchestration, Automation, and Response) to automate incident response.
- Train SOC teams to understand how AI tools prioritize alerts.
- Ensure humans can override AI decisions. If an AI-SOC mistakes a legitimate login for an attack, human intervention is required.
- Audit AI-SOC tools regularly to ensure they aren't being corrupted by poisoned training data (see Data Poisoning).

Final Takeaways

Attackers no longer focus on manual exploitation alone — they target the very AI models designed to stop them. Data poisoning corrupts machine learning models, causing them to misclassify threats or ignore genuine attacks. AI-augmented malware evolves in real time, bypassing traditional detection systems. And while AI-SOCs (Security Operations Centers) promise faster responses, they too are vulnerable to poisoned data and biased models.

To stay ahead, defenders must adopt smarter, AI-driven detection tools that are transparent, explainable, and adaptive. Explainable AI (XAI) reveals why AI models flag threats, reducing false positives and improving trust. Behavioral anomaly detection tracks deviations in normal user behavior, while SOAR (Security Orchestration, Automation, and Response) platforms automate containment, quarantine, and mitigation. Together, these technologies form a multi-layered approach to modern cybersecurity.

Chapter Conclusion: AI-Driven Detection & Response
The old days of relying on firewalls and signature-based antivirus tools are over. AI-driven detection and response is now the only way to keep up with modern threats like polymorphic malware, AI-guided phishing, and self-evolving malware. Attackers are automating every stage of the kill chain, from reconnaissance to ransomware delivery. Defenders must match this automation with XDR, EDR, SIEM, and SOAR platforms that can detect, respond, and adapt in real time.

This chapter focused on XDR, EDR, and SIEM as the ultimate trio of detection and response. XDR (Extended Detection and Response) ties together activity across endpoints, email, cloud services, and user behavior. EDR (Endpoint Detection and Response) protects individual devices (like phones and laptops) from malware and insider threats. SIEM (Security Information and Event Management) tracks every event across a network, creating a "master log" for post-incident analysis. Together, they create an interconnected security system that leaves fewer blind spots for attackers to exploit.

Key Takeaways from This Chapter

1. Explainable AI (XAI) — Making Threats Visible
Traditional AI models are often seen as "black boxes" — they make decisions, but no one knows why. This creates uncertainty when a threat is flagged. XAI (Explainable AI) changes that by revealing the logic behind alerts, making it clear why a file, login, or event was flagged as suspicious.

Why It Matters:
- Without XAI, human analysts can't explain why an alert was triggered, leading to distrust.
- With XAI, analysts can see exactly what prompted an alert (e.g., "Unusual Login Location") and take action faster.
- XAI reveals AI bias, helping companies audit their detection models to spot blind spots.

What You Should Do Next:
- Use security platforms with XAI capabilities. Tools like Darktrace and Microsoft Sentinel offer this functionality.
- Train analysts to understand XAI alerts so they can act quickly and accurately.
- Regularly audit XAI models for bias or gaps in logic.

2. XDR, EDR, and SIEM — The Trio That Stops 99% of Attacks

EDR, XDR, and SIEM are the "big three" in modern detection and response. EDR protects endpoints like laptops, phones, and tablets. XDR provides "big picture" detection by connecting endpoint activity with email, cloud, and network events. SIEM aggregates logs from all devices, giving security teams a unified view of activity across the network.

Why It Matters:
- Without EDR, an infected laptop can spread ransomware to the entire network.
- Without XDR, you miss the connection between an employee clicking a phishing link (email) and malware spreading to a device (endpoint).
- Without SIEM, there's no master log of events, making it hard to investigate attacks after the fact.

What You Should Do Next:
- Use tools that combine XDR, EDR, and SIEM into one platform (like CrowdStrike Falcon or SentinelOne).
- Demand that your SIEM can correlate logs from email, endpoint, and cloud services.
- Implement automated response (like quarantine or account lockouts) to act on alerts in real time.

3. Data Poisoning — Attackers Are Targeting AI Models

Data poisoning is a subtle but devastating threat. Attackers don't just target networks or endpoints — they target the AI models that detect threats. By feeding bad data into training models, attackers "teach" the AI to ignore specific threats or misclassify real attacks as "normal behavior." This is especially dangerous for anomaly detection models used in SIEM and XDR.

How Data Poisoning Works:
- Attackers trick AI models into accepting "clean" versions of malware during training.
- This causes the AI to view future versions of malware as "safe."
- Result: The AI system ignores real threats, letting attackers bypass security.

Why It Matters:
- If your AI models are trained on biased, outdated, or regional-specific data, they will misclassify threats.
- Data poisoning can cause security teams to miss new malware strains or social engineering attacks.
- Attackers will poison AI models before launching larger attacks, ensuring the attack goes undetected.

What You Should Do Next:
- Train AI models on a diverse set of global datasets (not just U.S. data).
- Use Explainable AI (XAI) to identify unusual patterns or sudden classification shifts.
- Deploy Human-in-the-Loop (HITL) training, allowing human analysts to correct errors and re-train models.

4. AI-Augmented Malware & Polymorphic Threats

Attackers now use mutation engines to evolve malware code in real time. Polymorphic malware creates new "versions" of itself after every infection, changing its code enough to bypass traditional antivirus software. AI-powered mutation engines make this process faster, cheaper, and more effective.

How It Works:
- Malware enters a system and "mutates" its code to avoid detection.
- Signature-based antivirus can't detect it because the malware "looks different" on every system.
- AI mutation engines like Emotet and TrickBot create thousands of versions of the same malware, bypassing antivirus scans.

Why It Matters:
- Traditional antivirus software can't keep up with polymorphic threats.
- Attackers are using AI-guided mutation engines to create malware that evolves at a pace no human can match.
- Without AI-driven EDR (like SentinelOne), you won't be able to detect these threats.

What You Should Do Next:
- Install AI-driven EDR on all endpoints (like laptops, phones, and servers).
- Use anomaly-based detection (like CrowdStrike Falcon) to detect changes in file behavior (not file names).
- Replace traditional antivirus with behavioral-based detection that doesn't rely on "known signatures."

5. AI-SOCs (Security Operations Centers)

AI-powered SOCs combine XDR, EDR, SIEM, and SOAR into one system. SOAR (Security Orchestration, Automation, and Response) automates threat response, which means when a ransomware attack is detected, the system can quarantine the infected device in real time.

How It Works:
- SOAR automates the incident response process. If malware is detected, the infected laptop is instantly quarantined.
- AI-SOCs use anomaly detection to spot abnormal activity (like a device encrypting thousands of files) and block encryption in real time.
- AI-SOCs also generate step-by-step attack playbooks to automate future responses.

Why It Matters:
- Without automation, it takes an average of 200 days for companies to detect a breach.
- AI-SOCs can detect and respond in seconds, shutting down attacks before data is stolen.

What You Should Do Next:
- Use tools like Microsoft Sentinel for end-to-end SOAR automation.
- Train security analysts to use SOAR platforms, teaching them how to review attack playbooks.
- Insist on AI-driven quarantine features, which block devices and IP addresses as soon as a threat is detected.

Final Thoughts

AI-driven threats like data poisoning, AI-augmented malware, and polymorphic attacks require a new approach to defense. The days of "black-box AI" are over — you need transparency, anomaly detection, and SOAR automation to stay ahead. With XDR, EDR, and SIEM working together, you'll have the power to see, predict, and stop threats in real time. As attackers evolve, so must you. Use XAI, behavioral anomaly detection, and automated response to stay ahead. Hackers only have to succeed once, but AI-driven defenses succeed every time.

Chapter 16: Incident Response & Disaster Recovery

Why Incident Response & Disaster Recovery Are Critical
"It's not about if you'll be attacked — it's about when."
Cyberattacks are inevitable. Hackers only need to succeed once, while defenders must succeed every single time. When an attack happens, the speed and precision of your Incident Response (IR) and Disaster Recovery (DR) efforts determine how much damage is done. If your team can detect, contain, and recover quickly, you may only experience a minor disruption. But if response times are slow, ransomware can encrypt critical files, exfiltrate sensitive data, and paralyze operations for days or even weeks.

This is why Incident Response and Disaster Recovery are essential components of every cybersecurity strategy. The faster you respond, the smaller the impact. The difference between a quick response and a delayed one could mean millions in damages.
What is Incident Response (IR)?

Incident Response (IR) refers to the immediate, real-time response to a cybersecurity attack. When an attack is detected, the primary goal of Incident Response is to contain, investigate, and neutralize the threat. This response is guided by a company's Incident Response Plan (IRP), which defines roles, responsibilities, and step-by-step actions to be taken.

Key Objectives of Incident Response:
1. Contain the Threat — Stop the attack from spreading (like quarantining an infected device).
2. Eradicate the Threat — Remove malware, patch vulnerabilities, and eliminate backdoors.
3. Restore Operations — Resume normal operations as quickly as possible.
4. Investigate the Cause — Identify how the attack happened and prevent it from happening again.

Example of Incident Response in Action:
- A phishing email containing ransomware is opened by an employee.
- The ransomware begins encrypting files on the employee's laptop.
- The EDR (Endpoint Detection and Response) tool detects unusual file activity and isolates the laptop from the network.
- The SOAR platform automatically triggers a playbook to lock shared file access and alert the Security Operations Center (SOC).

- IT investigates the origin of the ransomware and identifies a vulnerability in email filters, which is patched to prevent future attacks.

What is Disaster Recovery (DR)?
Disaster Recovery (DR) is the process of restoring normal business operations after a cyberattack, system failure, or disaster. While Incident Response (IR) focuses on immediate containment and neutralization, Disaster Recovery focuses on rebuilding and restoring. This includes restoring systems, files, and networks to a working state, often through data backups, failover systems, and restoration plans.

Key Objectives of Disaster Recovery:
1. Restore Business Operations — Get critical systems back online after an attack.
2. Recover Lost Data — Restore data from immutable backups (backups that can't be altered).
3. Rebuild Trust — Ensure that customers, employees, and stakeholders know the system is secure.
4. Test System Integrity — Ensure that no backdoors, malware, or vulnerabilities remain.

Example of Disaster Recovery in Action:
- A ransomware attack encrypts the main server of a financial company, taking down customer portals.
- The company activates its Disaster Recovery Plan (DRP), which triggers a failover to a backup server.
- Cloud-based immutable backups are restored within 30 minutes, and the customer portal is back online.
- The affected server is scanned, cleaned, and re-tested before being restored to production.

Incident Response = The Firefighters (Put out the fire immediately)

Disaster Recovery = The Rebuilders (Rebuild after the fire is out)

The Critical Role of Speed: The Golden Hour
In cybersecurity, there's a concept called the Golden Hour. This is the first 60 minutes after a cyberattack begins, and it's the most critical window of time for incident response. If you can detect, contain, and mitigate the attack within this window, you can prevent 90% of the potential damage.

Here's how speed makes a difference:
- 1-5 Minutes: If ransomware is detected early, it can be contained before it encrypts files.
- 5-15 Minutes: If containment is delayed, ransomware could start encrypting files, causing partial loss.
- 30+ Minutes: If containment takes too long, ransomware may have encrypted an entire network, paralyzing operations.
- 1+ Hour: After an hour, the attack has likely spread to other systems, and recovery costs skyrocket.

The faster you detect, contain, and recover, the less damage is done.

How AI Has Changed Incident Response & Disaster Recovery
Before AI, Incident Response and Disaster Recovery were entirely manual processes. IT teams would spend hours analyzing logs, quarantining devices, and restoring backups. But AI-driven tools have changed the game.

How AI Transforms Incident Response (IR):
1. Faster Threat Detection — AI models detect ransomware, phishing, and malware instantly (unlike human analysts who must review log files).
2. Automated Containment — AI-driven SOAR platforms automatically isolate infected devices, block malicious IPs, and lock file access.
3. Predictive Response — AI identifies attack patterns and predicts which systems may be targeted next, allowing preemptive defenses.
4. Autonomous Playbooks — Instead of waiting for human analysts to act, AI follows automated response playbooks to quarantine devices, notify IT, and block malware spread.

How AI Transforms Disaster Recovery (DR):
1. Automated Backup Restoration — AI can identify which files are most critical and prioritize their recovery.
2. Predictive Failover Activation — AI can identify when a server is about to fail and activate failover servers before the system goes down.
3. File Integrity Checks — AI scans recovered files for signs of malware, ensuring no backdoors remain.
4. Smart Testing of Restored Systems — AI tests restored servers and files for integrity and security before allowing them back into production.

The Role of SOAR in Incident Response & Disaster Recovery
What is SOAR (Security Orchestration, Automation, and Response)?
SOAR is an AI-driven system that automates incident response tasks like isolating devices, blocking IP addresses, and launching response playbooks. In the past, security teams had to analyze threats, make decisions, and implement response actions manually. SOAR automates all of this.

How SOAR Helps in Incident Response:
- Automated Quarantine — If ransomware is detected, SOAR automatically isolates infected devices.
- Malware Removal Playbooks — SOAR follows playbooks to automatically block malware, delete malicious files, and restore access.
- Threat Containment — SOAR locks down shared file drives, closes backdoors, and prevents malware from spreading.

How SOAR Helps in Disaster Recovery:
- File Restoration Playbooks — SOAR can automate the restoration of backups based on pre-built playbooks.
- System Integrity Checks — SOAR tests restored files and systems for vulnerabilities before releasing them back into production.
- Communication and Notifications — SOAR automatically notifies teams, stakeholders, and executives about recovery progress.

With SOAR, your IR and DR processes are faster, smarter, and more efficient.

The Difference Between Incident Response (IR) and Disaster Recovery (DR)

Many people confuse Incident Response with Disaster Recovery, but they serve distinct purposes:
- Incident Response (IR):
  - Focus: Stop the attack in real time.
  - Goal: Detect, contain, and neutralize the threat.
  - Example: If ransomware starts encrypting files, EDR quarantines the device.
- Disaster Recovery (DR):
  - Focus: Restore business operations.
  - Goal: Rebuild and recover from the damage.
  - Example: If ransomware encrypts a company's servers, DR restores the files from cloud backups.

Why Every Business Needs an IR and DR Plan
Here's the harsh reality:
- 43% of companies that experience a major data breach never reopen.
- Companies that have an IR and DR plan can recover in days, not weeks.
- Cyber insurance providers now require proof of an Incident Response Plan (IRP) and a Disaster Recovery Plan (DRP) to qualify for coverage.

Without a plan, your company may face:
- Permanent data loss.
- Extended downtime (which costs thousands per hour).
- Reputation damage and customer churn.

With a plan, you can bounce back in hours.

The 6 Phases of Incident Response
When a cyberattack strikes, every second matters. The ability to detect, contain, and recover from an attack quickly can mean the difference between a minor disruption and a catastrophic business shutdown. To stay prepared, organizations need a clearly defined process known as the Incident Response (IR) Lifecycle, which is broken into six critical phases.

These six phases provide a step-by-step roadmap for responding to cyberattacks, from the initial detection to the final post-incident review. Understanding these phases ensures that businesses can react swiftly, minimize damage, and continuously improve their defenses.

Phase 1: Preparation
"The best time to prepare for an attack is before it happens."
The Preparation phase is the most critical part of the Incident Response process because it lays the groundwork for everything that follows. Without a strong Incident Response Plan (IRP), teams will be forced to make decisions under stress, which often leads to mistakes.

Key Goals of the Preparation Phase:
- Develop an Incident Response Plan (IRP) that defines the exact steps to take in each phase.
- Establish clear roles and responsibilities for team members, including Incident Response Team (IRT) leads, SOC analysts, and executive stakeholders.

- Set up detection and monitoring systems like XDR, EDR, and SIEM to identify threats in real time.
- Create Incident Playbooks — Pre-built guides for handling specific attack types (like ransomware, phishing, and insider threats).
- Run Tabletop Exercises — Simulate attack scenarios to test your readiness.

How AI Enhances This Phase:
- AI-driven Playbooks: AI analyzes historical attack data to create automated playbooks for responding to threats.
- Predictive Threat Modeling: AI tools like Darktrace predict potential attack vectors, helping security teams strengthen weak points before they're attacked.

What You Should Do Next:
1. Draft an Incident Response Plan (IRP) and assign roles.
2. Set up AI-driven tools like SOAR to automate response actions.
3. Conduct a tabletop exercise to test how your team responds to a simulated cyberattack.

Phase 2: Detection & Analysis
"If you can't detect it, you can't stop it."
The Detection & Analysis phase is when an attack is first identified. This is often the most stressful part of the process, as teams scramble to identify the scope, severity, and origin of the threat. Speed is critical here because early detection can prevent ransomware from encrypting files or stop malware from spreading.

Key Goals of the Detection & Analysis Phase:
- Detect Threats in Real Time using AI-powered XDR, EDR, and SIEM tools.
- Analyze the Threat — What type of attack is it? (Ransomware? Phishing? Supply chain attack?)
- Determine the Scope — Which devices, systems, or users are affected?
- Collect Evidence — Save logs, file hashes, and malware samples for forensic analysis.
- Prioritize the Response — Is this a high-priority threat (like ransomware) or a low-priority anomaly?

How AI Enhances This Phase:
- Real-Time Threat Detection: AI-based systems like XDR and EDR can detect attacks the moment unusual activity (like file encryption) is detected.

- Anomaly Detection: AI systems monitor for unusual patterns (like login attempts from different countries) and flag them as threats.
- Threat Prioritization: AI assigns priority scores to threats, helping analysts focus on the most dangerous ones first.

What You Should Do Next:
1. Use AI-driven EDR to detect threats at the endpoint level.
2. Implement SIEM to analyze logs from cloud, network, and device activity.
3. Set up XDR to correlate events across multiple devices, systems, and email accounts.

Phase 3: Containment
"Contain it fast, or it spreads like wildfire."
Once an attack is detected, the next step is containment. The goal is to stop the spread of the attack and prevent it from causing further damage. This phase is crucial for stopping ransomware, malware, and insider threats from affecting more devices, users, or files.

Key Goals of the Containment Phase:
- Isolate Infected Devices — Quarantine devices that show signs of malware or ransomware.
- Block Suspicious IP Addresses — Use a firewall or SOAR playbook to block the attacker's IP address.
- Limit Data Access — Restrict access to shared file drives and cloud storage.
- Stop Malware Spread — Block malware communication (command and control) to prevent lateral movement.

How AI Enhances This Phase:
- Automated Quarantine: AI-driven SOAR platforms automatically isolate infected devices without human intervention.
- Predictive Containment: If AI detects unusual encryption activity (like ransomware), it can lock down shared drives to prevent data loss.
- Automated IP Blocking: AI systems like Cloudflare or Zscaler can block malicious IPs and command-and-control traffic instantly.

What You Should Do Next:
- Set up SOAR playbooks for automatic device quarantine.
- Use firewall rules to block malicious IP addresses.
- Restrict access to shared drives and cloud apps.

Phase 4: Eradication
"Containment stops it, but eradication kills it."
Once the attack is contained, the next step is to eliminate the threat entirely. This phase ensures that no malware, backdoors, or malicious files remain on the system. If eradication is incomplete, the attacker may regain access later.

Key Goals of the Eradication Phase:
- Remove Malware — Delete infected files and uninstall malware-infected software.
- Patch Vulnerabilities — Apply patches to fix software flaws that allowed the attack.
- Scan for Backdoors — Look for hidden backdoors left behind by hackers.
- Update Firewalls and Rules — Ensure that the attacker's IP addresses are permanently blocked.

How AI Enhances This Phase:
- Backdoor Detection: AI-based malware scanners detect hidden backdoors and eliminate them.
- Automated Patching: AI recommends and automates the installation of critical patches.

What You Should Do Next:
- Use malware scanners to identify backdoors and malicious files.
- Apply patches to eliminate known vulnerabilities.
- Use AI tools to scan and verify that no malware remains.

Phase 5: Recovery
"If you don't recover, you don't survive."
Once the threat is eliminated, the next step is to restore business operations. The goal is to restore all systems, files, and devices to normal operations.

Key Goals of the Recovery Phase:
- Restore from Backups — Use immutable backups that ransomware can't encrypt.
- Test System Integrity — Ensure that all devices are malware-free.
- Restore Business Operations — Get customers, employees, and stakeholders back online.
- Check for Backdoors — Look for hidden malware or credentials that attackers may have planted.

How AI Enhances This Phase:
- Automated Backup Restoration: AI restores only the critical files first, prioritizing what is most important.
- System Integrity Scans: AI scans all restored files for hidden malware.

What You Should Do Next:
- Ensure that backups are clean (no malware embedded).
- Restore systems using immutable backups to prevent re-infection.
- Test system integrity using AI-driven malware scanners.

Phase 6: Lessons Learned
"Every attack teaches you something. Don't waste it."
Once recovery is complete, you need to review what happened and make improvements to your Incident Response Plan (IRP). This phase ensures that the same attack won't succeed again.

Key Goals of the Lessons Learned Phase:
- Conduct a Post-Incident Review — What went right? What went wrong?
- Update the Incident Response Plan (IRP) — Revise your playbooks to address gaps.
- Review Logs and Attack Data — Study how the attacker moved laterally and what could have stopped them.
- Update Firewalls and Alerts — Add new detection rules to catch similar attacks in the future.

What You Should Do Next:
- Hold a post-incident review meeting.
- Update XDR and SIEM alerts.
- Revise SOAR playbooks to improve speed and automation.

These 6 phases make up the foundation of Incident Response. Next, we'll explore how AI-driven SOAR platforms automate response and reduce downtime.

AI-Driven SOAR (Security Orchestration, Automation, and Response) Tools

Cyberattacks happen fast — too fast for human teams to respond manually. Ransomware can encrypt an entire network in under 30 minutes, while phishing emails can lead to stolen credentials within seconds. Traditional Incident Response (IR) relies on human analysts to detect, investigate, and contain threats, but by the time analysts react, the damage is often done.

Enter SOAR: Security Orchestration, Automation, and Response. SOAR tools transform incident response from reactive to proactive. Powered by AI, SOAR platforms detect, contain, and neutralize threats automatically, reducing response times from hours to mere seconds. This section explores how SOAR works, how it's enhanced by AI, and why it's essential for modern cybersecurity.

What is SOAR?

SOAR (Security Orchestration, Automation, and Response) is a system that allows businesses to automate and orchestrate incident response tasks. Instead of waiting for human analysts to make decisions, SOAR triggers automatic playbooks — pre-built instructions on how to respond to specific threats like ransomware, phishing, or insider threats.

Key Objectives of SOAR:
- Automate Response Tasks — Quarantine infected devices, block malicious IP addresses, and alert the security team automatically.
- Orchestrate Multiple Tools — SOAR integrates with XDR, EDR, SIEM, firewalls, and email gateways to create a unified response system.
- Reduce Response Time — While human analysts may need 30-60 minutes to analyze an attack, SOAR responds in seconds.
- Centralized Incident Management — SOAR dashboards display real-time updates on containment, eradication, and recovery.

How SOAR Differs from SIEM, XDR, and EDR
- SIEM (Security Information and Event Management) collects and correlates log data, but it doesn't automate responses.
- XDR (Extended Detection and Response) tracks attacks across multiple vectors, like email, devices, and cloud, but it relies on SOAR to automate containment.
- EDR (Endpoint Detection and Response) detects threats at the device level, but it doesn't automate the containment of those threats.

SOAR is like the conductor of an orchestra, automating the response actions of XDR, EDR, and SIEM simultaneously.

How SOAR Works
SOAR systems are driven by three core concepts:
1. Security Orchestration — Combines multiple security tools (like EDR, XDR, and SIEM) into a unified platform.
2. Automation — Automates manual tasks like blocking IPs, quarantining devices, and triggering playbooks.
3. Response — Carries out real-time response actions, such as isolating devices, cutting off user access, and notifying security teams.

How It Works (Step-by-Step):
1. Threat Detected — A threat is detected by EDR, XDR, or SIEM (like a ransomware file or a phishing email).
2. SOAR Playbook Activated — The SOAR system triggers a specific playbook for that type of threat (like "Ransomware Response Playbook").
3. Automated Response Actions — The SOAR system:
   o Quarantines infected devices (EDR).
   o Blocks malicious IPs at the firewall.
   o Locks down file access in shared drives.
   o Alerts the SOC team and provides updates via Slack, Teams, or email.
4. Incident Resolution — The threat is neutralized and the system provides an audit trail of all actions taken.

AI Enhancements in SOAR Tools

How does AI make SOAR more effective?
Traditional SOAR platforms follow pre-built playbooks, but AI-powered SOAR platforms are adaptive and self-learning. They analyze threat patterns, prioritize incidents, and adjust their responses as new threats arise.

Here's how AI enhances SOAR tools:
- Anomaly Detection — AI tracks "normal" behavior and triggers a SOAR playbook if anomalies are detected (like unusual file transfers, logins from suspicious IPs, or failed login attempts).
- Automated Playbook Customization — AI can create or modify playbooks in real time. If the attack is a new type of ransomware, the AI customizes a response in seconds.
- Threat Prioritization — Instead of alerting the SOC for every threat, AI determines which threats are critical and prioritizes them.

- Self-Learning Models — The more threats the AI sees, the smarter it gets. AI-driven SOAR tools adapt their playbooks based on real-world attack data.
- AI-Powered Decision-Making — AI makes real-time decisions on whether to quarantine a device, block a URL, or lock shared files.

Without AI, SOAR follows static playbooks. With AI, SOAR becomes adaptive, smarter, and faster.

Common Use Cases for AI-Driven SOAR
1. Ransomware Response
Scenario: A ransomware attack begins encrypting files on an employee's laptop.

How SOAR Responds:
- Quarantine Device: The SOAR system detects unusual file encryption activity and isolates the laptop from the network.
- Lock File Access: The SOAR platform triggers a playbook to restrict file access to shared drives.
- Notify IT and Management: Sends a Slack or Teams message to the security team with real-time updates.

2. Phishing Email Containment
Scenario: A phishing email with a malicious link is sent to multiple employees.

How SOAR Responds:
- Email Quarantine: SOAR automatically isolates and removes the email from all inboxes.
- Block Malicious URL: The URL is added to the company's blocklist.
- User Notification: Sends employees a message that an email was flagged as phishing.

3. Insider Threat Response
Scenario: An employee suddenly begins downloading large amounts of data.

How SOAR Responds:
- User Quarantine: The SOAR platform locks the user's account.
- Monitor Data Access: Tracks all file downloads and movement.
- Generate Audit Report: Sends the audit log to human resources (HR) and the legal team for review.

Top AI-Powered SOAR Tools
- Splunk Phantom — One of the most popular SOAR platforms, with advanced automation and AI-based anomaly detection.
- Cortex XSOAR (Palo Alto Networks) — Known for its customizable playbooks and integrations with EDR, XDR, and SIEM.
- IBM Resilient — A SOAR tool with strong focus on AI-driven automation and incident response workflows.
- Swimlane — Offers no-code playbook design for companies that want customizable workflows without technical expertise.

Benefits of Using AI-Driven SOAR
1. Faster Response Times
- Without SOAR: It takes a human 30-60 minutes to detect, analyze, and isolate a ransomware attack.
- With AI-Driven SOAR: It takes 30 seconds to quarantine a device, block an IP, and lock down files.
2. 24/7 Automated Response
- Without SOAR: If an attack happens at 2 AM, analysts might not respond until 8 AM.
- With AI-Driven SOAR: Attacks are handled instantly with automated playbooks — no human needed.
3. Reduced Alert Fatigue
- Without SOAR: SOC teams are flooded with thousands of alerts, many of which are low-priority.
- With AI-Driven SOAR: AI prioritizes and resolves low-priority alerts automatically, so analysts focus only on high-priority issues.
4. Reduced Costs
- Without SOAR: Companies spend thousands on human analysts for incident response.
- With AI-Driven SOAR: Automation replaces manual tasks, reducing the need for human labor.

Challenges of Implementing SOAR
- High Cost — Some SOAR platforms are expensive to deploy and maintain.
- Integration Complexity — SOAR must integrate with EDR, XDR, SIEM, and firewalls.
- Customization — Companies must create and customize playbooks for different threat types.

Building a Comprehensive Disaster Recovery (DR) Plan
A Disaster Recovery (DR) Plan is your blueprint for surviving a cyberattack, ransomware incident, or catastrophic system failure. Without one, your business faces extended downtime, data loss, and potential closure. With a plan in place, you can restore operations quickly and avoid catastrophic consequences.

"If Incident Response is about stopping the attack, Disaster Recovery is about getting back on your feet."

A strong Disaster Recovery Plan (DRP) ensures your business can continue operating, even after a disaster. It's not just about restoring files — it's about having failover systems, backups, and communication strategies ready to go before disaster strikes.

What is a Disaster Recovery (DR) Plan?
A Disaster Recovery Plan (DRP) is a formal document that outlines how an organization will restore its systems, files, and services after a major cybersecurity incident, system failure, or natural disaster. This plan outlines:
- Which systems are critical and must be restored first.
- How and where data backups are stored (on-site, off-site, or in the cloud).
- Who is responsible for each step of the recovery process.
- How quickly systems need to be restored to avoid business disruption.

Why Do You Need a Disaster Recovery Plan?
- Cyberattacks Are Inevitable — Ransomware, malware, and zero-day attacks are happening at an increasing rate. 43% of businesses never recover after a major cyberattack.
- Data Loss is Expensive — The cost of downtime can range from $10,000 to $50,000 per hour, depending on the business.
- Cyber Insurance Requires a DR Plan — Insurers are now demanding proof of a DRP before issuing policies.
- Regulatory Compliance — Many industries (like finance and healthcare) are required to have formal DR plans as part of their compliance obligations.

"You don't create a Disaster Recovery Plan during an attack — you create it long before."

The Key Components of a Disaster Recovery Plan (DRP)
To build a comprehensive DRP, you need to include the following six key components:

1. Data Backup Strategy
If ransomware encrypts your data, your backups are your only hope. Backups ensure that you can restore systems, files, and business operations. But not all backups are equal. Traditional backups can be encrypted by ransomware too!

How to Build a Data Backup Strategy:
- Use Immutable Backups — Backups that cannot be changed, encrypted, or modified by ransomware.
- Follow the 3-2-1 Rule — 3 copies of your data, on 2 different storage types, with 1 copy stored offsite (like the cloud).
- Regular Backup Schedules — Back up critical files daily and full system backups weekly or monthly.
- Test Your Backups — Backups that fail to restore are worthless. Test them regularly.

AI Enhancements for Backups:
- AI-Powered Integrity Checks — AI scans restored files for backdoors, malware, or file corruption.
- Automated Backup Scheduling — AI schedules backups based on user activity (like after major software changes).

"Your backup is your last line of defense. Don't wait to find out it's broken."

2. Disaster Recovery Sites and Failover Systems
If your main systems go down, you need a failover system that takes over instantly. This can be a hot site, cold site, or cloud-based failover system.

Types of Disaster Recovery Sites:
- Hot Site — A fully functional backup system that mirrors your production system. If your primary system fails, operations switch to the hot site instantly.
- Cold Site — A physical space where you can set up new equipment, but it takes days or weeks to get operational.
- Cloud-Based Failover — The most modern option. If your on-premises system fails, the cloud takes over automatically.

How to Build a Failover Plan:
- Use cloud-based failover systems to ensure automatic failover.
- Test the failover process by simulating system failures.
- Identify which systems are mission-critical (customer-facing websites, financial services, etc.).

AI Enhancements for Failover:
- Predictive Failover Activation — AI can detect when systems are about to fail (like slow system performance) and activate failover before a crash happens.
- Automated System Failback — When your primary system comes back online, AI manages the transfer of files and processes from the backup system.

3. Business Impact Analysis (BIA)
A Business Impact Analysis (BIA) identifies which systems are mission-critical and determines how quickly they need to be restored. Some systems (like customer support chat) can be down for hours, but others (like payment systems) must be restored immediately.

How to Build a Business Impact Analysis:
- Identify Critical Systems — Which systems, files, or tools must be restored first?
- Set RTO and RPO Goals —
  - Recovery Time Objective (RTO): How fast does each system need to be restored? (Example: Payroll must be restored within 4 hours.)
  - Recovery Point Objective (RPO): How much data loss is acceptable? (Example: If your last backup was 12 hours ago, is that acceptable?)

AI Enhancements for BIA:
- AI-Powered System Prioritization — AI predicts which systems are most critical and which ones should be restored first.
- Automated RTO/RPO Reporting — AI tracks RTO and RPO performance in real time, showing you if goals are met.

"Not all systems are equal. Payment systems must be restored first. Email can wait."

4. Incident Response and Disaster Recovery Integration
Your Incident Response Plan (IRP) and Disaster Recovery Plan (DRP) must work together. While IR is about containment, DR is about restoration.

How to Integrate IR and DR:
- Link your SOAR playbooks to your DRP. For example, if a ransomware attack is detected, the DRP is automatically triggered to restore systems.
- Use AI to automate the switch from incident response to disaster recovery.

- Create a handoff process — Once the attack is contained (IR), the system automatically moves into recovery mode (DR).

5. Communication and Notification Plan
If your system is down, who needs to be notified? This could be IT teams, executives, customers, and third-party vendors.

How to Build a Communication Plan:
- Create a Contact List — Include IT staff, executives, and third-party vendors.
- Build Notification Templates — Pre-write email, Slack, and text message templates.
- Automate Notifications with SOAR — Use SOAR to send alert messages as soon as a major disaster begins.

6. Testing, Review, and Updates
A DRP is useless if it's never tested. You need to conduct tabletop exercises and live drills to ensure everything works.

How to Test a Disaster Recovery Plan:
- Conduct tabletop exercises to role-play ransomware attacks.
- Test the failover process to ensure that backups restore properly.
- Identify flaws in the DRP and update it after every test.

How AI Enhances Disaster Recovery
AI doesn't just help you detect threats — it helps you recover faster after an attack. Here's how:
- Backup Verification — AI scans restored files for malware.
- Automated Recovery Playbooks — When ransomware is detected, AI triggers a playbook to restore backups instantly.
- Data Prioritization — AI identifies which files are most critical (like payment files) and restores them first.
- Anomaly Detection — AI tracks restoration files for signs of hidden malware.

Best Practices for Incident Response & Disaster Recovery

Why Best Practices Matter
When a cyberattack happens, there's no time to "figure it out on the fly." You need to know exactly what to do and have a clear plan in place. The difference between a business that survives an attack and one that shuts down often comes down to one thing: preparation.

1. Create a Comprehensive Incident Response Plan (IRP)

Having a clear, step-by-step Incident Response Plan (IRP) ensures that your team knows exactly how to respond to a cyberattack. This plan should outline roles, responsibilities, and escalation procedures. Every second counts during a cyber incident, and delays caused by confusion can amplify damage.

Key Steps to Include in Your IRP:

- Identify key roles (like Incident Commander, Forensic Analyst, and Communications Lead).
- Create pre-written response templates for common threats (like ransomware or data breaches).
- Conduct regular tabletop exercises to ensure everyone knows their role.

2. Conduct Regular Cybersecurity Drills and Simulations

Cybersecurity drills aren't just for large enterprises — they are essential for businesses of every size. Simulated attacks (Red Team/Blue Team exercises) test your team's readiness and reveal gaps in your defenses.

How to Conduct Simulations:

- Use "live fire" scenarios to mimic real attacks (like ransomware or phishing breaches).
- Assign a "Red Team" (attackers) to simulate the attack and a "Blue Team" (defenders) to respond.
- Use AI-driven simulation platforms like RangeForce (https://www.rangeforce.com/) or CybSafe (https://www.cybsafe.com/) to train employees on threat response.
- After the drill, conduct a post-mortem analysis and revise your Incident Response Plan.

3. Establish Automated Threat Detection and Incident Alerts

By the time you "see" a threat, it's often too late. Automated threat detection tools monitor your environment 24/7, identifying threats before they become full-scale attacks.

Tools You Should Use:

- XDR (Extended Detection and Response) — Combines endpoint, network, and cloud threat detection into one dashboard (Example: CrowdStrike (https://www.crowdstrike.com/)).
- SOAR (Security Orchestration, Automation, and Response) — Automates responses like quarantining files or isolating devices (Example: Splunk SOAR (https://www.splunk.com/)).
- AI-Driven Alerts — AI tools like Darktrace (https://www.darktrace.com/) detect and predict anomalies, allowing you to stop threats early.

4. Back Up Everything and Follow the 3-2-1 Rule

Data backups are your best defense against ransomware and system failures. The 3-2-1 Rule means:

- Keep 3 copies of your data.
- Store it on 2 different media types (like cloud + local disk).
- Store 1 copy offsite (like offline cold storage).
- How to Do It Right:
- Use cloud services like Backblaze (https://www.backblaze.com/) or Carbonite (https://www.carbonite.com/) to automate daily backups.
- Regularly test your backups. A backup that can't be restored is useless.
- Encrypt your backups to prevent data theft, even if stolen.

5. Build a Disaster Recovery Plan (DRP) That Includes Critical Assets

A Disaster Recovery Plan (DRP) is more than a simple backup plan. It outlines how to restore your critical business functions after a disaster — whether it's a ransomware attack, natural disaster, or insider threat.

Essentials for Your DRP:

- Identify the Recovery Time Objective (RTO) (How fast do you need systems to be back online?)
- Identify the Recovery Point Objective (RPO) (How much data loss is acceptable, measured in time?)
- Prioritize which systems to restore first (like payment systems, customer data, etc.).
- Use cloud disaster recovery (CDR) platforms like AWS Disaster Recovery (https://aws.amazon.com/disaster-recovery/) to ensure rapid failover.

6. Adopt a Zero-Trust Security Model

Zero-Trust assumes that no user, device, or system can be trusted by default — even internal users. It's one of the most effective ways to prevent the lateral movement of attackers within your system.

How to Implement Zero-Trust:

- Require multi-factor authentication (MFA) for every login (including internal systems).
- Use AI-driven identity verification and risk-based conditional access.
- Monitor user behavior with User and Entity Behavior Analytics (UEBA).
- Grant users and applications the least privilege necessary to complete their tasks.

7. Use AI-Driven Tools for Incident Response Automation

Human response times are too slow for modern cyberattacks. That's why AI-driven SOAR platforms have become essential for automating incident response.

How AI Tools Help:
- AI can quarantine compromised devices before malware spreads.
- AI tools triage alerts to prevent alert fatigue.
- Automated Playbooks let AI respond to low-level incidents without human intervention.
- Tools to Use:
- Splunk SOAR (https://www.splunk.com/) — Automates incident response actions (like isolating devices) in real-time.
- Swimlane (https://swimlane.com/) — Customizable playbooks for responding to common incidents.
- Cortex XSOAR (https://www.paloaltonetworks.com/cortex/xsoar) — Integrated threat intelligence and automated threat response.

8. Regularly Audit and Test Your Incident Response Plan

A plan that isn't tested is just a theory. Regular audits ensure that your team stays ready.

What to Do:
- Schedule annual incident response audits to test for gaps.
- Conduct surprise "live attack" drills to see how teams respond.
- Update your plan with new attack methods and lessons learned.
- Use platforms like Cyberbit (https://www.cyberbit.com/) for live attack simulations.

Chapter Conclusion: Stay Ready, Not Reactive

Incident response and disaster recovery are no longer optional. As cyberattacks evolve, companies must assume they will be breached. What separates successful companies from failures is how fast they recover. The faster you detect, respond, and recover, the less damage you face.

Attackers are using AI to automate attacks, but you can use AI to automate your defense. AI-driven SOAR platforms can stop ransomware from spreading, quarantine infected devices, and execute pre-defined playbooks that stop attacks in their tracks. Backups protect your data; Zero-Trust protects your network; and disaster recovery plans ensure business continuity. Together, these elements create a defense-in-depth strategy.

Here's your next move:
- Automate incident response with SOAR tools like Splunk SOAR (https://www.splunk.com/) or Swimlane (https://swimlane.com/).
- Test your Disaster Recovery Plan and know your Recovery Time Objective (RTO) and Recovery Point Objective (RPO).
- Use the 3-2-1 backup rule with tools like Backblaze (https://www.backblaze.com/) or Carbonite (https://www.carbonite.com/) to ensure rapid data recovery.
- Embrace Zero-Trust and require MFA for all internal systems.

Don't wait for a disaster to happen. Prepare today so you don't panic tomorrow. A disaster you prepare for is an inconvenience; a disaster you don't prepare for is a catastrophe. Be ready.

Chapter 17: Cyber Insurance: Do You Need It?

Cyberattacks are no longer "if they happen" events — they're "when they happen" events. As attacks become more frequent and sophisticated, businesses must prepare for the potential financial fallout. This is where cyber insurance comes in.

Cyber insurance protects businesses from the financial consequences of cyberattacks like ransomware, data breaches, and business interruption. But cyber insurance isn't a one-size-fits-all solution. Some policies cover ransomware payments, while others only cover response costs. If your business isn't prepared, you could be left footing the bill for millions in damages.

In this chapter, we'll explore:
1. How cyber insurance works and what it covers.
2. How AI-driven risk reduction can lower your premiums.

1. What is Cyber Insurance?
Cyber insurance (also called cyber liability insurance) is a specialized insurance policy designed to cover financial losses caused by cyberattacks and data breaches. Traditional insurance policies (like property insurance) don't cover these losses, so businesses must purchase a dedicated cyber insurance policy.

Why You Need Cyber Insurance
- Cost of Ransomware — Ransomware demands can reach millions of dollars. Without insurance, you pay out of pocket.
- Data Breach Costs — Companies must pay for legal fees, data recovery, and credit monitoring for affected customers.
- Business Interruption — If your company is offline for hours or days, you lose revenue. Cyber insurance helps you recover lost income.

2. What Does Cyber Insurance Cover?
Every cyber insurance policy is different, but most cover these six key areas:

1. Ransomware Payments
If a ransomware attack encrypts your files, you may be forced to pay a ransom to get your data back. Cyber insurance can cover the cost of the ransom (up to a specified limit).

Example: If attackers demand a $250,000 ransom, your insurer might cover $200,000 of it (depending on your policy).

2. Business Interruption Costs

If a ransomware attack takes down your servers, websites, or payment systems, your business may not be able to operate. Cyber insurance can reimburse you for lost revenue during the downtime.

Example: If your e-commerce site is offline for 72 hours and you lose $50,000 in sales, cyber insurance will reimburse you for the lost revenue.

3. Legal and Regulatory Fines

When a breach occurs, companies are often required to notify affected customers. This can trigger fines under privacy laws like GDPR or CCPA. Cyber insurance covers the cost of fines, as well as legal fees.

Example: If your company is fined $50,000 for violating GDPR, cyber insurance will cover it.

4. Data Breach Response Costs

After a breach, you'll need to:
- Hire a forensic investigator to figure out how it happened.
- Notify affected customers.
- Provide credit monitoring services to affected customers.

Cyber insurance covers the cost of all of this, which can cost hundreds of thousands of dollars.

5. Extortion and Threat Costs

Sometimes, attackers don't encrypt files — they steal them. Then, they threaten to release sensitive files unless you pay. Cyber insurance may cover the cost of negotiating with attackers and paying them off.

Example: Hackers steal customer data and demand $100,000 to not release it. Your insurance policy may cover the payment.

6. Incident Response & Recovery

When an attack happens, you'll need to hire a forensics team, legal counsel, and PR consultants to recover. Cyber insurance helps you pay for:
- Incident Response Teams — Forensic investigators to analyze what happened.
- Public Relations (PR) — Damage control for customer trust and reputation.
- Data Recovery — Recovery of encrypted or stolen files.

3. What Does Cyber Insurance NOT Cover?

Not all policies cover everything. Exclusions matter. Here are some common exclusions in cyber insurance policies:

- Insider Threats — If a disgruntled employee steals data, some policies won't cover it.
- War Exclusion — If a cyberattack is deemed an act of war (like a nation-state attack), insurers may deny the claim.
- Outdated Systems — If your systems aren't updated or patched, insurers may deny your claim.
- Social Engineering Losses — If an employee is tricked into transferring funds to a scammer, the policy may not cover it.

Pro Tip: Read your policy closely and ask for clarification on what's included and what's excluded.

4. How to Qualify for Cyber Insurance

Insurance providers don't give coverage to everyone. You must prove that you're not a high-risk business. Here's what insurers look for:

1. Incident Response Plan (IRP)
Insurers want to know if you have a plan for responding to ransomware or data breaches. If you don't have one, you may pay higher premiums.

2. Security Controls
Companies with advanced security controls (like XDR, EDR, and SIEM) qualify for lower premiums.

3. Data Backup Plan
Insurers will ask if you have regular backups and if those backups are immutable (can't be encrypted by ransomware).

4. Multi-Factor Authentication (MFA)
If you don't have MFA for remote logins, you may be denied cyber insurance coverage.

5. Employee Training
If employees don't know how to spot phishing emails, you're a bigger risk. Train your staff on how to recognize scams.

Pro Tip: Insurers will send you a security questionnaire. The more controls you have in place (like backups, MFA, and XDR), the lower your premiums.

5. How AI Can Reduce Cyber Insurance Premiums
AI isn't just for hackers — it's also a tool for lowering your cyber insurance premiums. Insurance companies charge lower premiums to companies with strong defenses, and AI-driven security tools reduce your risk.

Here's how AI helps you save on premiums:

1. AI-Driven Anomaly Detection
AI tools like Darktrace detect unusual employee behavior (like large file transfers) and stop insider threats. Insurers see this as a sign that your company is well-defended, so they lower your premium.

2. AI-Based XDR (Extended Detection and Response)
XDR tools track threats across devices, cloud services, and email. Since XDR prevents ransomware from spreading, insurers reward companies with XDR by offering discounted premiums.

3. AI-Powered SOAR Automation
SOAR tools automate incident response actions (like quarantining ransomware-infected devices) so threats don't spread. Companies with SOAR tools qualify for lower premiums because they can respond to attacks instantly.

4. AI-Driven Vulnerability Scanning
Insurers want to know if you scan for vulnerabilities. AI-driven vulnerability scanners automatically detect weaknesses in your system and patch them. Businesses with strong scanning policies get lower premiums.

5. Use AI to Audit Compliance
Insurers offer lower premiums to companies that comply with regulations like GDPR and CCPA. AI-driven compliance tools automate audits, identify gaps, and keep you compliant.

6. How to Choose the Right Cyber Insurance Policy
Here's what to look for when shopping for a policy:
- Coverage Limits — Check how much they'll pay for ransomware, data breaches, and business interruption.
- Exclusions — Watch for exclusions on nation-state attacks and insider threats.
- Ransomware Coverage — Some policies only cover response costs, but not the ransom payment itself.
- Legal and PR Costs — Make sure your policy covers PR and brand damage costs.
- Recovery Costs — Ensure the policy covers data recovery and file restoration.

Pro Tip: Ask your insurer if they offer discounts for having AI-based detection, XDR, EDR, and SOAR.

Chapter Conclusion
Cyber insurance is no longer a "nice to have" — it's a must-have. As cyberattacks increase, so do the costs of recovery. But cyber insurance isn't free money. You'll need to prove that your business has a strong security posture, including:
- Incident Response and Disaster Recovery Plans
- AI-driven threat detection (like XDR, EDR, and SOAR)
- Immutable backups

"The attacker only needs to succeed once, but with cyber insurance, you can recover every time."

Chapter 18: Regulatory Compliance (GDPR, HIPAA, etc.)

Why Regulatory Compliance Matters
Compliance with regulatory frameworks like GDPR, HIPAA, PCI-DSS, and CCPA is no longer optional. Companies that fail to comply face massive fines, lawsuits, and loss of customer trust. The problem is, keeping up with regulatory requirements is complex, time-consuming, and ever-changing.

This is where AI-driven compliance tools come in. By automating audits, tracking regulatory changes, and monitoring risky activity, AI helps businesses maintain compliance in real time. Instead of relying on annual audits or manual checklists, AI offers continuous compliance monitoring, ensuring your business stays ahead of fines and penalties.

1. What is Regulatory Compliance?
Regulatory compliance refers to the process of ensuring that your organization follows the rules, laws, and standards set by regulatory bodies like the General Data Protection Regulation (GDPR), Health Insurance Portability and Accountability Act (HIPAA), and California Consumer Privacy Act (CCPA).

Why It Matters:
- Avoid Massive Fines: GDPR fines can reach €20M or 4% of global revenue.
- Protect Customer Trust: Customers are more likely to trust companies with transparent data privacy policies.
- Mitigate Legal Risk: Non-compliance can lead to lawsuits, government audits, and reputational damage.

2. Key Regulatory Frameworks You Need to Know

1. GDPR (General Data Protection Regulation)
Who It Affects: Any business that handles data from European Union (EU) citizens.

Core Requirements:
- Right to Be Forgotten: Customers can request that their personal data be deleted.
- Consent Management: Users must give consent for data collection (no pre-checked boxes).
- Data Breach Notification: Companies must notify authorities of a breach within 72 hours.

2. HIPAA (Health Insurance Portability and Accountability Act)

Who It Affects: Any business handling healthcare data, such as hospitals, insurers, and health tech companies.

Core Requirements:
- Data Encryption: All health data must be encrypted in transit and at rest.
- Access Control: Only authorized personnel should access sensitive healthcare data.
- Audit Trails: Companies must maintain audit logs to track all access to health records.

3. CCPA (California Consumer Privacy Act)

Who It Affects: Companies with customers in California that meet specific revenue or data processing thresholds.

Core Requirements:
- Right to Opt-Out: Customers can request to opt out of data sales.
- Access to Data: Consumers can request access to the personal data a company holds about them.
- Right to Delete Data: Similar to GDPR, consumers can request their data be deleted.

4. PCI-DSS (Payment Card Industry Data Security Standard)

Who It Affects: Any company that processes or stores payment card information (like credit card numbers).

Core Requirements:
- Data Encryption: Cardholder data must be encrypted.
- Access Controls: Only authorized employees should access cardholder data.
- Vulnerability Scanning: Businesses must regularly scan for system vulnerabilities.

Pro Tip: Companies may have to comply with multiple frameworks at once (like GDPR, CCPA, and PCI-DSS). This creates a "compliance overlap" that makes manual compliance extremely difficult.

3. How AI Helps Organizations Stay Compliant

Without AI, compliance is slow, manual, and prone to human error. Companies rely on annual audits, spreadsheets, and manual checklists, which often result in missed requirements and surprise fines. But with AI, compliance becomes continuous, automated, and real-time.

Here's how AI-driven compliance tools make compliance easier:

1. Continuous Compliance Monitoring
Instead of waiting for an annual audit, AI tracks compliance in real time. It monitors system logs, employee activity, and security configurations to ensure they meet regulatory standards. If it detects a misconfiguration (like a firewall being turned off), it alerts the compliance officer instantly.

How It Works:
- AI tracks changes to file permissions, firewall rules, and user access rights.
- It ensures that employee activities comply with regulations like HIPAA, GDPR, and PCI-DSS.
- It flags misconfigurations, such as unencrypted files or unauthorized user access.

Example: If an employee moves a healthcare file (protected under HIPAA) to a shared folder, the AI detects it and sends an alert to the compliance team.

2. AI-Driven Audits
Traditional audits are done once per year, but by then, it's too late to fix issues. AI allows for continuous audits. It scans your security settings, access logs, and encryption protocols daily to detect compliance gaps.

How It Works:
- AI runs daily audits on systems to ensure compliance with GDPR, HIPAA, and PCI-DSS.
- It tracks login attempts, file transfers, and access to sensitive data.
- It generates reports for regulators and auditors, making compliance reviews faster.

Example: If regulators request a GDPR compliance audit, you can generate an instant audit report instead of spending weeks gathering evidence.

3. Consent and Data Privacy Management
GDPR and CCPA require companies to track user consent for data collection. AI-based consent management platforms allow companies to track, log, and manage consent automatically.

How It Works:
- AI tracks user consent preferences and stores them in a compliance log.
- If a user withdraws consent, AI triggers a playbook to delete the user's personal data from all systems.
- AI generates logs of every user's consent, which can be used as proof of compliance in a legal case.

Example: If a customer requests to delete their data (as required by GDPR), AI identifies and deletes the data from all locations where it exists (databases, cloud storage, marketing platforms, etc.).

4. Automated Risk Assessments
AI tools can scan your system for risks (like unencrypted files or misconfigured servers) and rank them based on severity. This helps companies prioritize and fix the most critical issues first.

How It Works:
- AI scans your cloud storage, shared folders, and server logs.
- It flags risky behaviors, like open file shares or exposed databases.
- It recommends specific actions to reduce the risk.

Example: AI detects that a company's file storage system allows public access, which violates PCI-DSS. The AI triggers a playbook to restrict access automatically.

5. Predictive Compliance
Rather than react to non-compliance, AI predicts where future compliance issues may arise. For example, if a system change is about to violate PCI-DSS, the AI predicts the problem before it happens.

How It Works:
- AI tracks system changes (like software updates) and predicts whether they will cause compliance violations.
- If it identifies a high-risk change, it alerts the security team.
- AI recommends configuration adjustments to avoid violations.

Example: If an IT admin updates a server's firmware, AI predicts that the new firmware is not PCI-DSS compliant and warns the admin before the update is applied.

4. How to Use AI to Audit Compliance in Real Time
- Install AI-Driven Compliance Tools — Use tools like OneTrust, Vanta, or LogicGate to track GDPR, CCPA, and PCI-DSS compliance.
- Set Real-Time Alerts — Configure alerts for high-risk compliance issues (like unencrypted files or misconfigured permissions).
- Automate Consent Tracking — Use AI-based consent management systems to log and manage user consent for GDPR and CCPA compliance.
- Use Continuous Compliance Dashboards — AI compliance platforms have dashboards that show your compliance status in real time.

Pro Tip: Generate an instant compliance report for regulators, rather than wasting weeks on manual audits.

Chapter Conclusion
Compliance isn't a "one-and-done" process — it's a continuous, real-time effort. With regulations like GDPR, HIPAA, and PCI-DSS, companies must prove they are compliant every day, not just during an annual audit. AI makes this possible by enabling:
- Real-time compliance monitoring
- AI-driven audits
- Automated consent tracking

By using AI-based compliance platforms, companies can avoid fines, improve data privacy, and create audit-ready reports on demand.

"You don't wait for the auditor to knock on your door — you stay compliant 24/7."

Chapter 19: Threat Hunting & Red Teaming

The Rise of Proactive Cybersecurity

When it comes to cybersecurity, most companies are reactive — they respond only after an attack happens. But with the rise of self-evolving malware and AI-driven phishing scams, reactive security is no longer enough. Businesses need to shift to a proactive security strategy.

This is where Threat Hunting and Red Teaming come into play. Unlike reactive approaches, these strategies actively search for vulnerabilities before an attack happens. While Red Teaming simulates real-world attacks to expose weaknesses, Threat Hunting identifies and neutralizes potential threats before they become active attacks.

"The attacker only has to succeed once, but with proactive threat hunting, you can succeed every time."

In this chapter, you'll learn:
1. How AI-driven Red Teams run attack simulations.
2. How AI-driven Threat Hunting detects attacks before they happen.
3. How AI-based gamification platforms help train cybersecurity teams.

1. AI in Penetration Testing (Pentesting) — How AI-Driven Red Teams Run Attack Simulations

What is Red Teaming?

Red Teaming is the process of simulating a cyberattack on your own network. The goal is to think and act like a hacker, identifying weak points before real attackers do. Traditionally, Red Teams consist of human penetration testers who use hacker tactics to breach a company's defenses.

However, human Red Teams have limitations. They can only test during a set period (like once per quarter) and focus on a limited set of attack methods. In contrast, AI-driven Red Teams can simulate thousands of attack scenarios 24/7, identify weaknesses that human testers miss, and operate at a fraction of the cost.

What is AI-Driven Penetration Testing?

Traditional penetration testing (pentesting) is a manual process where human testers attempt to breach a system. While effective, it is slow, costly, and often leaves gaps in testing. AI-Driven Penetration Testing (AI Pentesting) takes this process to the next level by using AI to run attack simulations at scale.

Unlike human testers, AI-driven pentesting can:

- Continuously scan for vulnerabilities instead of waiting for quarterly tests.
- Use self-evolving attack strategies, similar to how polymorphic malware adapts.
- Launch thousands of attack paths simultaneously, ensuring every possible vector is tested.
- Simulate zero-day attacks (attacks that exploit unknown vulnerabilities) rather than focusing solely on known issues.

This allows companies to stay ahead of attackers, identify hidden flaws, and prioritize patching before attackers have a chance to exploit vulnerabilities.

How AI-Driven Red Teams Simulate Attacks

AI-driven Red Teams follow a multi-step approach to simulate real-world attacks. First, they generate a list of potential attack paths using AI-driven path prediction models. These models analyze network topology, known vulnerabilities, and historical data to determine which routes attackers are most likely to exploit.

Once attack paths are selected, AI-driven systems launch simulated attacks on the network. These attacks can take many forms, including:

- Fuzz Testing — The AI injects random inputs into software and applications to see if they crash. This reveals exploitable software bugs.
- Phishing Simulations — AI generates and sends personalized phishing emails to test if employees fall for them.
- Ransomware Simulations — AI deploys simulated ransomware to see how quickly Endpoint Detection and Response (EDR) tools can detect and contain the threat.
- Zero-Day Exploits — Instead of relying on known attack methods, AI creates new, previously unknown attack paths to identify unknown vulnerabilities.

By continuously generating new attack scenarios, AI-driven Red Teams are able to stay one step ahead of human hackers.

AI-Driven Red Team Tools
Several tools and platforms are used by AI-driven Red Teams to simulate real-world attacks. Some of the most common include:

1. Cobalt Strike — A platform for simulating attacker behavior like lateral movement, command-and-control (C2) channels, and privilege escalation. By incorporating AI-driven playbooks, Cobalt Strike can launch fully automated attack campaigns.

2. BloodHound — A tool used to visualize attack paths in Active Directory (AD) environments. BloodHound, enhanced with AI, can predict the most likely attack routes and prioritize which systems need protection.

3. Metasploit with AI Modules — Metasploit is a well-known tool for running exploit scripts on vulnerable systems. With AI, Metasploit automatically identifies which exploit scripts are most likely to succeed based on system scans.

4. Breach and Attack Simulation (BAS) Platforms — Tools like SafeBreach and AttackIQ run continuous attack simulations, generating ransomware, phishing, and malware attacks to test defenses.

Example of AI-Driven Penetration Testing in Action
A financial services company wants to test its resilience against ransomware. They deploy a Breach and Attack Simulation (BAS) platform to run a ransomware attack simulation.

The AI-driven platform generates multiple ransomware variants, each with different encryption methods and file paths. It launches the attack simulation and tracks how well the company's Endpoint Detection and Response (EDR) system reacts. The results reveal that the company's EDR software successfully blocks 80% of the attacks, but fails to detect 20% of the variants.

As a result, the company switches to an AI-based EDR system that offers better ransomware detection.

Benefits of AI-Driven Penetration Testing
- Faster Vulnerability Detection — Human testers work slowly, but AI-based tools scan hundreds of devices in parallel.
- 24/7 Testing — Instead of quarterly testing, AI-based pentesting runs continuously, identifying issues as soon as they arise.
- Cost Savings — Hiring human penetration testers costs tens of thousands of dollars. AI-driven pentesting tools operate 24/7 for a fraction of the cost.

- Better Accuracy — Human testers can only try a limited number of attack paths, while AI-based tools generate thousands of potential attack routes.
- Realistic Zero-Day Testing — Traditional testers focus on known vulnerabilities. AI-driven pentesting simulates zero-day vulnerabilities that no one has seen before.

Challenges of AI-Driven Pentesting
- False Positives — AI can mistakenly flag issues as vulnerabilities, wasting time and resources.
- Limited Creativity — While AI can identify paths that are logical, it can struggle to simulate creative attacks that human hackers might use.
- Playbook Customization — Customizing AI playbooks to match your company's network architecture takes time and effort.
- Over-Reliance on AI — Companies may assume that AI-driven pentesting is a "set it and forget it" solution, but it still requires oversight.

How to Implement AI-Driven Red Teaming in Your Business
- Deploy a Breach and Attack Simulation (BAS) Platform — Install platforms like SafeBreach or AttackIQ.
- Run Weekly Automated Tests — Schedule weekly attack simulations to detect new vulnerabilities as soon as they arise.
- Prioritize Patch Management — Act on the vulnerabilities identified in the reports, starting with the most critical ones.
- Use Polymorphic Malware Simulations — Simulate self-evolving malware and see how well your EDR, XDR, and antivirus tools respond.
- Train Staff on Attack Tactics — Train security teams on how to detect and respond to the attack paths used by AI-driven Red Teams.

Red Teaming vs. Threat Hunting
Although Red Teaming and Threat Hunting both aim to improve security, they focus on different objectives.
- Red Teaming is about simulating attacks. The goal is to test defenses by attacking the system like a hacker would.
- Threat Hunting is about detecting hidden threats that are already inside the system. The goal is to find threats before they become active attacks.

Red Teaming is proactive offense, while Threat Hunting is proactive defense.

How Threat Hunting with AI Detects Attacks Before They Happen

The Need for Proactive Threat Hunting
Imagine an attacker is inside your network, silently moving from system to system, gathering credentials, and planting backdoors. Traditional security tools like firewalls, SIEM, and antivirus can only detect threats when a known pattern or malware signature is present. But modern attacks, especially those powered by AI-driven malware or fileless attacks, don't leave behind the same predictable signatures.

This is where Threat Hunting comes in. While traditional tools focus on detecting known threats, Threat Hunting focuses on finding the unknown unknowns — threats that haven't been identified yet. By searching for unusual activity, anomalies, and subtle signs of compromise, Threat Hunters can detect threats before they launch an attack.

AI takes Threat Hunting to the next level. With machine learning, AI can recognize patterns of normal behavior and flag anything that deviates from that pattern. Unlike human Threat Hunters who may miss key signals, AI tracks millions of events simultaneously. The result? Faster threat detection, fewer missed attacks, and zero-day threats are stopped before they can act.

What is Threat Hunting?
Threat Hunting is the process of actively looking for threats that have not triggered an alert. Instead of waiting for a security tool (like an antivirus) to detect a virus, Threat Hunting involves manually and proactively looking for signs that an attack is already happening or is about to begin.

Threat Hunting is different from traditional security monitoring. Monitoring is passive — it waits for alerts. Hunting is active — it searches for threats before they strike.

How AI Enhances Threat Hunting
AI doesn't replace Threat Hunters — it makes them faster, smarter, and more effective. Traditional threat hunters rely on manual analysis, which is slow and prone to human error. AI-powered Threat Hunting uses machine learning, anomaly detection, and predictive analytics to automate this process.

Here's how AI makes Threat Hunting better:
- Behavioral Analysis — AI tracks what "normal" looks like for each user, system, and device. If a user suddenly starts logging in from another country at 2 AM, the AI flags it.
- Real-Time Anomaly Detection — AI detects unusual spikes in traffic, large data transfers, or unusual file executions that human threat hunters may not notice.
- Data Correlation — AI correlates logs, user activity, and network events from SIEM, EDR, and XDR tools. This helps identify patterns that no human could detect on their own.
- Continuous Hunting 24/7 — Unlike human threat hunters who work 9-5 shifts, AI runs continuously and tracks threats 24/7.
- Reduction of Alert Fatigue — Instead of sending every small anomaly to the security team, AI prioritizes alerts based on risk. High-risk threats are flagged first.
- Detection of Fileless Malware — Fileless malware doesn't leave behind traditional file signatures. AI tracks behavior instead of relying on malware signatures, detecting Living-off-the-Land (LotL) attacks that don't require malware files.

Pro Tip: Pair AI-based Threat Hunting with human Threat Hunters. Let AI handle the heavy lifting, while human experts analyze high-priority anomalies flagged by the AI.

How AI-Based Threat Hunting Works
AI-based Threat Hunting follows a clear process from start to finish. Here's a simple breakdown of the process:
- Baseline Creation — AI observes normal behavior for users, devices, and applications. For example, it tracks how often users log in, how they access files, and when certain applications are used.
- Anomaly Detection — Once the baseline is established, AI flags deviations from the norm. For instance, if a user who typically logs in from New York suddenly logs in from Moscow, AI flags it as an anomaly.
- Data Correlation — AI pulls in data from SIEM, EDR, and XDR tools. If a user logs in from an unusual location and simultaneously initiates a large data transfer, the system raises a higher-priority alert.
- Alert Prioritization — AI prioritizes threats based on the risk they pose. Anomalies that have multiple risk factors (like unauthorized access combined with large file transfers) are prioritized over single-factor anomalies.

- Automated Playbook Execution — Once a threat is detected, AI triggers an automated response playbook via SOAR (Security Orchestration, Automation, and Response). This playbook can quarantine a device, lock down shared files, or alert the Security Operations Center (SOC).
- Continuous Learning — After each attack, AI updates its knowledge base, making it more effective at spotting similar threats in the future.

Pro Tip: Continuous learning is what makes AI-driven Threat Hunting so powerful. Every time AI sees a new attack, it gets better at spotting the next one.

Threat Hunting Use Cases with AI

1. Insider Threat Detection
If an employee suddenly begins accessing files they don't normally use (like payroll files), AI will flag this behavior. Human threat hunters may miss these subtle signs, but AI identifies unusual file access immediately.

2. Advanced Persistent Threats (APTs)
Advanced Persistent Threats (APTs) often infiltrate a system, stay hidden for months, and only act when they're ready to exfiltrate data. AI-driven Threat Hunting looks for low and slow movements, like small data transfers over a long period, and detects early signs of an APT.

3. Fileless Malware Detection
Fileless malware attacks don't use files. Instead, they inject code directly into the memory of applications like PowerShell. AI-based Threat Hunting identifies abnormal activity in PowerShell scripts, command-line usage, and kernel-level changes.

4. Anomalous Login Activity
If a user logs in from New York at 9:00 AM and from China at 9:30 AM, that's impossible unless their credentials are stolen. AI spots impossible travel logins in real time and sends alerts to SOC teams.

5. Data Exfiltration Detection
If a user downloads thousands of files from a corporate drive at 3 AM, it's a red flag. AI correlates these data transfer anomalies with other user behavior to see if an insider threat or compromised user account is behind it.

How to Implement AI-Based Threat Hunting
- Deploy AI-Powered Threat Hunting Tools — Use tools like Microsoft Defender for Endpoint, Darktrace, or CrowdStrike Falcon. These tools monitor endpoints, cloud apps, and network traffic for anomalies.
- Use EDR, XDR, and SIEM Together — EDR detects threats at the device level, SIEM correlates security logs, and XDR connects everything. Together, they provide full visibility for AI-driven Threat Hunting.
- Set Alerts for High-Risk Behavior — Set up automated alerts for unusual login locations, large data transfers, and fileless malware attacks.
- Run Threat Hunting Playbooks — Use SOAR tools to create automated playbooks for threats like ransomware, lateral movement, and insider threats.
- Conduct Regular Threat Hunting Exercises — Run tabletop exercises where your team pretends to be attackers. This trains your team to recognize attack patterns and understand how AI spots anomalies.
- Enable Self-Learning AI Models — Use self-learning AI models that automatically adapt to new attack tactics (like polymorphic malware).

Benefits of AI-Driven Threat Hunting
- Faster Detection of Hidden Threats — Traditional detection relies on pre-built alerts. AI tracks anomalous behavior that pre-built alerts would miss.
- Reduced False Positives — AI correlates anomalies to reduce false positives. For example, one failed login might be normal, but if it's followed by unusual file transfers, AI sees a pattern.
- Detect Fileless Malware — Fileless malware doesn't have a file signature, so antivirus can't catch it. AI tracks PowerShell usage and kernel-level changes instead.
- 24/7 Threat Hunting — Unlike human hunters, AI works 24/7, 365 days a year.
- Improves Over Time — AI-based threat hunting systems improve after every attack. Each time a new technique is detected, AI remembers it for future threats.

AI-Driven Simulations and Gamification of Threat Hunting

Gamifying Cybersecurity to Build a Stronger Defense
How do you train cybersecurity teams to spot zero-day attacks, detect fileless malware, and track down Advanced Persistent Threats (APTs)? Traditional training, like lectures and classroom-style lessons, isn't enough. To develop real-world skills, cybersecurity professionals need hands-on experience in a realistic environment.

This is where AI-driven simulations and gamification come into play. By using gamified training platforms and AI-driven attack simulations, companies can turn threat hunting into an interactive, engaging experience. Trainees learn by doing, not just watching. They experience the same stress, urgency, and decision-making pressure they would face during a real attack.

Gamification isn't just for training beginners — even seasoned cybersecurity analysts benefit from this approach. When done right, gamification builds better decision-making, sharpens analytical skills, and keeps security teams battle-ready for real-world attacks.

"If you want to prepare for war, you need a battlefield. Gamified simulations are that battlefield."

What is AI-Driven Simulation in Threat Hunting?
AI-driven simulation is the use of artificial intelligence to create realistic, continuously evolving cyberattack scenarios. Unlike static training exercises, AI-based simulations use dynamic, adaptive attack paths to create unpredictable challenges for threat hunters.

AI-driven simulations provide:
- Real-World Scenarios — Participants must respond to realistic attacks, such as ransomware outbreaks, insider threats, and phishing attempts.
- Evolving Threats — AI generates attack paths that change every time, simulating how real-world attackers adapt their tactics.
- Gamified Feedback — Players receive scores and performance feedback, encouraging continuous learning and improvement.

AI-driven simulations are typically delivered via Cyber Ranges — virtual environments that mimic real-world networks, applications, and attack vectors. Players are tasked with defending these environments from simulated attackers.

What is Gamification in Threat Hunting?
Gamification is the process of turning threat hunting into a game-like experience, complete with:
- Scoring systems — Players earn points for detecting threats and mitigating attacks.
- Leaderboards — Teams compete to see who performs the best.
- Timed Challenges — Players must detect and contain threats within a certain time limit.
- Recognition and Rewards — High performers are recognized as "champions" and may receive awards or certifications.

Instead of feeling like "training," gamification feels like a cybersecurity competition. This competitive element motivates players to stay engaged, master advanced skills, and develop the confidence to handle real-world incidents.

Pro Tip: Gamification isn't just for beginners. Advanced threat hunters can compete in Capture The Flag (CTF) events, where they race to solve complex security challenges.

How AI Enhances Simulations and Gamification
AI enhances traditional cyber ranges, simulations, and Capture The Flag (CTF) competitions by making them smarter, faster, and more realistic. Here's how AI drives this innovation:
- Dynamic Attack Paths — AI evolves its attack strategy as participants play. If defenders block one path, AI finds a new one — just like a real hacker would.
- Scenario Randomization — AI generates unique attack scenarios for each player. One player may face a phishing attack, while another deals with Living-off-the-Land (LotL) malware. No two games are the same.
- Adaptive Difficulty — AI tracks a player's progress and adjusts the difficulty of the game. If the player performs well, the AI makes the next scenario harder.
- Performance Analytics — AI tracks how well players perform in each scenario. Metrics like detection speed, time to resolution, and accuracy are scored and displayed.
- Automated Feedback — AI provides personalized feedback on a player's decisions, offering suggestions for improvement.
- AI-Generated Threat Intelligence — AI-based simulations pull data from real-world threat intelligence feeds to create attack scenarios based on current threats. If a major ransomware attack (like LockBit) is happening in the real world, the simulation can recreate it.

Pro Tip: The best AI-driven gamification platforms update their scenarios weekly based on real-world threat intelligence feeds, so players always face current attack vectors.

Use Cases for AI-Driven Simulations and Gamification

1. Training for SOC (Security Operations Center) Analysts
When a SOC analyst is hired, they need to be prepared to detect threats as quickly as possible. Training them through AI-driven simulations gives them hands-on practice with realistic attack scenarios. AI-driven gamification ensures they learn by doing, not watching.

Example: A new SOC analyst must detect a phishing attack in progress. The AI generates a phishing email for the analyst to investigate. If the analyst correctly identifies it as a phishing email, they score points. If they miss it, the system explains what they missed and how to improve.

2. Capture the Flag (CTF) Competitions
CTF events are competitive games where players race to solve cybersecurity challenges. CTFs are used in cybersecurity certifications, industry conferences, and corporate training programs.

Example: A player may be asked to crack a steganography challenge (where sensitive data is hidden inside images) or reverse-engineer malware samples. AI-based CTF platforms generate new, unique challenges each time.

3. Incident Response Simulations
Instead of waiting for a real cyberattack, companies use incident response simulations to see how well their team responds to an attack. AI-driven simulations allow teams to practice containment, eradication, and recovery.

Example: The AI launches a simulated ransomware outbreak. Players must detect the ransomware, isolate infected devices, and recover files from backups — all within a strict time limit.

4. Gamification of Threat Hunting Tools
Threat hunting gamification happens when platforms like Microsoft Defender for Endpoint, Splunk, or CrowdStrike offer interactive threat-hunting challenges. Players get points for:
- Detecting anomalous logins.
- Spotting malware execution.
- Identifying insider threats.

At the end of the training, employees receive a "Threat Hunter Score" and personalized feedback on how to improve.

Benefits of AI-Driven Simulations and Gamification
- Realistic Attack Scenarios — Players experience real-world threats like phishing, ransomware, and insider threats.
- Continuous Learning — Each scenario is different, thanks to AI-driven scenario generation. Players never face the same challenge twice.
- High Engagement — Gamification increases participation and learning retention. Instead of reading PDFs or taking quizzes, players actively solve realistic attack scenarios.

- Real-Time Feedback — Players receive immediate feedback on their decisions. If they miss an alert, AI shows them how to detect it in the future.
- Competency Tracking — AI tracks player performance and generates detailed reports on how each player performed. These metrics can be used to promote high performers or identify areas where more training is needed.
- Attack Strategy Awareness — Players gain a deeper understanding of Red Team tactics, giving them better situational awareness.

AI-Powered Gamification Platforms for Threat Hunting
Several platforms use AI to gamify threat hunting. Here are some industry leaders:
- RangeForce — Cyber range platform where users practice detection, incident response, and threat hunting.
- Hack The Box — Gamified platform for practicing penetration testing and Red Team tactics.
- Immersive Labs — Real-time incident response and threat hunting training platform with gamification elements.
- Cyberbit — Provides full-scale cyber range simulations for corporations and military defense training.
- TryHackMe — Offers threat-hunting labs, CTF challenges, and security puzzles to prepare security analysts for real-world threats.

How to Measure Red Team Performance
Tracking the effectiveness of a Red Team operation is crucial for identifying gaps in your security posture and improving future attack simulations. Without proper measurement, it's impossible to know whether the Red Team was successful or if the organization's security controls need to be updated.

When measuring Red Team performance, companies should focus on three core areas:
- Attack Success Rate — Measure how many of the simulated attacks (like phishing, lateral movement, or privilege escalation) were successful. Did the Red Team achieve their objective, like stealing sensitive data or gaining admin access? The higher the success rate, the more gaps your security posture has.
- Time-to-Detection (TTD) — This metric tracks how long it took for the Blue Team (defenders) to detect the attack. If it takes hours or days to detect an attacker, it shows that detection tools (like SIEM, EDR, or XDR) need improvement. Ideally, threat detection should happen within minutes.

- Time-to-Response (TTR) — This measures how quickly defenders responded to the Red Team's attack after it was detected. Did they quarantine the affected device? Did they block a compromised user account? Fast containment of threats is essential to reduce damage.
- Vulnerability Detection Rate — This tracks how many vulnerabilities were detected by the Red Team versus how many were overlooked. If AI-driven Red Teams find 30 attack paths and the Blue Team only identifies 15, it reveals a major gap in visibility.
- Exploitation-to-Impact Ratio — Not every successful exploit results in serious damage. This ratio tells you how many exploits actually led to a serious security event, like data exfiltration or ransomware deployment. A low ratio means the organization was able to detect and neutralize threats before they became catastrophic.
- Dwell Time — Dwell time refers to the total time that an attacker spends undetected in a network. The longer the attacker remains inside, the more dangerous they become. Effective Red Team exercises aim to reduce dwell time to minutes, not days.

How to Track These Metrics
- Use SOAR platforms (like Cortex XSOAR or IBM Resilient) to measure how fast incident response playbooks are triggered.
- Track audit logs and system activity to see how long it took defenders to respond to Red Team actions.
- Review SIEM alerts and XDR dashboards to check how fast alerts were triggered and how long it took to close them.

Pro Tip: For companies using AI-driven Red Teams, request an automated "Attack Report" from the AI system. This report will automatically calculate the Attack Success Rate, Time-to-Detection, and other performance metrics.

UEBA Models for Threat Hunting
User and Entity Behavior Analytics (UEBA) is one of the most powerful tools for Threat Hunting. Unlike traditional tools that rely on known signatures to detect threats, UEBA tracks behavior patterns. It identifies what's normal for a user, device, or process — and flags anything unusual.

The goal of UEBA is to detect anomalies, insider threats, and zero-day attacks. It goes beyond traditional detection by focusing on behaviors, not just indicators of compromise (IOCs). This makes UEBA especially useful for catching threats like insider threats and fileless malware.

How UEBA Models Work
- Baseline Creation — The UEBA system observes normal behavior for each employee, device, and process. For example, it tracks:
  o User logins (what time they log in, from where, and how often).
  o File transfers (how many files they access and download per day).
  o Application usage (which apps they normally access).
- Anomaly Detection — Once the baseline is set, UEBA tracks any activity that deviates from the norm.
  o If a user suddenly accesses files they don't normally access, UEBA raises an alert.
  o If a user logs in from two different locations at the same time (like New York and China), UEBA detects an impossible travel scenario.
- Risk Scoring — Not every anomaly is a threat. UEBA assigns each anomaly a risk score based on its severity.
  o Anomalies like unusual logins may be flagged as "low risk."
  o Anomalies like large file transfers at 3:00 AM or access to confidential HR files may be flagged as "high risk."
- AI-Driven Threat Correlation — UEBA doesn't look at anomalies in isolation. It correlates anomalies across users, systems, and devices.
  o If one anomaly (like an unusual login) happens in isolation, it may not trigger an alert.
  o But if multiple anomalies happen at the same time (like a login from China and a large file transfer and access to a HR file), UEBA flags it as a major security incident.

Use Cases for UEBA in Threat Hunting
- Detecting Insider Threats — If an employee suddenly accesses files they have never touched before (like payroll files), UEBA flags it as a possible insider threat.
- Detecting Compromised Accounts — If an attacker steals user credentials and logs in from an unusual location, UEBA flags it as an impossible travel alert.
- Detecting Data Exfiltration — If a user downloads an unusually large number of files (like 10,000 files), UEBA treats it as a sign of data exfiltration.
- Detecting Fileless Malware — If an attacker uses a tool like PowerShell to execute commands directly in memory, UEBA tracks unusual PowerShell usage, even if no malware files are present.

Pro Tip: To implement UEBA, use tools like Splunk UEBA, Exabeam, or Microsoft Defender for Identity. These tools provide anomaly detection, risk scoring, and threat correlation for users, entities, and devices.

How Gamification Can Be Used for Talent Recruitment
The cybersecurity talent gap is one of the biggest challenges facing companies today. There aren't enough skilled security analysts to fill open positions. To solve this problem, companies are using gamification platforms and Capture The Flag (CTF) competitions to recruit top talent.

How Gamification Helps Recruit Talent

Showcase Real Skills, Not Resumes
- Traditional job interviews rely on resumes and past experience. But experience doesn't always reflect skill. With CTF competitions, companies can see how candidates perform in real-world attack scenarios. Instead of asking "Do you know how to reverse engineer malware?", companies can give them a malware challenge and watch how they solve it.

Identify High Performers
- By tracking scoring, speed, and problem-solving abilities, companies can see which candidates perform the best. Many companies hire directly from CTF leaderboards. If a candidate scores in the top 5%, they are often offered a job interview on the spot.

Recruit from Cybersecurity Competitions
- Companies like Microsoft, Google, and PwC recruit directly from CTF competitions and cybersecurity competitions like DEFCON, Hack The Box, and TryHackMe. These competitions showcase the best of the best, giving companies access to elite talent pools.

Build an Internal Cybersecurity Pipeline
- Companies can run internal gamification challenges for employees. By gamifying training, employees are encouraged to get better at threat hunting, malware detection, and incident response. High performers can be promoted or moved into new roles.

How to Use Gamification for Hiring

- Sponsor CTF Competitions — Companies can sponsor events like DEFCON, TryHackMe, and Hack The Box to recruit from the pool of participants.
- Run Internal Gamification Challenges — Run in-house competitions and track high performers.
- Host Private CTF Challenges — Create custom CTFs for job applicants. Instead of a traditional interview, give candidates real-world challenges and offer jobs to the top performers.
- Use Gamified Platforms — Use platforms like TryHackMe, RangeForce, or Hack The Box to recruit from the global talent pool of participants.

Pro Tip: Invite candidates to participate in a "Red Team vs. Blue Team" game. Candidates play as defenders while simulated attackers (AI) attack the system. Candidates who demonstrate quick decision-making and problem-solving abilities get moved to the next round of interviews.

Chapter Conclusion

Gamification and AI-driven simulations are transforming the way cybersecurity professionals learn, train, and prepare for real-world threats. By creating real-time attack scenarios, companies ensure their teams are ready for ransomware outbreaks, insider threats, and malware infections. With hands-on experience in AI-powered cyber ranges, analysts learn how to detect threats, respond under pressure, and improve their skills.

"The best way to prepare for war is to practice it every day."

Chapter 20: Future of AI in Cybersecurity

The Cybersecurity Future Shaped by AI
Cybersecurity is in the midst of a monumental shift. The emergence of AI-driven malware, autonomous cyber-weapons, and the pending arrival of quantum computing are transforming the threat landscape in ways we've never seen before. What once required teams of hackers working tirelessly can now be done by a single AI system with access to large language models, predictive analysis, and self-learning capabilities.

But it's not just the attackers who are evolving. The defenders are evolving too. AI is helping cybersecurity professionals detect threats faster, respond in real-time, and predict future attacks before they happen. Advanced AI models are transforming tools like SIEM, EDR, and XDR into predictive security platforms that spot anomalies before they become attacks.

The future of cybersecurity will be shaped by the interplay between AI on the offense (used by hackers) and AI on the defense (used by security teams). But what happens if AI becomes the attacker? What if AI itself turns rogue?

In this chapter, we'll explore:
1. Rogue AI & Autonomous Cyber-Weapons — What happens if AI turns against us?
2. How quantum computing will impact encryption and security.
3. Predicting the future of AI-driven cybersecurity tools.

1. Rogue AI & Autonomous Cyber-Weapons — What Happens If AI Turns Against Us?

What is Rogue AI?
Rogue AI refers to an AI system that operates outside of human control. It could be the result of:
- AI misalignment — The AI's goals are different from the goals of its human creators.
- Malicious actors — Hackers intentionally train AI to perform malicious tasks, like spreading malware.
- Autonomous learning gone wrong — An AI learns behaviors from its environment that were not originally intended by its creators.

Unlike traditional hacking tools, Rogue AI can act independently, evolving its own attack strategies over time. The scariest part is that Rogue AI can attack at scale, automating millions of attacks simultaneously without the need for a human operator.

Pro Tip: Rogue AI doesn't necessarily need to be "self-aware" to be dangerous. It just needs to be autonomous enough to operate without human control.

What Are Autonomous Cyber-Weapons?

An autonomous cyber-weapon is a self-operating cyberattack system driven by AI and machine learning. These cyber-weapons don't require a human hacker to operate them. They launch attacks, evolve their strategies, and adapt to network defenses all on their own.

Autonomous Cyber-Weapons Can:
- Scan and exploit vulnerabilities across millions of targets simultaneously.
- Evolve and mutate malware code to bypass antivirus and EDR detection.
- Use AI-generated deepfakes to impersonate voices and videos for social engineering.
- Launch supply chain attacks by infiltrating third-party vendors and suppliers.

Types of Autonomous Cyber-Weapons
- Self-Evolving Malware
  - What It Is: Malware that mutates its code every time it's scanned. It changes its signature, making it undetectable by antivirus.
  - How It Works: The AI-driven malware reads its environment and adapts to bypass firewalls, EDRs, and sandboxes.
  - Example: Polymorphic malware, like the Zeus Trojan, which mutates with every infection.
- AI-Driven Ransomware
  - What It Is: Ransomware powered by AI. It uses AI to pick targets, encrypt files faster, and negotiate ransom payments automatically.
  - How It Works: The AI chooses which files are most valuable (like financial records) and encrypts them first. It can even negotiate ransom payments via AI-powered chatbots.
  - Example: Future versions of ransomware like LockBit may use AI to automate ransom negotiations.

- Autonomous Phishing Bots
  - What It Is: AI bots that generate and send highly personalized phishing emails.
  - How It Works: AI reads emails, social media profiles, and public records to craft phishing emails that are tailored to the target's interests.
  - Example: An AI bot generates an email that looks like a message from your boss, asking for a wire transfer or login credentials.
- Adversarial AI for Evasion
  - What It Is: Attackers train adversarial AI models to trick defensive AI systems.
  - How It Works: The AI generates subtle changes in data (like small pixel changes in images) that fool security cameras, AI detection models, and biometric scanners.
  - Example: Attackers could use adversarial AI to fool facial recognition systems by altering images of faces so they can't be recognized.
- Supply Chain Attack Bots
  - What It Is: AI bots that infiltrate the supply chain by exploiting third-party vendor vulnerabilities.
  - How It Works: Instead of attacking the target directly, the AI identifies third-party vendors with weaker defenses. Once inside, the AI uses the vendor's access to infiltrate the main target.
  - Example: NotPetya exploited the supply chain by using compromised software updates to infect thousands of organizations.

What Would Happen If AI Turned Against Us?
If AI "turned against us," it wouldn't need to be sentient. All it takes is for an AI system to be misaligned or hijacked by bad actors. Here's how things could play out:
- AI Becomes a Hacker's Weapon — Hackers gain access to an AI-driven tool (like ChatGPT or Codex) and train it to create custom malware, phishing emails, and fake social media profiles.
- AI Launches Automated Attacks at Scale — Attackers unleash millions of AI-generated phishing attacks simultaneously, sending personalized phishing emails to every employee at every Fortune 500 company.
- AI-Led Insider Attacks — If an insider plants AI-powered malware inside a company, it can remain dormant for months. The malware would then activate and start learning from the company's environment, looking for sensitive files to steal.

- Rogue AI Leverages IoT Devices — Since most IoT devices have weak security, Rogue AI could turn them into botnets for DDoS attacks. Millions of smart cameras, smart TVs, and smart thermostats could be hijacked to launch attacks on banks, governments, and websites.
- Deepfakes and AI Voice Cloning — Attackers use AI to generate fake phone calls, fake Zoom meetings, and fake video calls to trick executives into transferring money or revealing login credentials. The victim thinks they're talking to their CEO, but it's really an AI-generated deepfake.

How to Defend Against Rogue AI and Autonomous Cyber-Weapons
- Zero Trust Architecture (ZTA) — Assume every user, device, and connection is a threat until verified.
- Behavioral Analytics with UEBA — Track user and device behavior for anomalies that may indicate AI-driven attacks.
- Endpoint Detection and Response (EDR) — Use EDR to identify and isolate AI-driven malware before it spreads.
- Digital Watermarking for Deepfakes — Use AI-detectable watermarks on video and audio to prevent fake deepfake videos.
- Supply Chain Verification — Verify that all software and updates come from trusted, verified sources.

Pro Tip: Organizations like DARPA are actively researching how to defend against autonomous cyber-weapons. Their focus is on systems that can self-patch vulnerabilities before AI-based malware can exploit them.

Real-World Example of Rogue AI
Case Study: AI-Driven Malware as a Service (MaaS)
Imagine a future where hackers rent AI-driven malware on the dark web, paying $100 per day to launch autonomous attacks. This isn't science fiction — there are already Malware-as-a-Service (MaaS) platforms offering pre-built malware for rent. The next evolution is adding AI-driven polymorphic malware that adapts to its targets in real time. Attackers no longer need to be technical experts. They simply pay for the AI system to do the work for them. AI writes the code, launches the attack, and negotiates ransoms — all on its own.

Rogue AI and autonomous cyber-weapons are not "science fiction." They exist right now. Hackers are already using AI-generated phishing emails, AI-built malware, and autonomous ransomware to attack businesses. As defenders, we must build systems that can detect rogue AI before it strikes. Tools like UEBA, EDR, and anomaly detection AI are critical to winning the fight.

"The war against rogue AI isn't coming — it's already here."

How Quantum Computing Will Impact Encryption and Security

The Quantum Threat to Cybersecurity
For decades, modern encryption has been the backbone of cybersecurity. From securing bank transactions to protecting personal messages, encryption is everywhere. Today, cryptographic methods like RSA, AES, and ECC are considered unbreakable — at least with classical computers. But the arrival of quantum computing threatens to shatter this security model.

Unlike traditional computers, which process one calculation at a time, quantum computers use qubits (quantum bits) to run millions of calculations simultaneously. This ability allows quantum computers to solve problems that would take classical computers thousands of years to complete.

One of the most alarming applications of quantum computing is its ability to break modern encryption. With a powerful enough quantum computer, hackers could decrypt even the most secure files, break into bank accounts, and render traditional cryptographic methods obsolete.

In this section, we'll explore:
1. How encryption works today.
2. How quantum computing threatens modern encryption.
3. What post-quantum encryption is and how to prepare for it.

1. How Encryption Works Today
Encryption is the process of converting readable data (plaintext) into unreadable data (ciphertext) using a key. Only someone with the decryption key can turn the ciphertext back into readable data. This process is the foundation of data privacy.

There are two main types of encryption used today:

Symmetric Encryption
- How It Works: The same key is used to encrypt and decrypt the message.
- Common Algorithm: AES (Advanced Encryption Standard).
- Where It's Used: VPNs, disk encryption, secure messaging (like WhatsApp).

290

Asymmetric Encryption
- How It Works: Two keys are used — a public key (for encryption) and a private key (for decryption).
- Common Algorithms: RSA (Rivest–Shamir–Adleman) and ECC (Elliptic Curve Cryptography).
- Where It's Used: SSL/TLS certificates, email encryption, and digital signatures.

Both symmetric and asymmetric encryption are considered secure today. For example, it would take a classical computer trillions of years to break a 256-bit AES key using brute-force methods. But with quantum computing, that timeline drops to just minutes or hours.

2. How Quantum Computing Threatens Modern Encryption

How Does Quantum Computing Work?
Quantum computing uses quantum bits (qubits) to store and process information. Unlike traditional bits (which are binary — 0s and 1s), qubits can exist in a state of superposition — meaning they can be both 0 and 1 at the same time. This allows quantum computers to compute many possibilities at once, rather than step-by-step like a classical computer.
This concept, combined with the ability to entangle qubits, enables quantum computers to solve complex problems that classical computers could never solve.

How Quantum Computing Breaks Encryption
Quantum computing threatens encryption in two major ways:
Breaking Asymmetric Encryption (RSA, ECC, DH)
- Classical computers would take thousands of years to factor the large prime numbers used in RSA.
- But quantum computers can use Shor's Algorithm to factor large prime numbers exponentially faster.
- What used to take a classical computer 1,000 years to break could be done by a quantum computer in a matter of hours.
- This impacts RSA (widely used in SSL/TLS), ECC (used in blockchain), and Diffie-Hellman (used in secure key exchanges).

Weakening Symmetric Encryption (AES)
- Symmetric encryption like AES is less vulnerable than RSA, but it's still at risk.
- Quantum computers use Grover's Algorithm, which speeds up brute-force key guessing.

- With Grover's Algorithm, a 256-bit key is reduced to the equivalent of a 128-bit key — still secure, but significantly weaker.
- If the quantum computer gets more qubits, even AES-256 could be brute-forced in a reasonable amount of time.

Pro Tip: Asymmetric encryption (like RSA and ECC) is more vulnerable than symmetric encryption (like AES). Shor's Algorithm poses the biggest threat to asymmetric encryption.

Real-World Example of the Quantum Threat
Breaking SSL/TLS — Today, your browser uses SSL/TLS to protect connections to websites. This encryption relies on RSA keys. If quantum computers become powerful enough, hackers could decrypt SSL/TLS traffic, exposing sensitive web data, such as bank logins, e-commerce purchases, and emails.

Compromising Blockchain — Blockchains like Bitcoin and Ethereum rely on Elliptic Curve Cryptography (ECC) to secure wallets. If quantum computers crack ECC, it could allow hackers to steal cryptocurrency from wallets.

Decrypting Private Communications — If hackers record your encrypted messages today, they could store them and decrypt them later once quantum computers become more powerful. This is known as a "store now, decrypt later" attack.

Pro Tip: Even though quantum computers aren't powerful enough yet, nation-states may already be recording encrypted communications in anticipation of decrypting them later.

3. How to Prepare for the Quantum Threat (Post-Quantum Encryption)

What is Post-Quantum Cryptography?
- Post-Quantum Cryptography (PQC) refers to cryptographic algorithms that are resistant to quantum attacks. Unlike traditional encryption (RSA, ECC), PQC algorithms are designed to be safe from Shor's Algorithm and Grover's Algorithm.
- The goal is to create encryption methods that remain strong even if quantum computers become a reality. Some of the algorithms being tested include:
- Lattice-based Cryptography — Uses complex lattice structures that quantum computers can't break.

- Hash-based Cryptography — Uses hash functions (like SHA-3) that are immune to quantum attacks.
- Multivariate Polynomial Cryptography — Relies on solving multivariate equations, which is hard for quantum computers to solve.

Pro Tip: The National Institute of Standards and Technology (NIST) is already working on standardizing post-quantum cryptographic methods.

How to Prepare for Quantum Computing Threats
- Use Larger Encryption Keys — For symmetric encryption (like AES), increase key sizes to 512 bits. While 256 bits is currently secure, it's better to future-proof systems now.
- Start Using Post-Quantum Algorithms — Prepare to transition from RSA and ECC to lattice-based encryption. Companies like Google have already tested New Hope (a quantum-safe encryption algorithm) in Chrome.
- Upgrade Certificates and Key Exchanges — SSL/TLS certificates use RSA keys that will be vulnerable to quantum attacks. Move to hybrid encryption that combines classical and post-quantum encryption.
- Data Segmentation — Encrypt sensitive files using multiple layers of encryption. Even if one layer is broken, the next layer is still secure.
- Zero-Trust Architecture (ZTA) — Assume every user and device is untrusted. This limits the damage that quantum attacks can do.
- Stay Informed About NIST Standards — NIST is developing post-quantum cryptographic standards. Follow their guidance to prepare for future changes.

How Long Do We Have Until Quantum Computers Break Encryption?
Quantum Supremacy has already been achieved by companies like Google and IBM. While quantum computers are still in the experimental phase, most experts predict that:
- Within 10-20 years, quantum computers will be strong enough to break RSA-2048.
- Within 5-10 years, businesses will need to switch to post-quantum encryption to remain secure.

Right now, nation-states like China and the U.S. are likely already collecting encrypted data, preparing to decrypt it once quantum computing advances.

Predicting the Future of AI-Driven Cybersecurity Tools

The New Era of AI-Driven Cybersecurity
Cybersecurity is no longer just a human effort. AI has become an essential force on both sides of the battle — used by defenders to protect systems and by attackers to exploit them. As AI technology advances, so do its applications in cybersecurity. But where is it all heading?

The future of AI-driven cybersecurity tools will be shaped by several major forces:
1. AI-Enhanced Detection and Response — Security tools will be more predictive, not just reactive.
2. Autonomous Cybersecurity Systems — Security tools will become fully autonomous, requiring minimal human oversight.
3. Human-AI Hybrid Teams — Security teams will rely on AI to handle repetitive tasks, while humans focus on strategy.
4. Offensive AI Used by Hackers — As attackers adopt AI, security tools will have to evolve to match and counter these threats.

In this section, we'll explore how AI-driven cybersecurity tools are expected to evolve over the next 5 to 10 years.

1. Predictive Cybersecurity: The Rise of AI-Enhanced Detection & Response
The Shift from Reactive to Predictive Security
Today's cybersecurity tools are largely reactive — they wait for an alert (like a malware signature match) and then take action. But in the future, AI will predict attacks before they happen. Instead of waiting for malware to be executed, AI will predict attack paths, recognize early indicators of compromise (IOCs), and block threats before they become active.

How Predictive Cybersecurity Will Work
- Attack Path Prediction
  - AI will create a "map" of all possible attack paths that hackers could take to breach a system.
  - The system will automatically deploy blockers, decoys, and honeytokens on the most likely attack paths.
- Proactive Patch Management
  - Instead of waiting for vulnerabilities to be discovered, AI will predict which systems are most likely to be targeted.
  - AI will recommend or automatically apply patches before attackers exploit them.

- Anomaly Prediction
  - AI won't just flag anomalies — it will predict anomalies before they happen.
  - Example: If an employee usually logs in at 9 AM, but AI sees they've booked a flight to another country, it may predict unusual login attempts and lock down their account temporarily.
- Cyber Threat Intelligence (CTI) Prediction
  - AI will scan dark web forums, hacker chats, and global malware feeds for early warning signs of future attacks.
  - When threat actors announce a new ransomware tool, AI will create YARA rules to detect similar threats before they spread.

Pro Tip: Predictive cybersecurity isn't science fiction. Companies like Darktrace, SentinelOne, and CrowdStrike are already using predictive AI to detect potential attacks before they happen.

2. Autonomous Cybersecurity Systems
What Are Autonomous Cybersecurity Systems?
Imagine a cybersecurity system that runs on autopilot. No human analyst is required. The system detects threats, responds to them, and adapts in real time. This is the vision for autonomous cybersecurity systems.

Pro Tip: Unlike traditional systems that require human intervention to handle alerts, autonomous systems use SOAR (Security Orchestration, Automation, and Response) to respond automatically.

How Will Autonomous Cybersecurity Systems Work?
- Self-Learning AI Models
  - AI models will learn from every new attack, adjusting their behavior automatically.
  - Example: If an attacker changes a malware file name to avoid detection, the AI system will still detect it because it tracks behavioral anomalies, not just file names.
- Automated Incident Response (SOAR 2.0)
  - Autonomous systems will detect threats and trigger automated playbooks to respond.
  - Instead of alerting a human to quarantine a device, the system will do it automatically.
- Zero-Touch Patching
  - Today, companies patch software once a month. In the future, AI-driven systems will run continuous patching — automatically applying micro-patches in real time.

- Attack Replication and Simulation
  - Autonomous systems will simulate attacks in real-time to identify weaknesses.
  - Example: An AI system might launch a simulated ransomware attack on a company's own servers to see how well its defenses respond.
- Continuous Compliance
  - Compliance audits (like GDPR, HIPAA) currently require manual checks. Autonomous AI systems will continuously audit compliance and self-correct policy violations.

Pro Tip: Companies like IBM, Palo Alto, and Microsoft are already experimenting with autonomous threat detection and automated playbooks in their XDR and SOAR platforms.

3. Human-AI Hybrid Teams: The Future of the SOC (Security Operations Center)

What is a Human-AI Hybrid Team?
In the future, human cybersecurity analysts won't work alone. Instead, they'll be part of a hybrid team where AI handles the repetitive, time-consuming tasks (like log analysis, anomaly detection, and alert triage), and humans handle the creative problem-solving and strategic decisions.

How Hybrid Teams Will Work
- AI-Powered Incident Response Assistants
  - Analysts will get help from AI co-pilots that suggest responses to incidents.
  - Example: If ransomware is detected, AI might suggest actions like quarantining the device, blocking user accounts, or rolling back files.
- AI-Driven Decision Support
  - AI will offer playbook recommendations to human analysts.
  - Example: During a phishing attack, the system may suggest actions like revoking access to email accounts or blocking incoming messages.
- Workload Automation
  - Routine tasks (like log review and alert triage) will be handled entirely by AI.
  - Humans will only be called in when an incident requires complex decision-making.
- Adaptive Learning from Human Feedback
  - Every time a human dismisses an alert, the system learns.
  - Over time, AI will know which alerts are "false positives" and automatically reduce noise.

4. The Role of AI in Offensive Hacking Tools
How Attackers Will Use AI
- AI-Powered Phishing Bots — Attackers will automate the creation of personalized phishing emails.
- AI-Generated Malware — Malware will adapt in real time to evade detection (like polymorphic malware).
- AI Voice Cloning — Attackers will impersonate executives to trick employees into wiring money (via voice cloning).
- Adversarial AI for Evasion — Attackers will use AI to create adversarial inputs that fool AI security tools.

Pro Tip: The best defense against offensive AI is to use AI to track adversarial inputs and detect anomalies that evade traditional detection methods.

5. Rogue AI & Cyber-Weapons
Rogue AI systems and AI-driven cyber-weapons are one of the most dangerous threats on the horizon. These are autonomous AI tools that no longer require human oversight to launch and manage attacks. Unlike traditional malware or human-controlled bots, Rogue AI can independently scan for vulnerabilities, deliver payloads, and even learn from failed attempts.

How It Works:
- Autonomous Ransomware: Imagine ransomware that can self-propagate, negotiate ransoms, and encrypt files without human involvement. Once deployed, it continues to evolve, changing its attack strategies on its own.
- AI-Controlled Bot Armies: Hackers can deploy botnets powered by AI to coordinate large-scale attacks, like Distributed Denial of Service (DDoS) attacks, without constant control from the attacker.
- AI-Driven Cyber-Weapons: These are AI-powered systems capable of scanning thousands of targets in seconds, identifying the weakest entry point, and launching precision attacks — all on autopilot.

Example:
An attacker deploys a self-evolving ransomware called "ShadowMind". This malware doesn't just encrypt files — it also tracks which ransom amounts are most likely to be paid, adjusts the ransom request accordingly, and evolves its encryption methods after each failed detection. Traditional ransomware needs human operators, but ShadowMind is fully autonomous, operating 24/7 to infect as many machines as possible.

How to Defend:
- Deploy AI-Driven EDR (Endpoint Detection and Response) — EDR solutions can recognize and respond to behaviors associated with rogue AI and autonomous ransomware.
- Use Zero-Trust Security Models — No device, user, or process is automatically trusted. This approach ensures that rogue AI bots can't move laterally through the network.
- Adopt SOAR (Security Orchestration, Automation, and Response) Tools — SOAR platforms use AI to automate incident response, allowing human analysts to shut down rogue AI-based attacks instantly.

6. Cloud Security and Quantum Risks

As more companies migrate to cloud environments, new vulnerabilities are emerging — especially with the rise of quantum computing. Cloud services like AWS, Google Cloud, and Microsoft Azure are vulnerable to both traditional attacks (like misconfigurations) and future quantum attacks that could break modern encryption. If RSA, AES, or ECC encryption is broken by quantum computing, millions of cloud-stored files and communications could be instantly decrypted.

How It Works:
- Cloud Misconfigurations: Attackers scan for misconfigured cloud buckets (like AWS S3) that are accidentally left public, exposing sensitive data.
- API Exploitation: APIs (application programming interfaces) are the "backdoors" of cloud apps. Attackers target weak API endpoints to steal data or execute commands.
- Quantum Attacks on Encryption: Traditional encryption methods like RSA-2048 can be cracked in seconds by quantum computers. Once quantum computers reach sufficient power, they could decrypt millions of stored files, including cloud backups, communications, and financial data.

Example:
A major financial institution stores sensitive customer data in the AWS cloud. Due to a misconfigured S3 bucket, the data becomes publicly accessible to anyone with the URL. Attackers quickly access the bucket, stealing customer banking details and personal data. If this same data were encrypted with RSA encryption, a future quantum computer could decrypt it instantly, exposing sensitive information that was previously "secure" under classical encryption.

How to Defend:
- Use Cloud Security Posture Management (CSPM) Tools — Tools like Palo Alto Prisma Cloud or Wiz can automatically detect and fix misconfigurations in AWS, GCP, and Azure.
- Adopt Post-Quantum Cryptography (PQC) — Use quantum-safe encryption algorithms like CRYSTALS-Kyber, NTRU, and Sike, which are designed to resist quantum attacks.
- Encrypt Cloud Backups with Quantum-Safe Methods — Ensure that backups stored in the cloud use post-quantum encryption, as they are a prime target for quantum attacks.
- Secure API Endpoints — Use API gateways and OAuth tokens to restrict access to sensitive API calls. Regularly audit cloud API permissions to prevent backdoor attacks.

Predictions for the Next 5-10 Years
Short-Term (1-3 Years)
- SOAR 2.0 — Security Orchestration, Automation, and Response (SOAR) tools will introduce more advanced AI-driven playbooks for incident response, allowing defenders to react in seconds instead of minutes.
- UEBA Expansion — User and Entity Behavior Analytics (UEBA) will become essential for spotting insider threats, with AI tracking user patterns, locations, and device activity to flag anomalies in real time.
- Gamification of Cybersecurity — Companies will train staff using gamified threat-hunting platforms. Employees will "level up" by completing challenges like stopping phishing attacks, spotting malware, and defending against simulated ransomware.
- Data Poisoning & Adversarial Attacks — Attackers will increase their use of data poisoning to corrupt machine learning models and adversarial inputs to fool AI-based threat detection systems.
- Deepfake Voice & Video Scams — Attackers will use deepfakes in video calls and phone scams to impersonate family members or company executives, tricking victims into sending money or exposing sensitive data.

Mid-Term (3-5 Years)
- Autonomous Cybersecurity Systems — Companies will deploy autonomous cybersecurity agents that can detect, respond, and patch vulnerabilities with zero human oversight. These agents will act as "always-on defenders" that run 24/7 without fatigue.
- Self-Patching Software — Software will automatically patch itself in real time, thanks to self-healing AI-driven code. Attackers will have to race against the clock to exploit vulnerabilities before they are automatically patched.

- Cyber-Physical Attacks on IoT & Infrastructure — Attacks on physical infrastructure (like power grids, water systems, and hospitals) will increase as attackers use AI-driven malware to breach IoT devices. This will lead to more attacks on critical infrastructure, like the Colonial Pipeline ransomware attack (2021).
- More Rogue AI Attacks — Attackers will develop rogue AI-driven malware that can think, learn, and evolve on its own. Expect to see autonomous ransomware capable of negotiating ransom amounts, hiding from EDR tools, and using AI to spot network weaknesses.

Long-Term (5-10 Years)
- AI vs. AI Battles — Cybersecurity will become an arms race between offensive AI vs. defensive AI. Attackers will deploy self-learning malware, while defenders will use self-evolving security systems. Expect AI-driven SOC bots (Security Operations Center bots) to fight AI-driven attack bots in real time.
- Post-Quantum Encryption — By this time, quantum computers may have become powerful enough to break RSA, AES, and ECC encryption, forcing companies to adopt post-quantum cryptography (PQC). Encryption methods like CRYSTALS-Kyber and NTRU will become standard across all sectors.
- Autonomous SOCs (Security Operations Centers) — The entire concept of a SOC will change. Human analysts will be replaced by autonomous AI-SOCs, where self-learning AI agents handle incident response, alert prioritization, and risk analysis.
- Quantum-Safe Cloud Storage — Cloud providers like AWS, Azure, and Google Cloud will be forced to adopt quantum-safe encryption to protect cloud-stored files. Cloud security threats will shift from misconfigurations and API flaws to quantum cryptography risks.

Chapter Conclusion: Prepare for the Unthinkable — When, Not If
The future of cybersecurity is no longer a battle of human vs.
human — it's AI vs. AI. Attackers are no longer lone hackers
hiding in basements; they're wielding autonomous malware, rogue
AI, and polymorphic ransomware that evolve in real time. The
defenders? They must adopt predictive threat detection, anomaly
detection, and self-healing systems to stay ahead. But one threat
looms larger than them all — Quantum Computing.

If you think today's encryption is invincible, think again. Quantum
computers have the potential to render all existing encryption —
RSA, ECC, SSL/TLS — obsolete. The result? Every encrypted
message, bank transaction, and online password becomes
vulnerable. Hackers, cybercriminals, and state-sponsored attackers
won't wait until quantum computers are "ready" — they're already
stockpiling encrypted data today, planning to decrypt it the
moment quantum computers become powerful enough.

The threat isn't distant. It's real. It's already happening. Nation-
states, like China, are believed to be collecting encrypted
communications right now, storing them for a future where
quantum computing can break it all. Imagine waking up one day to
find that every encrypted email, every bank transaction, every
password you've ever used is suddenly exposed. It won't be an "if"
— it will be a when.

A Warning for Families — Will You Be Ready?
If you think quantum attacks are just a "business problem," think
again. Cyber-physical attacks, like those on power grids, water
systems, and hospitals, are already happening. Imagine waking up
to find that power is out — not for a few hours, but for days or
even weeks. No lights. No refrigeration. No communication. No
access to cash or financial services. Sound far-fetched? It's not.
Cuba experienced this exact scenario in 2022, when over 10 million
people lost power for days following Hurricane Ian. But here's the
difference — in a cyber attack, there's no storm to pass. The outage
lasts until the hacker decides to give control back. If attackers seize
control of a national power grid, it could happen anywhere.

So, ask yourself this:
- If your family lost access to power for a week, would you be
  ready?
- Do you have cash on hand if ATMs and banks go offline?
- Do you have a supply of non-perishable food in case grocery
  stores close?
- Do you have a plan to communicate with loved ones if phones
  and internet go down?

The Cuba blackout was a natural disaster, but a cyber attack on critical infrastructure could have the same effect — but without warning. Attackers could freeze power grids, shut down water systems, and hold countries for ransom. This isn't science fiction — it's already happening. The Colonial Pipeline ransomware attack of 2021 disrupted fuel supplies across the eastern United States, causing gas shortages and panic buying. That attack was financially motivated, but imagine an attack with political motivations — one designed not for profit, but for power. The Cuba blackout of 2022 gives us a taste of how fragile these systems are. If it happened to them, it can happen to anyone.

The warning is simple: Prepare now. Keep extra cash, food, water, and emergency supplies ready. Think like a prepper, not a procrastinator. When the grid goes down, you don't want to be standing in line with thousands of others.

A Warning for Businesses — What's Your Plan?
For businesses, the risks are even greater. Your reputation, revenue, and customer trust are on the line. Cyber attacks don't just cause downtime — they destroy companies. If quantum computers break encryption, everything you rely on — VPNs, encrypted files, secure communications — becomes an open book. If you think you'll "fix it later," think again. If your company is down for even a few days, customers may never return.

Ask yourself this:
- Does your company have a disaster recovery plan?
- Do you have encrypted, offline backups of critical data?
- Are your employees trained to identify threats like deepfake video calls or AI-powered phishing scams?
- If your VPN encryption fails, how will you protect sensitive company data?

If your answer to any of the above is "I'm not sure," then you're already vulnerable. It's not enough to hope you won't be attacked. Attackers aren't hoping — they're preparing. The next big attack won't give you time to respond. It will happen in seconds. Your only choice is to have a plan ready before it happens.

What Can You Do Now?
Here's your checklist for personal and business cybersecurity preparation:

1. Adopt Post-Quantum Cryptography (PQC) — When quantum computers become powerful enough, RSA, ECC, and SSL/TLS will fail. Companies like Google, NIST, and IBM are already working on quantum-safe encryption, but it's not widespread yet. Ask your vendors and partners about PQC adoption — if they don't have a plan, find new vendors.

2. Zero-Trust Model — Whether for your home or business, the Zero-Trust model assumes that no user, file, or system is trusted by default. Require constant authentication and verification for all actions, whether it's a wire transfer or an employee logging into a system.

3. Backup Everything Offline — Ransomware encrypts your files. Self-evolving malware mutates to avoid detection. And if you rely on cloud backups, remember: clouds get hacked too. Create encrypted, offline backups on hard drives that aren't connected to the network.

4. Cyber-Physical Defense Plan — Power grids, water systems, and hospitals are being attacked because they're seen as easy targets. Work with IT security teams to install AI-driven device monitoring and deploy anomaly detection tools on OT (Operational Technology) systems. If you're a homeowner, ensure your smart home devices have changed default passwords and have software updates enabled.

5. Emergency Preparedness (For Families) — Power outages caused by cyber attacks can last for days or weeks. Stock up on emergency cash, water, food, flashlights, and phone power banks. Even if the lights come back on after a few hours, you'll have the peace of mind knowing you're prepared for the worst.

6. AI-Driven Defenses — For businesses, leverage AI-driven tools like SentinelOne (https://www.sentinelone.com/), CrowdStrike (https://www.crowdstrike.com/), and Darktrace (https://www.darktrace.com/) for predictive threat detection, behavioral analysis, and anomaly detection.

The Final Takeaway
The world of cybersecurity is no longer one of "good guys vs. bad guys." It's AI vs. AI. Attackers have access to AI-driven tools for phishing, polymorphic malware, and autonomous malware. But defenders have access to predictive detection, anomaly detection, and quantum-resistant encryption. The key difference is this: attackers only need to succeed once, but defenders must succeed every single time.

"If you fail to prepare, you prepare to fail." This is no longer a cliche — it's a fact of survival in the era of quantum threats, rogue AI, and cyber-physical warfare. Every company, every family, every person must have a plan. When the power goes out, when encryption breaks, and when ransomware locks you out, it's too late to "start preparing." By following the steps in this book, you're not just getting smarter — you're becoming prepared.

The future is unpredictable. Attacks will evolve. Technology will change. The only way to survive is to stay ahead.

Chapter 21: Careers in Cybersecurity (With AI Insights)

The Future of Cybersecurity Careers
The cybersecurity job market is one of the fastest-growing sectors in the world. With demand for cybersecurity professionals far exceeding supply, jobs like security analyst, SOC engineer, and threat hunter are in high demand. But as AI transforms the industry, the nature of these roles is changing.

Instead of eliminating jobs, AI will change how jobs are performed. Repetitive tasks (like log analysis, alert triage, and malware scanning) will be handled by AI tools, while human analysts will focus on strategy, creative problem-solving, and oversight of AI systems.

This chapter will explore:
1. How AI is changing the cybersecurity job market.
2. The top roles and skills that are "AI-proof."
3. The certifications and skills that future cybersecurity professionals will need.

1. How AI is Changing the Cybersecurity Job Market

Automation vs. Augmentation: Will AI Replace Cybersecurity Jobs?

There's a lot of fear that AI will replace human cybersecurity jobs, but the reality is more nuanced. While AI will handle routine tasks like alert triage, log analysis, and anomaly detection, humans will still be needed for:
- Strategic decision-making (which threats to prioritize)
- Creative problem-solving (finding non-traditional attack vectors)
- Supervising AI models (ensuring AI tools aren't making biased decisions)

Rather than eliminating jobs, AI will change them. Many of today's roles will be "augmented by AI", not replaced by it.

Pro Tip: The roles most at risk of being automated are those involving repetitive tasks (like alert triage) or jobs that rely solely on predefined rules. Jobs that require human creativity, intuition, and ethical reasoning are safe from AI disruption.

Cybersecurity Jobs That Will Be Automated by AI
These jobs are at risk of being automated or significantly reduced in scope:
- Level 1 SOC Analysts — AI tools like SOAR and XDR will handle low-level alerts automatically.
- Log Review Analysts — AI will scan 100% of system logs for anomalies, flagging only high-risk events for human review.
- Incident Response Playbook Handlers — AI-based SOAR platforms will automatically run playbooks to respond to incidents, like isolating infected devices or disabling compromised user accounts.

Cybersecurity Jobs That Will Be Augmented by AI
These jobs will not be eliminated but will change as AI takes over routine tasks:
- Threat Hunters — AI will handle 24/7 anomaly detection, but human threat hunters will analyze complex, multi-step attacks.
- SOC Managers — While Level 1 analysts will be reduced, SOC managers will supervise AI-driven threat hunting systems.
- Security Architects — AI will help architects design systems, but human creativity and experience will still be required.
- Incident Response Analysts — AI will automate containment (like quarantining infected endpoints), but human analysts will still manage crisis response and strategy.

Pro Tip: The more creative, complex, and strategic a role is, the safer it is from AI automation. Roles that require decision-making, ethical judgment, or "human intuition" will remain secure.

2. Skills, Certifications, and Roles That Are "AI-Proof"

What Does It Mean for a Role to Be "AI-Proof"?
An AI-proof role is one that can't be fully automated by AI tools. It may be "augmented" by AI, but the core responsibilities require human intelligence, critical thinking, and strategy. Examples of AI-proof roles include:
- Roles that require ethical decision-making (e.g., policy creation, governance, and compliance).
- Roles that require complex analysis (e.g., investigating multi-stage attacks).
- Roles that involve overseeing AI (e.g., training AI models, auditing AI performance, and mitigating AI bias).

AI-Proof Cybersecurity Roles
Here are the top AI-proof cybersecurity roles that will remain secure (and even grow) as AI becomes more powerful:

Threat Hunter (Human-Driven Investigations)
- Why It's Safe: AI tracks anomalies, but it takes a human to interpret context (like recognizing false positives).
- Required Skills: Anomaly detection, fileless malware analysis, attack path analysis, and knowledge of Living-off-the-Land (LotL) attacks.
- Tools to Learn: CrowdStrike Falcon, Darktrace, Microsoft Defender for Identity.

AI Auditor / Explainable AI (XAI) Specialist
- Why It's Safe: As companies rely on AI to make decisions, someone needs to audit AI's logic, spot bias, and ensure AI transparency.
- Required Skills: AI auditing, ethical AI principles, understanding of adversarial AI, and Explainable AI (XAI).
- Tools to Learn: SHAP (SHapley Additive exPlanations) and LIME (Local Interpretable Model-agnostic Explanations).

Cybersecurity Policy & Governance
- Why It's Safe: Governance roles rely on human judgment, ethical decision-making, and strategic thinking — all areas where AI struggles.
- Required Skills: Risk management, policy creation, knowledge of GDPR, HIPAA, and NIST standards.
- Tools to Learn: Governance, Risk, and Compliance (GRC) tools like OneTrust and RSA Archer.

Cybersecurity Consultant / Security Architect
- Why It's Safe: AI can recommend security designs, but only a human architect can make holistic design decisions.
- Required Skills: Network design, zero-trust architecture, security frameworks (like MITRE ATT&CK).
- Tools to Learn: AWS Security Hub, Azure Sentinel, and IBM QRadar.

Incident Response Leader
- Why It's Safe: AI can quarantine devices, but a human is still needed to oversee the response, negotiate ransom payments, and manage executive communication.
- Required Skills: Crisis management, forensics, malware analysis, decision-making under pressure.
- Tools to Learn: SOAR platforms (like Palo Alto Cortex XSOAR and Splunk Phantom).

3. Certifications and Skills That Future Cybersecurity Professionals Will Need

Certified Information Systems Security Professional (CISSP)
- Why It Matters: Teaches strategic, managerial, and architectural skills — all of which are AI-proof.
- AI Relevance: CISSP includes AI governance, policy creation, and risk management.

Certified Ethical Hacker (CEH)
- Why It Matters: Hackers use AI to create malware and attacks, so Ethical Hackers need to stay ahead of them.
- AI Relevance: AI-driven red teaming and pentesting are already becoming industry standards.

CompTIA CySA+ (Cybersecurity Analyst)
- Why It Matters: CySA+ focuses on threat hunting, incident detection, and response — all roles that are augmented (not replaced) by AI.

Certified Cloud Security Professional (CCSP)
- Why It Matters: As more companies move to the cloud, AI-driven security for cloud environments will be critical.
- AI Relevance: Cloud security roles involve XDR, EDR, and UEBA — all of which are AI-augmented.

AI-Specific Certifications
- Suggested Certs: AI Ethics and Governance Certifications from Coursera, AI For Business from MIT, and machine learning courses from Google.

Future Skills for Cybersecurity Professionals
- AI Model Oversight — Learn how to audit AI models, spot bias, and explain XAI (Explainable AI) decisions.
- Threat Hunting with AI — Learn how to use tools like CrowdStrike, Darktrace, and SentinelOne to hunt for AI-driven attacks.
- AI-Driven Incident Response — Learn how to manage and oversee incident response driven by SOAR platforms.
- Cloud Security with AI — Learn zero-trust cloud design and AI-enhanced cloud detection.

Chapter Conclusion
The future of cybersecurity careers is bright, but roles will shift as AI takes over repetitive tasks. Human intuition, ethical oversight, and collaboration between AI and humans will remain essential for advanced threat detection and strategic decisions. Success will be defined by humans working alongside AI.

Chapter 22: How to Perform a Cybersecurity Audit

Why Cybersecurity Audits Matter
A cybersecurity audit is a comprehensive review of your organization's security posture. It identifies vulnerabilities, evaluates the effectiveness of security controls, and ensures compliance with industry standards like GDPR, HIPAA, and NIST CSF. Traditionally, audits were performed manually by teams of security analysts. But in today's world of AI-driven automation, cybersecurity audits can be faster, more comprehensive, and more accurate.

With the rise of AI-driven auditing tools, companies can conduct automated risk assessments, detect vulnerabilities in real time, and generate audit reports without relying entirely on manual processes. Instead of waiting for a human to review logs, AI-driven tools continuously audit systems 24/7, identifying risks before they become major threats.

This chapter will walk you through:
1. How to conduct a cybersecurity audit step-by-step.
2. How AI-driven auditing tools and risk assessments work.
3. How to assess your business's security posture using AI.

1. How to Conduct a Cybersecurity Audit (Step-by-Step)
What is a Cybersecurity Audit?
A cybersecurity audit is like a "health check" for your company's security. Just as you would get a health check at a doctor's office, a cybersecurity audit identifies risks, analyzes past incidents, and creates a plan for future improvements. The goal is to ensure that your company meets cybersecurity compliance standards, mitigates risks, and stays ahead of attackers.

Step 1: Define the Scope of the Audit
Before you start, you need to know what you're auditing. Will you audit the entire system, or just a part of it (like cloud services, endpoints, or applications)?

Tasks for this Step
- Identify assets to audit (e.g., devices, software, data, and users).
- Decide on the audit type (internal audit, third-party audit, or regulatory compliance audit).
- List audit objectives (e.g., meet GDPR standards, reduce vulnerabilities, or prepare for ISO 27001 certification).

Pro Tip: If you're a small business, focus on auditing your high-risk areas first (like email, VPNs, and IoT devices).

Step 2: Identify Compliance Requirements
Compliance is one of the most common reasons companies conduct audits. GDPR, HIPAA, PCI-DSS, and other regulations require companies to conduct regular audits.

Tasks for this Step
- Identify compliance standards (like NIST, GDPR, or SOC 2) that apply to your industry.
- Use tools like OneTrust or RSA Archer to check for compliance gaps.
- If you're working in healthcare, check HIPAA standards. If you're in finance, check PCI-DSS standards.

Pro Tip: Even if your company doesn't have to comply with regulations, audit your own security posture to spot blind spots and reduce risk.

Step 3: Gather Evidence
To prove compliance, you'll need to collect evidence. Evidence includes screenshots, system logs, network diagrams, and vulnerability scans. This step is time-consuming, but AI-driven audit tools can collect evidence automatically.

Tasks for this Step
- Collect system logs from EDR, SIEM, and XDR platforms.
- Take screenshots of firewall configurations and access control policies.
- Review past incident response reports to see what lessons were learned.

Pro Tip: Tools like Splunk, Tenable, and Microsoft Sentinel can automatically collect and store audit evidence.

Step 4: Perform a Risk Assessment
A risk assessment identifies the biggest threats to your company and how likely they are to happen. AI-driven risk assessments can predict which attack vectors (like ransomware or phishing) are most likely to target your company.

Tasks for this Step
- Run a vulnerability scan using tools like Tenable.io or Rapid7 InsightVM.
- Use an AI-based risk assessment tool (like Darktrace or BitSight) to predict which threats are most likely.
- Document the risk level for each asset (like "high risk," "medium risk," or "low risk").

Pro Tip: Risk assessments aren't just about identifying threats. You also need to assign a risk score to each threat so you can prioritize what to fix first.

Step 5: Remediate Security Gaps
Once you know where the gaps are, you need to fix them. This could mean patching vulnerabilities, reconfiguring firewalls, or enforcing multi-factor authentication (MFA).

Tasks for this Step
- Prioritize the most critical vulnerabilities.
- Apply patches for known vulnerabilities (use AI-driven patch management tools to automate this process).
- Deploy additional security controls like endpoint protection, email filters, and MFA.

Pro Tip: Use SOAR platforms (like Cortex XSOAR or Splunk Phantom) to automate patching and remediation.

Step 6: Document Findings and Write a Report
The final step is to document everything. This report can be shared with executives, regulators, or auditors. It's also useful for internal training and for tracking progress over time.

Tasks for this Step
- Write an executive summary that non-technical people can understand.
- Create a list of key issues discovered and the actions you took to resolve them.
- Highlight the return on investment (ROI) for the audit.

Pro Tip: Use tools like OneTrust or AuditBoard to automatically generate compliance reports.

2. How AI-Driven Auditing Tools and Automated Risk Assessments Work

What Are AI-Driven Auditing Tools?

AI-driven auditing tools automate evidence collection, risk scoring, and report generation. Instead of waiting for humans to review logs, AI scans every log, configuration file, and user activity for anomalies.

How AI Enhances Cybersecurity Audits
- Automated Evidence Collection
  - AI scans EDR, XDR, and SIEM logs for key compliance data.
  - Example: AI can track user login logs from Microsoft Defender for Identity and link them to identity access control.
- Real-Time Risk Assessment
  - AI models predict which threats are most likely to target your company.
  - Tools like Darktrace detect unusual patterns that could lead to ransomware attacks.
- Automated Reporting
  - AI generates audit reports automatically, including risk scores, mitigation actions, and compliance metrics.
  - Example: AI creates a GDPR compliance report that auditors can review.
- Continuous Auditing (24/7 Monitoring)
  - Instead of performing an audit once a year, AI can run continuous audits 24/7.
  - When it detects non-compliance, it triggers a security alert.

AI-Driven Auditing Tools to Watch:
- Darktrace (for AI-driven anomaly detection)
- OneTrust (for compliance tracking and reporting)
- BitSight (for third-party risk audits)

3. How to Assess Your Business's Security Posture Using AI

What is a Security Posture?

A company's security posture is its overall level of readiness to detect, prevent, and respond to cyber threats. It includes all the technical, human, and procedural defenses in place.

Steps to Assess Security Posture Using AI
- Run an AI-Based Vulnerability Scan
  - Use tools like Nessus, Tenable.io, or Rapid7 InsightVM.
  - Look for outdated software, unpatched vulnerabilities, and misconfigured devices.

- Use AI to Score Security Posture
  - Tools like BitSight provide a security rating (like a credit score) for your company.
  - Review the score and prioritize high-risk areas first.
- Conduct Continuous Monitoring
  - Deploy XDR (Extended Detection and Response) to track threats 24/7.
  - Example: If AI detects unauthorized file access at 3 AM, it triggers an alert.
- Audit Identity and Access Control
  - Use AI to monitor login anomalies.
  - Example: If a user logs in from New York at 9 AM and from London at 9:30 AM, AI will flag it.

Chapter Conclusion

Cybersecurity audits are no longer manual processes. AI-driven auditing tools can perform continuous audits, collect evidence automatically, and generate compliance reports with minimal human intervention. Companies that implement AI-driven audits reduce risk, improve compliance, and save time.

"Don't wait for a breach to find gaps. Audit before the attack happens."

Chapter 23: Personalized AI Cybersecurity Assistants

The Rise of AI Cybersecurity Assistants
Imagine having a personal cybersecurity assistant who works 24/7, answers your security questions, helps you detect threats, and even automates tasks like updating passwords and scanning for vulnerabilities. With the rise of AI-driven assistants like Grok and ChatGPT, Bard, and custom-built AI chatbots, anyone can have access to a personal cybersecurity expert on demand.

For individuals and small businesses, AI assistants can act as a personal SOC analyst, risk advisor, and compliance consultant — all in one. Large enterprises have full-fledged Security Operations Centers (SOCs) with teams of analysts, but smaller organizations often lack the resources for constant monitoring. AI assistants fill this gap.

This chapter will teach you:
1. How to use AI assistants (like Grok and ChatGPT) to get security advice.
2. How to create DIY automation for home and small business security.

1. How to Use AI Assistants (Like Grok and ChatGPT) to Get Security Advice
What Is an AI Cybersecurity Assistant?
An AI cybersecurity assistant is a digital tool that provides personalized advice, guidance, and support on security issues. These AI-driven assistants use natural language processing (NLP) to understand questions and provide answers in plain, simple language.

Unlike traditional FAQ chatbots, AI assistants can:
- Answer complex technical questions (like "How do I block phishing emails?").
- Provide advice on security tools (like which antivirus or VPN to use).
- Help configure firewalls, VPNs, and security settings.
- Assist in writing security policies for businesses and teams.
- Explain cybersecurity concepts (like "What is ransomware?") in simple terms.

While general-purpose tools like Grok and ChatGPT can provide advice, enterprise-grade AI assistants like Microsoft Security Copilot offer more advanced, real-time support by integrating with threat detection and incident response tools.

How to Use AI Assistants for Cybersecurity Advice
To get the most out of an AI cybersecurity assistant, you should focus on the following use cases:

Ask Technical Questions — You can ask technical questions and receive step-by-step guidance. For example, you might ask, "How do I set up a firewall on my home network?" or "What's the difference between EDR and XDR security tools?" The AI assistant will provide step-by-step instructions for configuring firewalls, VPNs, and endpoint security.

Get Threat Alerts & Cybersecurity News — AI assistants can provide updates on the latest cyber threats. For example, you can ask, "What are the latest ransomware attacks this week?" or "Has there been a data breach affecting Microsoft users recently?" The AI assistant will provide a real-time summary of the latest cybersecurity news, threat intelligence, and breach reports.

Policy and Compliance Advice — If you're unsure how to write security policies, AI can provide templates and recommendations. You might ask, "How do I create a password policy for my business?" or "What are the key compliance steps for GDPR?" In response, the AI assistant will generate templates for password policies, compliance checklists, and detailed step-by-step instructions.

Incident Response Guidance — If you're facing an attack, AI assistants can provide guidance on how to respond. For example, you can ask, "My email has been hacked — what do I do now?" or "What should I do if ransomware is detected on my network?" The assistant will walk you through the incident response process, including quarantining devices, restoring backups, and notifying affected parties.

Which AI Assistants Should You Use?
Several AI cybersecurity assistants are available, each with unique features.
- ChatGPT — Best for general cybersecurity advice, how-tos, and simple templates. It excels at answering technical questions or generating templates for password policies, security guides, or checklists. ChatGPT is ideal for individuals or small businesses looking for quick, accessible support.
- Microsoft Security Copilot — Designed for enterprise-level threat detection, SOC support, and incident response. Unlike ChatGPT, it integrates directly with XDR and SIEM platforms, providing real-time threat intelligence and automation to help security teams manage incidents swiftly and effectively.

- Google Bard — Useful for phishing advice, consumer security tips, and general cybersecurity guidance. Bard is ideal for consumers seeking explanations of malware, phishing schemes, and security best practices, offering easy-to-understand advice for protecting personal data.
- Grok — A next-generation AI assistant designed for advanced cybersecurity tasks, including real-time threat analysis and proactive vulnerability detection. Grok can be integrated into a company's network infrastructure, providing tailored security insights and facilitating automated risk assessments. It's particularly useful for organizations looking for an AI that can adapt and respond to evolving threats in real-time.
- Custom AI Assistants — Some organizations create custom cybersecurity AI assistants trained on company-specific data. These AI assistants provide highly personalized advice, monitor network activity, and automate routine security tasks, ensuring a tailored approach to the organization's unique security needs.

2. DIY Automation for Home and Small Business Security
Why Automate Cybersecurity?
Manually checking every device, password, and connection is time-consuming. AI-driven automation allows you to:
- Continuously monitor your network for anomalies.
- Detect unauthorized logins and account takeovers.
- Automatically block phishing attempts.

By combining AI assistants with automation tools, you can create a mini-SOC (Security Operations Center) at home or for your small business. Automation also provides 24/7 protection, so you don't have to rely on manual checks.

DIY Security Automations You Can Set Up Today
Automated Phishing Protection
- One of the most important automations is protecting yourself from phishing attacks. AI-driven tools scan emails for phishing links, spoofed email addresses, and scam messages. To set this up:
  - Microsoft Defender for Office 365 detects and blocks phishing attempts.
  - Google Workspace has built-in phishing filters that automatically quarantine risky messages.
  - Third-party AI-powered email security solutions like SpamTitan, Avanan, and Mimecast offer more advanced protection.

316

Network Monitoring & Device Tracking
- IoT devices (like smart locks, cameras, and speakers) are common attack targets. DIY IoT security lets you track these devices for unusual behavior.
    - AI-driven tools like Fing, Domotz, or Bitdefender Box continuously monitor smart devices for abnormal activity (e.g., a camera sending data at 3 AM).
    - Set up a DIY network tracker on your Wi-Fi router to monitor connected devices in real-time.

Smart Password Management
- Use AI-driven password managers to create strong, unique passwords for every account.
    - Tools like 1Password and LastPass can detect if your passwords are part of a breach.
    - Sign up for alerts from HaveIBeenPwned.com, which notifies you when your email or passwords appear in data breaches.
    - Advanced users can train their own AI assistants to scan for leaked credentials on the dark web.

Intrusion Detection & Anomaly Tracking
- Use AI tools like Darktrace to monitor your home or business network for anomalies.
    - If unusual login behavior or excessive outbound traffic is detected, you'll receive an alert.
    - Set up DIY automation using free tools like Wireshark (for network packet capture) and Fail2Ban (to block suspicious logins).

DIY Backup & Recovery Automation
- Instead of waiting for ransomware to lock your files, set up automated backups that run daily.
    - Backblaze and Acronis Cyber Protect can automatically back up files every day.
    - Advanced users can automate this using cloud storage and simple Python scripts to create daily file snapshots.

Behavioral Anomaly Detection
- Some advanced DIY anomaly tracking solutions use AI-driven anomaly detection models.
    - These models learn "normal behavior" for devices and users, so if something abnormal occurs (e.g., data sent at 3 AM), an alert is triggered.
    - DIY users can set this up using open-source anomaly detection libraries like Scikit-learn or TensorFlow.

Chapter Conclusion

Cybersecurity doesn't have to be a solo effort. AI-powered cybersecurity assistants like Grok, ChatGPT, Microsoft Security Copilot, and Google Bard make it easier than ever to get answers, set up security measures, and automate protection. Small business owners, parents, and consumers can all benefit from these tools to protect their data, secure their devices, and prevent breaches before they happen.

AI assistants can help with incident response, policy creation, and threat detection, while DIY automation allows anyone to create a home-based Security Operations Center (SOC) for 24/7 protection. By leveraging tools like Bitdefender Box, SpamTitan, and network anomaly detection, individuals and small businesses can stay ahead of threats.

"Your personal AI assistant can be your first line of defense. Ask it questions, follow its guidance, and automate your security before an attacker makes their move."

Chapter 24: Cybersecurity Myths, Lies, and Misinformation

The Danger of Myths and Misinformation in Cybersecurity
There's a famous saying in cybersecurity:

"The greatest vulnerability is human ignorance."

Every day, businesses and individuals make decisions based on misconceptions and half-truths about cybersecurity. Some think, "I'm not a target", while others believe that "I have nothing hackers would want." These myths leave people vulnerable to attacks that could have been avoided.

At the same time, cybercriminals have found new ways to weaponize disinformation and fake news. From false data leaks to deepfake videos of executives, the rise of AI-generated disinformation is blurring the line between reality and deception. AI is both the attacker and defender in this battle, as AI-driven threat detection systems now track and flag disinformation campaigns.

This chapter will explore:
1. Debunking common cybersecurity myths and lies.
2. How AI spots disinformation and fake news online.

1. Debunking Common Cybersecurity Myths and Lies

Myth #1: "I'm Not a Target"

The Lie
Many people believe that hackers only target large corporations or high-profile individuals. The idea is, "I'm too small or insignificant for anyone to care about me."

The Reality
Hackers don't care how "important" you are. In fact, most cyberattacks are done through automated bots that scan for vulnerable systems — not specific people. If your device has an unpatched vulnerability, the bot will attack, regardless of your importance. Phishing emails, ransomware, and credential stuffing attacks target millions of people every day.

Why Hackers Love This Myth
Hackers know that small businesses and individuals think they aren't targets, so they leave their systems unprotected. Attackers focus on "low-hanging fruit" — users and companies who don't follow best practices.
319

How to Defend Yourself
- Use AI-Driven Vulnerability Scanners to identify weak spots on your network.
- Enable MFA (Multi-Factor Authentication) on all accounts, so even if your password is leaked, attackers can't access your accounts.
- Don't assume you're safe. Attackers use automation to target as many people as possible.

Pro Tip: Attackers don't choose targets manually. They scan thousands of devices at once and attack the most vulnerable ones — not necessarily the most valuable ones.

Myth #2: "I Use Antivirus, So I'm Safe"

The Lie
Some people believe that having an antivirus program installed is enough to protect them from all threats. They install antivirus software, click "scan," and assume they are invincible.

The Reality
Antivirus software only detects known threats using signature-based detection. Today's cybercriminals use polymorphic malware (malware that changes its code each time it spreads) to avoid signature-based detection. Additionally, fileless malware doesn't leave behind files for antivirus to scan.

Why Hackers Love This Myth
Hackers use fileless malware to avoid detection. Since the malware only runs in system memory (RAM) and doesn't leave files on the hard drive, traditional antivirus software can't detect it.

How to Defend Yourself
- Use EDR (Endpoint Detection and Response) instead of traditional antivirus. EDR tracks behavior, not just files.
- Avoid downloading email attachments and don't click on unknown links.
- Deploy AI-based malware detection (like SentinelOne or CrowdStrike) that tracks behavior instead of file signatures.

Pro Tip: Signature-based antivirus tools are no longer enough. Upgrade to AI-driven EDR or XDR tools that analyze behavior, not just files.

Myth #3: "I Have Nothing Hackers Would Want"

The Lie
This is one of the most dangerous misconceptions. People believe that they don't have any valuable information, so hackers won't bother targeting them.

The Reality
Hackers want more than bank account logins. They want access, control, and leverage. If a hacker gains access to your devices, they can:
- Turn your devices into a botnet (used in DDoS attacks).
- Steal personal information (like photos, messages, and tax info) to blackmail you.
- Use your email for spam campaigns.
- Sell your identity on the dark web.

Why Hackers Love This Myth
Hackers know that most people think they have nothing to steal, so they use easy-to-guess passwords, skip updates, and ignore security alerts. This makes them easy targets.

How to Defend Yourself
- Treat your personal information (like email, phone number, and photos) as valuable data.
- Use Dark Web Monitoring to check if your data is for sale.
- Enable MFA (Multi-Factor Authentication) on every major platform.

Pro Tip: Your personal information can be used in identity theft, sold on the dark web, or used in deepfake voice scams.

Myth #4: "Hackers Use Super-Advanced Tools"

The Lie
Movies and TV shows portray hackers as super-geniuses with access to ultra-advanced technology.

The Reality
Most attacks are done using off-the-shelf hacking tools available on the dark web. Attackers buy these tools as part of Malware-as-a-Service (MaaS), which allows them to launch attacks with minimal skill.

How to Defend Yourself
- Assume that attackers are using automated attack tools, not manually created attacks.
- Use patch management tools to keep software updated.
- Deploy AI-driven threat intelligence platforms (like Recorded Future) to detect attack trends.

Pro Tip: Hackers don't need to be geniuses. They can simply buy ready-to-use attack kits from the dark web.

AI-Driven Misinformation & Deepfakes: The Next Battlefront
The COVID-19 pandemic exposed a harsh truth: Misinformation is no longer a human-driven problem — it's AI-driven. The early days of the pandemic were filled with conflicting reports, sensationalized claims, and celebrity-endorsed falsehoods that influenced millions of people. News channels, social media platforms, and even government agencies repeated information that was later found to be false. From claims about the virus's origins to debates on mask effectiveness, the world watched as so-called "trusted sources" struggled to keep up with the truth.

This event taught us something critical: AI-driven misinformation can weaponize trust. And with the rise of AI-generated deepfakes, we are entering an era where video and audio "evidence" can be fabricated so convincingly that even experts can't spot the difference.

How It Works
- AI-Generated Fake News — Large Language Models (LLMs) like ChatGPT or other AI text generators can create fake news articles that look just like legitimate media reports. Attackers can generate articles in bulk, making it nearly impossible to fact-check every story.
- AI-Generated Deepfakes — Attackers use deepfake technology (like DeepFaceLab and D-ID) to create realistic videos of celebrities, politicians, or trusted figures. These videos are used to spread false narratives. Imagine seeing a "news clip" of a world leader announcing a war, only to discover it was a fake.
- AI-Social Media Amplification — Attackers create fake social media accounts and use AI bots to flood platforms like Twitter, TikTok, and YouTube with misinformation. The AI-driven recommendation engines then amplify the content, making it go viral.
- AI-Enhanced Propaganda — Propaganda campaigns no longer require massive human teams. AI tools can generate millions of posts, comments, and reviews that shape public perception. For example, bots can flood review sites with fake 5-star or 1-star reviews to discredit or promote specific agendas.

Real-World Example
1. COVID-19 Misinformation (2020-2021)
During COVID-19, major news channels like CNN, Fox News, and BBC repeatedly broadcast statements that were later proven false. Early reports claimed:

- "The virus came from a wet market" — This was presented as fact for months, while alternative theories (like the "lab leak" theory) were dismissed as conspiracy theories. Today, the lab leak theory is being seriously investigated.
- "Masks are unnecessary" — Early public health announcements stated that "You do not need to wear a mask" to protect yourself. Later, they reversed this guidance with some making in compulsory to wear, the inconsistency led to distrust.
- "The vaccines are 100% effective" — While COVID vaccines were marketed as being fully effective, later data revealed breakthrough infections and side effects that weren't discussed in early press conferences.

How It Relates to AI:
- AI played a role in misinformation spread by amplifying false information. Social media algorithms prioritize engagement, and fear-based content gets the most clicks.
- Deepfake videos of public health officials, fake "news anchors," and even celebrity endorsements have been used to promote health products, treatments, and scams.
- Bot networks flooded platforms like Twitter, Facebook, and YouTube, making fake stories "trend," which in turn was picked up by legitimate news outlets.

2. Deepfake Video of Ukrainian President Volodymyr Zelensky (2022)
During the Russia-Ukraine conflict, a deepfake video of Ukrainian President Volodymyr Zelensky was released, calling on Ukrainian troops to surrender. This video was shared on social media and messaging platforms. While experts quickly debunked it as a deepfake, many citizens initially believed it was real.

How It Relates to AI:
- The video was created using deepfake software that cloned the face and voice of Zelensky.
- Attackers uploaded the video to social media, where the AI-driven recommendation engines spread it to millions before it could be debunked.
- The deepfake was realistic enough that even experienced viewers were initially fooled.

How to Defend Against AI-Driven Misinformation & Deepfakes

1. Fact-Check Multiple Sources
   - When you see breaking news, check multiple sources before believing it. If only one source is reporting a story, it could be disinformation.
   - Use fact-checking platforms like Snopes (www.snopes.com) or FactCheck.org (www.factcheck.org) to verify claims.

2. Use Deepfake Detection Tools
   - Tools like Deepware Scanner (www.deepware.ai) can help you scan images and videos to detect signs of deepfake manipulation.
   - Platforms like Reality Defender (www.realitydefender.ai) specialize in scanning content for signs of deepfake tampering.

3. Don't Rely on Celebrity Endorsements
   - During COVID-19, celebrities repeated false claims from health agencies and news channels. Be cautious of any "celebrity-endorsed" news.
   - Attackers can use AI-generated celebrity deepfakes to endorse scams, fake products, and cryptocurrency schemes.

4. Be Wary of Highly Emotional Content
   - If content seems designed to provoke fear, anger, or outrage, it's likely disinformation. Attackers use emotional manipulation to trick users into clicking, sharing, and amplifying false content.

5. Check Video and Audio Sources
   - If you receive a voice message or video call that seems "off," ask yourself, "Could this be a deepfake?"
   - If a family member or boss calls you asking for money, verify it through a second channel (like a text message) before acting.

Call-to-Action: How to Stay Safe
   - Don't believe everything you see or hear. Misinformation campaigns use AI bots, social media amplifiers, and even AI-generated video calls to create panic.
   - Use Deepware Scanner to check if videos are deepfakes.
   - Teach your family to recognize deepfakes and scams.
   - Fact-Check information using multiple sources
   - Encourage family members to create a Family Password so they can verify calls from loved ones (see Chapter 12).

2. How AI Spots Disinformation and Fake News Online

How Attackers Use AI to Spread Disinformation
Attackers use AI to spread fake news, generate deepfakes, and manipulate public opinion. Here's how:
- Fake News Generators — Attackers use AI content generators (like ChatGPT-style models) to create convincing fake news articles.
- Deepfake Videos — AI can create fake videos of executives making statements they never said.
- Social Media Bots — Attackers deploy AI-driven bots to flood social media with fake news.

How AI Defends Against Disinformation
AI-Driven Disinformation Detection — AI can detect patterns in fake news articles. Tools like NewsGuard analyze word patterns, tone, and source reliability to determine if a news article is real or fake.

Deepfake Detection — AI tools like Deepware Scanner analyze facial movements, lighting inconsistencies, and voice irregularities to spot deepfake videos.

Bot Detection on Social Media — Social media platforms like Twitter and Facebook use AI models to detect bots and fake accounts. These models look for accounts that post at unnatural speeds or use copy-paste text patterns.

Pro Tip: If you see a viral story on social media, check if it's been verified by a reliable source. AI-driven bots often spread fake news during crises.

How to Protect Yourself from Disinformation
Disinformation is no longer just an internet problem — it's a global issue that affects how we view politics, health, business, and even cybersecurity. Today's disinformation campaigns are far more sophisticated, often powered by AI-generated content, social media bots, and highly targeted propaganda techniques. But perhaps the most alarming aspect is that the majority of mainstream media is controlled by a small handful of powerful corporations.

According to multiple studies, approximately 90% of U.S. media is controlled by just six corporations:

- Comcast
- Disney
- Warner Bros. Discovery
- Paramount Global
- News Corp
- Sony

This consolidation means that much of the information you see on news channels, social media, and websites is filtered through the interests of just a few corporate entities. While journalists are often dedicated to uncovering the truth, these large corporations have significant influence over editorial decisions, advertising revenue, and political agendas.

1. Understand How Centralized Media Control Affects Disinformation

When only a few corporations control the majority of media, it becomes much easier for disinformation to spread, even if it's unintentional. Here's how it happens:

1. Echo Chambers — News stories are shared across networks, and since most networks are owned by the same corporations, the message remains consistent, even if it's incorrect. This makes it harder for independent voices to challenge the narrative.
2. Commercial Interests — Media outlets rely on advertisers for revenue. Stories that affect advertisers negatively (like data privacy or corporate negligence) are often downplayed or not reported at all.
3. Mistakes Are Amplified — If one major outlet publishes a flawed report, it is repeated across partner stations. When CNN, Fox News, or MSNBC make mistakes, those errors get amplified because other outlets pick up the story.

2. Don't Believe Everything You Read (or See)

The first and most important rule of disinformation defense is don't believe everything you see or hear. Just because a major media outlet or social media account shares a story, it doesn't make it true.

Here's how you can apply this principle:

- Question Headlines and Soundbites — Headlines are designed to be sensational to drive clicks. If something seems too shocking to be true, it probably is.
- Read the Full Story — Headlines often oversimplify or misrepresent the true message of an article. Take time to read the entire story before forming an opinion.

- Beware of One-Source Stories — If a story is only being reported by one source, be skeptical. The strongest stories are verified by multiple, independent news organizations.
- Look for the Source — Is the source of the claim a government press release, a leaked document, or an anonymous insider? Evaluate the credibility of the source.

Pro Tip: Disinformation campaigns thrive on "hot takes" and "breaking news" announcements. Wait for more information before drawing conclusions.

3. Use Fact-Checking Sites (But Be Cautious With Them Too)
Fact-checking sites like Snopes and FactCheck.org are useful, but they are not infallible. While they often provide excellent context, they are not immune to bias. Fact-checkers rely on human editors, and like any human, they can make mistakes or be influenced by their own beliefs.

Here's how to use fact-checking sites effectively:
- Cross-Check Claims Using Multiple Fact-Checkers — Don't rely on a single source. Check multiple fact-checking websites to see if they all agree.
- Look at Primary Sources — If the fact-check cites a scientific paper, read the abstract or executive summary. Primary sources often contain nuance that fact-checkers miss.
- Be Wary of "Partially True" Claims — If a fact-checker rates something as "partially true," it means part of the story is false. Focus on the parts that were wrong.

Pro Tip: Instead of relying on fact-checking sites alone, look for the original source (like the press release, court filing, or study) and see what it says.

4. Watch for AI-Generated Deepfakes
Deepfakes are AI-generated fake videos or audio clips. Attackers create them to mimic the appearance, voice, and movements of real people. Deepfakes have been used to:
- Impersonate executives during phone calls, tricking employees into sending money.
- Fake video evidence of people making statements they never made.
- Spread disinformation in the form of video "proof" of political figures doing things they never did.

Here's how to detect deepfakes:
- Look for Visual Artifacts — Watch for unnatural blurring around the eyes, teeth, or hair.

- Look for Lighting Inconsistencies — AI often struggles to get natural lighting correct. If the shadows on a person's face seem off, it may be a deepfake.
- Check for Lip-Sync Errors — Deepfakes sometimes have imperfect lip movement. If the mouth movements don't match the words, it's a red flag.
- Use Deepfake Detection Tools — Tools like Deepware Scanner allow you to upload a video and scan it for signs of AI generation.

Pro Tip: Pay attention to eyes, teeth, and lip movement — these are the most common places where deepfakes fail.

5. Recognize Propaganda Disguised as News

One of the most dangerous forms of disinformation is propaganda disguised as news. Unlike fake news, propaganda is created with the intent to manipulate. It's designed to create fear, hatred, or division.

Signs of propaganda:
- Emotional Headlines — If a headline makes you angry, afraid, or outraged, it might be propaganda.
- Lack of Specific Sources — Propaganda often says "experts say" or "some believe" without naming the source.
- Over-Simplification — Real stories are complex. Propaganda tries to reduce the story to a simple, black-and-white conflict.

Pro Tip: Ask yourself, "Who benefits if I believe this story?" Propaganda is often designed to divide people or push a specific agenda.

6. Tools to Fight Disinformation

- Deepware Scanner — Detects deepfakes by scanning for signs of AI manipulation.
- NewsGuard — Rates the trustworthiness of online news sources.
- CrowdTangle — Tracks how stories are shared on social media, helping you identify viral disinformation.
- Bot Sentinel — Detects social media bots that spread disinformation.

Pro Tip: When you see a viral story, check if it has been verified by NewsGuard, Deepware Scanner, or Bot Sentinel.

Case Study: COVID-19 and Media-Driven Disinformation
The COVID-19 pandemic wasn't just a health crisis, but also a disinformation crisis. Conflicting messages from media outlets, health agencies, and government officials led to widespread confusion and eroded public trust. Key narratives evolved over time, often without clear explanations, and dissenting voices were censored.

Origin of the Virus: Initially, COVID-19 was believed to have originated from a wet market in Wuhan, China. However, later evidence suggested a possible lab leak, a theory that was dismissed early on and censored. As the possibility gained traction, it highlighted the dangers of silencing alternative viewpoints.

Mask Effectiveness: Early guidance from health officials claimed masks weren't necessary, but this later changed to a universal recommendation. Studies eventually showed that cloth masks had little impact on virus transmission, leading to skepticism and a loss of trust in health advice.

Social Distancing: The 6-foot rule, which was widely implemented, was based on outdated research and later deemed arbitrary. This revelation, along with the lack of solid evidence, led to public doubts about the scientific basis for many pandemic measures.
Vaccine Testing and Side Effects: Initially, COVID-19 vaccines were marketed as 100% effective and safe, but it later emerged that they had not been fully tested for transmission prevention, and side effects like myocarditis were discovered. The perception of a double standard, with exemptions for officials, further undermined trust.

Lessons Learned: The pandemic demonstrated how misinformation spreads when institutions repeat unverified claims, refuse to acknowledge mistakes, and censor alternative perspectives. This situation has set a precedent for future disinformation campaigns, especially with the rise of AI-driven misinformation and deepfakes.

Key Takeaways
1. Misinformation Comes From "Trusted Sources"
Misinformation isn't limited to social media trolls. It can come from mainstream news, government officials, and even health experts. The COVID-19 pandemic showed that even trusted authorities can be wrong — and when their mistakes aren't acknowledged, public trust collapses.

2. Silencing Dissent Fuels Distrust
When the lab-leak theory was banned on platforms like Facebook and Twitter, people grew suspicious. When it was later re-opened as a plausible theory, many felt betrayed. This event showed that silencing alternative views often backfires and increases distrust.

"The truth in science thrives when questioned; lies fear the light of scrutiny and seek the shadow of censorship."

3. AI-Driven Misinformation Will Get Worse
The next generation of misinformation won't come from government officials or celebrities. It will come from AI-generated deepfake videos, synthetic voices, and AI-generated news articles. Attackers will use voice cloning and deepfake video impersonations to manipulate public perception, promote fake products, or influence elections.

How to Protect Yourself
- Question the Source — Just because something comes from a "trusted source" doesn't mean it's accurate. COVID-19 taught us that even government agencies and major news outlets can be wrong. Seek multiple sources before you believe any claim.
- Be Aware of Deepfakes — Tools like Deepware Scanner (www.deepware.ai) can detect signs of deepfake manipulation. If you see a viral video or hear a shocking "leaked audio" clip, check its authenticity.
- Think Critically — Always ask yourself: Who benefits from this story? Is the media trying to inform you — or manipulate you? Remember that large corporations, pharmaceutical companies, and even media outlets have financial incentives to shape public narratives.

Conclusion
The COVID-19 pandemic revealed the dangers of centralized information control and the erosion of trust when alternative theories were dismissed and later quietly reversed. The failure to admit mistakes fueled conspiracy theories and deepened skepticism, a pattern that will likely repeat with AI-driven misinformation. With tools like DeepFaceLab and ElevenLabs voice cloning now publicly available, attackers can easily create hyper-realistic deepfakes, blurring the line between fact and fiction. As deepfakes and AI-powered deception become more prevalent, the lesson is clear: don't believe everything you see or hear. Misinformation thrives in environments where critical thinking is lacking, and AI will only amplify this risk.

"If you don't control what you believe, someone else will."

Chapter 25: The Ultimate Cybersecurity Checklist

Your Mission to Level Up Your Cybersecurity
Cybersecurity can feel overwhelming with constant threats, complex technologies, and endless tasks. But what if you could approach it like a game? Gamification in cybersecurity turns what would otherwise be a daunting checklist into an engaging and rewarding experience. Instead of simply reading guides or watching videos, gamified platforms allow you to actively participate in simulated cybersecurity challenges. These platforms offer hands-on experience in detecting threats, defending systems, and responding to attacks, all while providing real-time feedback on your progress.

The beauty of gamification is that it makes learning interactive and fun, which is crucial when mastering a subject as complex as cybersecurity. With AI-powered learning platforms, the process becomes even more personalized, adapting challenges based on your strengths and weaknesses. Whether you're a beginner or an experienced user, gamification ensures that the skills you develop are not only remembered but practiced repeatedly—building muscle memory that will prepare you for real-world threats.

By turning cybersecurity tasks into missions, levels, and achievements, gamification helps keep you motivated. It builds essential skills—like threat hunting, incident response, and ethical hacking—while tracking your progress toward becoming a true Cybersecurity Champion.

Cybersecurity Gamification: Learn Cybersecurity Through AI-Powered Platforms
Gamification in cybersecurity transforms traditional learning into a dynamic, engaging experience. Platforms use game mechanics—such as challenges, rewards, and real-time feedback—to teach essential cybersecurity skills. Instead of passively absorbing information, you're actively solving problems, simulating real-world cyberattacks, and applying your knowledge in a safe environment.

Why Gamification Works
Gamification works because it taps into fundamental human psychology: people are naturally drawn to games. The competitive, reward-driven nature of games boosts motivation and focus, making learning feel less like a chore and more like an accomplishment. You're more likely to stick with cybersecurity tasks when they're framed as challenges to overcome, whether it's spotting a phishing email or defending against a simulated ransomware attack.

Additionally, gamified platforms offer immediate feedback, which is essential for improving skills. Unlike traditional study methods, where mistakes may go unnoticed, these platforms highlight errors in real-time, allowing you to learn from them and try again. Over time, you build the confidence to tackle more complex cybersecurity issues.

How Gamification Helps You Learn Cybersecurity
Gamified platforms bring a hands-on approach to learning. Instead of just reading about phishing scams or malware, you're put into scenarios where you must identify threats, block attacks, and prevent breaches. This practical experience helps you internalize critical skills like threat hunting, penetration testing, and incident response.

Key cybersecurity skills learned through gamification include:
- Threat Hunting: Identifying hidden threats by analyzing logs, network traffic, and anomalies.
- Incident Response: Practicing real-time responses to ransomware, malware, and data breaches.
- Penetration Testing: Learning ethical hacking techniques to test the security of systems.
- Social Engineering: Recognizing phishing, deepfakes, and other social engineering tactics.
- Encryption and Decryption: Understanding encryption methods and how hackers exploit weak encryption.

Gamified learning also helps you think like a hacker, teaching you how attackers view and exploit vulnerabilities. This "offensive" perspective helps you better protect your systems by anticipating potential threats.

By engaging with these platforms, you can level up your cybersecurity skills progressively—moving from simple tasks to more complex challenges as you gain experience.

Best Cybersecurity Gamification Platforms
There are several powerful gamification platforms designed to help individuals, families, and businesses level up their cybersecurity skills. These platforms provide hands-on, real-time learning through simulated cyberattacks, vulnerability testing, and problem-solving challenges. Each platform offers unique features suited to different skill levels and learning goals. Below are some of the best platforms to help you master cybersecurity through gamification.

1. TryHackMe
- Who It's For: Beginners to intermediate learners
- What It Offers: TryHackMe offers "capture-the-flag" (CTF) style challenges, where users solve real-world cybersecurity problems in a safe, virtual environment. The platform walks you through missions like penetration testing, malware analysis, and network security. It's designed to teach you ethical hacking skills through hands-on experience.

Key Features:
- Beginner-friendly lessons with guided walkthroughs
- A variety of real-world attack scenarios to practice on
- Points and ranks to track your progress

2. Hack The Box (HTB)
- Who It's For: Advanced learners, penetration testers, red teamers
- What It Offers: Hack The Box is designed for more advanced users. It allows you to hack into virtual systems, exploit vulnerabilities, and "capture flags" to prove your skills. HTB regularly updates its "machines" (virtual environments) to challenge users with new scenarios. This platform is ideal for those looking to dive deep into penetration testing and ethical hacking.

Key Features:
- Advanced challenges and real-world systems to hack into
- Regularly updated content with new machines and challenges
- Leaderboards that let you compete with others

3. CyberStart
- Who It's For: Students, beginners, and those new to cybersecurity
- What It Offers: CyberStart is a great platform for students or beginners just getting into cybersecurity. It uses gamification to teach core concepts like threat detection, network security, and incident response. Players take on the role of cyber agents tasked with defending against cyberattacks in a story-driven world.

Key Features:
- Advanced challenges and real-world systems to hack into
- Regularly updated content with new machines and challenges
- Leaderboards that let you compete with others

4. CyberStart
- <u>Who It's For:</u> Students, beginners, and those new to cybersecurity
- <u>What It Offers:</u> CyberStart is a great platform for students or beginners just getting into cybersecurity. It uses gamification to teach core concepts like threat detection, network security, and incident response. Players take on the role of cyber agents tasked with defending against cyberattacks in a story-driven world.

Key Features:
- Story-based challenges to engage users
- Interactive puzzles to build foundational cybersecurity skills
- A great starting point for students or those new to the field

5. RangeForce
- <u>Who It's For:</u> Businesses and corporate teams
- <u>What It Offers:</u> RangeForce is a gamified platform tailored for corporate cybersecurity training. It is perfect for businesses looking to train employees in threat detection, incident response, and secure network management. The platform simulates real-world attacks, giving teams the opportunity to practice defensive measures in a controlled environment.

Key Features:
- Team-based training scenarios for businesses
- Real-time response simulations for various cyberattacks
- Customizable training based on corporate needs

6. Immersive Labs
- <u>Who It's For:</u> Individuals, students, and businesses
- <u>What It Offers:</u> Immersive Labs offers hands-on labs that walk users through various attack scenarios like ransomware, phishing, and malware analysis. These labs are designed to simulate real-world incidents, allowing you to learn how to handle cyberattacks in a practical environment. It's suitable for both individuals and businesses looking to improve their cybersecurity readiness.

Key Features:
- Story-driven, interactive cyberattack simulations
- Real-world scenarios for practicing incident response
- Detailed feedback to improve your skills

Final Action Steps to Protect Your Family, Business, and Personal Data

By now, you've learned how gamified platforms can help you level up your cybersecurity skills, but it's essential to apply those skills to real-world scenarios. Here's your final checklist of actionable steps to ensure you and your loved ones are protected from cyber threats. Whether you're securing personal devices, protecting your family's digital presence, or safeguarding business data, these steps will help you stay ahead of potential attacks.

For Individuals

1. Enable Multi-Factor Authentication (MFA): Always activate MFA on your accounts, especially for email, banking, and social media. This adds an extra layer of protection against unauthorized access.
2. Use a Password Manager: Store and generate unique passwords for each account to avoid reusing passwords and reduce the risk of breaches.
3. Update Software Regularly: Ensure your operating systems, apps, and antivirus software are always up to date to protect against vulnerabilities.
4. Encrypt Sensitive Data: Use tools like full-disk encryption or encrypted messaging apps to protect sensitive information, especially on mobile devices and laptops.
5. Be Cautious of Phishing: Train yourself to recognize phishing attempts by analyzing email addresses, links, and grammar carefully.

For Families

1. Create a Family Password System: Protect your household against AI-driven scams like voice cloning by having a unique family password for verification in suspicious situations.
2. Set Parental Controls: Use parental control software to monitor your children's online activity, keeping them safe from inappropriate content and online predators.
3. Secure IoT Devices: Make sure that all connected devices in your home, such as cameras, smart locks, and thermostats, have strong passwords and are updated regularly.
4. Monitor for Cyberbullying and Scams: Educate your kids about the dangers of online scams and social media manipulation, and encourage them to come to you with any concerns.
5. Backup Family Data Regularly: Store important family photos, documents, and other sensitive data in a secure cloud or external backup to prevent loss due to ransomware or system failures.

For Businesses

- Implement a Zero-Trust Model: Ensure that all users, devices, and networks are continuously verified, minimizing the chances of a breach from within.
- Train Employees Regularly: Keep employees up-to-date with cybersecurity best practices by using gamified platforms or simulated phishing campaigns to improve their ability to detect threats.
- Adopt AI-Driven Threat Detection Tools: Invest in tools like EDR or XDR to monitor and respond to threats in real time.
- Create an Incident Response Plan: Have a clear, tested plan for how your business will respond to various types of cyberattacks, including data breaches, ransomware, and insider threats.
- Backup Business Data Daily: Use automated cloud backup solutions to ensure that business-critical data is always recoverable in case of an attack.

Conclusion: Level Up Your Cybersecurity Skills

As you've seen, cybersecurity doesn't have to be a complex or overwhelming task. By approaching it as a game, you can transform the process of learning and protecting yourself, your family, and your business into an engaging, rewarding journey. Gamification not only makes learning fun, but it also ensures that you retain critical skills and knowledge, preparing you for the real-world threats that lie ahead.

The best part is that the more you engage with these platforms and complete challenges, the more confident you'll become in handling potential cyber threats. Whether you're protecting personal data, securing your home network, or managing a business's security operations, every step you take towards improving your cybersecurity brings you closer to becoming a true Cybersecurity Champion.

The key takeaway? Cybersecurity is an ongoing process, not a one-time fix. Keep leveling up, stay informed, and don't stop learning. The world of cyber threats is constantly evolving, and by embracing gamification, you'll be ready to face any challenge that comes your way.

Remember, in cybersecurity, just like in a game, every mission completed and every challenge conquered brings you closer to success. Keep advancing, and you'll always be one step ahead of the attackers.

Chapter 26: Cyber-Physical Attacks & Critical Infrastructure Security

What Are Cyber-Physical Attacks?
Imagine a hacker shutting down an entire power grid, leaving millions of homes in darkness. Picture a ransomware attack on a hospital, where doctors are suddenly unable to access patient records or use critical life-saving equipment. Consider the chaos caused when traffic lights in a smart city all turn green at once, triggering mass collisions at intersections. These aren't scenes from a sci-fi movie — they're real-world examples of cyber-physical attacks.

A cyber-physical attack occurs when a cyberattack disrupts or takes control of a physical process or device, often with life-threatening consequences. Unlike traditional cyberattacks that target data, files, or money, cyber-physical attacks impact the physical world. They target critical infrastructure such as power grids, hospitals, water treatment plants, factories, and smart cities. When these systems fail, the results aren't just financial losses — they can include blackouts, delays in medical care, and even loss of life.

Cyber-physical attacks have been on the rise for the last decade, but the stakes are even higher now. As more infrastructure systems become "smart" and AI-driven, the attack surface grows exponentially. From self-driving cars to automated power grids, each system is an entry point for AI-powered hackers. While attackers use AI to automate and amplify attacks, defenders must counter with AI-driven anomaly detection, threat intelligence, and Zero Trust frameworks.

Why Do Cyber-Physical Attacks Matter?
The critical nature of these attacks is rooted in the fact that they target systems we rely on for our daily lives — electricity, water, healthcare, and transportation. If a cyberattack shuts down a social media platform, it's frustrating. But if it shuts down a hospital's life-support system, it's catastrophic.

These attacks matter because they impact both national security and daily life. Cyber-physical attacks affect physical systems, not just data. Unlike data breaches, which result in information theft, cyber-physical attacks result in power outages, production halts, traffic collisions, and interruptions to medical care. Hackers target the systems that power society itself, making cyber-physical security one of the most critical areas of modern cybersecurity.

These attacks are also a national security concern. Instead of launching missiles, adversaries can now attack a country's power grid, water supply, or emergency response systems with nothing more than a laptop and an internet connection. As the world becomes more connected, attack surfaces increase. Smart cities, autonomous vehicles, and smart factories are all new entry points for attackers.

AI plays a major role in this evolution. Attackers use AI to automate reconnaissance, scan for vulnerable systems, and create polymorphic malware that adapts to avoid detection. On the defense side, AI-driven tools like anomaly detection, automated patching, and Zero Trust verification are being used to mitigate the threat. However, as attackers and defenders both use AI, the battle becomes AI vs. AI in the race to protect physical systems from disruption.

How Cyber-Physical Attacks Differ from Traditional Cyberattacks
Cyber-physical attacks are not like typical ransomware or phishing attacks. While those attacks steal or lock up data, cyber-physical attacks target the systems that control the physical world. Instead of leaking private information, these attacks can lead to loss of life, large-scale financial loss, and damage to critical infrastructure.

Traditional cyberattacks usually target IT networks, websites, and databases, while cyber-physical attacks target OT (Operational Technology) systems, like power grids, water treatment facilities, hospitals, and traffic control systems. These systems are run by SCADA (Supervisory Control and Data Acquisition) systems and ICS (Industrial Control Systems), which are much more difficult to patch and secure. Traditional IT systems receive regular software updates, but many OT systems can't be updated without taking them offline, which makes them a prime target for attack.

Cyber-physical attacks often have a larger and more long-term impact. If hackers breach an email system, the company may have to reset passwords. But if hackers infiltrate a power grid, the blackout could impact millions of people for days or weeks. Cyber-physical attacks go beyond the digital realm and have very real, tangible consequences.

Key Systems Targeted in Cyber-Physical Attacks
Power grids are one of the most critical targets for hackers. Disrupting a power grid can cause blackouts that impact homes, hospitals, and businesses. A well-known example of this is the Ukraine Power Grid Attack. Hackers used BlackEnergy malware to breach Ukraine's power grid and cut off electricity to 230,000 people for six hours. By manipulating SCADA systems, hackers were able to control electrical substations remotely, cutting power at will.

Hospitals and healthcare facilities are also prime targets for cyber-physical attacks. Hackers target hospitals because they know that lives are at stake, making it more likely that hospitals will pay ransoms quickly. In 2020, a ransomware attack on a hospital in Germany caused the first known death related to a cyberattack. When the attack locked the hospital's patient record system, emergency care was delayed for a patient, resulting in death. Attackers often go after connected medical devices, such as ventilators, heart monitors, and insulin pumps, all of which can be controlled or disabled remotely.

Smart cities have become a growing target due to their reliance on automated public services like smart traffic lights, smart streetlights, and public Wi-Fi networks. By hacking a city's urban control center, attackers can manipulate traffic lights, cause traffic jams, or even prevent emergency services from responding to calls. In 2019, Johannesburg, South Africa experienced a ransomware attack that took down its municipal services, including public service payment portals and emergency hotlines. The attack caused widespread disruption, highlighting the vulnerability of smart city systems.

Factories and manufacturing facilities are vulnerable because of the Industrial Control Systems (ICS) and Programmable Logic Controllers (PLCs) that control industrial processes. An infamous example is Stuxnet, a digital weapon that targeted Iranian nuclear facilities. Stuxnet was designed to make centrifuges spin at abnormal speeds, causing physical destruction while sending fake "all-clear" signals to operators. This attack revealed how malware could be used to cause physical sabotage in industrial operations.

How AI Changes the Game for Cyber-Physical Attacks

AI allows attackers to automate, scale, and supercharge cyber-physical attacks. Attackers no longer have to spend weeks manually scanning networks or looking for entry points. With AI, attackers can scan for thousands of vulnerabilities in real time, prioritize high-value targets, and automate attacks with self-learning malware.

One key innovation is AI-driven polymorphic malware. Traditional malware can be detected because its code matches known virus signatures. Polymorphic malware, however, changes its code every few minutes, making it impossible for traditional antivirus programs to recognize. Attackers now use mutation engines powered by AI to create malware that evolves constantly, ensuring it is never detected the same way twice.

Another threat is the use of deepfake videos and AI-generated voices. Attackers can use AI to create realistic fake videos of CEOs, executives, or public officials. These deepfakes can be used to manipulate public opinion, cause confusion, or trick employees into following false orders. A famous example of this is the rise of deepfake phone calls, where attackers use AI-cloned voices to trick employees into sending wire transfers.

Call-to-Action for the Reader

Cyber-physical attacks are no longer isolated incidents. They have become one of the biggest threats to national security, public health, and the global economy. Critical infrastructure systems like power grids, hospitals, and transportation networks are no longer immune to the digital threats once limited to email scams or password theft. Attackers are using AI to automate attacks, evade detection, and cause physical destruction.

"If your email gets hacked, it's an inconvenience. But if a hospital is hacked, lives are at stake."

Take action now by learning how to identify threats, protect critical infrastructure, and adopt Zero Trust principles to protect vital systems. As smart cities, smart factories, and connected hospitals continue to grow, so does the attack surface. Your knowledge could be the only thing standing between safety and chaos.

Real-World Case Studies: Attacks That Changed Everything
To understand the reality of cyber-physical attacks, it's essential to examine real-world incidents. These cases show how hackers have infiltrated power grids, healthcare systems, factories, and smart cities, causing massive financial, operational, and human impact. Each case highlights a unique tactic, from malware and ransomware to direct control over industrial systems.

Case Study 1: Stuxnet (2010) — The World's First Cyber Weapon
Target: Iranian Nuclear Enrichment Facility (Natanz)
Type of Attack: Malware-based sabotage targeting SCADA/ICS systems

What Happened:
- The Stuxnet worm is widely regarded as the world's first known cyber-physical weapon. Its primary goal was to target SCADA (Supervisory Control and Data Acquisition) systems used to control centrifuges in Iranian nuclear facilities. The malware was highly sophisticated, with a built-in capability to identify specific Siemens PLC (Programmable Logic Controller) systems. Once it infected the targeted SCADA system, it altered the speed of the centrifuges, causing them to spin at unsafe speeds. This physical stress caused the machines to break down, slowing down Iran's uranium enrichment program.

AI's Role:
Although AI-driven automation wasn't explicitly part of Stuxnet, its logic functioned similarly to AI models. The malware identified its target, waited until specific conditions were met, and then launched an automated, covert attack while sending "all-clear" signals to human operators. Modern malware, like self-learning AI malware, now mimics this tactic.

Impact:
Stuxnet is widely regarded as a turning point in cyber warfare. It demonstrated how cyberattacks could cause physical damage without firing a single bullet. It also set a precedent for using digital tools as weapons of war, inspiring other nation-states to develop similar cyber capabilities.

Lesson Learned:
Cyber-physical attacks can be disguised as normal system activity, making them hard to detect. The lesson is that anomaly detection systems powered by AI are essential to spot abnormal system behavior, such as changes in machine spin rates or system delays.

Case Study 2: Colonial Pipeline Ransomware Attack (2021) — Fuel Crisis in the U.S.
Target: Colonial Pipeline (largest U.S. fuel pipeline)
Type of Attack: Ransomware attack on pipeline control systems

What Happened:
- In 2021, Colonial Pipeline suffered a devastating ransomware attack carried out by the DarkSide ransomware group. Hackers infiltrated the company's IT network, encrypted critical files, and demanded a ransom of $4.4 million in Bitcoin. As a result, Colonial Pipeline shut down its pipeline operations for six days, halting the flow of fuel to the U.S. East Coast. This led to widespread fuel shortages, long gas station lines, and a surge in fuel prices.

AI's Role:
Attackers used AI-enhanced reconnaissance tools to identify network vulnerabilities and weak points in Colonial Pipeline's remote work infrastructure. The attackers also relied on AI-driven ransomware kits that automate encryption, ransom generation, and communication with victims.

Impact:
This attack exposed the vulnerability of the U.S. energy supply chain. It led to fuel shortages across multiple states, panic buying, and price increases. The U.S. government was forced to declare a state of emergency.

Lesson Learned:
Ransomware doesn't just affect IT systems — it can shut down entire physical supply chains. Companies must use Zero Trust principles to control access, and they should rely on AI-driven anomaly detection to spot unusual activity in both IT and OT networks.

Case Study 3: Ukraine Power Grid Attack (2015 & 2016) — Turning Off the Lights in a Nation
Target: Ukrainian Power Grid (distribution substations)
Type of Attack: Remote access attack on SCADA/ICS systems

What Happened:
- In December 2015, hackers launched an attack on Ukraine's power grid, successfully shutting down power to 230,000 homes for six hours. The attackers infiltrated three regional electric distribution companies, remotely taking control of the grid's SCADA (Supervisory Control and Data Acquisition) systems. They turned off 30 substations, causing widespread power outages.

- The following year, in 2016, a similar attack struck Ukraine's Pivnichna electrical substation, causing further outages. This time, the attackers used malware called Industroyer, which specifically targeted protocols for power grid communication.

AI's Role:
While AI wasn't explicitly mentioned in the 2015 attack, it has since become a key tool for both attackers and defenders. Today, attackers use AI to automate network scans to identify vulnerabilities in SCADA/ICS systems. Defenders now use AI-driven threat detection to analyze network traffic, spot anomalies, and detect intrusions.

Impact:
The attack caused six-hour blackouts across multiple Ukrainian regions. It demonstrated how hackers could cause blackouts on a national scale, sparking global fear of power grid attacks. This event served as a wake-up call for other nations, leading to increased investment in AI-driven grid anomaly detection.

Lesson Learned:
Attackers can use SCADA-specific malware to control electrical substations remotely. Defenders must ensure network segmentation between IT and OT systems and deploy AI-driven anomaly detection to flag unusual power fluctuations or command overrides.

Case Study 4: Attack on the Healthcare System (2020) — When a Cyber Attack Becomes Deadly
Target: German hospital (Dusseldorf University Hospital)
Type of Attack: Ransomware attack on hospital IT systems

What Happened:
- In 2020, ransomware attackers targeted a German hospital in Düsseldorf, Germany. Attackers infiltrated the hospital's IT network and encrypted critical files related to patient care. Doctors and nurses were unable to access patient records, treatment schedules, and medical devices. Tragically, a patient in urgent need of care was rerouted to another hospital, causing a fatal delay. This marked the first death attributed to a ransomware attack.

AI's Role:
Attackers used AI-enhanced ransomware kits to encrypt the hospital's systems and automated payment demands. On the defensive side, hospitals have since adopted AI-driven threat detection to spot abnormal network traffic and block ransomware attacks in real time.

Impact:
The attack revealed how cyber-physical attacks are not just a financial threat — they are a life-threatening issue. As hospitals adopt more connected devices (like ventilators and smart heart monitors), cyber-physical risk increases.

Lesson Learned:
Healthcare systems must prioritize cyber-physical security by isolating connected devices, conducting regular vulnerability scans, and adopting AI-based ransomware detection. Defenders must prioritize air-gapped backup systems to ensure patient data can be restored after an attack.

Case Study 5: Smart City Attack on Johannesburg (2019) — The Day a City Was Held Hostage
Target: City of Johannesburg, South Africa (municipal services)
Type of Attack: Ransomware attack on city services

What Happened:
- Hackers launched a ransomware attack on Johannesburg's municipal systems, affecting public services like bill payments, emergency response hotlines, and public Wi-Fi access. The city's administrative portal went offline, and the hackers demanded a ransom payment in Bitcoin to restore access. Emergency services, like police hotlines, were interrupted, causing panic.

AI's Role:
Attackers used AI-driven reconnaissance tools to scan for vulnerable endpoints. They also used AI-enhanced ransomware automation to lock down critical city services.

Impact:
This attack highlighted the danger of smart cities. The more connected a city becomes, the more targets hackers have. The attack on Johannesburg exposed how ransomware attacks can disrupt daily life, from 911 services to online payments.

Lesson Learned:
Smart cities must deploy AI anomaly detection and Zero Trust access for municipal systems. Public service portals should undergo regular penetration testing, and 24/7 monitoring is required to prevent city-wide service shutdowns.

Types of Cyber-Physical Attacks
Cyber-physical attacks target the systems that bridge the gap between the digital and physical worlds. These attacks don't just corrupt files or steal data — they disrupt physical processes, destroy critical systems, and in some cases, endanger human lives. The more our world integrates IoT (Internet of Things), smart devices, and automated infrastructure, the larger the attack surface becomes.

While there are many subcategories of cyber-physical attacks, the following types are the most prevalent and dangerous:

1. Industrial Control System (ICS) Attacks
Industrial Control Systems (ICS) manage essential operations in factories, power grids, oil refineries, and manufacturing plants. ICS includes tools like Supervisory Control and Data Acquisition (SCADA) systems and Programmable Logic Controllers (PLCs), which allow operators to control physical processes remotely.

How It Works:
Attackers compromise ICS to gain control of key processes like assembly lines, production systems, and factory robots. Once they have access, they can send false commands to devices or tamper with sensor readings to make systems think everything is normal. This allows hackers to:
- Shut down production lines.
- Cause unsafe machine speeds (like in the Stuxnet attack).
- Spoil production materials (overheating, misalignment, or over/under processing).
- Trigger physical damage to factory equipment.

Real-World Example:
The Stuxnet attack on Iranian nuclear centrifuges was the most famous ICS attack. The malware caused centrifuges to spin at abnormal speeds, causing them to break. Attackers can also target power grids, as seen in the Ukraine Power Grid Attack where hackers remotely shut down electricity to 230,000 homes.

How AI Plays a Role:
Attackers use AI-driven reconnaissance to scan thousands of ICS devices looking for unpatched vulnerabilities. Once inside, AI-driven malware automates the attack, allowing the attacker to control multiple PLCs at once. Defenders now use AI anomaly detection to spot unusual commands sent to ICS devices, like a centrifuge suddenly spinning faster than normal.

2. Ransomware on Critical Infrastructure

Ransomware encrypts files, but when applied to cyber-physical systems, it locks down entire hospitals, power grids, and factories. While ransomware on IT systems is already devastating, it becomes life-threatening when applied to hospitals, police services, or emergency hotlines.

How It Works:
Attackers use ransomware kits to lock down control systems, disable networked devices, and demand payment for a decryption key. This type of attack is especially effective on hospitals and healthcare systems, where the urgency to restore operations forces hospitals to pay the ransom. Colonial Pipeline's ransomware attack is an example of how ransomware can impact physical infrastructure, in this case, cutting off the fuel supply to the entire U.S. East Coast.

Real-World Example:
The Colonial Pipeline ransomware attack in 2021 forced the largest U.S. fuel pipeline to shut down for six days, causing fuel shortages across multiple states. Another example is the attack on the Dusseldorf University Hospital in Germany, where ransomware delayed emergency care for a critical patient, resulting in a fatality.

How AI Plays a Role:
AI tools are used by attackers to automate ransomware delivery and to encrypt files at scale. Ransomware kits like REvil use AI-driven mutation engines to avoid detection, creating polymorphic malware that changes its code every few minutes. Defenders use AI-based ransomware detection to spot encryption activity on file systems and isolate affected devices in real time.

3. Smart City Attacks

Smart cities are interconnected urban areas with digital infrastructure like smart traffic lights, public Wi-Fi, and smart surveillance cameras. By hacking into a city's control systems, attackers can disrupt public services, overload traffic systems, and cause chaos.

How It Works:
Attackers breach city control centers that manage public services. Once inside, they can:
- Shut down traffic lights, causing major congestion and accidents.
- Take over public surveillance cameras, gaining visual access to streets, intersections, and public areas.

- Shut down 911 emergency call centers, preventing emergency calls.
- Disable payment portals for public services, as seen in the 2019 Johannesburg ransomware attack.

Real-World Example:
In 2019, hackers attacked Johannesburg, South Africa, taking down essential services like payment systems and emergency response services. The attack crippled city operations for days.

How AI Plays a Role:
AI is used by attackers to scan for open ports on smart city systems, like exposed Wi-Fi hotspots or public kiosks. Attackers can also create AI-driven ransomware that specifically targets connected systems like smart traffic lights. Defenders are now deploying AI anomaly detection to flag unusual behavior, such as all traffic lights switching green at once.

4. Cyber-Physical IoT Device Attacks
IoT (Internet of Things) devices like smart locks, thermostats, cameras, and home assistants are everywhere. These devices, while convenient, create massive security risks because they are often shipped with default passwords or have unpatched vulnerabilities.

How It Works:
Attackers scan for exposed IoT devices connected to the internet. Once inside, they can:
- Unlock smart locks remotely to gain physical access to homes.
- Disable security cameras to hide their movements.
- Overheat smart thermostats, causing home temperatures to rise to unsafe levels.
- Hijack voice assistants to give voice commands like opening doors or placing orders.

Real-World Example:
A famous example of IoT vulnerabilities occurred when hackers launched the Mirai botnet attack, infecting millions of IoT devices (like security cameras) and using them to launch massive DDoS attacks on major websites like Netflix, Twitter, and Amazon.

How AI Plays a Role:
Attackers use AI-guided network scanning to identify vulnerable IoT devices with exposed ports. Attackers also use AI to generate default passwords to brute-force devices. Defenders are now using AI-driven home security tools like Norton Core to monitor IoT device behavior and flag unusual connections.

5. Cyber Attacks on Critical Infrastructure (Power Grids, Hospitals, Airports)

Attackers target critical infrastructure like power grids, hospitals, airports, and water treatment plants. These systems operate on legacy Operational Technology (OT) networks that aren't designed for modern cybersecurity.

How It Works:
Attackers compromise power grids, airports, and healthcare systems by attacking their SCADA and ICS systems. Once inside, they can:

- Shut down power substations, leading to blackouts (like in Ukraine).
- Lock down hospitals' IT networks, causing delays in patient care (like in Dusseldorf).
- Interrupt airport control towers, delaying flights and affecting air traffic.

Real-World Example:
The Ukraine Power Grid Attack is a prime example. Attackers used BlackEnergy malware to access SCADA control systems and shut down power to 230,000 people. Other examples include ransomware attacks on hospitals and airports, where patient care and flight schedules were disrupted.

How AI Plays a Role:
Attackers use AI to predict weak points in power grids and automate scanning for vulnerable SCADA devices. AI also enables adaptive malware that learns how to bypass firewalls and anomaly detection. On the defensive side, AI-driven predictive threat intelligence platforms now track and analyze attack patterns in real time, allowing power grid operators to detect and respond to intrusions.

Cyber-physical attacks aren't just "digital threats" — they're threats to human life. From shutting down hospitals to taking over entire power grids, attackers are no longer just stealing data — they're seizing control of the real world. The evolution of AI has amplified these attacks, with AI-driven malware and automated attack tools allowing hackers to launch attacks at scale.

While the types of attacks may vary — from ransomware on hospitals to polymorphic malware in power grids — the goal remains the same: control physical infrastructure. Governments, hospitals, and businesses must prioritize defense strategies like Zero Trust models, network segmentation, and AI-based anomaly detection to combat this growing threat.

How Attackers Use AI in Cyber-Physical Attacks
Attackers are no longer relying on human ingenuity alone —
they're unleashing AI-driven attack tools to infiltrate, disrupt, and
manipulate critical infrastructure. From power grids and smart
factories to hospitals and water treatment plants, cyber-physical
systems are prime targets for AI-powered attacks. Unlike
traditional malware that requires manual input from hackers, AI-
augmented attacks can learn, evolve, and adapt in real time.

Here's a closer look at the key ways attackers are weaponizing AI
in cyber-physical attacks:

**1. AI-Driven Malware (Polymorphic Malware for ICS/SCADA
Systems)**
What It Is:
Traditional malware follows static patterns that can be detected by
signature-based antivirus tools. But AI-driven malware is
polymorphic, meaning it continuously changes its code, behavior,
and even its "appearance" to avoid detection. When used against
SCADA systems (Supervisory Control and Data Acquisition) and
ICS (Industrial Control Systems), this malware becomes nearly
impossible to detect.

How It Works:
- Mutation Engines: AI "mutates" the malware code every few
  minutes, creating an entirely new "signature" for the file.
- AI-Driven Adaptation: If the malware detects it's being
  analyzed in a sandbox environment, it plays dead to avoid
  detection.
- Context-Aware Malware: The malware "learns" how to exploit
  its environment, such as targeting specific SCADA controllers,
  changing pressure levels, or altering commands to physical
  devices.

Example:
The Industroyer/CrashOverride malware was designed to attack
Ukraine's power grid in 2016. It had built-in capabilities to control
circuit breakers, disrupt electric substations, and mimic SCADA
commands. A polymorphic AI-driven version of this malware
would be even more dangerous because it would constantly evolve
to avoid detection.

How to Defend:
- Use AI-based anomaly detection to spot behavioral changes in
  SCADA systems.
- Deploy EDR (Endpoint Detection and Response) for SCADA
  endpoints.
- Use Zero-Trust architecture to ensure malware can't spread
  laterally.

2. AI-Guided Exploitation (AI Finds Vulnerabilities Faster Than Hackers)

What It Is:

Instead of hackers scanning a target system for vulnerabilities, AI-guided exploitation tools automate this entire process. AI uses algorithms to search for unpatched vulnerabilities, open ports, default passwords, and misconfigured firewalls in SCADA and ICS environments.

How It Works:
- Vulnerability Scanning: AI automatically scans thousands of targets at once, prioritizing systems with known flaws (like the Log4j vulnerability).
- Attack Path Mapping: AI models predict the easiest route to exploit an environment (like lateral movement from an IoT device to an ICS network).
- Exploitation as a Service (EaaS): Attackers rent access to AI-driven vulnerability scanners on the dark web.

Example:

A hacker using Shodan (IoT search engine) could locate vulnerable SCADA systems, but it would take manual effort to identify which devices are most at risk. AI-guided exploitation tools like Metasploit + AI plugins could automate this process, scanning 10,000 targets in minutes and automatically launching known exploits.

How to Defend:
- Use AI vulnerability scanners to identify misconfigured firewalls, open ports, and insecure PLCs.
- Apply the "Patch Early, Patch Often" strategy.
- Deploy Zero-Trust micro-segmentation to isolate devices from each other.

3. AI Voice Cloning & Deepfake Attacks (Tricking Operators Into Authorizing Access)

What It Is:

AI voice cloning technology can mimic the voice of control room operators, IT admins, and even C-suite executives. Attackers use voice clones to make phone calls and trick employees into issuing dangerous commands, such as disabling critical alarms, allowing remote access, or authorizing a ransomware payment.

How It Works:
- Voice Cloning: Attackers use tools like ElevenLabs, Resemble AI, or Voice.ai to clone a voice with just 10-20 seconds of sample audio.

- Call Spoofing: Attackers spoof the caller ID, making it look like the call is coming from a trusted source (like the factory manager's phone).
- Social Engineering: The "voice" of the manager gives the operator an urgent task like "disable that pressure valve" or "send the password for remote access."

Example:
A deepfake voice attack occurred in 2020 when an AI-generated clone of a CEO's voice convinced an employee to transfer $243,000 to a hacker's account. Imagine if that same attack targeted a SCADA operator, instructing them to disable safety protocols for a pressure valve in a refinery.

How to Defend:
- Use a "family password" system where operators use secret challenge phrases to verify identity.
- Deploy AI anomaly detection for operator commands.
- Use call-back verification for any remote requests that affect critical safety systems.

4. AI-Guided DDoS Attacks on Critical Systems
What It Is:
A Distributed Denial of Service (DDoS) attack floods a system with traffic, making it impossible for legitimate users to access it. But with AI, these attacks are faster, more dynamic, and harder to stop. Attackers use AI bots to flood critical infrastructure like hospital networks, factory control panels, and smart city sensors.

How It Works:
- AI-Swarm Attacks: Attackers launch AI-coordinated "swarm" attacks from thousands of IoT devices, like smart cameras and smart locks.
- Evasive Techniques: AI can detect when DDoS mitigation tools are active and change attack patterns to avoid detection.
- Botnet Automation: AI automates the process of identifying and recruiting new IoT devices to join the DDoS botnet.

Example:
The Mirai botnet used infected IoT devices (like IP cameras) to flood internet services with traffic, causing global internet outages. A future AI-driven Mirai 2.0 could automatically adapt to mitigation tools like Cloudflare, altering its attack strategy in real time.

How to Defend:
- Use AI-driven DDoS protection services like Cloudflare and AWS Shield.
- Disable remote access on IoT devices to prevent botnet recruitment.
- Deploy rate-limiting controls on ICS network traffic.

5. AI-Based Ransomware That Targets ICS and SCADA
What It Is:
While traditional ransomware encrypts files, AI-based ransomware goes beyond file encryption — it targets SCADA controllers, ICS commands, and operational settings. Attackers don't just lock files; they lock operational processes. Imagine a power grid operator being locked out of their own control room.

How It Works:
- Command Hijacking: Attackers hijack SCADA commands, such as "disable cooling system" or "increase turbine speed."
- AI-Driven Decision Making: The ransomware decides which SCADA commands to disable, making it impossible for operators to regain control.
- Extortion + Sabotage: Attackers demand a ransom, but even if the ransom is paid, the attacker can leave behind logic bombs to trigger future outages.

Example:
A ransomware attack on a water treatment plant could lock operators out of the system, while AI-driven ransomware changes the chemical dosage, making the water unsafe to drink.

How to Defend:
- Deploy EDR and SIEM for ICS endpoints.
- Store encrypted backups of PLC configurations.
- Use AI-based anomaly detection to spot unusual SCADA commands.

The Takeaway
Cyber-physical attacks are no longer launched by humans alone. Attackers are using AI to automate every step of the attack process, from reconnaissance to payload delivery. Key tactics include:
- AI-driven malware that evolves in real-time.
- AI-guided exploitation tools that scan for misconfigurations and zero-days.
- AI voice cloning to trick control room operators.
- AI-driven DDoS swarms that overwhelm smart grids.
- AI ransomware that locks down industrial processes.

How Do We Defend?
- Deploy AI-powered anomaly detection.
- Use Zero-Trust models to stop lateral movement.
- Deploy multi-factor authentication for SCADA, ICS, and OT systems.

Attackers are using AI, and so must defenders. AI vs. AI will define the future of cyber-physical warfare.

How to Defend Critical Infrastructure Using AI
As attackers become more sophisticated with AI-driven malware, deepfakes, and polymorphic ransomware, the only way to effectively defend critical infrastructure is by using AI-powered defense systems. Unlike traditional cybersecurity methods, which react after an attack is detected, AI-driven defenses predict, prevent, and self-heal in real time. This section outlines how to protect critical infrastructure using AI and the latest strategies to safeguard power grids, water systems, hospitals, and other essential services.

1. AI-Driven Anomaly Detection (Spot Threats Before They Attack)
What It Is:
AI-driven anomaly detection tracks the behavior of devices, users, and network traffic to spot unusual patterns in real-time. Instead of relying on rules and signatures, AI uses machine learning to recognize when a system behaves abnormally (like a SCADA system suddenly activating at midnight).

How It Works:
- Behavioral Baselines: AI observes "normal" behavior for ICS (Industrial Control Systems), OT (Operational Technology), and SCADA devices.
- Pattern Recognition: AI models recognize deviations from the baseline (like a pump that suddenly increases pressure at an unusual time of day).
- Alerts and Automation: When anomalies are detected, AI sends an alert and, in some cases, triggers an automatic lockdown or quarantine of the affected system.

Example:
An AI-powered anomaly detection system at a water treatment plant notices that a valve is being opened at midnight (when no employees are present). Since this action deviates from normal activity, the AI system automatically disconnects the affected valve and locks it down until a human operator can investigate.

How It Defends:
- Prevents sabotage of SCADA controllers and PLC devices.
- Detects attacks in progress, like malware attempting to modify operational commands.
- Blocks rogue employees, hackers, or insiders from manipulating OT devices.

2. Zero-Trust Architecture for SCADA, ICS, and OT Systems

What It Is:

Unlike traditional security (where devices inside the network are "trusted" by default), a Zero-Trust security model assumes that no user, device, or system is trustworthy. In SCADA, ICS, and OT systems, this means that every device, command, and operator request must be authenticated and verified.

How It Works:
- Micro-Segmentation: Every part of the SCADA network is isolated, so even if one part is breached, attackers can't move laterally.
- Identity and Access Management (IAM): Only devices with verified, cryptographic identities are allowed access to the network.
- Continuous Verification: Every user, device, and system must re-verify its access every few minutes.

Example:

If attackers infiltrate a power plant's HVAC system, traditional security allows them to move laterally to the power grid's SCADA system. But under a Zero-Trust model, every lateral movement requires new identity verification, and devices are prevented from communicating directly with other segments.

How It Defends:
- Stops lateral movement by isolating devices, PLCs, and SCADA controllers.
- Reduces the impact of ransomware by restricting file movement across network zones.
- Ensures that even if an operator's credentials are stolen, the attacker still can't access other devices.

3. AI-Driven Self-Healing Systems (Repair Systems Without Human Input)
What It Is:
Self-healing systems are AI-powered repair mechanisms that detect cyberattacks in real time, quarantine the infected devices, and automatically repair any damage done. These systems work like "digital immune systems" that heal themselves after a breach, ensuring that the critical infrastructure continues to function.

How It Works:
- Detect & Quarantine: If AI detects ransomware encrypting files, it instantly disconnects the device from the network.
- Rollback to Clean State: Self-healing systems roll back ICS and SCADA devices to their last known "clean" state, using backup snapshots.
- Patch & Secure: If the attack exploited a known vulnerability, AI patches the affected system to prevent reinfection.

Example:
An attack on a power grid SCADA system locks out operators and takes control of the circuit breakers. A self-healing system automatically restores control to the operators, reverts the SCADA settings to their pre-attack state, and applies security patches to prevent the same attack vector from being used again.

How It Defends:
- Stops ransomware attacks from locking down SCADA and ICS devices.
- Rolls back files, control settings, and PLC logic to "pre-attack" states.
- Automates security patching for known vulnerabilities.

4. AI-Powered Threat Hunting and Attack Prediction
What It Is:
Traditional threat hunting is manual and reactive. With AI, threat hunting becomes predictive, proactive, and fully automated. AI identifies attack patterns, attack paths, and likely targets before the attack happens.

How It Works:
- Attack Path Prediction: AI predicts how an attacker would move from one vulnerable device to another.
- Automated Threat Hunting: AI scans millions of IoC (Indicators of Compromise) from dark web forums, ransom sites, and malware feeds.
- Threat Maps: AI generates a "heat map" of which parts of your SCADA network are most likely to be attacked.

Example:
A predictive defense system scans the dark web for leaked SCADA passwords. When it finds one related to your company, it triggers an alert. It also maps out where that password could be used (like accessing HMI terminals) and identifies which systems need to be patched.

How It Defends:
- Prepares for attacks before they happen by patching at-risk systems.
- Detects threats as they emerge in real time (not after the breach).
- Provides threat intel from the dark web, ransomware forums, and leaked credential dumps.

5. AI-Driven DDoS Protection (Stop Swarm Attacks on Power Grids and IoT Systems)
What It Is:
Distributed Denial of Service (DDoS) attacks overwhelm systems with fake traffic. AI-driven DDoS protection tools detect and block swarm attacks on critical infrastructure, ensuring that power grids, hospitals, and traffic control systems remain operational.

How It Works:
- Rate Limiting: AI analyzes network traffic and automatically drops traffic that doesn't fit normal usage patterns.
- Botnet Detection: AI identifies IoT devices that are part of a botnet (like Mirai) and blocks them in real time.
- Geo-Blocking: AI geolocates malicious traffic (like requests from unusual countries) and blocks it.

Example:
A DDoS attack on a hospital network could prevent emergency responders from communicating with ambulances. An AI-driven DDoS mitigation system, like AWS Shield, automatically detects and blocks malicious requests before they affect the system.

How It Defends:
- Prevents attacks from disabling hospitals, water treatment plants, and public safety systems.
- Blocks malicious IoT devices from joining botnets like Mirai.
- Identifies DDoS patterns in real time and drops the attack traffic before it causes downtime.

6. AI-Powered Device Authentication and Secure Access (Decentralized Identity)

What It Is:

Traditional authentication relies on usernames and passwords, but AI-powered device authentication ensures that only verified devices and users can access SCADA, ICS, and OT systems. Every device is assigned a tamper-proof decentralized identity (DID) that attackers can't fake.

How It Works:
- Tamper-Proof IDs: Every SCADA controller, PLC, and device gets a cryptographic ID.
- AI Authentication: AI verifies devices before they can send control commands.
- Continuous Verification: The device must constantly "prove" its ID, preventing attackers from impersonating SCADA controllers.

Example:

If malware hijacks a smart lock in a smart city, it can use that access to spread ransomware. But with decentralized identity (DID), the hijacked smart lock is rejected, since it no longer has its verified ID.

How It Defends:
- Stops attackers from hijacking SCADA devices with fake commands.
- Prevents PLC hijacking and smart device impersonation.
- Adds multi-factor authentication for SCADA devices.

AI is the only force capable of defending against AI-powered threats. Defenders must leverage:
- AI-driven anomaly detection to catch changes in SCADA behavior.
- Zero-Trust architecture to stop lateral movement.
- Self-healing systems to repair malware infections automatically.
- Predictive AI to anticipate future attacks.

As attackers get smarter, defenders must stay one step ahead. Cyber-physical security is now AI vs. AI.

AI-Generated Bioweapons and Explosives

The integration of AI into bioweapons and explosives introduces a terrifying new chapter in the evolution of cyber-physical warfare. Unlike traditional explosives and chemical weapons, which require direct human oversight to design, build, and deploy, AI systems can autonomously generate, enhance, and refine these weapons with little to no human intervention. This threat is not theoretical — it's a growing concern for national security agencies and intelligence communities worldwide.

From AI-driven chemical synthesis to autonomous drone explosives, AI weaponization poses a unique danger. By automating key aspects of design, development, and deployment, bad actors can now create weapons faster, smarter, and more efficiently than ever before.

1. How AI Is Used to Create Bioweapons

What It Is:
AI can analyze vast datasets on biological structures, predict the properties of unknown molecules, and even create synthetic pathogens that are more potent than those found in nature. This process, known as AI-driven chemical synthesis, is already being used in pharmaceutical research to create new life-saving drugs. Unfortunately, the same technology can be misused to create bioweapons.

How It Works:
- AI-Powered Drug Discovery Software: AI systems like AlphaFold, ChemBL, and MoleculeNet are used by pharmaceutical companies to create new drugs.
- Weaponization of Pharmaceutical AI: In 2021, researchers tested how AI drug-discovery models could be misused to identify toxins and lethal chemical compounds. In just a few hours, AI had identified over 40,000 potential chemical bioweapons.
- Synthesis of New Viruses: AI can "design" new pathogens that target specific genetic profiles, creating viruses that may only impact certain populations or regions.

Example:
A pharmaceutical AI system designed to discover new antibiotics could be reconfigured to generate a new toxin. In an experiment, AI generated a list of potential nerve agents (like VX gas) in a matter of hours. This was done to highlight the potential risks of dual-use AI. Imagine if a rogue nation-state or cybercriminal group misused these tools to create a bioweapon that targets specific genetic markers.

358

How to Defend:
- Strict Regulation: Governments must enforce "dual-use AI" restrictions on pharmaceutical AI tools to prevent misuse.
- AI Model Safeguards: Backdoors and kill switches should be placed into AI models, allowing developers to disable harmful functionality.
- Monitoring & Auditing: Implement AI usage audits to track how AI drug discovery tools are being used by research labs, universities, and pharmaceutical companies.

2. How AI Powers Smart Explosives and Autonomous Drone Weapons

What It Is:

Autonomous drones and AI-driven explosives represent the next wave of AI-controlled warfare. Attackers are no longer restricted to crude, remote-controlled devices. Today, drones can independently select targets, identify human faces, and even dodge countermeasures. Attackers use AI to create drones that can navigate complex terrain, recognize faces, and identify structural weak points in buildings or vehicles.

How It Works:
- AI-Driven Targeting: AI models recognize human faces, vehicles, and buildings through facial recognition and computer vision.
- Swarm Attacks: Instead of one drone, an attacker can launch a swarm of mini-drones that communicate with each other in real time, attacking targets in waves.
- Autonomous Decision-Making: Modern drones, equipped with AI neural networks, no longer need remote control. They identify targets and make real-time decisions about who, where, and when to strike.

Example:

In 2020, Killer Drones (Loitering Munitions) were reportedly used in the Libyan conflict, where autonomous drones pursued retreating soldiers without requiring human input. The drones used AI-based facial recognition to track and target specific individuals.

How to Defend:
- AI Jamming Technology: Deploy jamming devices to block drone communications and interfere with AI-driven navigation.
- Anti-Swarm Defense Systems: Use AI-driven counter-swarm technology to identify and intercept drone swarms.
- Geofencing: Implement geofencing systems that prevent unauthorized drones from flying near critical sites like power grids, airports, and military bases.

3. Weaponization of AI Algorithms (Attackers Use AI to Design Explosives)

What It Is:

Just as AI models predict the outcome of football games or stock prices, AI can predict the chemical interactions required to make explosives. By using physics engines, chemistry datasets, and machine learning models, attackers can design new explosives that are more powerful, safer to transport, or easier to manufacture.

How It Works:
- AI-Powered Chemistry Simulation: Attackers use AI-based chemistry platforms to simulate explosive reactions in virtual environments.
- Designing New Explosives: AI models can create new, more effective explosives by modeling the impact of different chemicals and optimizing for maximum destructive power.
- Open-Source Explosive Designs: Criminals can access open-source libraries and AI-driven design models to develop new versions of explosives.

Example:

Attackers could modify the explosive properties of TATP (triacetone triperoxide) — a common material in homemade bombs. AI can predict more effective recipes, making them more stable, smaller, and harder to detect.

How to Defend:
- AI Model Restrictions: Governments should impose restrictions on public AI models used for chemical synthesis.
- Digital Fingerprints: Develop "explosive design detection" algorithms that flag specific simulations of chemical reactions in online chemistry labs.
- Monitor Online Collaboration Platforms: Track activity on open-source collaboration platforms like GitHub, where threat actors may upload AI-based chemistry models.

4. How Attackers Can Use AI to Deliver Bioweapons and Explosives

What It Is:

Attackers are combining AI, robotics, and drones to create delivery systems for bioweapons and explosives. These systems can release toxic gases or explosives at specific times, locations, or populations. Unlike human-delivered attacks, these delivery systems operate independently.

How It Works:
- Drone-Based Dispersal: Attackers launch drones loaded with explosives or chemical agents that can be dispersed remotely.

- Targeted Release: AI predicts the best weather and wind conditions to ensure maximum coverage for airborne toxins.
- AI-Controlled Release Mechanism: The drones release gas or toxins once they reach their designated coordinates.

Example:
A drone could release a cloud of toxic gas over a power plant or military base, rendering it uninhabitable. AI could analyze wind speed, air currents, and weather forecasts to optimize dispersal.

How to Defend:
- Use AI-driven air quality sensors to detect and track airborne toxins.
- Deploy anti-drone weapons to detect and destroy drones in restricted areas.
- Install emergency ventilation shut-off systems in power plants and military bases to stop airborne contaminants from spreading.

5. AI-Driven Cyber-Warfare Meets Physical Destruction (The Hybrid Threat)
What It Is:
Some attacks use a combination of cyberattacks and physical sabotage. Attackers use AI to launch cyberattacks (like disabling a water treatment plant's alarms) and then deploy explosives or bioweapons to destroy physical systems.

How It Works:
- Cyber-Physical Hybrid Attacks: First, attackers hack into SCADA or ICS systems to weaken defenses.
- Physical Attack Launch: Once defenses are disabled, the attacker deploys a physical bomb, drone, or other explosive to damage the infrastructure.

Example:
In 2010, the Stuxnet malware sabotaged Iranian centrifuges by manipulating SCADA commands. Imagine a modern attack where AI controls both the cyberattack and a physical explosive payload released by drones.

How to Defend:
- Isolate critical ICS systems from the internet (Air-gapping).
- Use AI-based attack path mapping to predict which devices attackers would compromise first.
- Deploy redundant physical safety mechanisms to prevent chemical leaks or explosions.

Chapter Conclusion: The Real and Present Danger of Cyber-Physical Attacks

The intersection of AI and critical infrastructure is no longer a futuristic concern, but a very real and growing threat. From power grids to hospitals, cyber-physical attacks are becoming increasingly sophisticated, with AI technologies now being used by malicious actors to exploit vulnerabilities in vital systems. The rise of AI-generated bioweapons and explosives only heightens the potential for devastation, signaling a new level of complexity in these attacks.

Case studies like Stuxnet and the Colonial Pipeline attack highlight the immense damage cyber-physical attacks can cause, disrupting economies, threatening public health, and endangering lives. These events have already reshaped our understanding of the risks, and the next attack could be even more catastrophic. As Elon Musk and other experts have warned, this threat is real, and we must act with urgency to address it.

While the danger is significant, with the right leadership and understanding, we can limit the chaos AI might bring. By fostering collaboration between governments, industry leaders, and cybersecurity experts, we can create a framework that mitigates risks while harnessing AI's benefits. If we approach the issue proactively, ensuring strong safeguards are in place, we can protect our critical infrastructure and build a safer future for all.

Chapter 27: Practice & Exercises

From Theory to Practice
By now, you've learned about threats, defenses, and the tools used by both attackers and defenders. But knowing isn't enough — you have to practice.

This chapter gives you the opportunity to put your knowledge into action. By completing hands-on exercises, you'll gain practical skills that go beyond theory. These exercises simulate real-world challenges like password cracking, phishing defense, and red team/blue team scenarios. You'll also complete a capstone challenge where you'll design your own AI-powered cybersecurity system.

Chapter Overview:
- 10+ Hands-On Exercises — These challenges are designed to simulate real-world scenarios.
- Red Team / Blue Team Scenarios — You'll experience the roles of attacker (red team) and defender (blue team) in live attack simulations.
- Capstone Challenge — Your ultimate test: design a fully functional AI-powered security system to protect a fictional organization.

1. Hands-On Cybersecurity Activities (10+ Challenges)
The following exercises are designed to give you hands-on experience with key concepts. Each task builds on the skills you've learned throughout this book.

Exercise 1: Password Cracking Challenge
Objective: See how quickly passwords can be cracked using automated tools like Hashcat or John the Ripper. This will help you understand how weak passwords are exploited by attackers.

Steps:
1. Download Hashcat (a free password-cracking tool).
2. Create a list of 10 common passwords (like "123456" or "password").
3. Run Hashcat to crack the passwords in your list.
4. Repeat the process with a 12-character password containing letters, numbers, and symbols.

Key Takeaways:
- Learn why short passwords are dangerous.
- See how complexity and length increase security.
- Understand the power of password managers to generate stronger passwords.

Exercise 2: Phishing Awareness Simulation
Objective: Learn how to spot a phishing email.

Steps:
- Create a fake phishing email using a phishing email generator like GoPhish.
- Send it to a test email account (do NOT send to friends or coworkers without permission).
- Examine the phishing email — identify red flags (like typos, odd URLs, and requests for personal data).
- Review the telltale signs of phishing.

Key Takeaways:
- Learn how to spot common phishing tactics (like fake login pages).
- See how phishing emails bypass spam filters.
- Learn how to report phishing attempts on platforms like Gmail, Outlook, and corporate inboxes.

Pro Tip: This is one of the most common attack methods hackers use — mastering this skill will protect you from 90% of phishing attempts.

Exercise 3: Red Team / Blue Team Attack Simulation
Objective: Experience what it's like to be both an attacker (red team) and defender (blue team) in a cybersecurity scenario.

Scenario: Your company has been hit with a ransomware attack. As a red teamer, you'll attempt to "hack" into a system. As a blue teamer, you'll detect and respond to the attack.

Red Team Steps:
- Use a free penetration testing tool like Metasploit.
- Try to exploit a vulnerability in a sample virtual machine (VM) like Metasploitable.
- "Capture the flag" by planting a file on the system.

Blue Team Steps:
- Use Wireshark or ELK Stack (Elasticsearch, Logstash, Kibana) to analyze network traffic.
- Detect unusual activity and quarantine affected machines.
- Track and block the attacker's IP address.

Key Takeaways:
- Understand the "attacker vs. defender" dynamic.
- Learn to recognize the patterns of ransomware, malware, and DDoS attacks.
- Practice the critical skills of incident response and real-time defense.

Pro Tip: Red team/blue team scenarios are used by professional cybersecurity teams to strengthen security measures and train employees.

Exercise 4: Design a Zero-Trust Model for Your Home Network
Objective: Implement a zero-trust model for your home network, treating every device as untrusted.

Steps:
- Identify all devices on your home network (laptops, phones, smart devices, etc.).
- Create a guest Wi-Fi network for IoT devices like smart speakers and cameras.
- Use a firewall (like Bitdefender Box) to block all non-essential traffic.
- Enable network segmentation so that IoT devices can't access your work devices.

Key Takeaways:
- Understand how to build a zero-trust network.
- Learn how network segmentation limits the scope of an attack.
- Create a safer home network for your family.

Pro Tip: Hackers often target smart devices (like Ring cameras and Alexa devices) because they are poorly protected. A zero-trust network stops them from reaching your laptops, phones, and work devices.

Exercise 5: Identify and Remove Your Digital Footprint
Objective: Use online tools to find and delete your personal information from data broker websites.

Steps:
- Use services like Deseat.me or DeleteMe to identify where your personal data is stored.
- Submit opt-out requests to data brokers like Spokeo, MyLife, and Whitepages.
- Delete old online accounts with JustDelete.me.

Key Takeaways:
- Reduce your visibility to attackers, hackers, and identity thieves.
- Limit the amount of personal information that can be found online.

Pro Tip: Data brokers sell your personal information to advertisers, spammers, and hackers. Deleting this information makes you less of a target.

2. Red Team / Blue Team Scenarios
This section lets you take on the roles of both red team (attacker) and blue team (defender).
Scenario 1: Ransomware Attack Simulation
- Red Team Goal: Deploy ransomware on a network and lock all devices.
- Blue Team Goal: Detect, isolate, and stop the ransomware from spreading.

Scenario 2: Phishing Email Intrusion
- Red Team Goal: Send a phishing email to gain login credentials.
- Blue Team Goal: Spot the phishing attack, report it, and prevent credential theft.

Scenario 3: Insider Threat Simulation
- Red Team Goal: Act as a rogue employee trying to steal customer data.
- Blue Team Goal: Detect suspicious employee behavior and prevent the data breach.

Pro Tip: Many companies conduct red team/blue team exercises every 6 months to train employees on real-world threats.

3. Capstone Challenge: Design Your AI-Powered Cybersecurity System
The ultimate challenge — design a fully functional, AI-powered security system to protect a business.

Scenario:
You are hired as the Chief Information Security Officer (CISO) for a large tech company. Your mission is to design a cybersecurity system that:
- Protects the company from ransomware, phishing, and insider threats.
- Uses AI-driven threat detection to spot unusual user behavior.
- Follows a zero-trust security model.

Steps to Complete:
- Design a Security Plan — Identify the tools you'll need (like EDR, SIEM, and AI threat detection).
- Create Incident Response Playbooks — Write a plan for responding to phishing attacks, ransomware, and data breaches.
- Build a Red Team / Blue Team Schedule — Schedule attack/defense training for employees.
- Present Your Strategy — Write a 1-page executive summary to present your security plan to the CEO.

Pro Tip: This capstone challenge is modeled after what companies expect from CISOs and security architects. It's great for your resume if you want to pursue a job in cybersecurity.

Chapter Conclusion
This chapter turned you from a reader into a hands-on cybersecurity expert. You've cracked passwords, defended against ransomware, and experienced the thrill of red team/blue team simulations. Your final challenge — creating an AI-powered security system — mirrors what real-world companies expect from CISOs.

"Knowing is not enough. Doing makes you unstoppable."

Chapter 28: Appendix & Resources

Your Go-To Cybersecurity Resource Hub
This appendix is your "all-in-one toolkit" for everything you've learned in this book. Here, you'll find essential resources, definitions, templates, and tools that will help you apply everything you've learned. No need to search the web for extra info — it's all right here.

This chapter includes:
1. Glossary of Essential Cybersecurity & AI Terms — Definitions of key terms and acronyms you've encountered in the book.
2. Recommended Tools & Software — A complete list of tools, platforms, and software to level up your cybersecurity game.

Glossary of Essential Cybersecurity & AI Terms
Here's a list of essential terms and definitions that were introduced in this book. These definitions will help you understand the language of cybersecurity professionals and AI experts.

A-C
- Adversarial AI — An attack method where hackers trick an AI model into making a mistake, like confusing facial recognition software.
- AI Bias — When AI models make flawed decisions due to incomplete, skewed, or biased training data.
- Authentication — The process of verifying a user's identity, often done through passwords, biometrics, or multi-factor authentication (MFA).
- Blue Team — A defensive cybersecurity team responsible for detecting, responding to, and mitigating attacks.
- Botnet — A network of malware-infected devices controlled by a hacker to launch attacks like DDoS.
- Brute-Force Attack — An attack where an attacker tries every possible password combination until they guess the right one.

D-F
- DDoS (Distributed Denial of Service) — An attack where hackers overload a website or server with fake traffic, causing it to crash.
- Data Breach — The theft, exposure, or unauthorized access of confidential data.
- Encryption — The process of converting data into an unreadable format to protect it from unauthorized access.
- Endpoint Detection and Response (EDR) — A security system that detects and responds to threats on endpoint devices like laptops and phones.

- Exploit — A tool, code, or process used by attackers to take advantage of vulnerabilities in software or systems.
- False Positive — A system alert that incorrectly flags normal activity as suspicious, often seen in SIEM or anomaly detection systems.

G-K
- Gamification — Turning learning into a game-like experience to increase engagement and memory retention.
- Hashing — Converting a password or file into a fixed-length string of characters (called a "hash") for secure storage.
- Incident Response (IR) — The process of responding to and mitigating a cyberattack or data breach.
- Insider Threat — A threat caused by employees, contractors, or partners with access to sensitive company data.
- Keylogger — Malicious software that records every keystroke you type to steal passwords or private information.

L-P
- Malware — Malicious software, like viruses, trojans, and ransomware, designed to harm, steal, or spy on your systems.
- Multi-Factor Authentication (MFA) — A login method requiring two or more verification methods, like a password and a fingerprint.
- Penetration Testing (Pentesting) — Ethical hacking where security professionals attempt to break into systems to find vulnerabilities before hackers do.
- Phishing — A scam where attackers trick victims into revealing sensitive information through fake emails, websites, or text messages.

Q-Z
- Quarantine — The process of isolating infected devices, files, or applications to prevent malware from spreading.
- Red Team — An offensive cybersecurity team that simulates attacks to test an organization's defenses.
- Rogue AI — A theoretical concept where an AI system operates beyond human control, often with malicious intent.
- SIEM (Security Information and Event Management) — A system that collects, analyzes, and responds to security alerts from devices and networks.
- Social Engineering — Manipulating people to gain access to information or systems, often done via phishing or pretexting.
- Zero-Trust Model — A security strategy where no user, device, or network is trusted by default — all access must be verified.

Recommended Tools & Software
Here are the essential tools and software mentioned throughout this book. Use this list to build your Cybersecurity Toolkit.

Personal Security Tools (Individuals & Families)
- 1Password / LastPass — Password managers for creating strong, unique passwords.
- HaveIBeenPwned — Check if your email or passwords have been leaked. (https://haveibeenpwned.com/)
- Bitdefender Box — AI-driven home firewall for securing smart home devices. (https://www.bitdefender.com/box/)
- Deseat.me — Helps users delete old accounts and reduce their digital footprint. (https://www.deseat.me/)
- Qustodio / Bark — Parental control tools for monitoring children's online activity. (https://www.qustodio.com/ & https://www.bark.us/)

Business Security Tools
- CrowdStrike / SentinelOne — EDR (Endpoint Detection and Response) systems for detecting and stopping malware and ransomware.
- Tenable.io / Qualys — Vulnerability scanning tools for auditing business networks.
- SIEM Systems (Splunk, IBM QRadar) — Centralized platforms to collect, analyze, and respond to system alerts.
- RangeForce / Immersive Labs — Gamification platforms for employee training.

Pro Tip: Bookmark or print this list. Each tool was selected for its effectiveness, ease of use, and industry reputation.

The Appendix & Resources section of this book serves as a reference guide that readers can return to for years to come. From the glossary of key terms to the downloadable templates, every tool you need to protect yourself, your family, and your business is here.

"Cybersecurity isn't a one-time event — it's a lifestyle."

Final Thoughts: Stay Vigilant, Stay Secure

Congratulations!

You've reached the end of "A.I Teaches You Cybersecurity Fundamentals: AI-Driven Cybersecurity to Protect Your Family, Business & Identity in Today's Online World."

But let's be clear — this is not the end of your journey. Cybersecurity is a living, evolving challenge that requires constant vigilance, adaptation, and learning. The threats of today may not be the threats of tomorrow. Attackers are always innovating, and AI is making them faster, smarter, and more unpredictable.

That's why the lessons in this book are meant to stay with you for life. If you've applied even half of the strategies, tools, and concepts you've learned here, you're already ahead of 90% of the population.

But staying ahead requires continuous growth. Technology changes, threats evolve, and hackers only need to succeed once. Your mission is to ensure that they never get that chance.

What You've Accomplished
Over the course of this book, you've:
- Mastered the core principles of AI-driven cybersecurity — From self-evolving malware to rogue AI threats, you now know how to spot, defend, and counter these emerging risks.
- Secured your personal devices, family, and business — Your laptops, phones, smart home devices, and business infrastructure are now significantly harder targets.
- Learned how to "think like a hacker" — By understanding the psychology of cybercriminals and the tactics they use (like phishing, social engineering, and ransomware), you've become better equipped to anticipate and prevent attacks.
- Designed your own cybersecurity system — Through hands-on exercises and a capstone challenge, you've done something that few others have done: planned and built an AI-powered cybersecurity strategy.
- Achieved mastery over core tools and concepts — From using SIEMs and EDRs to deploying zero-trust networks and mastering red team/blue team tactics, you've learned to protect your home, family, and business like a professional.

But remember — what got you here won't get you there. Cybersecurity is a continuous process, not a one-time event. Attackers evolve, and so must you.

3 Critical Rules to Follow Moving Forward
1. Stay Updated on Emerging Threats
   - Hackers are relentless. New attacks like deepfakes, supply chain attacks, and rogue AI threats are becoming more sophisticated. Stay ahead of them.
   - How to stay updated: Follow trusted security blogs like Krebs on Security, DarkReading, and the Cybersecurity & Infrastructure Security Agency (CISA).

2. Keep a Critical Mindset
   - The biggest cybersecurity weapon you have is your mind. Social engineering, fake news, and misinformation thrive on people who don't think critically.
   - Always ask:
     - "Why am I being asked to do this?"
     - "Is this too good to be true?"
     - "Does this message feel urgent, rushed, or threatening?"

If it feels urgent or too good to be true, it probably is. Slow down, think, and verify.

3. Practice the Principles of Zero Trust
   - Trust nobody, no device, and no network by default. Assume every email, link, and message is malicious until proven safe.
   - This principle applies to family, employees, and even your own accounts.
   - How to apply this in real life:
     - Verify unknown senders before clicking links.
     - Don't assume phone calls from "official sources" are legitimate.
     - Use multi-factor authentication (MFA) for every account.

Your New Role: Defender of Your Family, Business & Identity
This isn't just about protecting your devices — it's about protecting your family, your privacy, and your livelihood. Hackers don't just want access to your accounts; they want control of your data, financial information, and trust.

Here's your final mission:
1. Apply what you've learned — Don't leave it in theory. Take action.
2. Lead your family and business — You're now the cybersecurity leader in your circle. Share this knowledge with your loved ones, employees, and friends.
3. Keep improving — Your skills are sharper now, but they must be constantly refined. Stay sharp by practicing exercises from Chapter 26.

One Last Word of Wisdom

"The attacker only has to succeed once, but you have to succeed every time."

That's the uncomfortable truth about cybersecurity. Hackers are patient, creative, and relentless. But you now have the tools to outthink, outprepare, and outlast them.

If you take one thing from this book, remember this: The strongest defense is a prepared mind. No software, AI tool, or firewall can protect you from poor decisions. That's why critical thinking is your most powerful weapon.
- If you receive a suspicious phone call — think critically.
- If you see an email urging "immediate action" — think critically.
- If you're asked for private information online — think critically.

You now have the knowledge, skills, and mindset to protect yourself, your family, and your business. Don't let it go to waste.

Next Steps
- Stay updated on new threats — Cybersecurity evolves daily. Follow blogs, news, and threat intelligence.
- Take action on your checklist — Use Chapter 25: The Ultimate Cybersecurity Checklist and finish any items you may have missed.
- Share what you've learned — Teach your family, colleagues, and community how to protect themselves. Every person you help becomes part of a stronger, safer world.

You Are a Cybersecurity Champion
This isn't just a title — it's your new identity. You are no longer an ordinary user or bystander. You are now the front line of defense. With the knowledge, tools, and strategies from this book, you're no longer the prey. You're the one hackers fear.

Congratulations on taking this step to protect your family, your business, and your identity. Stay safe, stay sharp, and stay ahead.

"The only thing stronger than an attacker's code is your critical thinking."

Thank you for reading!